A COLLECTION OF PAPERS RELATIVE TO THE DISPUTE BETWEEN GREAT BRITAIN AND AMERICA 1764-1775

A Da Capo Press Reprint Series

THE ERA OF THE AMERICAN REVOLUTION

GENERAL EDITOR: LEONARD W. LEVY
Claremont Graduate School

A COLLECTION OF
PAPERS RELATIVE TO THE
DISPUTE BETWEEN
GREAT BRITAIN AND AMERICA
1764-1775

Edited by John Almon

DA CAPO PRESS · NEW YORK · 1971

A Da Capo Press Reprint Edition

This Da Capo Press edition of
*A Collection of Papers Relative to the Dispute
Between Great Britain and America, 1764-1775,*
is an unabridged republication of the first
edition published in London in 1777. It is
reprinted from a copy of the original edition
in the collection of the Oberlin College Library.

Library of Congress Catalog Card Number 70-146272

SBN 306-70127-8

Published by Da Capo Press, Inc.
A Subsidiary of Plenum Publishing Corporation
227 West 17th Street, New York, N.Y. 10011

A COLLECTION OF
PAPERS RELATIVE TO THE
DISPUTE BETWEEN
GREAT BRITAIN AND AMERICA
1764-1775

A

COLLECTION

OF

INTERESTING, AUTHENTIC

PAPERS,

RELATIVE TO THE

DISPUTE

BETWEEN

GREAT BRITAIN AND AMERICA;

SHEWING THE

CAUSES AND PROGRESS

OF THAT

MISUNDERSTANDING,

FROM

1764 TO 1775.

LONDON:

PRINTED FOR J. ALMON, OPPOSITE BURLINGTON-HOUSE,
IN PICCADILLY.

M.DCC.LXXVII.

ADVERTISEMENT.

AT the Requeſt of many Gentlemen, a Collection is here preſented to the Public, of the principal Facts and Papers reſpecting the Diſpute between Great Britain and America before the Commencement of Hoſtilities. The RE-MEMBRANCER beginning with the firſt Hoſtilities, this Collection of PRIOR DOCUMENTS has been deſired, as neceſſary to accompany that Work.

PRIOR DOCUMENTS.

THE difpute between Great Britain and America commenced in the year 1764, with an attempt to prevent fmuggling in America. There are fome perfons who apprehend the feeds of it were fown much earlier.* They may be right.—But it is not the defign of this compilation to explain motives, or explore latent caufes. The object here is, to prefent an impartial collection of authentic Documents; with fuch additions only, as are abfolutely neceffary to connect the narrative.

In 1764, the Britifh miniftry having come to a refolution, to prevent, as much as poffible, the practice of fmuggling, not only the commanders of the armed cutters ftationed on the Britifh coafts, but of the fhips fent to America, were ordered to act in the capacity of revenue officers, to take the ufual Cuftom-houfe oaths, and obferve the Cuftom-houfe regulations; by which that enterprifing fpirit of theirs, which had been lately, with great fuccefs, exerted againft the common enemy, was now directed and encouraged againft the fubject. Trade was injured by this meafure. The gentlemen of the navy were not acquainted with Cuftom-houfe laws, and therefore many illegal feizures were made. The fubject in America could get no redrefs but from England, which was tedious and difficult to obtain.

See Remembrancer, vol. 1, page 24.

A trade had for many years been carried on between the Britifh and Spanifh colonies, confifting of the manufactures of Great Britain, imported by the Britifh colonies for their own confumption, and bought with their own produce; for which they were paid by the Spaniards in gold and filver, fometimes in bullion and fometimes in coin, and with cochineal, &c. occafionally. This trade was not literally and ftrictly according to law, yet the advantage of it being obvioufly on the fide of Great Britain and her colonies, it had been connived at. But the armed fhips, under the new regulations, feized the veffels; and this beneficial traffic was fuddenly almoft deftroyed. Another trade had been carried on between the North American colonies and the French Weft India iflands, to the great difadvantage of both, as well as to the mother country. Thefe matters had been winked at many years, in confideration of the quantity of manufactures our North American colonies were thereby enabled to take from us. This advantageous commerce not only prevented the Britifh colonies being drained of their current fpecie by the calls of the mother country, but added to their common circulation of cafh; which encreafed in proportion with the trade. But this trade being alfo cut off, by the cruizers, all America became uneafy.

On the 10th of March, 1764, the Houfe of Commons agreed to a number

number of resolutions respecting the American trade; upon a number of which, a bill was brought in, and passed into a law, laying heavy duties on the articles imported into the colonies from the French and other islands in the West Indies; and ordering these duties to be paid, in specie, into the Exchequer of Great Britain. As to the Spanish trade, the Court of Madrid had always been against it; and in complaisance to that Court, as well as in compliance with the old law, and treaties with Spain, it continued to be prevented, as much as possible.

The Americans complained much of this new law; and of the unexampled hardship, of first being deprived of obtaining specie, and next being ordered to pay the new duties, in specie, into the Treasury at London; which they said must speedily drain them of all the specie they had. But what seemed more particularly hard upon them, was, a bill brought in the same session, and passed into a law, " To restrain the currency of paper money in the colonies."

At the end of the session, the King thanked the House of Commons, for the " wise regulations which had been established to augment the public revenues, to unite the interests of the most distant possessions of his crown, and to encourage and secure their commerce with Great Britain."

Extract of a letter from Pensacola, West Florida, dated Dec. 13, 1764.

" Every thing here is put into a dull state, by the men of war obstructing the Spaniards from trading with us. We had four vessels here lately, but they were not permitted to trade, which is the greatest misfortune that could have befallen us in this young settlement, and which I think at the same time will be no small loss to our mother country,

being thereby prevented from vending a very considerable quantity of its manufactures."

Letters to the same purport came from all the colonies.

Extract of a letter from Kingston, in Jamaica, dated Jan. 27, 1765.

" Kingston, which used to be a place of great trade and hurry, is become as still as a desart, since we were so wise to banish our best friends the Spaniards, and now the current of that valuable commerce is turned in favour of the French and Dutch, who have made their ports free, and taking the advantage of our misconduct, have promised them safety, and so deal with them for all the European goods, upon the same terms the English did. Were I to depend on the sale of goods I had from you, I should not be able to remit the money these two or three years."

Part of a letter from Jamaica to a friend in London, dated May 12, 1775.

" We are in the most deplorable state ever known in this island: that channel through which all the money we had came among us, is entirely stopped up; and, what is most astonishing, is, that this measure should be taken with you, who receive so much benefit from the encouragement of it."

The Continental Colonies were exceedingly offended. In several places the inhabitants had meetings, and they resolved, in resentment, not to buy any cloathing they could possibly do without, that was not of their own manufacturing. Several associations were formed, and it was resolved, every where, to consume as few British manufactures as possible; and to set about manufacturing some articles themselves, the materials of which they had in great plenty of their own production.

Boston,

Boston, (in New-England) March 30, 1765. Funerals without mourning, or the giving of English gloves, is become so fashionable, that there has been but one burial for many months past in the old fashion way. We are much indebted to those patriots who first set this example of frugality, by which this town only has made a saving last year of near 19,000l. sterling. Other towns and provinces have copied the example, and experience its utility. It is a pleasure to behold what other savings are made by laying aside a multitude of superfluous articles of British manufactures and British produce.

At the same time (March 10, 1764) the House of Commons resolved, that it was proper to charge certain stamp duties in the colonies and plantations.

This resolution was not this year followed by any bill, being only to be held out as an *intention,* for next year. It was proposed, and agreed to, in a thin House, late at night, and just at the rising, without any debate.

The assemblies of Massachusetts-Bay and New-York, were alarmed at this resolution. They came to some resolutions upon it; which, with a petition from each, to the House of Commons, against it, were transmitted to the Board of Trade in England. They were laid before the Privy Council on the 11th of December, 1764. The Privy Council advised the King to lay them before Parliament. They were never laid before Parliament—they were suppressed.

In the spring of 1765, the American agents in London were informed by administration, That if the colonies would propose any other mode of raising the sum intended to be raised by stamp duties, their proposal would be accepted,

and the stamp duty laid aside. *(See third volume of* Remembrancer, *page* 253). The agents said they were not authorized to give any answer, but that they were ordered to oppose the bill when it should be brought into the House, by petitions questioning the right claimed by parliament of taxing the colonies.

The bill laying a stamp duty in America, passed in March 1765.

The following was printed at the time as part of the Debates on the bill:

Mr. *Grenville*, after speaking long in favour of the bill, concluded with saying, "These children of our own planting (speaking of the Americans) nourished by our indulgence, until they are grown to a good degree of strength and opulence, and protected by our arms, will they grudge to contribute their mite to relieve us from the heavy load of national expence, which we lie under?"

Colonel *Barré* replied, "*Children planted by your care!* No! your oppression planted them in America; they fled from your tyranny, into a then uncultivated land, where they were exposed to almost all the hardships to which human nature are liable, and among others, to the savage cruelty of the enemy of the country, a people the most subtle, and I take upon me to say, the most truly terrible, of any people that ever inhabited any part of GOD's EARTH; and yet, actuated by principles of true English liberty, they met all these hardships with pleasure, compared with those they suffered in their own country, from the hands of those that should have been their friends.

"*They nourished up by your indulgence?* They grew by your neglect of them: as soon as you began to care about them, that care was exercised

(margin, handwritten) Reasons for Stamp Act

ercised in sending persons to rule over them, in one department and another, who were, perhaps, the deputies of some deputy, sent to spy out their liberty, to misrepresent their actions, and to prey upon them; men, whose behaviour, on many occasions, has caused the blood of those sons of liberty to recoil within them; men promoted to the highest seats of justice, some, to my knowledge, were glad, by going to foreign countries, to escape being brought to a bar of justice in their own.

" *They protected by your arms?* They have nobly taken up arms in your defence, have exerted their valour amidst their constant and laborious industry, for the defence of a country, whose frontiers, while drenched in blood, its interior parts have yielded all its little savings to your enlargement; and *believe me, remember I this day told you so,* That the same spirit which actuated that people at first, will continue with them still; but prudence forbids me to explain myself any further. God knows, I do not at this time speak from motives of party heat. However superior to me, in general knowledge and experience, any one here may be, yet I claim to know more of America, having seen and been more conversant in that country. The people there are as truly loyal, I believe, as any subjects the King has; but a people jealous of their liberties, and who will vindicate them if they should be violated; —but the subject is delicate. I will say no more."

At the end of the session, the King said to the House of Commons, " I have seen, with the most perfect approbation, that you have employed this season of tranquility in promoting those objects which I have recommended to your attention, and

in framing such regulations as may best inforce the just authority of the legislature, and, at the same time, secure and extend the commerce, and unite the interests of every part of my dominions."

The objections of the people of America to the stamp act, were of three kinds.

First, The powers given by the act to Vice-Admiralty courts in America, they said, would prove exceedingly grievous to the subject, by the distance of them; and more so, by depriving the subject of his trial by jury, which was allowed in England.

Secondly, Because the stamp duty would entirely drain the colonies of their specie.

Thirdly, Not being represented in the Parliament of Great Britain, that Parliament, they affirmed, had no right to tax them. Themselves only were the proper, and best judges of their ability; they claimed a right to the exercise of this judgment, and to the sole and exclusive right of imposing taxes upon themselves.

As soon as they were informed the stamp act had passed, the whole continent of America was thrown into a flame.

The province of Virginia took the lead. On the 29th of May, 1765, the House of Burgesses of Virginia, came to the following resolutions:

Whereas the Honourable House of Commons in England, have of late drawn into question, how far the General Assembly of this colony hath power to enact laws for laying taxes and imposing duties, payable by the people of this, his Majesty's most ancient colony; for settling and ascertaining the same to all future times, the House of Burgesses of this present General Assembly

have

have come to the several following resolutions:

Resolved, That the first adventurers and settlers of this his Majesty's colony and dominion of Virginia, brought with them, and transmitted to their posterity, and all other his Majesty's subjects since inhabiting in this his Majesty's colony, all the privileges and immunities that have at any time been held, enjoyed, and possessed by the people of Great Britain.

Resolved, That by the two royal charters granted by King James the First, the colonists aforesaid are declared entitled to all privileges of faithful liege and natural born subjects, to all intents and purposes, as if they had been abiding and born within the realm of England.

Resolved, That his Majesty's liege people of this his most ancient colony, have enjoyed the right of being thus governed by their own assembly, in the article of taxes and internal police, and that the same have never been forfeited, or any other way yielded up, but have been constantly recognized by the King and people of Great Britain.

Resolved, Therefore, that the General Assemby of this colony, together with his Majesty or his substitute, have, in their representative capacity, the only exclusive right and power to lay taxes and impositions upon the inhabitants of this colony; and that every attempt to rest such a power in any person or persons whatsoever, other than the General Assembly aforesaid, is illegal, unconstitutional, and unjust, and has a manifest tendency to destroy British, as well as American freedom.

The following Resolves were not passed, only drawn up by the Committee.

Resolved, That his Majesty's liege people, the inhabitants of this colony, are not bound to yield obedience to any law or ordinance whatsoever, designed to impose any taxation whatsoever upon them, other than the laws and ordinances of the General Assembly aforesaid.

Resolved, That any person who shall, by speaking or writing, maintain that any person or persons, other than the General Assembly of this colony, have any right or power to impose or lay any taxation whatsoever on the people here, shall be deemed an enemy to this his Majesty's colony.

The stamp act was printed and cried about the streets at New York by the title of *The Folly of England, and Ruin of America*. On the 14th of April, the guns at Philadelphia were discovered to be all spiked up, and on looking at those of the barracks, they were found to be served in the same manner, to the great surprize and uneasiness of the inhabitants. Letters arrived in London, from Boston, in New England, dated the 1st and 6th of April, expressing the alarm that the news of the stamp act had thrown the people into, the heart-burnings encreased during the summer, and the New York paper, in the beginning of June, 1765, gave sufficient proofs of the temper with which the colonists beheld the approach of the 1st of November, on which day the act was to take place. Letters of the same tenor came from Virginia, dated in June, and from Philadelphia, of the same date.

It was not the populace alone who were discontented, men of property took the alarm. The General Assembly of Virginia having debated on the stamp act, come to the preceding resolutions; the Governor thought fit to dissolve them. But when a new election took place, it did not seem to be composed of

men

men of more paffive principles, fince the electors excluded all thofe members who did not affent to thofe refolves, while thofe who did were all re-elected.

At Bofton, in New England, upon the meeting of the Affembly, Sir Francis Bernard, the Governor, delivered the following fpeech to them :

" Soon after my arrival to this government, I formed in my mind an idea of three improvements which this country was capable of making, profitable to itfelf and convenient to Great Britain : I mean pot-afh, hemp, and the carrying lumber to the Britifh markets. They are all proper ftaples for New England, and muft be very acceptable to Great Britain, as fhe is at prefent fupplied with them from foreigners, by a lofing trade.

" I have already had the pleafure to fee the firft of thefe eftablifhed with effect, and wanting now nothing but care to preferve its credit, and prevent the general quality of the goods, which is of a fuperior kind, being rendered doubtful and fufpicious, by the fraudulent practices of particulars. This is a neceffary caution at the commencement of a new trade ; for upon its firft reputation depends its future fuccefs. There is already a law for the regulation of this trade, but it wants to be carried into execution ; this I muft defire may be done this feffion, as it is now becoming immediately wanting.

" You have lately given a public teftimony of your defire to promote the production of hemp ; I am equally perfuaded of your good intentions to the improvement of the lumber trade ; as you muft be fenfible of the infufficiency of the prefent markets for the reception of the great quantity of lumber which is now produced, and which will be continually encreafing. The Parliament of Great Britain has already given encouragement to the one ; and it is hoped that it will alfo extend its bounty to the other.

" Thefe are proper objects of your concern ; works, which naturally arife in your own country, ftrengthen your connection with Great Britain, may eafily be confined within yourfelves, and will foon be fuperior to thofe of foreign rivals. When thefe are added to your own refources, they will form a fund, which, with the bleffing of God, upon your induftry and frugality, will be adequate to the expence of all neceffary imports ; and you will have no occafion, as you have hitherto fhewn no difpofition, vainly to attempt to transfer manufactories from their fettled abode ; an undertaking at all times difficult, but, under the difadvantage of high-priced labour, impracticable.

" The general fettlement of the American provinces, which has been long ago propofed, and now probably will be profecuted to its utmoft completion, muft neceffarily produce fome regulations, which, from their novelty only, will appear difagreeable. But I am convinced, and doubt not but experience will confirm it, that they will operate as they are defigned, for the benefit and advantage of the colonies. In the mean time a refpectful fubmiffion to the decrees of the Parliament, is their intereft, as well as their duty.

" In an empire, extended and diverfified as that of Great Britain, there muft be a fupreme legiflature, to which all other powers muft be fubordinate. It is our happinefs that the fupreme legiflature, the parliament of Great Britain, is the fanctuary of liberty and juftice ; and

that

that the prince, who prefides over it, realizes the idea of a patriot King. Surely then, we fhould fubmit our opinions to the determinations of fo auguft a body; and acquiefce in a perfect confidence, that the rights of the members of the Britifh empire will ever be fafe in the hands of the confervators of the liberty of the whole."

Extract of a letter from Bofton, in New England, Auguft 5, 1765.

" As to public affairs, it would take me up a week's time to write all I could fay: as to the impofition of the ftamp act, (which takes place the 1ft of November) it will, I believe, be of fhort continuance; for it is univerfally efteemed here as arbitrary and unconftitutional, and as a breach of charter and compact between K—— and fubject; and we think we have a right to refufe fubmiffion to it.—However, I believe moft of the ftamp mafters will be afraid to act in fuch ftation as will ftab their country.

" We have two hundred thoufand inhabitants in this province, and the others in proportion; fo that it is computed there are about two millions in the whole: from hence you will think it is too late in the day to be dragoon'd out of our rights.

" I have been here above fixteen years, and I don't know of one fingle man but would rifque his life and property to ferve King George the Third; and would do the fame to maintain his rights, liberty, and property.—Touch our Birth-right, and our body politick, like the human body, fenfibly feels it, and would do its utmoft to fhake it off.

" The Cuftom-houfe books will fhew, that 3000l. lefs is collected fince the duty of molaffes has been three-pence, than when one penny: your fmall men of war have eat the King's provifions in guarding the coafts; but have brought neither profit nor credit to their employers."

Thefe difcontents were general; and they were encreafed by what they ftiled an utter inability to pay the tax in fpecie.

About the beginning of Auguft, the colonifts began ferioufly to think of the fteps they were to take. A General Congrefs of reprefentatives of all the Colonies, was agreed on, to meet at New York. The freemen of Providence, in Rhode Ifland, were called together, " to confer on fuch meafures, " as " fhould appear to them necef- " fary, relative to the *ftamp act*; " whereby the liberties, the darling " boaft of the Englifh North Ame- " rican fubjects, which were once " deemed indefeafible, muft be " greatly abridged, if not totally " annihilated." And accordingly they met, and appointed a committee to prepare fuitable *inftructions* to be given their reprefentatives, for their conduct in the General Congrefs, on that occafion. Thefe inftructions were prepared, and the freemen being again convened the next day, were laid before them, and approved of. The fame fteps were alfo taken by the province of South Carolina.

The houfe of reprefentatives at Bofton, refolved, That the honourable James Otis, Thomas Ruggles, and Oliver Partridge, Efqrs. be a committe, to meet the committees of the *Affemblies of the whole continent*, at New York, October 1, to unite in a petition to his Majefty and the Britifh parliament, for relief under the infupportable grievance of the ftamp act.—This was the Firft Congrefs of the American Continent.

On the 10th of September, the affembly of Philadelphia, having

C   appointed

appointed a committee to attend at the general congress at New York, a letter from the speaker of the Massachusett's assembly was read, and the house came to the following resolutions on the questions :

First, Whether the house are of opinion, that, in duty to their constituents, they ought to remonstrate to the crown against the stamp act, and other late acts of parliament, by which heavy burdens have been laid on the colonies.

Resolved in the affirmative.

Secondly, Whether this house will appoint a committee of three, or more of their members, to attend the congress proposed in the foregoing letter, to be held at New York on the first of October next, for the purposes therein mentioned.

Resolved in the affirmative.

Extract of a letter from Boston, in New England, August 26.

" Very early on Wednesday morning, the 14th instant, were discovered hanging, on a limb of the great trees, so called, at the South part of this town, two effigies, one of which, by the labels, appeared to be designed to represent a stamp officer, the other a jack boot with a head and horns peeping out of the top. The report of the images soon spread through the town, brought a vast number of spectators, and had such an effect on them, that they were immediately inspired with a spirit of enthusiasm, which diffused itself through the whole concourse ; so much were they affected with a sense of liberty, that scarce any could attend to the task of day-labour. About dusk the images were taken down, placed on a bier (not covered with a sheet, except a sheet of paper which bore the inscription) supported in procession by six men, followed by a great con-

course of people, and in the greatest order, echoing forth, Liberty and Property ! No Stamp, &c.—Having passed through the town-house, they proceeded with their pageantry down King-street, and thro' Kilby-street, where an edifice had been lately erected, which was supposed to be designed for a stamp-office. Here they halted, and went to work to demolish that building, which they soon effected, without receiving any hurt, excepting one of the spectators, who happened to be rather too nigh the brick wall when it fell. This being finished, many of them them loaded themselves with the wooden trophies, and proceeded (bearing the two effigies) to the top of Fort-hill, where a fire was soon kindled, in which one of them was burnt. The populace after this went to work on the barn, fence, garden, &c. and here it would have ended, had not some indiscretions, to say the least, been committed by his friends within, which so enraged the people they were not to be restrained, though hitherto no violence had been offered to any one. But it is very remarkable, though they entered the lower part of the house in multitudes, yet the damage done to it was not so great as might have been expected.

" The next day the honourable gentleman, who had been appointed to the duty of distributor of the stamps when they should arrive, supposing himself to be the object of their derision, informed the principal gentlemen of the town, that as it appeared so disagreeable to the people, he should request the liberty of being excused from that office ; and in the evening the populace re-assembled, erected a pyramid, intending a second bonfire ; but upon hearing of the resignation, they desisted, and repaired to the

gentleman's

gentleman's gate, gave three cheers, and took their departure without damage; but having heard it propagated that an honourable gentleman, at the north part of the town, had been acceſſary in laying on the ſtamp duties, &c. they repaired to his houſe, where, upon being informed by ſome gentlemen of integrity and reputation, that he had not only ſpoke, but wrote to the contrary, they retired, and having patroled the ſtreets, returned to their reſpective habitations, as quietly as they had done the night before."

Extract of a letter from a gentleman in Philadelphia, to his friend in Briſtol, Sept. 7, 1765.

" I make no doubt you have been informed, by letters from your friends, as well as by our public news-papers, of the great commotions throughout our colonies in general, which daily increaſe on account of the late ſtamp act for raiſing money amongſt us: What adds to our uneaſineſs is, that we hear our brethren in England cenſure us ſeverely, from a miſtaken opinion that we are unwilling to pay our proportion towards relieving the nation from the heavy burden of debt it now groans under, This is by no means the caſe: We are, and always have been, ready and willing to pay our yearly proportion of that debt. What occaſions this general uneaſineſs and commotion is,—1ſt. That we are to be taxed by this act, without being repreſented on your ſide of the water, or being firſt heard for ourſelves.—2d. That all the monies to be raiſed by this act are to be remitted home to the King's Exchequer in ſpecie, and not by bills of exchange, or any other remittance.—3d. That if any offence is committed againſt the act, the offender, if the proſecutor chuſes it,

is to be tried by a Court of Admiralty.

" The 1ſt, the coloniſts ſay, is an infringement on the rights and privileges they have ever been entitled to, and enjoyed by their Royal Charter. Had the government at home fixed on any particular ſum to be yearly raiſed and paid by them, and adjuſted their ſeveral proportions, which they well know how to do, and left it to their ſeveral aſſemblies to raiſe the money by ſuch ways and means as they ſhould think moſt eaſy, it might have been readily complied with.—To the 2d, it is impoſſible for the colonies to raiſe one fourth part of ſo much ſpecie as their tax would amount to, as they do not from all their trade import it. Were the remittance to be made in bills of exchange, they might poſſibly make it by them.— This third article is ſo great a ſtride to arbitrary power, and ſo great a violation and infringement on Engliſh liberty, that no Engliſhman can ſubmit tamely to it. Why ſhould the King's ſubjects on this ſide of the water be deprived of the liberty of being tried by civil authority and twelve honeſt jurymen more than in England? Were an attempt to be made of this kind with you, every Engliſhman who has the leaſt ſenſe of his right of liberty would riſe in oppoſition; and you may depend upon it, that unleſs theſe three particulars are altered, the coloniſts will grow more and more uneaſy."

In the midſt of theſe heats, Governor Fauquieur prorogued the General Aſſembly of Virginia, till the 17th of October; and Governor Wentworth prorogued that of New Hampſhire to the 19th of November (eighteen days after the ſtamp act was to be in force).

Mr. Meſſerve, the ſtamp-officer for New Hampſhire, was ſurrounded

by

by above three hundred perfons (feveral of whom were men of property) and obliged to engage not to
act in his office.

At Providence, a Gazette Extraordinary was publifhed, on the 24th
of Auguft, with VOX POPULI, VOX
DEI, in large letters, for the fron-
tifpiece; and underneath, *Where
the Spirit of the Lord is, there is Liberty*. St. Paul.—It congratulated
them on the fpirit of oppofition that
had already been fhewn in divers parts
of North America; and went on in
thefe words : " We have glorious accounts from all parts, of the noble
fpirit of the people in the caufe of liberty," and concluded an addrefs to
the people of New England, thus :
" Let me draw towards a conclufion,
by obferving the univerfal fpirit
which now prevails thro' the colonies,
to take all *lawful* meafures to prevent the execution of the ftamp act
here.   This laudable zeal hath burft
into a flame in Bofton, and the exertions of the people in that ancient
town, who have heretofore been
obliged to ftruggle for their liberties,
when infamoufly attacked, as their
their hiftory fhews, plainly indicate
that the fpirit of their fathers reft
upon them, and that they preferve
in their breafts the noble fenfations
of freedom."

The flame now ran from province
to province, and the fpirit of oppofition was almoft univerfal ; Mr. In-
gerfoll, ftamp officer of Connecticut,
had fent to Wyndham to a perfon
whom he had appointed to be his
deputy, to come to him at New Haven, to receive his commiffion ; but
the inhabitants at Wyndham, having
knowledge of the letter he had received, furrounded his houfe, demanded the letter from him, and
warned him not to accept the office,
which fo terrified him, that the very
fame poft he fent back an abfolute

refufal of taking the charge upon
him.

The fame fate awaited his principal at New Haven, whofe refignation of the place of ftamp officer was
printed in the Bofton Poft Boy of
Aug. 24, in the following words :

To the good People of CONNECTICUT.

" When I undertook the office of
diftributor of ftamps for this colony,
I meant a fervice to you, and really
thought vou would have viewed it
in that light, when you came to underftand the nature of the ftamp act,
and that of the office ; but fince it
gives you fo much uneafinefs, you
may be affured, if I find (after the
act takes place, which is the firft of
November) that you fhall not incline
to purchafe or make ufe of any
ftampt paper, I fhall not force it
upon you, nor think it worth my
while to trouble you or myfelf with
any exercife of my office ; but if by
that time I fhall find you generally
in much need of the ftampt paper,
and very anxious to obtain it, I fhall
hope you will be willing to receive
it of me (if I fhall happen to have
any) at leaft until another perfon
more agreeable to you can be appointed in my room.

" I cannot but wifh you would
think more how to get rid of the
ftamp act, than of the officers who
are to fupply you with paper, and
that you had learnt more of the nature of my office before you had undertaken to be fo very angry at it."

New Haven,   J. INGERSOLL.
Aug. 1765.

This refignation was much applauded, but feems rather to have
been the effect of fear, than a hearty
defire of complying with the temper
of the times ; for, when the people
affembled round his houfe, and demanded, whether he intended to act
in that office, or refign, he an-
                                    fwered,

swered, that as he had accepted the office in person, he did not think he had power to resign. They next demanded whether, when the stampt paper arrived, he would deliver it to them, to make a bonfire ? Or— have his house pulled down. To this question he strove to evade giving an answer, by desiring them to wait the meeting of the assembly, and several other pretences ; but when he found all unavailing, he then promised, " that when they arrived, he would either re-ship them to be sent back ;- or, when they were in his house, he would leave his doors open, that they might then act as they thought proper ; this satisfied them, and they dispersed ; and the above advertisement appeared in the paper.

On the 26th of August, about twilight, a small bonfire was kindled in King-street, Boston, and surrounded only by a few boys and children ; but when the fireward endeavoured to extinguish it, he was whispered, by an unknown person, to desist ; which he not regarding, received a blow on his arm, and such other marks of displeasure, as obliged him to withdraw. But presently after a particular whistle and whoop was heard from several quarters, which instantly drew together a great number of persons, disguised, and armed with clubs, sticks, &c. who assaulted the house of William Story, Esq; deputy register of the Vice-Admiralty, opposite the north side of the Court-House, the lower part of which, being his office, was broke open, the files and public records of that court were seized, and condemned to the flames.

This did not take up half an hour, when they rushed onwards (encreasing in their numbers) to the

new-built house of Benjamin Hallowell, jun. Esq; the furniture of which they destroyed. About ten o'clock, they attacked the house of the Lieut. Governor, which, in a few hours, they stript of its furniture ; and even his apparel, books, &c. were destroyed. After which they dispersed.

The next morning was the time for holding the assize and the supreme court of judicature, when the chief justice was obliged to attend in his only suit, while the gentlemen of the bench and bar were in their respective robes. But the chief inhabitants were very strenuous to distinguish " that tumultuous and outrageous behaviour, from a truly noble opposition to the imposition of internal taxes, without the intervention of the respective legislatures of the colonies." The peace and good order of the town was restored, and preserved by a nightly military watch, and several persons were apprehended and committed to goal, on suspicion of being concerned in the late riots.

It is proper to remark, that the outrages on the 26th were not only disavowed by the reputable part of the inhabitants, but, on a short notice, they met at Fanueil-hall in great numbers, and testified their utter detestation of the extraordinary and violent proceedings of the unknown persons the preceding night; and they unanimously voted " That the select men, and magistrates of the town, be desired to use their utmost endeavours, agreeable to law, to suppress such disorders for the future ; and that the freeholders, and other inhabitants, will do every thing in their power to assist them therein." The next day a proclamation was published by the governor, offering a reward of 300l. for the discovery of any of the ring-

leaders,

leaders, and 100l. for any of the other perfons concerned in that riot.

On Tuefday the 27th of Auguft (for, as if it had been previoufly concerted, the commotions throughout the provinces all happened within a few days of each other) about nine o'clock in the morning, the people of Newport, in Rhode Ifland, brought forth the effigies of three perfons, in a cart, with halters about their necks, to a gallows, twenty feet high, placed near the Town-houfe, where they were hung to public view till near night, when they were cut down, and burnt under the gallows, amidft the acclamations of thoufands.

The next evening they affembled again, and befet the houfe of Martin Howard, jun. Efq; the furniture, &c. thereof they burnt and deftroyed, as they did next that of Dr. Thomas Moffat, leaving the houfes mere fhells. They then proceeded towards the houfe of Auguftus Johnfton, Efq; who had been appointed ftamp-mafter for Rhode Ifland, but were met and parleyed with by a gentleman, who, telling them the houfe was not Mr. Johnfton's property, they defifted from any farther attempts, but infifted that Mr. Johnfton's effects fhould be delivered to them next day, unlefs he would refign his place, which he did on his coming to town next day, in the following terms, and then they difperfed:

To the Inhabitants of the town of Newport,

Gentlemen,

" As I find my being appointed the ftamp-officer of this colony has irritated the people of this town againft me, though the office was beftowed on me unafked and unthought of; and being willing, as far as it is in my power, to reftore tranquility to the town, do engage, upon my honour, that I will not accept of the faid office, upon any terms, unlefs I have your confent for the fame.

AUGUSTINE JOHNSTON."
Auguft 29, 1765.

On thefe outrages, Mr. Howard and Mr. Moffat, finding the refentment of the people was very high againft them, and fearing their perfons would not be fafe in Newport, took fhelter in the Signet man of war, and foon after departed for Great Britain.

On the 10th of September, the ftamp papers for the ufe of the New England Government, arrived at Bofton; of which the Governor informed the Affembly in the following fpeech:

Gentlemen of the Council and Gentlemen of the Houfe of Reprefentatives,

" A fhip is arrived in the harbour with ftamped papers on board for the King's ufe in this province, and alfo with other ftamped papers for the like ufe for the province of New Hampfhire and colony of Rhode Ifland; as Mr. Oliver has declined the office of diftributor of ftamped papers, and cannot fafely meddle with what are arrived, the care of them devolves to this government, as having a general c arge of the King's intereft within it. I have already laid this matter before the Council, and they refer it to a General Court; I therefore now apply to you jointly to defire your advice and affiftance, in order to preferve the ftamped papers defigned for this government, being the King's property, of very confiderable value, fafe and fecure for his Majefty's further orders. I muft alfo defire you at the fame time to confider of the like prefervative of the ftamped papers defigned for New Hampfhire

and

and Rhode Island, if the diftributors appointed for thofe governments fhould decline to have the charge of them, and in fuch cafe the care of them will devolve to this government, equally with others."

To which the Affembly replied.

May it pleafe your Excellency,

" The Houfe having given all due attention to your Excellency's meffage of this day, beg leave to acquaint your Excellency, that the ftamped papers mentioned in your meffage are brought here without any directions to this government : it is the fenfe of the Houfe, that it may prove of ill confequence for them any ways to intereft themfelves in this matter; we hope therefore your Excellency will excufe us, if we cannot fee our way clear enough to give you any advice or affiftance therein."

The General Affembly having thus declined to interfere in the direction of the ftamp paper, the Governor again applied to the Council, who advifed him to lodge the ftamp papers in the Caftle; but various reports having been fpread concerning this meafure, his Excellency on the firft of October made the following fpeech to the Council :

Gentlemen,

" I have been informed that it is reported about the town, that the ftamped papers are to be lodged in the Caftle, there to be unpacked and diftributed. I have frequently in converfation fhewn the abfurdity of fuch a fuppofition ; but as what I have faid is perhaps not much known, I make this declaration to you : That I have no warrant, order, or authority whatfoever, to diftribute the ftamped papers, or to unpack the bales, or feparate the parcels, or order any perfon whatfoever

fo to do ; that it cannot be conceived that I fhould be fo imprudent as to undertake a bufinefs to which I have no appointment, and make myfelf anfwerable for large fums of money, the receipt of which I cannot attend to, and have no power to direct or order : What I have done in purfuance of your advice, in ordering the ftamped papers to be depofited in the Caftle, and there to be defended with all the force of that fortrefs, was to preferve them entire and unpacked for his Majefty's ufe. In this I have had two things in view, to prevent imprudent people committing an high infult upon the King, an indignity which would be fure to meet with particular refentment; and to fave the town and province, as it may happen, from being made anfwerable for fo great a fum as the value of the ftamped papers will amount to ; as they certainly will be, if the ftamped papers fhould be taken away. In providing againft thefe two evils, furely we are endeavouring to do the town and province real and important fervice, whatever people, in their prefent temper, may think."

" His Excellency having made the foregoing declaration to the Board, they fignified their unanimous defire to his Excellency, that he would permit the fame to be publifhed ; and his Excellency thereupon gave permiffion for publifhing the fame accordingly."

A. OLIVER, Sec.

About this time the following advertifement appeared in the New York Gazette :

To Meffrs. GREEN *and* RIND.

Gentlemen,

" I am informed that the ftamplaw takes place the firft day of November next ; I therefore hereby give notice to all officers whatfoever
that

that may be appointed by virtue of that moft grievous and unconftitutional act (to prevent them trouble) that I will pay no tax whatever, but what is laid upon me by my reprefentatives. I am, gentlemen,

Your humble fervant,

BENJAMIN WELSH."

While the colonies fhewed the ftrongeft marks of diflike to thofe whom they fuppofed to be the promoters of the ftamp-act, they were as ftrong in their marks of approbation of thofe who had oppofed its paffing. On the 18th of September, at a meeting of the freeholders and inhabitants of Bofton, a committee of feven gentlemen was chofen " to draw up and tranfmit to Mr. Secretary Conway and Colonel Ifaac Barré, feveral addreffes of thanks for their patriotic fpeeches in parliament, in favour of the rights and privileges of the colonifts; and to defire correct copies thereof to be placed among their moft precious archives." And they voted the pictures of thofe gentlemen to be placed in their Town-hall.

On Saturday, Sept. 21, there was publifhed a new news-paper in America, under the following title, " The CONSTITUTIONAL COURANT, containing matters interefting to *Liberty*, and no ways repugnant to *Loyalty :*" It had an emblematical head-piece, of a fnake cut into feveral pieces, on each of which were the initial letters of the names of the feveral colonies, and over it, " JOIN OR DIE" in large letters, and the imprint was, " Printed by *Andrew Marvel*, at the fign of the *Bribe refufed*, on *Conftitution-hill*, North America."

The 25th of September the General Affembly of the province at Maffachufett's-Bay, in New Eng-

land, met at Bofton, when his Excellency Francis Bernard, Efq; Governor of the faid province, made the following fpeech to them :

Gentlemen of the Council, and Gentlemen of the Houfe of Reprefentatives,

" I have called you together at this unufual time, in purfuance of the unanimous advice of a very full Council, that you may take into confideration the prefent ftate of the province, and determine what is to be done at this difficult and dangerous conjuncture. I need not recount to you the violences which have been committed in this town, nor the declarations which have been made and ftill fubfift, that the act of parliament for granting ftampduties in the Britifh colonies fhall not be executed within this province. The ordinary executive authority of this government is much too weak to contradict fuch declarations, or oppofe the force by which they are fupported : It has therefore been found neceffary to call the whole legiflative power in aid of the executive government. From this time this arduous bufinefs will be put into your hands, and it will become a provincial concern.

" Upon this occafion it is my duty to ftate to you what will probably be the confequences, if you fhould fuffer a confirmed difobedience of this act of parliament to take place. I am fenfible how dangerous it is to fpeak out at this time, and upon this fubject ; but my ftation will not allow me to be awed or reftrained in what I have to fay to the General Court ; not only my duty to the King, but my duty to the Province, my love to it, my concern for it, oblige me to be plain and explicit upon this occafion. And I hope no advocate for liberty will violate that effential conftitutional right, freedom of fpeech in the General Affembly.

" As

" As I defire not to dictate to you, and would avoid all appearance of it, I fhall refolve what I have to recommend to your confideration into mere queftions, and avoid affertions of my own in matters which are doubtful. I fhall not enter into any difquifition of the policy of the act: it has never been a part of my bufinefs to enter into any judgment of it; and as I have not hitherto had any opportunity to exprefs any fentiments of it, I fhall not do it now. I have only to fay, that it is an act of the parliament of Great Britain, and as fuch ought to be obeyed by the fubjects of Great Britain. And I truft that the fupremacy of that parliament, over all the members of their wide and diffufed empire, never was, and never will be denied within thefe walls.

" The Right of the parliament of Great Britian to make laws for the American colonies, however it has been controverted in America, remains indifputable at Weftminfter. If it is yet to be made a queftion, who fhall determine it but the parliament? If the parliament declares that this right is inherent in them, are they like to acquiefce in an open and forcible oppofition to the exercife of it? Will they not more probably maintain fuch right, and fupport their own authority? Is it in the will or in the power, or for the intereft of this province to oppofe fuch authority? If fuch oppofition fhould be made, may it not bring on a conteft, which may prove the moft detrimental and ruinous event which could happen to this people?

" It is faid, that the gentleman who oppofed this act in the Houfe of Commons, did not difpute the authority of parliament to make fuch a law, but argued upon the inexpediency of it at this time, and the inability of the colonies to bear fuch an impofition. Thefe are two distinct queftions, which may receive different anfwers. The power of the parliament to tax the colonies may be admitted, and yet the expediency of exercifing that power at fuch a time, and in fuch a manner, may be denied. But if the queftions are blended together, fo as to admit of but one anfwer, the affirmative of the right of parliament will conclude for the expediency of the act. Confider therefore, gentlemen, if you found your application for relief upon denying the parliament's right to make fuch a law, whether you will not take from your friends and advocates the ufe of thofe arguments, which are moft like to procure the relief you defire?

" You, Gentlemen of the Houfe of Reprefentatives, have propofed a congrefs of committees from the reprefentatives of feveral colonies, to confider of a general, united, dutiful, loyal and humble reprefentation which you have propofed? Will the denying the power and authority of the King and Parliament, be the proper means to obtain their favour? If the parliament fhould be difpofed to repeal this act, will they probably do it whilft there fubfifts a forcible oppofition to the execution of it? Is it not more probable, that they will require a fubmiffion to their authority as a preliminary to their granting you any relief? Confider then, whether the oppofition to the execution of the act has not a direct tendency to defeat the meafures you have taken to procure a repeal of it, if you do not interpofe to prevent it.

" By this act, all papers which are not duly ftamped are to be null and void; and all perfons who fhall fign, engrofs, or write any fuch papers, will forfeit, for each fact, ten pounds. If therefore ftamps are not to be ufed, all public offices muft be fhut up: for it cannot be expected,

D that

that any officer should incur penalties much beyond all he is worth, for the sake of doing what must be null and void when it is done. I would therefore desire you to consider what effects the stopping two kinds of offices only, the Courts of Justice and the Custom-houses, will have upon the generality of the people. When the Courts of Justice are shut up, no one will be able to sue for a debt due to him. Must not then all credit and mutual faith cease of course, and fraud and rapine take their place? Will any one's person or property be safe, when their sole protector, the law, is debased to act? Must not the hand of violence be then let loose, and force of arms become the only governing power? It is easy to form an adequate idea of a state of general outlawry: And may not the reality exceed the worst idea you can form of it?

"If trade and navigation shall cease by the shutting up the ports of this province for want of legal clearances; are you sure that all other ports which can rival these will be shut up also? Can you depend upon recovering your trade again entire and undiminished, when you shall be pleased to resume it? Can the people of this province subsist within navigation for any long time? What will become of the seamen who will be put out of employment? What will become of the tradesmen who immediately depend upon the navigation for their daily bread? Will these people endure want quietly without troubling their neighbours? What will become of the numberless families which depend upon fishery? Will they be able to turn the produce of their year's work into the necessaries of life without navigation? Are there not numberless other families who do not appear immediately concerned in trade,

and yet ultimately depend upon it? Do you think it possible to provide for the infinite chain of the dependants upon trade, who will be brought to want by the stopping of it? It is certain that this province has a stock of provisions within itself sufficient for all its inhabitants, without the usual imports? If there should be a sufficiency in general, can it be distributed among all the individuals without great violence and confusion? In short, can this province bear a cessation of law and justice, and of trade and navigation, at a time when the business of the year is to be wound up, and the severe season is hastily approaching? These are serious and alarming questions, which deserve a cool and dispassionate consideration.

"I would not willingly aggravate the dangers which are before you: I do not think it very easy to do it: This province seems to me to be upon the brink of a precipice; and that it depends upon you to prevent its falling. Possibly I may fear more for you than you do for yourselves; but in the situation you now stand, a sight of your danger is necessary to your preservation! and it is my business to open it to you. But I do not pretend to enumerate all the evils which may possibly happen; several, and some of no little importance, will occur to you, tho' they have been omitted by me. In a word, gentlemen, never were your judgment and prudence so put to a trial, as they are like to be upon the present occasion.

"I am aware that endeavours have been, or may be used, to lessen my credit with you, which I have hitherto always studied to improve to the advantage of the province. Violences seldom come alone: The same spirit which pulls down houses attacks reputations. The best men

in

in the province have been much injured in this way; I myself have not escaped this malignity. But I shall not lower myself so as to answer such accusers: To you I shall always owe such explanations as shall be necessary to the improvement of a good understanding between us. However, I will take this opportunity to declare publicly, that ever since I have sat in this chair, I have been constantly attentive to the true interests of this province, according to the best of my understanding, and have endeavoured to promote them by all means in my power. The welfare of this people is still uppermost in my heart : and I believe no man feels more for them than I do at this present time.

Gentlemen of the House of Representatives,

" I must recommend you to do an act of justice, which at the same time will reflect credit upon yourselves; I mean to order a compensation to be made to the sufferers by the late dreadful disturbances. Their losses are too great for them to sit down with; one of them amounts to a very large sum. You must be sensible that it will be expected that these damages be made good; and it will be better for you to do it of your own accord before any requisition is made to you. An estimate of these damages is made by a committee of the council, pursuant to order, which will be laid before you.

Gentlemen,

" I am sensible of the difficulty of the part you have to act; it may not be sufficient for you to be convinced of a submission to the law for the present, unless the same conviction shall be extended to the people in general. If this should be so, I can only desire you to use all means to make

yourselves well acquainted with the exigency of the present time; and if you shall be persuaded that a disobedience of the act is productive of much more evil than a submission to it can be, you must endeavour to convince your constituents of the truth of such persuasion. In such case I shall readily grant you a recess for a sufficient time; and I shall be ready to concur with you in all other legal measures to provide for the safety of the people in the best manner.
Council Chamber, FRA. BERNARD."
Sept. 25, 1765.

The House of Representatives immediately appointed a committee to prepare an address in answer to his Excellency's speech, and the draught was to have been reported the 28th; on the preceding day, both the houses of assembly received the astonishing, sudden, and unexpected message to adjourn to the 23d of October.

The 26th of September the hon. Thomas Finch, Esq; governor of Connecticut, issued a proclamation, " requiring all officers, civil and military, to use their utmost endeavours for preventing and suppressing all riots and tumultuous assemblies :" but so great was the dread of the peoples resentment, that William Storey, Esq; resigned his office of deputy-register of the court of Vice-Admiralty; as some days before, William Cox, Esq; had resigned his office as stamp-master for New-Jersey.

About the same time, fourteen boxes more of stampt paper arrived at Boston for the use of that province; and of New Hampshire and Rhode Island; but the ships that brought them were obliged to be guarded in by a man of war sloop and a cutter, and brought to under

D 2 the

the protection of the guns of the castle.

The inhabitants of Connecticut not being fully satisfied with the first declaration of Mr. Ingersoll, a great number of the inhabitants from the eastern parts of the province came on horseback to Hartford on the 18th of September, and declared they were on their way to Newhaven, to demand of Mr. Ingersoll a total resignation of his office, as were also a number of their companions on the lower roads, who were all to rendezvous at Brentford the next day; they then separated to get lodgings in Hartford for that night. In the evening they received information that Mr. Ingersoll was to be in town the next day, to apply to the assembly for protection; but left he should come in the night, to shun them, they kept a patrole in the streets all that night to prevent his coming unnoticed; but he not arriving the next morning, the whole body set off, and in about an hour met Mr. Ingersoll at the lower end of Wethersfield, and told him their business, when, after many evasions and debates, he read his resignation to the multitude, who desired him to cry out *Liberty and Property* three times, which he did; and they returned three loud huzzas. Mr. Ingersoll then went and dined at the tavern with many of the company, and a party of about five hundred escorted him to Hartford, where he again publicly read his resignation, which they again applauded with three huzzas, and then they all dispersed without any disturbance. His resignation was as follows:

Wethersfield, Sept. 9, 1765.

" I do hereby promise, that I will never receive any stamped papers, which may arrive from Europe, in consequence of an act lately passed in the parliament of Great Britain, nor officiate in any manner as stamp-master, or distributor of stamps, within this colony of Connecticut, either directly or indirectly. And I do hereby notify to all the inhabitants of his Majesty's colony of Connecticut, (notwithstanding the said office or trust has been committed to me) not to apply to me, ever after, for any such stamped papers, hereby declaring, that I do resign the said office, and execute these presents of my own free will and accord, without any equivocation, or mental reservation.

In witness whereof I have hereunto set my hand,

J. INGERSOLL."

In Philadelphia, the house of assembly met on the 21st of September, and came to the following resolutions:

" The House taking into consideration, that an act of parliament has lately passed in England, for imposing certain stamp duties, and other duties on his Majesty's subjects in America, whereby they conceive some of their most essential and valuable rights, as British subjects, to be deeply affected, think it a duty they owe to themselves, and their posterity, to come to the following resolutions, viz.

Resolved, N. C. D. That the assemblies of this province have, from time to time, whenever requisitions have been made by his Majesty, for carrying on military operations for the defence of America, most chearfully and liberally contributed their full proportion of men and money for those services.

Resolved, N. C. D. That whenever his Majesty's service shall, for the future, require the aids of the inhabitants of this province, and they shall be called upon for that purpose, in a CONSTITUTIONAL WAY, it will be their indispensable
duty

duty moſt chearfully and liberally to grant to his Majeſty their proportion of men and money, for the defence, ſecurity, and other public ſervices of the Britiſh American colonies.

Reſolved, N. C. D. That the inhabitants of this province are intitled to all the rights and privileges of his Majeſty's ſubjects in Great Britain, or elſewhere; and that the conſtitution of government in this province is founded on the natural rights of mankind, and the noble principles of Engliſh liberty, and therefore is, or ought to be, perfectly free.

Reſolved, N. C. D. That it is the inherent birth-right, and indubitable privilege of every Britiſh ſubject, to be taxed only by his own conſent, or that of his legal repreſentotives, in conjunction with his Majeſty, or his ſubſtitutes.

Reſolved, N. C. D. That the only legal repreſentatives of the inhabitants of this province, are the perſons they annually elect to ſerve as members of aſſembly.

Reſolved therefore, N. C. D. That the taxation of the people of this province, by any other perſons whatſoever than ſuch their repreſentatives in aſſembly, is UNCONSTITUTIONAL, and ſubverſive of their moſt valuable rights.

Reſolved, N. C. D. That the laying taxes upon the inhabitants of this province *in any other manner*, being manifeſtly ſubverſive of public liberty, muſt, of neceſſary conſequence, be utterly deſtructive of public happineſs.

Reſolved, N. C. D. That the veſting an authority in the courts of admiralty to decide in ſuits relating to the ſtamp duties, and other matters, foreign to their proper juriſdiction, is highly dangerous to the liberties of his Majeſty's American ſubjects, contrary to Magna Charta,

the great charter and fountain of Engliſh liberty, and deſtructive of one of their moſt *darling and acknowledged rights*, that of TRIALS BY JURIES.

Reſolved, N C. D. That it is the opinion of this houſe, that the reſtraints impoſed by ſeveral acts of parliament on the trade of this province, at a time when the people labour under an enormous load of debt, muſt of neceſſity be attended with the moſt fatal conſequences, not only to this province, but to the trade of our mother country.

Reſolved, N. C. D. That this houſe think it their duty thus firmly to aſſert, with modeſty and decency, their inherent rights, that their poſterity may learn and know, that it was not with their conſent and acquieſcence, that any taxes ſhould be levied on them by any perſons but their own repreſentatives; and are deſirous that theſe their reſolves ſhould remain on their minutes, as a teſtimony of the zeal and ardent deſire of the preſent houſe of aſſembly to preſerve their *ineſtimable rights*, which, as Engliſhmen, they have poſſeſſed ever ſince this province was ſettled, and to tranſmit them to their lateſt poſterity."

The ſame day, the following addreſs was preſented to the Governor of Maryland:

To his Excellency HORATIO SHARPE, *Eſq; Governor and Commander in Chief in and over the province of* Maryland.

The humble Addreſs of the Houſe of Delegates.

May it pleaſe your Excellency,

" We, his majeſty's moſt dutiful and loyal ſubjects, the delegates of the freemen of the province of Maryland, in aſſembly convened, return your excellency our thanks for your ſpeech at the opening of this ſeſſion;

and

and beg leave to affure you, that the opportunity your excellency has now afforded us, of promoting the true intereft of our country, is extremely agreeable to us.

As we have thought it our indifpenfible duty to our conftituents, at this time to appoint a committee of fome of our members, to join committees from the houfe of reprefentatives of the other colonies on the continent, who are to meet at the city of New York, on the firft Tuefday in October next, in order to to join in a general and united dutiful, loyal and humble reprefentation to his majefty, and the Britifh parliament, of the circumftances and condition of the Britifh colonies and plantations, and to implore relief againft fome acts of parliaments, we are informed have lately paffed in England, whereby it is apprehended the liberty of the colonies will be greatly abridged, which, with the matters neceffarily relative to, and dependant upon it, (wherein we have met with fome very unexpected delays) has fo wholly engroffed our attention, that we have not yet even fettled any of our ordinary rules for proceeding, we cannot doubt but we fhall ftand excufed for being thus late in anfwering your excellency's fpeech ; and having now very nearly completed that affair, and as the next month will be chiefly taken up in adjourned country courts, by which means feveral of our members muft be taken from the bufinefs of the houfe, or great numbers fuffer much by their fuits continuing open at this time, we hope your excellency will, as foon as the prefent important bufinefs is finifhed, give us a fhort recefs of a few weeks, that thofe inconveniences may be removed, when we fhall be very glad to have an opportunity of proceeding to the difpatch of the interefting matters your excellency has been pleafed to recommend to us, and to concur with the other branches of the legiflature, in every meafure tending to produce the general welfare of our country, which we are much pleafed to be affured by your excellency, you alfo confider as your own."

Robert Lloyd, Speaker. Sept. 21, 1765.

To which he returned the following Anfwer, on Sept. 28:

Gentlemen of the Lower Houfe of Affembly.

" As I perceive by your addrefs, which hath been juft prefented to me, that you are defirous to have a fhort recefs of a few weeks, I fhall comply with your requeft ; but it being probable that the ftamped paper deftined for this province, in confequence of the act of parliament that was made laft feffion, by the legiflature of Great Britain, will arrive here before I fhall have an opportunity of advifing with you again, and that the mafter of the veffel who may give charge thereof, will defire me to give orders for its being landed, and lodged in a place of fecurity, efpecially as the perfon appointed to diftribute the ftamps here, has, I underftand, left the province, I fhould be glad to know how you would advife me to act on fuch an occafion. Sept. 28. Horatio Sharpe."

And the houfe then came to the following refoluitons, which they ordered to be printed :

By the Lower Houfe of Affembly.

Sept. 28, 1765.

Ordered, That Mr. Jonas Green, printer, do publifh in the Maryland Gazette, next week, the following refolves of this houfs :

Signed per order.

M. Macnemara, Cl. Lo. Ho.

I. Re-

I. Refolved unanimoufly, That the firft adventurers and fettlers of this province of Maryland brought with them, and tranfmitted to their pofterity, and all other his Majefty's fubjeĉts fince inhabiting in this province, all the liberties, privileges, franchifes, and immunities, that at any time have been held, enjoyed and poffeffed, by the people of Great Britain.

II. Refolved unanimoufly, That it was granted by Magna Charta, and other the good laws and ftatutes of England, and confirmed by the petition and Bill of Rights, that the fubjeĉt fhould not be compelled to contribute to any tax, tallage, aid, or other like charge, not fet by common confent of parliament.

III. Refolved unanimoufly, That by a royal charter, granted by his majefty king Charles I. in the eighth year of his reign, and in the year of our Lord 1632, to Cæcilius, then lord Baltimore, it was for the encouragement of people to tranfport themfelves and families into this province, amongft other things covenanted and granted by his faid majefty, for himfelf, his heirs and fucceffors, as followeth:

[Here is recited fuch parts of their charter as may be feen in the 10th and 20th claufes of the Maryland charter.] After which they proceeded thus:

IV. Refolved that it is the unanimous opinion of this houfe, That the faid charter is declaratory of the conftitutional rights and privileges of the freemen of this province.

V. Refolved unanimoufly, That trials by juries is the grand bulwark of liberty, the undoubted birthright of every Englifhman, and confequently of every Britifh fubjeĉt in America: And that the ereĉting other jurifdiĉtions for the trial of matters of faĉt, is unconftitutional,

and renders the fubjeĉt infecure in his liberty and property.

VI. Refolved, That it is the unanimous opinion of this houfe, That it cannot with any truth or propriety be faid, That the freemen of this province of Maryland are reprefented in the Britifh parliament.

VII. Refolved unanimoufly, That his majefty's liege people of this ancient province, have always enjoyed the right of being governed by laws, to which they themfelves have confented in the article of taxes, and internal policy; and that the fame hath never been forfeited, or any other way yielded up; but hath been conftantly recognized by the king and people of Great Britain.

VIII. Refolved, That it is the unanimous opinion of this houfe, that the reprefentatives of the freemen of this province, in their legiflative capacity, together with the other part of the legiflature, hath the fole right to lay taxes and impofitions on the inhabitants of this province, or their property and effeĉts: And that the laying, impofing, levying or colleĉting, any tax on or from the inhabitants of Maryland, under colour of any other authority, is unconftitutional, and a direĉt violation of the rights of the freemen of this province.

On the 5th of Oĉtober the ftamps arrived at Philadelphia, the fhip which brought them having laid fome time at Newcaftle upon Delaware, under proteĉtion of a man of war. When the fhips firft appeared round Gloucefter-point, all the veffels in the harbour hoifted their colours half-ftaff high, the bells were muffled, and continued to toll till evening, and every countenance added to the appearance of fincere mourning. At four in the afternoon, feveral several thousands of citizens met at the State-house to consult on proper measures to prevent the execution of the stamp-act. It was agreed to send a deputation of seven persons to Mr. Hughes, the stamp-master for that province, (who was then sick in bed) to request he would resign his office. He readily declared, that no act of his should assist the carrying of that law into execution, till it was generally complied with in the other colonies, but refused to sign any resignation. When this report was made by the deputies to the State-house, the citizens were enraged to that degree, that it is hard to say to what lengths their fury would have carried them, had not the deputies represented Mr. Hughes as at the point of death; this moved their compassion, and they agreed to make their demand in writing, and give Mr. Hughes till the Monday following to make a reply. And on Monday the deputies read the following answer aloud to all the multitude assembled:

Philadelphia, Monday morning, Oct. 7, 1765.

" Whereas about six o'clock, on Saturday evening last, a paper was sent to me, expressing, that ' a great number of the citizens of Philadelphia, assembled at the State-house, to demand of Mr. John Hughes, distributor of stamps for Pensylvania, that he will give them assurance, under his hand, that he will not execute that office; and expect that he will give them a fair, candid, and direct answer, by Monday next, at ten o'clock, when he will be waited on for that purpose. Saturday, October 5, 1765.'

" I do therefore return for answer to those gentlemen, and all their associates, that I have not hitherto taken any step tending to put the late act of parliament into execution

in this province; and that I will not, either by myself or my deputies, do any act or thing that shall have the least tendency to put the said act into execution in this province, until the said act shall be put into execution generally in the neighbouring colonies, and this I am determined to abide by.

" And whereas my commission includes the three counties of New-Castle, Kent, and Sussex, upon Delaware, I do, therefore, hereby voluntarily inform the good people of those counties, that no act of mine shall, either directly or indirectly, involve them in any difficulties with respect to the said stamp act, before the same shall take place generally in the neighbouring colonies.

JOHN HUGHES."

It is necessary sometimes, in this narration, to neglect a strict observance of the order of time, that each separate account may have a proper continuation:—to return them a little back; on the 20th of September, all the lawyers of the supreme court, held at Perth Amboy, assembled, and the Chief Justice having proposed the following queries, they agreed and came to these several resolutions: First, Whether, if the stamps should arrive, and be placed at the city of Burlington, by or after the first of November, they would, as practitioners, agree to purchase them, for the necessary proceedings in the law?

Resolved by the whole body, N. C. D. they would not, but rather suffer their private interest to give way to the public opinion, protesting at the same time against all riotous and indecent behaviour, which they will discountenance by every means in their power, to preserve order, and by an absolute refusal to make use ufe of the ftamps, and other quiet methods, endeavour to obtain a repeal of the law.

Second. Whether it was their opinion, that fhould the aft take place, the duties could poffibly be paid in gold and filver.

Anfwered by the whole body, It could not be paid in gold and filver even for one year.

Third. Their opinion was defired, whether, as the aft required the Governor and Chief Juftice to fuperintend the diftributor, he fhould be obliged to take charge of the diftribution of the ftamps, by order and appointment of the Governor, if he fhould think proper to fix upon him for that office?

Anfwered and advifed, not to take it upon him, the Governor not being impowered by the aft to appoint; or if he was, it was left to the Chief Juftice's option, and that it would be incompatible with his office as Chief Juftice.

The lawyers alfo of New Jerfey met, and refolved to lofe all their bufinefs, rather than make ufe of any ftamps.

When the Commiffioners from Bofton came to the Congrefs at New-York, they waited on Lieutenant-Governor Colden, who received them very coldly; and told them, that " fuch a Congrefs was unconftitutional, unprecedented, and unlawful, and that he fhould give them no countenance."

On the 21ft of Oftober, the freeholders and other inhabitants of the town of Plymouth had a meeting, and unanimoufly agreed on inftructions to Thomas Forfter, Efq. their reprefentative in the General Affembly of Maffachufet's Bay. In which, after expreffing the higheft efteem for the Britifh conftitution, fhewing how far the people of America have exerted themfelves in fupport thereof, and

fetting forth their grievances, they proceed as follows:

" You, Sir, reprefent a people who are not only defcended from the firft fettlers of this country, but inhabit the very fpot they firft poffeffed. Here was firft laid the foundation of the Britifh empire in this part of America, which from a very fmall beginning, has increafed and fpread in a manner very furprifing, and almoft incredible; efpecially when we confider that all this has been effefted without the aid or affiftance of any power on earth, that we have *defended*, *protefted*, and *fecured* ourfelves againft the invafions and cruelty of favages, and the fubtilty and inhumanity of our inveterate and natural enemies the French; and all this without the appropriation of any tax by ftamps, or ftamp afts laid upon our fellow fubjefts in any part of the king's dominions, for defraying the expences thereof. This place, Sir, was at firft the afylum of liberty, and we hope will ever be preferved facred to it; though it was then no more than a forlorn wildernefs, inhabited only by favage men and beafts. To this place our fathers (whofe memories be revered) poffeffed of the principles of liberty in their purity, difdaining flavery, fled to enjoy thofe privileges which they had an undoubted right to, but were deprived of by the hands of violence and oppreffion in their native country. We, Sir, their pofterity, the freeholders and other inhabitants of this town, legally affembly for that purpofe, poffeffed of the fame fentiments, and retaining the fame ardour for liberty, think it our indifpenfable duty, on this occafion, to exprefs to you thefe our fentiments of the ftamp aft, and its fatal confequences to this country, and to enjoin upon you, as you regard not only the welfare, but the very being of this people, that you (confiftent with our allegiance to the king, and re-

E   lation

lation to the government of Great-Britain) difregarding all propofals for that purpofe, exert all your power and influence in relation to the ftamp act, at leaft until we hear the fuccefs of our petitions for relief. We likewife, to avoid difgracing the memories of our anceftors, as well as the reproaches of our own confciences, and the curfes of pofterity, recommended it to you to obtain, if poffible, in the honourable houfe of reprefentatives of this province, a full and explicit affertion of our rights, and to have the fame entered on their public records, that all generations yet to come, may be convinced, that we have not only a juft fenfe of our rights and liberties, but that we never (with fubmiffion to divine providence) will be flaves to any power on earth ; and as we have at all times an abhorrence of tumults and diforders, we think ourfelves happy in being at prefent under no apprehenfions of any, and in having good and wholefome laws fufficient to preferve the peace of the province in all future times, unlefs provoked by fome imprudent meafure : fo we think it by no means advifeable for you to intereft yourfelf in the protection of ftamp papers, or ftamp officers.

" The only thing we have further to recommend to you at this time, is to obferve on all occafions a fuitable frugality and œconomy in the public expences; and that you confent to no unneceffary or unufual grant at this time of diftrefs, when the people are groaning under the burthen of heavy taxes : and that you ufe your endeavours to enquire into, and bear teftimony againft, any paft, and to prevent any future unconftitutional draughts on the public treafury."

Authentic Account of the Proceedings of the Congrefs * held at New-York in 1765, on the Subject of the Stamp Act.

Bofton, June 1765.

Sir,

The houfe of reprefentatives of this province, in the prefent feffion of the general court, have unanimoufly agreed to propofe a meeting, as foon as may be, of committees, from the houfes of reprefentatives or burgeffes of the feveral Britifh colonies on this continent, to confult together on the prefent circumftances of the colonies, and the difficulties to which they are, and muft be reduced, by the operation of the acts of parliament for levying duties and taxes on the colonies ; and to confider of a general, and united, dutiful, loyal and humble reprefentation of their condition, to his Majefty and the Parliament, and to implore relief. The houfe of reprefentatives of this province have alfo voted to propofe, 'That fuch meeting be at the city of New-York, in the province of New-York, on the firft Tuefday in October next ; and have appointed a committee of three of their members to attend that fervice, with fuch as the other houfes of reprefentatives, or burgeffes, in the feveral colonies, may think fit to appoint to meet them. And the committee of the houfe of reprefentatives of this province, are directed to repair to faid New-York, on faid firft Tuefday in October next, accordingly.

If, therefore, your honourable houfe fhould agree to this propofal, it would be acceptable, that as early notice of it as poffible, might be tranfmitted to the fpeaker of the houfe of reprefentatives of this province.

SAMUEL WHITE, Speaker.

In confequence of the foregoing circular letter, the following gentlemen met at New-York, in the province of New-York, on Monday the feventh day of October, 1765, viz.

From

---

* This was the firft Congrefs of the American Continent.

From the province of the Maſſachuſetts-bay,

James Otis,
Oliver Patridge, } Eſquires.
Timothy Ruggles,

From the colony of Rhode-Iſland,
and Providence plantations,

Metcalf Bowler, } Eſquires.
Henry Ward,

From the colony of Connecticut,

Eliphalet Dyer,
David Rowland, } Eſquires.
Wm. Samuel Johnſon,

From the colony of New-York,

Robert R. Livingſton,
John Cruger,
Philip Livingſton, } Eſquires.
William Byard,
Leonard Liſpenard,

From the colony of New-Jerſey,

Robert Ogden,
Hendrick Fiſher, } Eſquires.
Joſeph Borden,

From the province of Pennſylvania,

John Dickenſen,
John Morton, } Eſquires.
George Bryan,

From the government of the counties of Newcaſtle, Kent, and Suſſex,
on Delaware,

Cæſar Rodney, } Eſquires.
Thomas M'Kean,

From the province of Maryland,

William Murdock,
Edward Tilghman, } Eſquires.
Thomas Ringgold,

From the province of South-Carolina,

Thomas Lynch,
Chriſtoph. Gadſden, } Eſquires.
John Rutledge,

Then the ſaid committees proceeded to chuſe a chairman by ballot, and
Timothy Ruggles, Eſq. on ſorting
and counting the votes, appeared to
have a majority, and thereupon was
placed in the chair.

Saturday, Oct. 19, 1765, A. M.
The Congreſs met according to
adjournment, and reſumed, &c. as
yeſterday. And, upon mature deliberation, agreed to the following de-

clarations of the rights and grievances
of the coloniſts in America, which
were ordered to be inſerted.

The members of this Congreſs,
ſincerely devoted, with the warmeſt
ſentiments of affection and duty to his
Majeſty's perſon and government,
inviolably attached to the preſent
happy eſtabliſhment of the Proteſtant
ſucceſſion, and with minds deeply
impreſſed by a ſenſe of the preſent
and impending misfortunes of the
Britiſh colonies on this continent;
having conſidered as maturely as time
will permit, the circumſtances of the
ſaid colonies, eſteem it our indiſpenſible duty to make the following declarations of our humble opinion, reſpecting the moſt eſſential rights and
liberties of the coloniſts, and of the
grievances under which they labour,
by reaſon of ſeveral late acts of parliament.

I. That his Majeſty's ſubjects in
theſe colonies, owe the ſame allegiance to the crown of Great Britain,
that is owing from his ſubjects born
within the realm, and all due ſubordination to that auguſt body the parliament of Great-Britain.

II. That his Majeſty's liege ſubjects in theſe colonies, are entitled to
all the inherent rights and liberties
of his natural born ſubjects, within
the kingdom of Great-Britain.

III. That it is inſeparably eſſential
to the freedom of a people, and the
undoubted right of Engliſhmen, that
no taxes be impoſed on them but with
their own conſent, given perſonally,
or by their repreſentatives.

IV. That the people of theſe colonies are not, and, from their local
circumſtances, cannot be, repreſented
in the Houſe of Commons in Great-
Britain.

V. That the only repreſentatives
of the people of theſe colonies are
perſons choſen therein by themſelves,
and that no taxes ever have been, or
can be conſtitutionally impoſed on
them, but by their reſpective legiſlatures. E 2 VI.

VI. That all supplies to the crown being free gifts of the people, it is unreasonable and inconsistent with the principles and spirit of the British constitution, for the people of Great-Britain to grant to his Majesty the property of the colonists.

VII. That trial by jury, is the inherent and invaluable right of every British subject in these colonies.

VIII. That the late act of parliament, entitled, *An act for granting and applying certain stamp duties, and other duties, in the British colonies and plantations in America, &c.* by imposing taxes on the inhabitants of these colonies, and the said act, and several other acts, by extending the jurisdiction of the courts of admiralty beyond its ancient limits, have a manifest tendency to subvert the rights and liberties of the colonists.

IX. That the duties imposed by several late acts of parliament, from the peculiar circumstances of these colonies, will be extremely burthensome and grievous; and from the scarcity of specie, the payment of them absolutely impracticable.

X. That as the profits of the trade of these colonies ultimately center in Great-Britain, to pay for the manufactures which they are obliged to take from thence, they eventually contribute very largely to all supplies granted there to the crown.

XI. That the restrictions imposed by several late acts of parliament on the trade of these colonies, will render them unable to purchase the manufactures of Great-Britain.

XII. That the increase, prosperity and happiness of these colonies, depend on the full and free enjoyments of their rights and liberties, and an intercourse with Great-Britain mutually affectionate and advantageous.

XIII. That it is the right of the British subjects in these colonies to petition the king, or either house of parliament.

Lastly, That it is the indispensible duty of these colonies, to the best of sovereigns, to the mother country, and to themselves, to endeavour by a loyal and dutiful address to his Majesty, and humble applications to both houses of parliament, to procure the repeal of the act for granting and applying certain stamp duties, of all clauses of any other acts of parliament, whereby the jurisdiction of the admiralty is extended as aforesaid, and of the other late acts for the restriction of American commerce.

Upon motion, voted, That Robert R. Livingston, William Samuel Johnson, and William Murdock, Esqrs. be a committee to prepare an address to his Majesty, and lay the same before the congress on Monday next.

Voted also, That John Rutledge, Edward Tilghman, and Philip Livingston, Esquires, be a committee to prepare a memorial and petition to the lords in parliament, and lay the same before the congress on Monday next.

Voted also, That Thomas Lynch, James Otis, and Thomas M'Kean, Esquires, be a committee to prepare a petition to the house of commons of Great-Britain, and lay the same before the congress on Monday next.

Then the congress adjourned to Monday next at twelve o'clock.

Monday, Oct. 21, 1765, A. M.

The congress met according to adjournment.

The committee appointed to prepare and bring in an address to his Majesty, did report, that they had essayed a draught for that purpose, which they laid on the table, and humbly submitted to the correction of the congress.

The said address was read, and after sundry amendments, the same was approved of by the congress, and ordered to be ingrossed.

The committee appointed to prepare and bring in a memorial and petition to the lords in parliament, did report, That they had essayed a draught

draught for that purpose, which they laid on the table, and humbly submitted to the correction of the congress.

The said address was read, and after sundry amendments, the same was approved of by the congress, and ordered to be ingrossed.

The committee appointed to prepare and bring in a petition to the house of commons of Great-Britain, did report, That they had essayed a draught for that purpose, which they laid on the table, and humbly submitted to the correction of the congress.

The said address was read, and after sundry amendments, the same was approved of by the congress, and ordered to be ingrossed.

The congress adjourn to to-morrow morning, nine o'clock.

Tuesday, Oct. 22, 1765, A. M.

The congress met according to adjournment.

The address to his Majesty being ingrossed, was read and compared, and is as follows, viz.

To the King's most excellent Majesty.

The Petition of the freeholders and other inhabitants of the Massachusets-bay, Rhode-Island, and Providence plantations, New-Jersey, Pennsylvania, the government of the counties of Newcastle, Kent, and Sussex, upon Delaware, province of Maryland,

Most humbly sheweth,

That the inhabitants of these colonies, unanimously devoted with the warmest sentiments of duty and affection to your Majesty's sacred person and government, inviolably attached to the present happy establishment of the protestant succession in your illustrious house, and deeply sensible of your royal attention to their prosperity and happiness, humbly beg leave to approach the throne, by representing to your Majesty, that these colonies were originally planted by subjects of the British crown, who, ani-

mated with the spirit of liberty, encouraged by your Majesty's royal predecessors, and confiding in the public faith, for the enjoyment of all the rights and liberties essential to freedom, emigrated from their native country to this continent, and by their successful perseverance in the midst of innumerable dangers and difficulties, together with a profusion of their blood and treasure, have happily added these vast and valuable dominions to the empire of Great-Britain. That for the enjoyment of these rights and liberties, several governments were early formed in the said colonies, with full power of legislation, agreeable to the principles of the English constitution.

That under those governments, these liberties, thus vested in their ancestors, and transmitted to their posterity, have been exercised and enjoyed, and by the inestimable blessings thereof (under the favour of Almighty God) the inhospitable deserts of America have been converted into flourishing countries; science, humanity, and the knowledge of divine truths, diffused through remote regions of ignorance, infidelity, and barbarism; the number of British subjects wonderfully increased, and the wealth and power of Great-Britain proportionably augmented.

That by means of these settlements, and the unparalleled success of your Majesty's arms, a foundation is now laid for rendering the British empire the most extensive and powerful of any recorded in history. Our connection with this empire, we esteem our greatest happiness and security, and humbly conceive it may now be so established by your royal wisdom, as to endure to the latest period of time; this, with most humble submission to your Majesty, we apprehend will be most effectually accomplished, by fixing the pillars thereof on liberty and justice, and securing the inherent rights and liberties of

your

your subjects here, upon the principles of the English constitution. To this constitution these two principles are essential, the right of your faithful subjects, freely to grant to your Majesty, such aids as are required for the support of your government over them, and other public exigencies, and trials by their peers : by the one they are secured from unreasonable impositions ; and by the other from arbitrary decisions of the executive power.

The continuation of these liberties to the inhabitants of America we ardently implore, as absolutely necessary to unite the several parts of your wide extended dominions, in that harmony so essential to the preservation and happiness of the whole. Protected in these liberties, the emoluments Great Britain receives from us, however great at present, are inconsiderable, compared with those she has the fairest prospect of acquiring. By this protection she will for ever secure to herself the advantage of conveying to all Europe, the merchandises which America furnishes, and of supplying through the same channel whatever is wanted from thence. Here opens a boundless source of wealth and naval strength ; yet these immense advantages, by the abridgment of those invaluable rights and liberties, by which our growth has been nourished, are in danger of being for ever lost ; and our subordinate legislatures, in effect, rendered useless, by the late acts of parliament imposing duties and taxes on these colonies, and extending the jurisdiction of the courts of admiralty here, beyond its ancient limits : statutes by which your Majesty's commons in Britain undertake absolutely to dispose of the property of their fellow subjects in America, without their consent, and for the enforcing whereof, they are subjected to the determination of a single judge in a court unrestrained by the wise rules of the common law, the birth-

right of Englishmen, and the safeguard of their persons and properties.

The invaluable rights of taxing ourselves, and trial by our peers, of which we implore your Majesty's protection, are not, we most humbly conceive unconstitutional ; but confirmed by the great Charter of English liberty. On the first of these rights the honourable the house of commons found their practice of originating money bills, a right enjoyed by the kingdom of Ireland, by the clergy of England, until relinquished by themselves, a right, in fine, which all other your Majesty's English subjects, both within and without the realm, have hitherto enjoyed.

With hearts, therefore, impressed with the most indelible characters of gratitude to your Majesty, and to the memory of the kings of your illustrious house, whose reigns have been signally distinguished by their auspicious influence on the prosperity of the British dominions, and convinced by the most affecting proofs of your Majesty's paternal love to all your people, however distant, and your unceasing and benevolent desires to promote their happiness, we most humbly beseech your Majesty, that you will be graciously pleased to take into your royal consideration the distresses of your faithful subjects on this continent, and to lay the same before your Majesty's parliament, and to afford them such relief, as in your royal wisdom their unhappy circumstances shall be judged to require.

And your petitioners as in duty bound will pray.

The memorial to the lords in parliament was read and compared, and is as follows, viz.

To the right honourable the Lords spiritual and temporal of Great-Britain, in parliament assembled.

The Memorial of the freeholders and others inhabitants of the Massachusetts-bay, Rhode-Island, and Providence plantations, ,

New-

New-Jerfey, Pennfylvania, the government of the counties of New-caftle, Kent, and Suffex, upon Delaware, province of Maryland.

Moft humbly fheweth,

That his Majefty's liege fubjects in his American colonies, though they acknowledge a due fubordination to that auguft body the Britifh parliament, are entitled, in the opinion of your memorialifts, to all the inherent rights and liberties of the natives of Great-Britain, and have ever fince the fettlement of the faid colonies exercifed thofe rights and liberties, as far as their local circumftances would permit.

That your memorialifts humbly conceive one of the moft effential rights of thefe colonies, which they have ever, till lately, uninterruptedly enjoyed, to be trial by jury.

That your memorialifts alfo humbly conceive another of thefe effential rights to be, the exemption from all taxes, but fuch as are impofed on the people by the feveral legiflatures in thefe colonies, which right alfo they have till of late, freely enjoyed.

But your memorialifts humbly beg leave to reprefent to your lordfhips, that the act for granting certain ftamp-duties in the Britifh colonies in America, &c. fills his Majefty's American fubjects with the deepeft concern, as it tends to deprive them of the two fundamental and invaluable rights and liberties above-mentioned, and that feveral other late acts of parliament, which extend the jurifdiction and powers of courts of admiralty in the plantations, beyond their limits in Great-Britain, thereby make an unneceffary and unhappy diftinction as to the modes of trial, between us and our fellow fubjects there, by whom we never have been excelled in duty and loyalty to our Sovereign.

That from the natural connection between Great-Britain and America, the perpetual continuance of which

your memorialifts moft ardently defire, they conceive that nothing can conduce more to the intereft of both, than the colonifts free enjoyment of their rights and liberties, and an affectionate intercourfe between Great Britain and them. But your memorialifts (not waving their claim to thefe rights, of which with the moft becoming veneration 'and deference to the wifdom and juftice of your lordfhips, they apprehend they cannot reafonably be deprived) humbly reprefent, That from the peculiar circumftances of thefe colonies, the duties impofed by the aforefaid act, and feveral other late acts of parliament, are extremely grievous and burthenfome, and the payment of the faid duties will very foon, for want of fpecie, become abfolutely impracticable; and that the reftrictions on trade, by the faid acts, will not only greatly diftrefs the colonies, but muft be extremely detrimental to the trade and true intereft of Great-Britain.

Your memorialifts, therefore, impreffed with a juft fenfe of the unfortunate circumftances of the colonies, and the impending deftructive confequences which muft neceffarily enfue from the execution of thofe acts, animated with the warmeft fentiments of filial affection for their mothercountry, moft earneftly and humbly entreat, That your lordfhips will be pleafed to hear their counfel in fupport of this memorial, and take the premiffes into your moft ferious confideration, and that your lordfhips will alfo be thereupon pleafed to purfue fuch meafures for reftoring the juft rights and liberties of the colonies, and preferving them for ever inviolate, for redreffing their prefent, and preventing future grievances, thereby promoting the united intereft of Great-Britain and America, as to your lordfhips, in your great wifdom, fhall feem moft conducive and effectual to that important end.

And

And your memorialists as in duty bound will ever pray.

Wednesday, Oct. 23, 1765, A. M.

The congress met according to adjournment.

The petition to the house of commons being ingrossed, was read and compared, and is as follows, viz.

To the honourable the knights, citizens, and burgesses of Great-Britain, in parliament assembled.

The Petition of his Majesty's dutiful and loyal subjects, the freeholders and other inhabitants of the colonies of the Massachusetts-bay, Rhode-Island, and Providence plantations, , , New-Jersey, Pennsylvania, the government of the counties of Newcastle, Kent, and Sussex, upon Delaware, Maryland.

Most humbly sheweth,

That the several late acts of parliament, imposing divers duties and taxes on the colonies, and laying the trade and commerce thereof under very burthensome restrictions, but above all the act for granting and applying certain stamp duties, &c. in America, have filled them with the deepest concern and surprize; and they humbly conceive the execution of them will be attended with consequences very injurious to the commercial interest of Great-Britain and her colonies, and must terminate in the eventual ruin of the latter.

Your petitioners therefore most ardently implore the attention of the honourable house, to the united and dutiful representation of their circumstances, and to their earnest supplications for relief, from those regulations which have already involved this continent in anxiety, confusion, and distress.

We most sincerely recognize our allegiance to the crown, and acknowledge all due subordination to the parliament of Great-Britain, and shall always retain the most grateful sense of their assistance and protection. It is from and under the English constitution, we derive all our civil and religious rights and liberties: we glory in being subjects of the best of kings, and having been born under the most perfect form of government; but it is with most ineffable and humiliating sorrow, that we find ourselves, of late, deprived of the right of granting our own property for his Majesty's service, to which our lives and fortunes are entirely devoted, and to which, on his royal requisitions, we have ever been ready to contribute to the utmost of our abilities.

We have also the misfortune to find, that all the penalties and forfeitures mentioned in the stamp act, and in divers late acts of trade extending to the plantations, are, at the election of the informer, recoverable in any court of admiralty in America. This, as the newly erected court of admiralty has a general jurisdiction over all British America, renders his Majesty's subjects in these colonies, liable to be carried, at an immense expence, from one end of the continent to the other.

It gives us also great pain to see a manifest distinction made therein, between the subjects of our mother-country, and those in the colonies, in that the like penalties and forfeitures recoverable there only in his Majesty's court of record, are made cognizable here by a court of admiralty: by these means we seem to be, in effect, unhappily deprived of two privileges essential to freedom, and which all Englishmen have ever considered as their best birthrights, that of being free from all taxes but such as they have consented to in person, or by their representatives, and of trial by their peers.

Your petitioners further shew, That the remote situation, and other circumstances of the colonies, render it impracticable that they should be represented, but in their respective subordinate legislature; and they humbly

humbly conceive, that the parliament, adhering ftrictly to the principles of the conftitution, have never hitherto taxed any but thofe who were actually therein reprefented; for this reafon, we humbly apprehend, they never have taxed Ireland, or any other of the fubjects without the realm.

But were it ever fo clear, that the colonies might in law be reafonably deemed to be reprefented in the honourable houfe of commons, yet we conceive, that very good reafons, from inconvenience, from the principles of true policy, and from the fpirit of the Britifh conftitution, may be adduced to fhew, that it would be for the real intereft of Great-Britain, as well as her colonies, that the late regulations fhould be refcinded, and the feveral acts of parliament impofing duties and taxes on the colonies, and extending the jurifdiction of the courts of admiralty here, beyond their ancient limits, fhould be repealed.

We fhall not attempt a minute detail of all the reafons which the wifdom of the honourable houfe may fuggeft, on this occafion, but would humbly fubmit the following particulars to their confideration.

That money is already become very fcarce in thefe colonies, and is ftill decreafing by the neceffary exportation of fpecie from the continent, for the difcharge of our debts to Britifh merchants.

That an immenfely heavy debt is yet due from the colonies for Britifh manufactures, and that they are ftill heavily burthened with taxes to difcharge the arrearages due for aids granted by them in the late war.

That the balance of trade will ever be much againft the colonies, and in favour of Great-Britain, whilft we confume her manufactures, the demand for which muft ever increafe in proportion to the number of inhabitants fettled here, with the means of purchafing them. We therefore humbly conceive it to be the intereft of Great-Britain, to increafe, rather than diminifh, thofe means, as the profits of all the trade of the colonies ultimately center there to pay for her manufactures, as we are not allowed to purchafe elfewhere; and by the confumption of which, at the advanced prices the Britifh taxes oblige the makers and venders to fet on them, we eventually contribute very largely to the revenue of the crown.

That from the nature of American bufinefs, the multiplicity of fuits and papers ufed in matters of fmall value, in a country where freeholds are fo minutely divided, and property fo frequently transferred, a ftamp duty muft ever be very burthemfome and unequal.

That it is extremely improbable that the honourable houfe of commons fhould, at all times, be thoroughly acquainted with our condition, and all facts requifite to a juft and equal taxation of the colonies.

It is alfo humbly fubmitted, Whether there be not a material diftinction in reafon and found policy, at leaft, between the neceffary exercife of parliamentary jurifdiction in general acts, for the amendment of the common law, and the regulation of trade and commerce through the whole empire, and the exercife of that jurifdiction, by impofing taxes on the colonies.

That the feveral fubordinate provincial legiflatures have been moulded into forms, as nearly refembling that of their mother-country, as by his Majefty's royal predeceffors was thought convenient; and their legiflatures feem to have been wifely and gracioufly eftablifhed, that the fubjects in the colonies might, under the due adminiftration thereof, enjoy the happy fruits of the Britifh government, which in their prefent circumftances they cannot be fo fully and clearly availed of, any other way under thefe forms of government we and our

F   anceftors

anceftors have been born or fettled, and have had our lives, liberties and properties protected. The people here, as every where elfe, retain a great fondnefs for their old cuftoms and ufages, and we truft that his Majefty's fervice, and the intereft of the nation, fo far from being obftructed, have been vaftly promoted by the provincial legiflatures.

That we efteem our connections with, and dependance on Great-Britain, as one of our greateft bleffings, and apprehend the latter will appear to be fufficiently fecure, when it is confidered, that the inhabitants in the colonies have the moft unbounded affection for his Majefty's perfon, family and government, as well as for the mother-country, and that their fubordination to the parliament, is univerfally acknowledged.

We, therefore, moft humbly entreat, That the honourable houfe would be pleafed to hear our counfel in fupport of this petition, and take our diftreffed and deplorable cafe into their ferious confideration, and that the acts and claufes of acts, fo grievoufly reftraining our trade and commerce, impofing duties and taxes on our property, and extending the jurifdiction of the court of admiralty beyond its ancient limits, may be repealed ; or that the honourable houfe would otherwife relieve your petitioners, as in your great wifdom and goodnefs fhall feem meet.

And your petitioners as in duty bound fhall ever pray.

Then the congrefs adjourned till to-morrow morning, ten o'clock.

Thurfday, October 24, 1765.

The congrefs met according to adjournment.

The congrefs took into confideration the manner in which their feveral petitions fhould be preferred and folicited in Great-Britain, and came to the following determination, viz.

It is recommended by the congrefs, to the feveral colonies, to appoint fpecial agents for foliciting relief from their great grievances, and unite their utmoft intereft and endeavours for that purpofe.

Voted unanimoufly, That the clerk of this congrefs fign the minutes of their proceedings, and deliver a copy for the ufe of each colony and province.

By order of the congrefs,

JOHN COTTON, Clerk.

Savannah in Georgia, Sept. 6, 1765.

(C O P Y.)

Sir,

Your letter dated in June laft, acquainting me, that the houfe of reprefentatives of your province, had unanimoufly agreed to propofe a meeting at the city of New-York, of committees, from the houfes of reprefentatives of the feveral Britifh colonies on this continent, on the firft Tuefday in October next, to confult together on the prefent circumftances of the colonies, and the difficulties to which they are, and muft be reduced, by the operation of the acts of parliament for laying duties and taxes on the colonies, and to confider of an humble reprefentation of their condition to his Majefty and the parliament, and to implore relief, came to hand at an unlucky feafon, it being in the recefs of the general affembly of this province; neverthelefs, immediately upon the receipt of your letter, I difpatched expreffes to the feveral reprefentatives of this province, acquainting them with the purport thereof, and requefting them to meet at this place without delay, and accordingly they met here on Monday laft, to the number of fixteen, being a large majority of the reprefentatives of this province, the whole confifting of twenty-five perfons ; but his excellency our governor being applied to, did not think it expedient to call them together on the occafion, which is the reafon of their not fending a committee, as propofed by your houfe, for you may

be

be affured, Sir, that no reprefentatives on this continent can more fincerely concur in the meafures propofed, than do the reprefentatives of this province now met together, neither can any people, as individuals, more warmly efpoufe the common caufe of the colonies, than do the people of this province.

The gentlemen now prefent, requeft it as a favour, you'll be pleafed to fend me a copy of fuch reprefentation as may be agreed upon by the feveral committees at New-York, and to acquaint me how, and in what manner, the fame is to be lain before the king and parliament, whether by any perfon particularly authorifed for that purpofe, or by the colony agents. The general affembly of this province ftands prorogued to the 22d day of October next, which is the time it generally meets for the difpatch of the ordinary bufinefs of the province; and I doubt not the reprefentatives of this province will then, in their legiflative capacity, take under confideration the grievances fo juftly complained of, and tranfmit their fenfe of the fame to Great-Britain, in fuch way as may feem beft calculated to obtain redrefs, and fo as to convince the fifter colonies of their inviolable attachment to the common caufe. I am, Sir, your moft obedient, and moft humble fervant,
ALEXANDER WILLY.
To Samuel White, Efq. Speaker of the Houfe of Reprefentatives of Maffachufetts, &c.

New-Hampfhire.
Mr. Speaker laid before the houfe a letter from the honourable Speaker of the honourable houfe of reprefentatives of the province of the Maffachufetts-bay, to the Speaker of this affembly, propofing a meeting of committees, from the feveral affemblies of the British colonies on the continent, at New-York, to confider of a general, united, dutiful, loyal,

and humble reprefentation of our circumftances, and for imploring his Majefty and the parliament for relief: which being read,

Refolved, That notwithftanding we are fenfible fuch reprefentation ought to be made, and approve of the propofed method for obtaining thereof, yet the prefent fituation of our governmental affairs will not permit us to appoint a committee to attend fuch meeting, but fhall be ready to join in any addrefs to his Majefty and the parliament we may be honoured with the knowledge of, probable to anfwer the propofed end.
A. CLARKSON, Clerk.
The two foregoing letters are true copies from the original.
Atteft. JOHN COTTON, Clerk.
Adjourned to to-morrow morning nine o'clock.

Friday, October 25, 1765.
The congrefs met according to adjournment.

Time not permitting the clerk to make copies at large, of the proceedings of the congrefs, for all the colonies, they think it proper, fhould be furnifhed therewith;

Refolved, That the gentlemen from the Maffachufetts-bay be requefted to fend a copy thereof to the colony of New Hampfhire; the gentlemen of Maryland to Virginia; and the gentlemen of South Carolina to Georgia, and North Carolina. Signed per order, J. COTTON, Clerk.

An account of the difpofition of the £.500 granted by ordinance, and received of the treafurer, by William Murdock, Edward Tilghman, and Thomas Ringgold.

	£.	s.	d.
To cafh paid the whole expences of the committee to New-York, there and back again.	138	14	1
To cafh paid exprefs to New York, to give notice of our coming.	15		

To

	£.	s.	d.
Brought over -	153	14	1
To paid for expreſs, to ſend a copy of our proceedings to the Speaker of Virginia.	1	10	
To paid for a bill of exchange, to remit to Charles Garth, Eſq; with the addreſs and petitions 150*l.* ſterling, at 65 per cent. exchange.	247	10	
Caſh remaining in hand 127 piſtoles, and 18/8.	172	7	8
	575	1	9

By caſh received of the Treaſurer in gold, £.500, at 5/6 per dwt. as follows :

	£.	s.	d.
409 Spaniſh piſtoles, at 27*ſ.*	532	3	
5 Half Johannes, at 57/6.	14	7	6
4 French piſtoles, at 26/6.	5		6
1 Moidore, - - -	2	3	6
1 Half ditto, - - -	1	1	9
	575	1	9

SIR,   *October* 26, 1765.

We had the honour to be appointed by the houſe of repreſentatives of the province of Maryland, a committee, to meet committees of the members of aſſembly of the other colonies on this continent, at New York, the firſt of this inſtant, to join in a general, and united, dutiful, loyal, and humble repreſentation of the condition of thoſe colonies, to his Majeſty and the parliament, and to implore relief from the grievous burthens lately laid upon our trade, and the taxes and duties lately impoſed on us, eſpecially by the Stamp-act.

Accordingly members from nine colonies met, to wit, from the Maſſachuſetts-bay, Connecticut, Rhode-iſland and Providence plantations, New-York, New-Jerſey, Pennſylvania, the government of the counties of Newcaſtle, Kent, and Suſſex, upon Delaware, Maryland, and South Carolina, but as you'll find the addreſs, &c. ſigned only by members from ſix of thoſe colonies, it may be proper to acquaint you with the reaſons why they did not all ſign, though they all concurred with the proceedings.

The lieutenant-governor of New-York prorogued their aſſembly from time to time, ſo that their houſe had not an opportunity of appointing members with full powers to join, and ſign the addreſs, &c. Yet the aſſembly of New-York having, at their laſt meeting, appointed five of their members as a committee, not only to correſpond with their agent at home, but alſo during the receſs of the houſe, to write to and correſpond with the ſeveral aſſemblies, or committees of aſſemblies on this continent, on the ſubject matter of the ſeveral late acts of parliament, ſo grievous and dangerous to their colonies, it was thought proper to admit this committee to join in the conferences, and they agreed to what was done, and promiſed to uſe their endeavours with their aſſembly to concur alſo whenever they ſhould be permitted to meet.

The South-Carolina aſſembly, not rightly viewing the propoſal (which originally came from the aſſembly of the government of the Maſſachuſetts-bay) as it was intended that the ſeveral committees, when met, ſhould frame and ſign an addreſs to his Majeſty, and memorial and petition to the parliament, to be immediately diſpatched by the congreſs, inſtructed their members (Meſſrs. Lynch, Rutledge, and Gadſden) to return their proceedings to them for approbation. The Connecticut aſſembly made the ſame reſtrictions in their inſtructions.

The

The affembly alfo of New Hampfhire wrote, that they had refolved, That notwithftanding they were fenfible fuch a reprefentation ought to be made, and approved of the propofed method for obtaining thereof, yet the prefent fituation of their governmental affairs would not permit them to appoint a committee to attend fuch meeting, but fhould be ready to join in any addrefs to his Majefty and the parliament they might be honoured with the knowledge of, probable to anfwer the propofed end: and the Speaker of the affembly of Georgia wrote, that a majority of their members had applied to the governor to call their affembly, and he did not think it expedient, which was the reafon they did not fend a committee as propofed, but requefled us to tranfmit a copy of our proceedings to them (which will be done) and that their affembly would meet about this time, and he did not doubt but they fhould act fo as to convince the fifter colonies of their inviolable attachment to the common caufe : we alfo underftood the North-Carolina, and we know the Virginia affembly was prorogued, whereby they could not have the opportunity of joining us ; fo that we doubt not but the colonies who have not figned, will very fpeedily tranfmit fimilar addreffes, &c. if their affemblies fhould not be hindered from meeting: and to this purpofe, we hope you'll foon hear from the affembly of South-Carolina. By the gentlemen of that colony we were favoured with a fight of your late letters, and informed of your careful and fpirited conduct with regard to the interefts of that colony, and that, together with your declaration which we find in thofe letters, that you enjoy an independent feat in the Britifh parliament, induced us (as we have no eftablifhed agent at prefent, for this province, nor have yet been able to obtain a law to tax ourfelves for that purpofe) to trouble you with our requeft, that you will prefent the inclofed addrefs to his Majefty, and memorial and petition to the houfes of parliament, and exert your utmoft intereft and abilities in behalf of this poor diftreffed country, and of this province in particular.

We hope, as there is a change in the miniftry, and as the gentlemen in the houfe of commons may, at their next meeting, take a more enlarged view of the true intereft of Great-Britain and her colonies, they will find it to be in fupporting the rights and encouraging the trade of the latter, and that the happinefs of the mother-country and her colonies muft be infeparable, and that we fhall obtain relief.

The feveral committees agreed to recommend it to their refpective colonies, to appoint fpecial agents on this occafion, and to inftruct them to unite their utmoft intereft and endeavours for that purpofe. One addrefs, &c. was tranfmitted by the gentlemen of the Maffachufetts government, immediately to their agent (Mr. Jackfon we underftood) and we expect the other colonies will have duplicates fent to their agents, and we hope will all unite in expence and inftructions, to have able counfel before both the lords and commons, as our petitions pray.

We were intrufted with the difpofition of fome money upon this occafion, and inclofe you a bill of exchange, on Meffrs. Capel and Ofgood Hanbury, for one hundred and fifty pounds fterling, as a compenfation for your trouble and expence in this affair. We doubt not our affembly will approve of what we do in this matter ; and as they are to meet the laft of this month, we fhall lay our proceedings before them, and it is probable they will write you more fully, and furnifh you with fuch further inftructions and arguments as may appear to them to be proper to be given and urged on this occafion, in behalf of the colonies. We are, your moft obedient fervants.

(End of the proceedings of the Congrefs.)

The

The fum expected to be raifed by the ftamp-duty, was £.100,000 *per annum.*

On the 9th of July 1765, the board of treafury (in London) entered upon their books the following minute: "That, in order to obviate the inconvenience of bringing into this kingdom the money to be raifed by the ftamp duties, all the produce of the American duties, arifing or to arife by virtue of any Britifh act of parliament, fhould from time to time be paid to the deputy pay-mafter in America, to defray the fubfiftence of the troops, and any military expences incurred in the colonies."

In June 1765, the king thought proper to difmifs his minifters. The Marquis of Rockingham was appointed firft lord of the treafury, and others, his lordfhip's friends, fucceeded to the vacant places.

The refolutions of the houfe of burgeffes of Virginia (in pages 6 and 7) being laid before the new board of trade, they, on the 27th of Auguft, reprefented to the king in council, "That the refolutions, as they contain an abfolute difavowal of the right of the parliament of Great-Britain to impofe taxes upon her colonies, and a daring attack upon the conftitution of this country, appear to us to require an immediate and ferious attention; and whatever further meafures your Majefty may, with the advice of your council, judge proper to be taken either for expreffing your royal difapprobation of thefe proceedings, or for preventing the fatal confequences which they naturally tend to produce, we think it our duty to fubmit to your Majefty's confideration, whether, in the mean time, it may not be expedient to difpatch immediate inftructions to your Majefty's fervants in your Majefty's colony of Virginia, who may be concerned in enforcing the execution of the law for levying the duty upon ftamps, that they do each in their feveral department, in fupport of the authority of parliament, vigoroufly exert themfelves, and, with

becoming refolution upon every occafion, exact a due obedience to all the laws of the land."

This reprefentation was referred to the privy council.

On the 3d of October, 1765, the privy council reported to the king, "That this is a matter of the utmoft importance to the kingdom and legiflature of Great Britain; and of too high a nature for the determination of your Majefty in your privy council, and is proper only for the confideration of Parliament."

The refolutions of the other affemblies of the colonies were in like manner reprefented to the king by the new board of trade, and referred to the privy council, who reported of them in fimilar terms.

———————

Parliament, however, did not meet for bufinefs till January 1766, when the following papers were laid before both houfes.

Copy of a letter from Mr. Secretary Conway, to Lieutenant Governor Fauquier.

SIR,   *Sept.* 14, 1765.

It is with the greateft pleafure I received his Majefty's commands to declare to you his moft gracious approbation of your conduct. His Majefty and his fervants are fatisfied, that the precipitate refolutions you fent home did not take their rife from any remifnefs or inattention in you; nor is his Majefty at all inclined to fuppofe, that any inftance of diffidence or diffatisfaction could be founded in the general inclination of his antient and loyal colony of Virginia; the nature of the thing and your reprefentations induce a perfuafion, that thofe ill-advifed refolutions owed their birth to the violence of fome individuals, who taking the advantage of a thin affembly, fo far prevailed, as to publifh their own unformed opinions to the world as the fentiments of the colony. But his Majefty, Sir, will not, by the prevalence of a few men, at a certain moment,

moment, be perfuaded to change the opinion, or leffen the confidence, he has always entertained of the colony of Virginia ; which has always experienced the protection of the crown. His Majefty's fervants, therefore, with entire reliance on your prudence, and on the virtue and wifdom of the colony entrufted to your care, perfuade themfelves, that when a full affembly fhall calmly and maturely deliberate upon thofe refolutions, they will fee, and be themfelves alarmed at, the dangerous tendency and mifchievous confequences which they might be productive of, both to the mother country and the colonies, which are the equal objects of his Majefty's parental care ; and whofe mutual happinefs and profperity certainly require a confidential reliance of the colonies upon the mother country.

Upon thefe principles, Sir, and upon your prudent management, and a proper reprefentation to the wife and fober part of the people, how earneft his Majefty is to extend the happy influence of his fatherly care over every part of his dominions, it is expected that a full affembly will form very different refolutions, fuch as may cement that union, which alone can eftablifh the fafety and profperity of the colonies and the mother country.

As there is no intention in the crown to attempt, nor in the king's fervants to advife, any incroachments on the real rights and liberties of any part of his Majefty's fubjects ; fo neither will his Majefty undoubtedly fubmit, or his fervants advife, under any circumftances, that the refpect which is due to parliament, and which is neceffary for the good of the whole Britifh empire, fhould any where be made a facrifice to local and dangerous prejudices.

As this important matter is, however, now before his Majefty's privy council, as well as the other confideration of the dangerous riot and mutinous behaviour of the people on the frontiers, I fhall not pretend to give any advice or inftructions on thefe fubjects ; not doubting, but you will foon have the fulleft from the wifdom of that board, in all thofe things, in which, by your laft accounts, the moft effential interefts of the colony are fo deeply concerned.

You will therefore, in the mean time, be very attentive, by every prudent meafure in your power, at once to maintain the juft rights of the Britifh government, and to preferve the peace and tranquillity of the provinces committed to your care.

But as thefe appear to me matters of government fit for his Majefty's more immediate notice and information, I muft beg you will not fail to tranfmit to me fuch occurrences, from time to time, on thefe heads, as you may deem of importance in the light I mention. I am, &c.

H. S. CONWAY.

Extract of a letter from Mr. Secretary Conway, to Major General Gage.

SIR,   *October* 24, 1765.

It is with the greateft concern, that his Majefty learns the difturbances which have arifen in fome of the North American Colonies: thefe events will probably create application to you, in which the utmoft exertion of your prudence may be neceffary ; fo as juftly to temper your conduct between that caution and coolnefs, which the delicacy of fuch a fituation may demand on one hand, and the vigour neceffary to fupprefs outrage and violence on the other. It is impoffible, at this diftance, to affift you by any particular or pofitive inftruction, becaufe you will find yourfelf neceffarily obliged to take your refolution as particular circumftances and emergencies may require.

It is hoped, and expected, that this want of confidence in the juftice and tendernefs of the mother country, and this open refiftance to its authority,

thority, can only have found place among the lower and more ignorant of the people. The better and wiser part of the colonies will know, that decency and submission may prevail, not only to redress grievances, but to obtain grace and favour, while the outrage of a public violence can expect nothing but severity and chastisement. You, and all his Majesty's servants, from a sense of your duty to, and love of, your country, will endeavour to excite and encourage these sentiments.

If, by lenient and persuasive methods, you can contribute to restore that peace and tranquillity to the provinces, on which their welfare and happiness depend, you will do a most acceptable and essential service to your country: but having taken every step which the utmost prudence and lenity can dictate, in compassion to the folly and ignorance of some misguided people, you will not, on the other hand, where your assistance may be wanted to strengthen the hands of government, fail to concur in every proper measure for its support, by such a timely exertion of force, as may be necessary to repel acts of outrage and violence, and to provide for the maintenance of peace and good order in the provinces.

Copy of a Letter from Mr. Secretary Conway, to Governor Bernard.

SIR,   *October* 24, 1765.

Your letters of the 15th, 16th, 22d, and 31st of August, have been received; the three former not till yesterday.

It is with the greatest concern his Majesty learns the disturbances which have lately arisen in your province, the general confusion that seems to reign there, and the total languor and want of energy, in your government, to exert itself with any dignity or efficacy, for the suppression of tumults, which seem to strike at the very being of all authority and subor-

dination among you. His Majesty cannot but, with the greatest surprize, hear of the refusal of your council to call for the aid of any regular force to the support of the civil magistracy, at a time when, it seems, you had reason to think, there was no other power capable of providing for the peace and quiet of the province.

Nothing can, certainly, exceed the ill-advised and intemperate conduct held by a party in your province, which can in no way contribute to the removal of any real grievance they might labour under, but may tend to obstruct and impede the exertion of his Majesty's benevolent attention to the ease and comfort, as well as the welfare, of all his people.

It is hoped, and expected, that this want of confidence in the justice and tenderness of the mother country, and this open resistance to its authority, can only have found place among the lower and more ignorant of the people; the better and more wise part of the colonies will know, that decency and submission may prevail, not only to redress grievances, but to obtain grace and favour, while the outrage of a public violence can expect nothing but severity and chastisement. These sentiments, you, and all his Majesty's servants, from a sense of your duty to, and love of, your country, will endeavour to excite and encourage: you will all, in a particular manner, call upon them not to render their case desperate; you will, in the strongest colours, represent to them the dreadful consequences that must inevitably attend the forcible and violent resistance to acts of the British parliament, and the scene of misery and distraction to both countries, inseparable from such a conduct.

If, by lenient and persuasive methods, you can contribute to restore that peace and tranquillity to the provinces, on which their welfare and happiness depend, you will do a most acceptable and essential service to your country;

country; but having taken every ftep which the utmoft prudence and lenity can dictate, in compaffion to the folly and ignorance of fome mifguided people, you will not, on the other hand, fail to ufe your utmoft power for repelling all acts of outrage and violence, and to provide for the maintenance of peace and good order in the province, by fuch a timely exertion of force, as the occafion may require; for which purpofe, you will make the proper applications to General Gage, or Lord Colvil, commanders of his Majefty's land and naval forces in America: for however unwilling his Majefty may confent to the exertion of fuch powers as may endanger the fafety of a fingle fubject, yet can he not permit his own dignity, and the authority of the Britifh legiflature, to be trampled on by force and violence, and in avowed contempt of all order, duty and decorum.

If the fubject is aggrieved, he knows in what manner legally and conftitutionally to apply for relief: but it is not fuitable, either to the fafety or dignity of the Britifh empire, that any individuals, under the pretence of redreffing grievances, fhould prefume to violate the public peace. I am, &c.

H. S. CONWAY.

P. S. The floop which carries this will carry orders to Lord Colvil, and to the Governor of Nova-Scotia, to fend to your affiftance any force which may be thought neceffary from thence, and which that province can fupply.

Copy of Mr. Secretary Conway's circular letter to the Governors in North-America.

SIR, *October* 24, 1765.

It is with the greateft concern, that his Majefty learns the difturbances which have arifen in fome of the North-American colonies: if this evil fhould fpread to the Government of ———, where you prefide, the utmoft exertion of your prudence will be neceffary, fo as juftly to temper your conduct between that caution and coolnefs which the delicacy of fuch a fituation may demand, on the one hand, and the vigour neceffary to fupprefs outrage and violence, on the other. It is impoffible, at this diftance, to affift you, by any particular or pofitive inftruction; becaufe you will find yourfelf neceffarily obliged to take your refolution, as particular circumftances and emergencies may require.

His Majefty, and the fervants he honours with his confidence, cannot but lament the ill-advifed intemperance fhewn already in fome of the provinces, by taking up a conduct, which can in no way contribute to the removal of any real grievance they might labour under, but may tend to obftruct and impede the exertion of his Majefty's benevolence and attention to the eafe and comfort, as well as the welfare, of all his people.

It is hoped and expected, that this want of confidence in the juftice and tendernefs of the mother-country, and this open refiftance to its authority, can only have found place among the lower and more ignorant of the people. The better and wifer part of the colonies will know, that decency and fubmiffion may prevail, not only to redrefs grievances, but to obtain grace and favour, while the outrage of a public violence can expect nothing but feverity and chaftifement. Thefe fentiments you, and all his Majefty's fervants, from a fenfe of your duty to, and love of, your country, will endeavour to excite and encourage.

You will all, in a particular manner, call upon them not to render their cafe defperate. You will, in the ftrongeft colours, reprefent to them the dreadful confequences that muft inevitably attend the forcible and violent refiftance to acts of the Britifh parliament, and the fcene of mifery and calamity to themfelves, and of

G   mutual

mutual weaknefs and diftraction to both countries, infeparable from fuch a conduct.

If, by lenient and perfuafive methods, you can contribute to reftore that peace and tranquillity to the provinces, on which their welfare and happinefs depend, you will do a moft acceptable and effential fervice to your country : but having taken every ftep which the utmoft prudence and lenity can dictate, in compaffion to the folly and ignorance of fome mifguided people, you will not, on the other hand, fail to ufe your utmoft power, for repelling all acts of outrage and violence, and to provide for the maintenance of peace and good order in the province, by fuch a timely exertion of force as the occafion may require ; for which purpofe, you will make the proper applications to general Gage, or lord Colville, commanders of his Majefty's land and naval forces in America. For however unwillingly his Majefty may confent to the exertion of fuch powers as may endanger the fafety of a fingle fubject ; yet can he not permit his own dignity, and the authority of the Britifh legiflature, to be trampled on by force and violence, and in avowed contempt of all order, duty and decorum.

If the fubject is aggrieved, he knows in what manner legally and conftitutionally to apply for relief; but it is not fuitable, either to the fafety or dignity of the Britifh empire, that any individuals, under the pretence of redreffing grievances, fhould prefume to violate the public peace. I am, &c.

H. S. CONWAY.

P. S. *To Governor Wilmot.*

You will probably receive application from governor Bernard, to fend him part of the force which may be within your government. Lord Colville has command to tranfport them ; and you will be very attentive, that the public fervice fhould

fuffer no impediment from any delay in you, when fuch application is made.

Extract of a letter from Mr. Secretary Conway, to Major-General Gage.

SIR,   *December* 15, 1765.

I Had the favour of your letters of the 4th, 8th, and 9th of November laft, by which I learn, with the utmoft concern, the difordered ftate of the province where you refide, and the very riotous and outrageous behaviour of too many of the inhabitants.

I did not fail to lay your difpatches, together with thofe of lieutenant-governor Colden, before his Majefty, who, though highly provoked by fuch an infult offered to his governor there, is however pleafed to hear, that matters were not pufhed to fuch extremity, as might have coft the lives of many of his fubjects, and perhaps have tended, as you feem apprehenfive, to the great detriment, if not ruin, of the town of New-York ; particularly if the fort had fired on that infolent and infatuated mob which fo provokingly approached. The temper fhewn, as well by lieutenant-governor Colden, as by the officers there, is highly to be commended. His Majefty is willing to fuppofe, that both yourfelf and governor Colden have acted on principles of duty to his fervice, in the advice and refolution formed to put the ftampt paper into the hands of the magiftrates of New-York ; which, however, unlefs the neceffity for it appeared very preffing, muft certainly be looked upon as a ftep greatly humiliating and derogating to his Majefty's government.

If the poft was not tenable, or the papers infecure there, it fhould feem much preferable to have put them on board the man of war, as was propofed : nor does there appear any good reafon, why captain Kennedy refufed to take them. It is difficult, at this diftance, to judge with the fame propriety of conduct, to be held on occafion;

occasions of such difficulty and importance, as on the spot. Had the personal safety of those in the fort alone been considered, I am persuaded, there would not have been a moment's hesitation about the defence of it, against any attack that might rashly have been attempted: nor can his Majesty suppose any want of resolution for his service, in those who have, in their different stations, given so many proofs of their regard to it. It should otherwise seem, that the reality of the mobs being armed, and prepared for an actual attack, should have been well ascertained before the papers were given up.

The step you have thought fit to take, in drawing together such forces as their situation allowed, was certainly prudent, and could not be too soon determined, on any positive grounds, to suspect an insurrection; and especially in regard to the securing his Majesty's stores, a circumstance which will still demand your greatest attention; and particularly those arms, which may be seized by the mob for their own mutinous purposes.

Your situation is certainly delicate and difficult, it requires both prudence and firmness in the conduct of all employed in his Majesty's service there; especially, considering what you say of the difficulty, or rather impossibility, of drawing any considerable number of men together, and of the impracticability of attempting any thing by force, in the present disposition of the people, without a respectable body of troops.

You seem to think there are still hopes, that as the spirits of those unhappy people have time to cool, there will be more submission shewn; your will not fail, I am persuaded, in your station, to avail yourself of every favourable symptom for the improvement of such favourable dispositions, any more than to exert yourself, where the necessity of the case may require, in support of the

honour of government, and for suppressing any riotous or rebellious resistance offered to the laws, or those magistrates who have the execution of them.

I hope my former letters are come safe, *as they will have conveyed to you his Majesty's sentiments and commands for your conduct, on the first notice of these disturbances.*

Copy of a letter from Mr. Secretary Conway, to Lieutenant-Governor Colden.

SIR,   *December* 15, 1765.

I have received your letter of the 5th of November by major James, and that of the 9th of the same month by the pacquet, with the minutes of the council of New-York, from the 31st of October to the 6th of November, &c.—From your last letter, I have hopes that time will produce a recollection, which may lead these unhappy people back to a sense of their duty; and that, in the mean time, every proper and practicable measure will be taken to awe that licentious spirit, which has hurried them to those acts of outrage and violence, equally dangerous to the sober and well-disposed part of the people, the ease and quiet of the city, and subversive of all order and authority among them.

Sir Henry Moore will certainly be arrived before this reaches you; it is expected, therefore, Sir, from your knowledge of the country and people, that you should inform the new governor of every thing necessary for his knowledge, as well respecting the state of things, as the characters and dispositions of men in that country. He will see that, by his instructions, he is empowered to suspend members of the council, and officers of the law, who shall appear to desire it; being, in that case, only obliged to send home immediately the reasons and causes of such suspension. It is not improbable, that such times as these

may

may require the exercise of that power: as it is not doubted the governor will use it with discretion, so it is expected he should not want firmness to use it boldly, whenever it may seem useful to the King's service and the public peace.

————

October 1, 1765.

Copy of a Representation of the Lords Commissioners for Trade and Plantations, touching the Proceedings and Resolutions of the House of Representatives of Massachuset's Bay, with respect to the Act for levying a Duty upon Stamps in America, and to other Acts of the Parliament of Great Britain.

To the King's Most Excellent Majesty.

May it please your Majesty,

The house of representatives of your Majesty's province of Massachuset's Bay having, last year, printed and published, in the journals of their proceedings, a letter from a committee of that house to their agent here; in which letter the acts and resolutions of the parliament of Great-Britain were treated with the most indecent disrespect, and principles tending to a denial of the right of parliament to levy taxes upon your Majesty's subjects in the colonies, were openly avowed; our predecessors in office thought it their duty to transmit this transaction to your Majesty's consideration, to the end that such directions might be given, as the nature and importance of the matter should appear to require.

Since this, and since the passing the act of parliament for levying a stamp duty in America, the grounds of which act gave rise to the reflexions contained in the above-mentioned letter, the same spirit that dictated the sentiments it expresses, has appeared throughout the whole proceedings of the said house of representatives.

Upon the election of counsellors, who, by the constitution of this colony, are annually chosen by the house of representatives, the strongest endeavours were used to preclude your Majesty's secretary of state, who has always been a member of the council from his seat at that board; and this, as your Majesty's governor represents, merely on account of his having received an appointment (unsolicited) to be a distributor of the stamps: and the motion made in that house, to discontinue the annual salary allowed for the support of your Majesty's governor, upon which proceeding we have this day made a separate representation to your Majesty, seems to have arisen from the same motives.

These, however, being only attempts of individuals in the community, would not either have required or deserved your Majesty's attention, in the light in which we view them; but it further appears, from the journals of the house of representatives in their last session, that " this assembly, having thought fit to make the propriety and expediency of the stamp-act, and of other acts of parliament, a subject of open question and discussion," came to several resolutions and proceedings thereupon, which they kept secret till the last day of their session, when they published them in their printed journals —Then follow the resolutions—Then the board of trade proceeds thus: The object of the resolutions and proceedings of the house of representatives of Massachuset's Bay, is to recommend to, and induce, the rest of your Majesty's colonies in America, to join in a general congress of committees from the several assemblies, independent of the other branches of the legislature, and without any previous application to your Majesty, to consider and deliberate upon the acts of the parliament of this kingdom. As this appears to us to be the first instance of a general congress, appointed by the assemblies of the colonies without the authority of the

the crown ; a meafure which we conceive of dangerous tendency in itfelf, and more efpecially fo, when taken for the purpofes expreffed in the above-mentioned refolution, and connected with the fpirit that has appeared throughout the whole conduct of this particular affembly ; we therefore think it our indifpenfible duty to fubmit this matter to your Majefty's confideration, for fuch directions as your Majefty, with the advice of your council, may think proper and expedient to give thereupon.

All which is moft humbly fubmitted, &c.

Whitehall, Oct. 1, 1765.

Copy of a Reprefentation from the Board of Trade, with feveral Papers tranfmitted, relative to the outrageous Behaviour of the People at the Town of Bofton, in Oppofition to the Stamp-Duty Act. Dated October 10, 1765. *To the King's Moft Excellent Majefty.*

May it pleafe your Majefty,

Since our humble reprefentation to your Majefty of the 1ft inftant, in confequence of fome alarming proceedings in the houfe of reprefentatives, in the province of Maffachufet's Bay, we have received letters from ———, giving an account of a riot of a moft dangerous tendency, which had arifen in the town of Bofton, and which, directing its fury againft the houfes and perfons of the lieutenant-governor, and other principal officers of government, continued with repeated acts of extraordinary violence, from the 15th of Auguft to the 26th of the fame month ; at which period the tumult feemed fufpended, rather than allayed.

In whatever light thefe difturbances may be viewed, whether in refpect of the avowed object, which the perpetrators and abettors of them declare to be a general refolution, to oppofe and prevent the execution of an act of the parliament of Great-Britain, or in refpect of the ftate of government and magiftracy there, which ——— reprefents to be utterly incapable of refifting or fuppreffing thefe tumults and diforders, they feem to us of fuch high importance, that we lofe no time in laying the letters and papers relating thereunto before your Majefty, that your Majefty may direct fuch meafures to be purfued, as your Majefty, with the advice of your council, fhall think moft prudent and effectual.

Which is moft humbly fubmitted, &c.

Philadelphia, Oct. 12, 1765.
Gentlemen,

Having been confined to my bed twenty-five days paft, with a violent diforder that was expected would have proved mortal, but thank God am now able to fet up in bed, I fhall attempt to give you a fketch of not only my own conduct, but alfo that of the prefbyterians and proprietary party here, relative to the ftamp-office.

In May laft I received information by a letter from Doctor Franklin, that he had recommended me for chief diftributor of the ftamps in this province, and thus the matter refted, until fome gentlemen to the eaftward received their commiffions, whereupon mobs arofe in feveral of the eaftern provinces, and the officers were obliged to refign ; but as a prelude to the deftruction and diforder made by thofe mobs, the printers in each colony, almoft without exception, ftuffed their papers weekly, for fome time before, with the moft inflammatory pieces they could procure, and excluded every thing that tended to cool the minds of the people ; thefe meafures they purfued, until the prefbyterians in particular, in every colony, began to threaten the ftamp-officers ; and thofe gentry in this province, about the beginning of September, began to be very noify, and fome of them faid, I ought to refign ;

I gave

I gave them for anfwer, I had as yet no commiffion, therefore could not refign what I had not. However, about the middle of September, it was reported that the ftamps would arrive in captain Friend, who was then expected, and thefe riotous gentry began to threaten they would deftroy the ftamps as foon as they arrived; I therefore being defirous, or as far as in me lay, to preferve the ftamps, wrote on the 17th the letter (No. I.) to his honour the governor, but received no anfwer, and as the ftamps did not arrive in Capt. Friend, matters refted until October the 2d, when I received the paper, (No. II.) being a note from Captain William Dovel, a tool of the party, and therefore I wrote my anfwer (No. III.) to Mr. Dickefon, the owner of the fhip, and on the next day I wrote my letter (No. IV.) to his honour the governor, but received no anfwer, and here matters refted until Saturday the 5th of October, when I received information, that the fhip with the ftamps was come up to the town that day, and that a mob would be collected, by beating muffled drums through the ftreet, and ringing the ftate-houfe and church-bells muffled, which was accordingly done all the afternoon, but at two o'clock the poft arrived with the mail and packet, and, among other things, my commiffion; this the party ventured to alledge, becaufe there was a large packet for me; accordingly the mob collected, chiefly prefbyterians and proprietary emiffaries, with the Chief Juftice's (Mr. William Allen) fon at their head, animating and encouraging the lower clafs.

About three o'clock, the following perfons; viz. James Tilghman, Efq. attorney at law, Meffieurs Robert Morris, Charles Thompfon, Archibald M'Call, John Cox, William Richards, merchants, and Mr. William Bradford, printers, came to me on a deputation from a great number

collected at the State-houfe, to requeft my refignation. I anfwered, it is true, I now have my commiffion, but as two gentlemen are bound for my performance, in the fum of £.5000, I could not refign, unlefs indemnify my bail. Altercations on this head took up near an hour (low as I was), and at laft they faid, all that was expected of me, was, that I would not put the act in execution in this province, until his Majefty's further pleafure was known, or until the act fhould be put in execution in the neighbouring colonies; to this I thought proper to fignify fome difpofition to comply, becaufe I had many informations by my friends, that the mob intended to proceed to the laft extremities, if I did not refign; upon this the deputation withdrew to confult their affociates, and at fix o'clock I received the paper, (No. V.) being a peremptory demand; then the matter refted until Sunday morning, when having recovered my fpirits a little from the fatigue of that long altercation aforefaid, I looked over the paper, and found it more pofitive than what had been mentioned the day before, and therefore fent for Mr. Charles Thompfon, one of the deputation, and afked him if they were fincere the day before, or whether they came to wiredraw what they would firft, and then force the reft, becaufe I obferved the paper fent me did not agree with the propofition made to me; he faid he was fincere, and could only anfwer for himfelf: I replied, well, gentlemen, you muft look to yourfelves, for this is a high affair; he made anfwer, thus I do not know, but hope it will not be deemed rebellion. Indeed, Sir, I know no other name for it—Well, fays he, I know not how it may end, for we have not yet determined, whether we will ever fuffer the act to take place here or not, and took his leave. On Monday morning, at ten o'clock, the whole deputation

deputation came, and I offered them the paper (No. VI.), and after some consultation among themselves, they objected to their names being inserted. I said, why, sure gentlemen, you have not done a thing you are ashamed to own; not in the least they said, but there was no necessity for their names being inserted, nor would they receive that resignation; whereupon I said to Mr. Tilghman, come, Sir, take the pen and please yourself, for I see you are determined to be arbitrary; he then took the pen, and formed the paper, (No. VII.) and when it was transcribing, I asked them what they intended to do with the stamps, as they assumed the supreme power in the province; they then looked at one another for a while, and seemed somewhat confused; but, at last, Mr. Tilghman replied, we did not come prepared to speak to that head; then another replied, let Mr. Hughes take care of them. I answered, gentlemen, that cannot be, as you have now fixed matters; for were I to take the stamps into my care, I should have your party come about my house, and pull it down, and destroy both me and them. Well, says another, let the governor take care of them; another then says, perhaps the governor will call upon Mr. Hughes to put the act in execution, and when he declines, the governor perhaps will appoint an officer, and the act may take place. Here a general pause ensued, but at last one and all cried out, let us see who will dare put the act in execution; upon the governor's appointment we will take care of that; by this time the paper (No. VII.) was transcribed, and after I had signed it, they went away to proclaim it to their friends, and the next day I wrote the letter (No. VIII.) to the governor, and received the under-written verbal answer by my son.

" My health, at this time, will not permit me to be more expeditious on this very extraordinary transaction; what I have said, is sufficient to inform you, gentlemen, and the lords commissioners, that unless my hands are strengthened, it will never be in my power to put the act in execution.

" Perhaps their lordships, and you, gentlemen, may expect that the governor will exert himself on the occasion, and strengthen my hands; but this will not happen, for on the day that the mob were collecting, and after the drums began to beat, I am informed his honour left the city, and presently after the attorney-general, who is recorder of the city, left it also; whether the mayor and chief justice were out of the city, I cannot say, but this is certain, that no one magistrate or public officer appeared abroad the whole day, to discourage the mob, or to give the least aid or protection. All, therefore, that I shall add on this head, is, that if ever my hands are strengthened, so as it will be in my power to do my duty, as chief distributor of the stamps, I shall not fail to comply with the duties of my office in the strictest manner, and then I hope will sufficiently save my securities in their lordships and your opinion, as it is now out of my power to discharge my duty until the face of affairs are changed.

" In paper (No. 7.) you will observe the three counties upon Delaware included in my resignation, the reason of which was, that on Saturday the 6th of October, a friend of mine privately sent up a little boy to inform me, that he had reason to believe a mob was uniting in those counties, and would soon be up at Philadelphia. This I knew would raise a second mob, and therefore I did not prevent it, and it has had the desired effect.

" I am now to acknowledge the receipt of a letter from the secretary of the stamp-office, and also a bill of lading for three cases and seven packs of stamps for this province, exclusive

clusive of those for New Jersey and Maryland, but there is neither invoice nor bills of parcels, nor any account of the prices the stampt paper or parchment is to be sold at. I have seen a printed paper, said to be the prices of the stamps, &c. but as the bill of lading makes me liable to the freight, I should be glad to know whether the freight is included in these printed papers, or not; if I had received the stamps, I should have been at a loss on the 1st of November how to proceed, but as things now stand, there is time for my being fully informed, and especially with respect to the invoice of bills of parcels, without which it is impossible for me to know what I am charged with at the stamp-office, and how far the goods received agree with the charge.

"I am further to inform you, that I received in the packet sent by your secretary, a bond, which in his letter he directed, I should execute before the governor, or some other person of note, and sent it back to the stamp-office by the first conveyance, which I should have punctually complied with, had I been in health, and had not our over-ruling gentry the mob thought fit to direct otherwise; however, I have the bond in my custody, and whenever there is a prospect of carrying the act into execution, shall not fail to execute the bond, and transmit it to the stamp-office by the first opportunity, and also do every thing in my power faithfully to discharge my duty.

"I am further to inform you, gentlemen, that I am extremely obnoxious to the governor, men in power, and that for no other reason, than that I have constantly, while I have been in the assembly, endeavoured to promote the king's interest, and given opposition to some favourite schemes that tended to retard his Majesty's service.

"I am also unfortunate enough to be particularly hateful to the chief justice, because I have charged him in the house of assembly with being a rebel, upon his saying, " That if ever the government was changed, we should find the king's little finger heavier than the proprietor's loins." This declaration he made in the house of assembly more than once, and I as often alledged, that his allegation tended to alienate the affection of the subject from the king, and therefore was treason, and that none but a rebel would be guilty of it. I also am particularly hateful to the proprietary party, because it was my interest, assiduity, and influence in the house of assembly, that enabled the province to send home Doctor Franklin, to present our petitions for a change of government, from propriety to royal, which I hope is effected by this time.

"Since writing the above, I am informed that Benjamin Shoemaker, Esq. who is one of the people called quakers, also an alderman of this city, met with the drummers as they were alarming the city, and took them to task, requiring to know by what authority they were endeavouring to raise a mob, they answered, if he would go to the State-house, he might know; he then asked who ordered them to beat about the streets, they said, they had their orders from the coffee-house. [N. B. Kept by the before-mentioned Mr. Bradford.] Mr. Shoemaker then forbid them to proceed any further, and he said he would go immediately to the mayor and have them committed; they answered they could get the mayor's orders when they pleased. But Mr. Shoemaker could not find the mayor, nor any officer to assist him, and therefore was obliged to desist, lest he should draw the mob upon himself and family, and so have his house pulled down.

"If some rule and order does not take place in America, I am very sure

sure every person who has been named to the stamp-office, must leave North America shortly, or they and their families will fall a sacrifice to the deluded populace.

" Common justice calls upon me to say, the body of people called quakers, seemed disposed to pay obedience to the stamp-act, and so do that part of the Church of England, and baptists, that are not some way under proprietary influence. But presbyterians, and proprietary minions, spare no pains to engage the Dutch and lower class of people, and render the royal government odious, but at the same time profess great loyalty to the best of kings, and yet insinuate that his immediate government is intolerable. If his Majesty and his ministers knew the pains taken by the proprietary partisans to give a wrong bias to the minds of his Majesty's subjects, I am confident they would not suffer the powers of government to remain six months in the hands of any proprietor on the continent; neither ought the powers of government to be lodged in any private person, it being disadvantageous to both his Majesty's subjects.

" I shall conclude with the following observation; viz. That if Great-Britain can, or will suffer such kind of conduct in her colonies to pass unpunished, a man need not be a prophet, nor the son of a prophet, to see clearly, that her empire in North-America is at an end; for I dare say the mobbing gentry will immediately proceed to other extravagancies, as they will then begin to think their united power irresistable.

" That God, of his infinite goodness, may direct the councils and measures of his Majesty, of his ministers, to that which may be best for Great Britain and North America, is, and shall be the constant prayer of, Gentlemen, your most obedient and most humble servant,

To the Commissioners JOHN HUGHES.
of the stamp-office.

Philadelphia, September 17, 1765.
No. I.

As great riots and disturbances has happened in some of the neighbouring colonies, occasioned by a dislike the people have to the stamp-act, and it being reported that the stampt papers, &c. for the province, may be expected in a little time, and, as his Majesty's revenue is deeply interested in the preservation thereof, think it my duty to acquaint you, that notwithstanding of any reports spread of my being named by the officers for this province, that I have not received either bond, commission, nor any other information whatsoever, of my appointment from the stamp-office, or lords of the treasury, and therefore I can have no pretension whatever, to take charge of the paper should they arrive. This information I have thought necessary to give you, that you may take such measures in the premises, as you shall think consistent with your duty and judgment. I am, Sir, your most obedient humble servant,   JOHN HUGHES.
To the Hon. John Penn, Esq.
Lieutenant Governor of
Pennsylvania.

No. II.

Sir,

Mr. Dickenson is is town from London, and the ship Charlotte is at Newcastle, and do not chuse to bring her up till you give orders about the stamp-papers, as she is a valuable ship.

WILLIAM DOWELL.
I pray send an answer by bearer.
Philadelphia, 5 *o'clock, 2d of Oct.* 1765.
No. III.

Mr. Dickenson,

I received your kind notice by Mr. Bradford, and for answer, am to inform you, that I have not received from the lords of the treasury, nor from any other person appointed by his Majesty, any commission or public information of my being the officer of the province of Pennsylvania, and

H   therefore

therefore cannot pretend to any right to take charge of thofe papers, nor fhould I, were they now at the wharf; the governor is the officer of the crown, whofe duty it is to preferve and fecure thofe papers; to him I refer you for directions how to proceed in the premifes, and I make no doubt but his honour the governor will take care to fee that the papers are landed in a place of fecurity, and there kept fafe until fome perfon properly commiffioned fhall appear to demand them. Signed by order of my father.

JOHN HUGHES, jun.

To Mr. Dickenfon. Copy of a Letter fent by Mr. Bradford's fon.

No. IV.

Sir,

I inclofe you a letter I received laft evening from Mr. William Dovel, by which I underftand that the ftamped papers are arrived at Newcaftle in the Charlotte, that the owner of the veffel does not care to order his fhip into the port while thefe papers are on board, left fome violence fhould be done to her; and as I have not the leaft power from the lords of his Majefty's treafury, or any other public board, authorizing me to receive them, and as his Majefty's revenue is in concerned in their prefervation, I thought it my duty to give you the information, that you might take fuch meafures therein as your prudence fhould fuggeft. I am, Sir, yours,

To John Penn, Efq." JOHN HUGHES.

No. V.

A great number of the citizens of Philadelphia affembled at the ftate-houfe do demand of Mr. John Hughes, diftributor of ftamps for Pennfylvania, that he will give them affurance under his hand that he will not execute that office, and expect that he will give them a fair, candid, and direct anfwer by Monday next ten o'clock, when he will be waited on for that purpofe.

Saturday, Oct. 5, 1765.

No. VI.

Philadelphia, Monday Morning, October 7, 1765.

Whereas I was applied to on Saturday laft, about three o'clock in the afternoon, by the following gentlemen, viz. James Tilghman, Efq. attorney at law, Meffrs. Robert Morris, Charles Thompfon, Archibald M'Call, John Cox, and William Richards, merchants; Mr. William Bradford, Printer, who affured me they were fent by a great number of people then affembled at the ftate-houfe, in order to requeft me to refign the ftamp-office; and after fome converfation on the fubject, Mr. Robert Morris, and fome others, declared, that it was not expected or defired that my refignation fhould be any other than the not accepting the office, and declaring every ftep or meafure that fhould tend to put the late ftamp-act into execution, until his Majefty's further pleafure fhould be known, or until the act fhould be generally carried into execution in the neighbouring colonies; and if that fhould happen, I was then at liberty to do as I thought proper: and whereas about fix o'clock the fame evening, a paper was fent me by fome of thefe fame gentlemen, in behalf, as I underftand, of all thofe collected at the ftate-houfe as aforefaid, declaring, that a great number of the citizens of Philadelphia affembled at the ftate-houfe, do demand of Mr. John Hughes, diftributor of ftamps for Pennfylvania, that he will give them affurance under his hand that he will not execute that office, and expect that he will give them a fair, candid, and direct anfwer by Monday next at ten o'clock, where he will be waited on for that purpofe.

Saturday, Oct. 5, 1765.

I do therefore return for anfwer to thofe gentlemen and all their affociates, that I have not hitherto taken any ftep tending to put the late act of par-

parliament in execution in this province, and that I will not either by myself or my deputies, do any act or thing that shall have the least tendency to put the said act into execution in this province, until his Majesty's future pleasure shall be known, or until the said act shall be put in execution in the neighbouring colonies, and this I am determined to abide by, unless either the governor or commander in chief of this province for the time being shall call upon me to execute the said act.

And whereas my commission includes the three counties of Newcastle, Kent, and Suffex, upon Delaware, I do therefore hereby voluntarily inform the good people of those counties, that no act of mine shall either directly or indirectly involve them into any difficulties with respect to the said stamp-act, before the same shall take place in the neighbouring colonies, or until his Majesty's future pleasure shall be known, or until the governor and commander in chief for the time being of those counties shall call upon me as aforesaid, to execute the said act.

(Copy)   JOHN HUGHES,

No. VII.

Philadelphia, Monday Morning,
October 7, 1765.

Whereas about six o'clock on Saturday evening last a paper was sent to me, expressing, that a great number of citizens of Philadelphia, &c. (this paper of resignation has been published verbatim.)

No. VIII.

Philadelphia, Tuesday Morning,
October 8, 1765.

Sir,

I make no doubt but you have heard that a great number of people were collected at the state-house on Saturday last, by causing muffled drums to beat through the streets of this city, and by ringing the state-house bell muffled, and by directing all enquirers to repair to the state-

house for information; and that after the people were collected, a deputation was sent to me demanding my resignation of the office of chief distributor of stamps for this province. I am well informed, that great numbers of the ringleaders and promoters of this meeting declared and vowed destruction to my person and property if I refused to gratify them in their demands.

My resignation is accordingly made, and I beg you will be so kind as to inform me where the stamps are deposited, that I may by this day's post inform the lords of the treasury what situation they are in. This you must know it is my duty to do, as the stamps were consigned to me by their lordships, and I have the bill of lading. But as I am confined to my bed, and also restrained by the people from executing my office, it is not in my power to know what is to be done in the premisses, I therefore pray your answer by the bearer, my son, which will oblige, Sir, your humble servant,   JOHN HUGHES.

To the Hon. John Penn, Esq.
The Governor returned the following
verbal Answer, viz.

Let Mr. Hughes know the stamps are on board the man of war.

Philadelphia, Nov. 2, 1765.
Gentlemen,

Since my last, a copy whereof is herewith sent, nothing very extraordinary has been attempted by the mob, as the great men here would fain have it termed and believed on your side the water, and I make no doubt but it will be so represented by the proprietary governor, and his friends; but the truth is, that if the governor, or any half dozen of the magistrates, had called the sheriff and constable to their assistance, it would have been very easy for them, with the assistance of my friends then collected about my house, to the amount of not less than seven or eight hundred men of reputation, who would

have

have affifted the civil officers at the rifque of their lives, as I did to fupprefs the Paxton riot, that intended to deftroy the Indians at the barracks.

I am now informed the governor has taken the oath prefcribed by the ftamp-act, but his friends keep it a fecret, and fay, 'who knows that he has,' but it will foon appear here, for that will alter his conduct; the commiffioners and government may depend that I will communicate things as they happen, though it is at the rifque of my life; for the party, by their tools, frequently give out, that if they knew the man that would fo far affift Britain as to inform againft any man, in this or any other province, he fhould not live many hours; and I do affure the government and commiffioners, that all pofitive charges made by me, can be proved by reputable witneffes. But whether his Majefty or his miniftry can, or will wink at and overlook thefe infults and outrages, and permit their colonifts to refufe obedience to an act of parliament, and alfo declare it illegal and unconftitutional, and alfo permit the printers here to publifh weekly the moft violent and inflammatory pieces that ever were wrote, and I am of opinion, that if thefe continental papers for the two or three months paft were examined, many of them would be found rather to exceed the North Briton, (No. XLV.) in alienating the affections of the people from his Majefty, and animating them to rebellion, and yet at the fame time call themfelves Englifhmen, and profefs the higheft degree of loyalty to his Majefty. I fome time tell fome of our warm blades, that it is a piece of inconfiftency to call themfelves Englifhmen, becaufe gentlemen, fay I, if you are Englifhmen, you muft be bound by acts of parliament, until that parliament releafes you from that obedience, which has not yet been done as I know of. To this they reply our charters have done it abfolutely. No, gentlemen, your charters are but the declarations of the kings that granted them, and they cannot be   to mean no more, than that the king of Great Britain would not arbitrarily, and without law, raife money on the fubject in America, and this all our forefathers feemed to have afked—when they left Britain, and indeed it is all the kings of Great Britain can legally promife, for the king cannot bar the rights of the lords and commons, any more than they can his prerogatives. The anfwer then is, you are an enemy to America, and ought to have your brains beat out, &c. And indeed there is nothing has faved me but the great number of friends and relations that I have in this country, and, had it not been for their numbers, I muft have refigned my office abfolutely, or elfe not only me but my family and fortune would have fallen a facrifice. I believe I am the only ftamp diftributor that has not either refigned abfolutely, or fled the province between Virginia and Hallifax, and if the Virginia officer had been there, I think he muft have refigned alfo, for there the fire began. It is my private opinion, that if the province of Pennfylvania was changed from proprietary to a royal government, and fome perfon appointed to govern it, that had both intereft among the people, and a perfect knowledge of them, fo as to be able to difplace the difloyal, and put in power and commiffion fuch only as could be depended on, and have demonftrated their loyalty to their king; fuch a perfon, after the changes aforefaid, might eafily govern this province, and preferve the peace of it, and keep it in fubjection to his Majefty, which I think we hardly are at this time. One reafon affigned for not paying obedience to this act of parliament, is, that we have no reprefentative in parliament; I then fay, let us petition for reprefentatives. O, no, we will not agree to that, becaufe we have reprefentatives of our own, and have always given money

when

when we have been called on by the king or his minifters, and if that will not do, let us have a houfe of Commons in America, to fettle what fhall be the quota of each colony when money is wanted—No, gentlemen, you have foreclofed yourfelves of that, for you have demonftrated your propenfity to rebellion, to that degree, that in my opinion the miniftry never can advife his Majefty to unite you more than you now are; but if they knew our circumftances rightly, they would divide us yet more, by forming new colonies out of Virginia, and perhaps fome others that are already but too large; but thefe things are at a diftance, for Great Britain muft firft determine whether fhe is to govern or not, and whether fhe will permit us to put ourfelves under the protection of France, or Spain, as many upon the continent declare they will ward off the ftamp-act, until they can get France or Spain to protect them; and fome few have gone fo far in this province. I muft now contradict your allegation of our giving money when called upon. Pray has Maryland given one fhilling all the laft war, and did not moft of the colonies, except Pennfylvania, refufe both men and money for Colonel Bouquet's laft expedition againft the Indians to the weftward; and when Col. Bouquet, by his friends, got fome volunteers raifed for the purpofe in Virginia, was he not obliged to apply to the commiffioners of this province to pay them, or elfe he muft have paid them out of his private fortune; although the war was on the Virginia frontier, and their people frequently murdered at that time.

November the 3d, being Saturday evening, I was called upon by the collector, to let me know that he and the other cuftom-houfe officers would call upon me next day, but they afterwards changed their plan; and on

Tuefday the 5th, I received the paper, (No. I.) and that afternoon returned for anfwer the paper (No. II.) and I now underftand that the party are much diffatisfied with my anfwer, and fay I had no need to fay more than three words; viz. I have none —This they could have protefted upon and fent home to the cuftom-houfe, but I believe they have no great inclination to fend home this letter; however, I think it my duty to fend it you with a copy of theirs; alfo I wifh I knew whether the act would be enforced or not, for if it is to be repealed, I might refign voluntarily in time, and thereby efcape the violence of the party, for if the act is not enforced, nor I do not refign in time, I fhall not be able to go into fome of the neighbouring colonies, and look after my intereft during my life-time, for they threaten me already in Maryland and Virginia, that if they ever catch me there they will make a facrifice of me; but if they fhould be made fubject to Great Britain, I fhall then be in no danger, for the iffue of this act will abfolutely determine Britain's fovereignty in America. For, if by thefe rebellious actions we can get this act repealed, I have no doubt but fome of my children may live to fee a duty laid by Americans on fome things imported from Britain, for I do not know an inftance of a mob's fitting down contented with one thing, unlefs they have a force able to quell them.

I prefume when the remonftrances from the grand committee (who meet at New-York) come here, it will be eafy to judge what we would be at; for even in this province fome few fay, if we ftick by one another, it is not in the power of Britain to enforce it, and fay that Ireland did the fame formerly, and by that means have efcaped the burthen as they call it. I am unable at this time to give a more full account of the proceedings in America, being not recovered from

my

my late illnefs. I am, gentlemen, with refpect, your moft obedient, humble fervant,

Nov. 7, 1765, JOHN HUGHES.
To the commiffioners of the ftamp-office.

No. I.

Mr. John Hughes,

Sir, We have heard from public report, that you are the officer appointed to diftribute ftamp-papers and parchment in the province, purfuant to an act of parliament lately publifhed in England, and we now apply to you, to know whether you can fupply us with ftamp papers proper for cockets and clearances, on which the duty of four-pence fterling is impofed (if the copy we have feen of the act be genuine). We apprehend it is our duty to apply to you for them, as we cannot proceed regularly in the bufinefs of our office without them. Pleafe to let us have your anfwer in writing as foon as poffible, in order to prevent any miftake or mifunderftanding that may happen from a verbal conference between us. We beg you will be pleafed to have a direct anfwer, whether you will or not let us have the ftamp papers for the purpofes above-mentioned. We are, Sir, your moft humble fervants,

Cuftom-Houfe, J. SWIFT, Dep. Collr.
Philadelphia, A. BARCLAY, Comptr.
Nov. 4, 1764. T. Grame, Naval Offr.

No. II.

Gentlemen,

I received yours of the 4th inftant, and cannot but infer from the contents, that you are a ftranger in Pennfylvania, fince by the tenor of your letter, you feem to be unacquainted with the things that are come to pafs in thefe our days. Therefore, I think it neceffary, before I proceed in anfwer, to give you a brief detail of what has happened. Firft then, I am to inform you, that on Saturday the 5th of October laft, the State-houfe and Chrift-church bells were rung muffled, and two Negro-drummers, one of whom belonged to alderman Samuel Mifflin, beat through all parts of the city with muffled drums, thereby alarming the inhabitants. In confequence whereof, a large number of people was raifed and affembled at the State-houfe, where it was publicly declared (as I am informed), that if I did not immediately refign my office, my houfe fhould be pulled down and my fubftance deftroyed, but before the convention broke up, the gentlemen affembled there, in part changed their refolution, and by a note they at night fent me, indulged me till ten o'clock the Monday morning following, to fatisfy them whether I would or not refign my office as ftamp-diftributor for this province. Secondly, although it was currently reported through the city on the 4th of October laft, that Capt. Halland, with the ftamp papers, &c. would be up next day, and that a mob would be raifed to deftroy them, yet neither the governor, the fupreme judges, the mayor, recorder, aldermen, nor any other jufticiary officers. (Benjamin Shoemaker, Efq. excepted) took the leaft notice thereof, nor ufed any means to preferve the peace of the city. Thirdly, although on Monday the 7th of October, when the people collected at the Free Mafons lodge, and their delegates, who need not here be named, came to my houfe and demanded of me my anfwer, whether I would or would not refign my office as ftamp-diftributor of this province, yet neither the governor, the judges of the fupreme court, although then fitting, the mayor, recorder, aldermen, nor any of the peace-officers of this city, teftified the leaft difapprobation thereof, but permitted thofe gentlemen and their affociates, to compel me to make the declaration which you may fee printed in the Gazette and Pennfylvania Journal of the 10th of October laft. Fourthly, thefe gentlemen delegates and their affociates have therefore

therefore prevented any stamp from coming into my possession. Of consequence, it is not in my power to supply you. But as you may be unacquainted with the situation of the stamp papers, I do myself the pleasure of informing you, that his honour the governor, has committed them to the care of Capt. Hawker, commander of his Majesty's ship Sardine. And I would likewise, gentlemen, beg leave to acquaint you, that he has taken, as I am informed, a solemn oath, " to do to his utmost, that all and every of the clauses contained in the stamp-act shall be *bona fide* observed ;" wherefore I must refer you to him, as I am for the reasons already assigned, at present incapacitated to supply you with stampt papers, &c. for a more full answer, if necessary, to your letter. Fifthly, if any inconveniencies or damages, therefore, should happen to any person or persons for want of the stampt papers, the blame neither can nor does lie at my door, whatever it may of those of the gentlemen delegates and their associates. I am sorry, gentlemen, that you suffered an insinuation to escape your pen, as if I would not afford you a direct answer to your letter, for I am perswaded no part of my conduct has given you or any other person cause to suspect either my candor or integrity, therefore, permit me to say, I must look upon this insinuation both ungenerous and unfriendly. I am, Sirs, your humble servant,

Philadelphia, Nov.   J. HUGHES.
5, 1765.
John Swift, Alex. Barclay, and Thomas Grame, Esquires.

Philadelphia, Sept. 1765.
Extract of Letters from John Hughes, Esq. appointed Distributor of the Stamps for Pennsylvania, to Benjamin Franklin, Esq. Agent for said Province, by him, per Order, laid before the Parliament.

" You are now from letter to letter to suppose each may be the last that you will receive from your old friend, as the spirit or flame of rebellion is got to a high pitch among the North Americans, and it seems to me, that a sort of frenzy, or madness, has got such hold of the people of all ranks, that I fancy some lives will be lost before this fire is put out ; I am at present much perplexed what course to steer ; for, as I have given you reason to expect, I would endeavour to put the act in execution, and you no doubt have informed the commissioners I cannot in point of honor go back, until something or other is done by the people to render it impossible for me to proceed ; but, perhaps when a mob is on foot, my interest may fall a sacrifice to an infatuated multitude, and I know of no other way to prevent it, but absolutely declaring off as all the rest have done to the eastward, but as yet I cannot prevail upon myself, notwithstanding the threats of some, and the persuasions of others, to do an act that appears to me neither loyal nor reputable.

" I had hitherto kept matters easy, by saying I had nothing to resign, for I have neither received any commission or any other kind of writing from the stamp-office ; but when it is known I have received my commission, I fancy I shall not escape the storm of presbyterian rage, and as Capt. Friend is expected every day, my doom will soon be known, but whether I may live to inform you, is yet in the womb of futurity.

" By Governor Franklin's letters, and by my last, you will see that Mr. Cox has resigned the stamp-office for New-Jersey, and there is scarce a day goes over my head, but many people call on me to resign, and say I am an enemy to North-America if I do not ; but since I am now   and must abide by consequences, be they what they will, I shall be exceedingly obliged to you, if it is consistent with
your

your judgment, to recommend my son Hugh for Mr. Cox's fucceffor. My fon is married, and fettled in New Jerfey, has a good eftate, both real and perfonal, and can give any fecurity that may be required—I am the more induced to afk this favour, as I think there will be no difficulty in putting the act in execution in that province; and, if my property, and perhaps my life may be loft in this province, my fon I hope will be the better for the office in that province, which may be fome compenfation for what property may be loft out of the family.

Sept. 10, 1765.

" Our affembly met yefterday, and this day a majority of fifteen againft fourteen, were for fending a committee to New-York, to meet the committee of Bofton on the firft of October, where they infinuate there will be men fent from every colony, in order to unite and become, as they exprefs it, like a bundle of rods, alluding to the fable of the old man and his fons. This fcheme, or plan of union, is not only begun, but indefatigably pufhed forward, by the prefbyterians principally.

Sept. 11. This afternoon Capt. Friend arrived, and as he fays he has no ftamp papers on board, all feems pretty quiet at prefent. The affembly have named Jofeph Fox, Geo. Bryan, John Morton and John Dickinfon, as a committee to go to the Congrefs at New-York.

Sept. 12. Our clamours run very high, and I am told my houfe fhall be pulled down and the ftamps burnt, to which I give no other anfwer than that I will defend my houfe at the rifque of my life. I muft fay that all the fenfible quakers behave prudently.

Sept. 16. in the evening—Common report threatens my houfe this night, as there are bonfires and rejoicings for the change of miniftry. The fober and fenfible part of the people are doing every thing in readinefs to fup-

prefs a mob, if there fhould be any intention of rifing. I, for my part, am well armed with fire-arms, and am determined to ftand a fiege. If I live till to-morrow morning, fhall give you a further account, but as it is now about eight o'clock I am on my guard, and only write this between whiles, as every noife or buftle of the people calls me off.

Nine o'clock. Several friends that patrole between my houfe and the coffee-houfe, came in juft now, and fay the collection of rabble begins to decreafe vifibly in the ftreets, and the appearance of danger feems a good deal lefs than it did.

Twelve o'clock. There are now feveral hundreds of our friends about the ftreet ready to fupprefs any mob, if it fhould attempt to rife, and the rabble are difperfing.

Sept. 17. five in the morning—We are all yet in the land of the living, and our properties fafe, thank God.

Extract of a Letter from Jofeph Galloway, Efq. dated Philadelphia, September 29, 1765, to Benjamin Franklin, Efq.

" The public papers will inform you of the prefent diftracted ftate of the colonies, and the many outrages and riots that have been occafioned by a diflike to the ftamp-act, all which have been incited by the principal members of the colonies where they have been committed—Meafures have not been wanting to create the fame temper in the people here, in which fome have been very active. In hopes to prevent their ill effects, I wrote a moderate piece, figned Americanus, publifhed here and at New-York, and fince in Virginia, wherein you will fee my fentiments on the fubject. I am told it had good effect in thofe places as well as here, being much approved by the moderate part of the people ; yet we fhould not have been free from riots here, if another method had not been taken to prevent them, viz. By

By affembling quietly at the inftance of Mr. Hughes's friends (and not by order from the government of the city), near eight hundred fober inhabitants were pofted in different parts, ready to prevent any mifchief that fhould be attempted by the mob, which effectually intimidated them and kept all tolerable quiet, only they burnt a figure that they called a ftampman, and about midnight difperfed. Great pains have been taken to perfuade and frighten Mr. Hughes into a refignation of his office, but he continues firm, and will not refign in any manner that fhall do difhonour to his appointment, and I think will be able to put his commiffion into execution, notwithftanding the example fet by other colonies.

———————

The King having, in his fpeech, recommended to the confideration of parliament the affairs of America, a debate naturally followed on the addrefs.

The new minifters fpoke tenderly of the difturbances and confufions in America. The late minifters (at this time in oppofition) were quite the reverfe.

Earl Nugent (then Mr. Nugent) infifted, ' That the honour and dignity of the kingdom, obliged us to compel the execution of the ftamp-act, except the right was acknowledged, and the repeal follicited as a favour. He computed the expence of the troops now employed in America for their defence, as he called it, to amount to nine-pence in the pound of our land tax; while the produce of the ftamp-act would not raife a fhilling a head on the inhabitants of America; but that a pepper-corn, in acknowledgment of the right, was of more value, than millions without. He expatiated on the extreme ingratitude of the colonies; and concluded, with charging the miniftry with encouraging petitions to parliament, and inftructions to members from trading

and manufacturing towns, againft the act.'

Mr. Pitt (now Lord Chatham) fpoke next. As he always begins very low, and as every body was in agitation at his firft rifing, his introduction was not heard, 'till he faid, ' I came to town but to-day; I was a ftranger to the tenor of his Majefty's fpeech, and the propofed addrefs, 'till I heard them read in this houfe. Unconnected and unconfulted, I have not the means of information; I am fearful of offending through miftake, and therefore beg to be indulged with a fecond reading of the propofed addrefs.' The addrefs being read, Mr. Pitt went on :—He commended the King's fpeech, approved of the addrefs in anfwer, as it decided nothing, every gentleman being left at perfect liberty to take fuch a part concerning America, as he might afterwards fee fit. One word only he could not approve of, an *early*, is a word that does not belong to the notice the miniftry has given to parliament of the troubles in America. In a matter of fuch importance, the communication ought to have been immediate : I fpeak not with refpect to parties; I ftand up in this place fingle and unconnected. As to the late miniftry, (turning himfelf to Mr. Grenville, who fat within one of him) every capital meafure they have taken, has been entirely wrong!

' As to the prefent gentlemen, to thofe at leaft whom I have in my eye (looking at the bench where Mr. Conway fat, with the lords of the treafury) I have no objection; I have never been made a facrifice by any of them. Their characters are fair; and I am always glad when men of fair character engage in his Majefty's fervice. Some of them have done me the honour to afk my poor opinion, before they would engage. Thefe will do me the juftice to own, I advifed them to engage; but notwithftanding —I love to be explicit—I cannot give

I   them

them my confidence; pardon me, gentlemen, (bowing to the miniftry) confidence is a plant of flow growth in an aged bofom : youth is the feafon of credulity ; by comparing events with each other, reafoning from effects to caufes, methinks, I plainly dif-cover the traces of an over-ruling in-fluence.

' There is a claufe in the act of fet-tlement, to oblige every minifter to fign his name to the advice which he gives his fovereign. Would it were obferved!—I have had the honour to ferve the crown, and if I could have fubmitted to influence, I might have ftill continued to ferve ; but I would not be refponfible for others.——I have no local attachments: it is in-different to me, whether a man was rocked in his cradle on this fide or that fide of the Tweed.—I fought for merit wherever it was to be found.— It is my boaft, that I was the firft minifter who looked for it, and I found it in the mountains of the north. I called it forth, and drew it into your fervice, an hardy and in-trepid race of men! men, who, when left by your jealoufy, became a prey to the artifices of your enemies, and had gone nigh to have overturned the ftate, in the war before the laft. Thefe men, in the laft war, were brought to combat on your fide: they ferved with fidelity, as they fought with valour, and conquered for you in every part of the world : detefted be the national reflections againft them !——they are unjuft, ground-lefs, illiberal, unmanly. When I ceafed to ferve his Majefty as a mi-nifter, it was not the country of the man by which I was moved—but the man of that country wanted wifdom, and held principles incompatible with freedom.

' It is a long time, Mr. Speaker, fince I have attended in parliament. When the refolution was taken in the houfe to tax America, I was ill in bed. If I could have endured to have been carried in my bed, fo great was the agitation of my mind for the con-fequences ! I would have follicited fome kind hand to have laid me down on this floor, to have borne my teftimony againft it. It is now an act that had paffed—I would fpeak with decency of every act of this houfe, but I muft beg the indulgence of the houfe to fpeak of it with freedom.

' I hope a day may be foon ap-pointed to confider the ftate of the nation with refpect to America.—I hope, gentlemen will come to this debate with all the temper and im-partiality his majefty recommends, and the importance of the fubject requires. A fubject of greater importance than ever engaged the attention of this houfe ! that fubject only excepted, when, near a century ago, it was the queftion, whether you yourfelves were to be bound, or free. In the mean time, as I cannot depend upon health for any future day, fuch is the nature of my infirmities, I will beg to fay a few words at prefent, leaving the juftice, the equity, the policy, the ex-pediency of the act, to another time. I will only fpeak to one point, a point which feems not to have been gene-rally underftood—I mean to the right. Some gentlemen (alluding to Mr. Nugent) feem to have confidered it as a point of honor. If gentlemen confider it in that light, they leave all meafures of right and wrong, to follow a delufion that may lead to deftruction. It is my opinion that this kingdom has no right to lay a tax upon the colonies. At the fame time, I affert the authority of this kingdom over the colonies, to be fovereign and fupreme, in every circumftance of government and legiflation whatfoever.——They are the fubjects of this kingdom, equally entitled with yourfelves to all the natural rights of mankind and the peculiar privileges of Englifhmen. Equally bound by its laws, and equally participating of the conftitution of

this

this free country. The Americans are the sons, not the bastards, of England. Taxation is no part of the governing or legislative power.—The taxes are a voluntary gift and grant of the commons alone. In legislation the three estates of the realm are alike concerned, but the concurrence of the peers and the crown to a tax, is only necessary to close with the form of a law. The gift and grant is of the commons alone. In antient days, the crown, the barons, and the clergy possessed the lands. In those days, the barons and the clergy gave and granted to the crown. They gave and granted what was their own. At present, since the discovery of America, and other circumstances permitting, the commons are become the proprietors of the land. The crown has divested itself of its great estates. The church (God bless it) has but a pittance. The property of the lords, compared with that of the commons, is as a drop of water in the ocean: and this house represents those commons, the proprietors of the lands; and those proprietors virtually represent the rest of the inhabitants. When, therefore, in this house we give and grant, we give and grant what is our own. But in an American tax, what do we do? We, your Majesty's commons of Great Britain, give and grant to your Majesty, what? Our own property?—No. We give and grant to your Majesty, the property of your Majesty's commons of America.—It is an absurdity in terms.—

'The distinction between legislation and taxation is essentially necessary to liberty. The crown, the peers, are equally legislative powers with the commons. If taxation be a part of simple legislation, the crown, the peers have rights in taxation as well as yourselves: rights which they will claim, which they will exercise, whenever the principle can be supported by power.

'There is an idea in some, that the colonies are virtually represented in this house. I would fain know by whom an American is represented here? Is he represented by any knight of the shire, in any county in this kingdom? Would to God that respectable representations was augmented to a greater number! Or will you tell him that he is represented by any representative of a borough—a borough, which perhaps no man ever saw—This is what is called, the rotten part of the constitution.——It cannot continue the century—If it does not drop, it must be amputated.—The idea of a virtual representation of America in this house, is the most contemptible idea that ever entered into the head of a man—It does not deserve a serious refutation.

'The commons of America, represented in their several assemblies, have ever been in possession of the exercise of this, their constitutional right, of giving and granting their own money. They would have been slaves if they had not enjoyed it. At the same time, this kingdom, as the supreme governing and legislative power, has always bound the colonies by her laws, by her regulations, and restrictions in trade, in navigation, in manufactures—in every thing, except that of taking their money out of their pockets without their consent.—Here I would draw the line, *Quam ultra citraque nequit consistere rectum.*'

He concluded with a familiar voice and tone, but so low that it was not easy to distinguish what he said. A considerable pause ensued after Mr. Pitt had done speaking.

Mr. Conway at length got up. He said, 'he had been waiting to see whether any answer would be given to what had been advanced by the right honourable gentleman, reserving himself for the reply: but as none had been given, he had only to declare, that his own sentiments were entirely conformable to those of the right honourable

honourable gentleman.—That they are fo conformable, he faid, is a circumftance that affects me with moft fenfible pleafure, and does me the greateft honour. But two things fell from that gentleman which give me pain, as whatever falls from that gentleman, falls from fo great a height as to make a deep impreffion. I muft endeavour to remove it. It was objected, that the notice given to parliament of the troubles in America was not early. I can affure the houfe, the firft accounts were too vague and imperfect to be worth the notice of parliament. It is only of late that they have been precife and full. An over-ruling influence has alfo been hinted at. I fee nothing of it. I feel nothing of it. I difclaim it for myfelf, and (as far as my difcernment can reach) for all the reft of his Majefty's minifters.'

Mr. Pitt faid, in anfwer to Mr. Conway, ' The excufe is a valid one, if it is a juft one. That muft appear from the papers now before the houfe.' Mr. Grenville next ftood up. He began with cenfuring the miniftry very feverely, for delaying to give earlier notice to parliament of the difturbances in America. He faid, ' They began in July, and now we are in the middle of January; lately they were only occurrences, they are now grown to difturbances, to tumults and riots. I doubt they border on open rebellion; and if the doctrine I have heard this day be confirmed, I fear they will lofe that name to take that of revolution. The government over them being diffolved, a revolution will take place in America. I cannot underftand the difference between external and internal taxes. They are the fame in effect, and only differ in name. That this kingdom has the fovereign, the fupreme legiflative power over America, is granted. It cannot be denied; and taxation is a part of that fovereign power. It is one branch

of the legiflation. It is, it has been exercifed, over thofe who are not, who were never reprefented. It is exercifed over the India company, the merchants of London, the proprietors of the ftocks, and over many great manufacturing towns. It was exercifed over the palatinate of Chefter, and the bifhoprick of Durham, before they fent any reprefentatives to parliament. I appeal for proof to the preambles of the acts which gave them reprefentatives: the one in the reign of Henry VIII. the other in that of Charles II.' Mr. Grenville then quoted the acts, and defired that they might be read; which being done, he faid: ' When I propofed to tax America, I afked the houfe, if any gentleman would object to the right; I repeatedly afked it, and no man would attempt to deny it. Protection and obedience are reciprocal. Great-Britain protects America: America is bound to yield obedience. If not, tell me where the Americans were emancipated? When they want the protection of this kingdom, they are always very ready to afk it. That protection has always been afforded them in the moft full and ample manner. The nation has run itfelf into an immenfe debt to give them their protection; and now they are called upon to contribute a fmall fhare towards the public expence, an expence arifing from themfelves, they renounce your authority, infult your officers, and break out, I might almoft fay, into open rebellion. The feditious fpirit of the colonies owes its birth to the factions in the houfe. Gentlemen are carelefs of the confequences of what they fay, provided it anfwers the purpofes of oppofition. We were told we trod on tender ground; we were bid to expect difobedience. What was this, but telling the Americans to ftand out againft the law, to encourage their obftinacy with the expectation of fupport from hence? Let us only hold out a little, they would

would fay, our friends will foon be in power. Ungrateful people of America! Bounties have been extended to them. When I had the honour of ferving the crown, while you yourfelves were loaded with an enormous debt, you have given bounties on their lumber, on their iron, their hemp, and many other articles. You have relaxed, in their favour, the act of navigation, that palladium of the Britifh commerce; and yet I have been abufed in all the public papers as an enemy to the trade of America. I have been particularly charged with giving orders and inftructions to prevent the Spanifh trade, and thereby ftopping the channel, by which alone North-America ufed to be fupplied with cafh for remittances to this country. I defy any man to produce any fuch orders or inftructions. I difcouraged no trade but what was illicit, what was prohibited by act of parliament. I defire a Weft-India merchant, well known in the city (Mr. Long) a gentleman of character, may be examined. He will tell you, that I offered to do every thing in my power to advance the trade of America. I was above giving an anfwer to anonymous calumnies; but in this place, it becomes one to wipe off the afperfion.'

Here Mr. Grenville ceafed. Several members got up to fpeak, but Mr. Pitt feeming to rife, the houfe was fo clamorous for Mr. Pitt, Mr. Pitt, that the fpeaker was obliged to call to order. After obtaining a little quiet, he faid, 'Mr. Pitt was up;' who began with informing the houfe, 'That he did not mean to have gone any further upon the fubject that day; that he had only defigned to have thrown out a few hints, which, gentlemen who were fo confident of the right of this kingdom to fend taxes to America, might confider; might, perhaps, reflect, in a cooler moment, that the right was at leaft equivocal. But fince the

gentleman, who fpoke laft, had not ftopped on that ground, but had gone into the whole; into the juftice, the equity, the policy, the expediency of the ftamp-act, as well as into the right, he would follow him through the whole field, and combat his arguments on every point.'

He was going on, when the late Lord Strange got up, and called both the gentlemen, Mr. Pitt, and Mr. Grenville, to order. He faid, ' they had both departed from the matter before the houfe, which was the King's fpeech; and that Mr. Pitt was going to fpeak twice on the fame debate, although the houfe was not in a committee.'

Mr. Onflow (now Lord Onflow) anfwered, ' That they were both in order, as nothing had been faid, but what was fairly deducible from the King's fpeech;' and appealed to the Speaker. The Speaker decided in Mr. Onflow's favour.

Mr. Pitt faid, ' I do not apprehend I am fpeaking twice: I did exprefsly referve a part of my fubject, in order to fave the time of this houfe, but I am compelled to proceed in it. I do not fpeak twice; I only finifhed what I defignedly left imperfect. But if the houfe is of a different opinion, far be it from me to indulge a wifh of tranfgreffion, againft order. I am content, if it be your pleafure, to be filent.'—Here he paufed.—The houfe refounding with, Go on, go on; he proceeded:

' Gentlemen, Sir, (to the Speaker) I have been charged with giving birth to fedition in America. They have fpoken their fentiments with freedom, againft this unhappy act, and that freedom has become their crime. Sorry I am to hear the liberty of fpeech in this houfe, imputed as a crime. But the imputation fhall not difcourage me. It is a liberty I mean to exercife. No gentleman ought to be afraid to exercife it. It is a liberty by which the gentleman who

who calumniates it might have profited. He ought to have profited.
He ought to have defifted from his
project. The gentleman tells us,
America is obftinate ; America is
almoft in open rebellion. I rejoice
that America has refifted. Three
millions of people, fo dead to all the
feelings of liberty, as voluntarily to
fubmit to be flaves, would have been
fit inftruments to make flaves of the
reft. I come not here armed at all
points, with law cafes and acts of
parliament, with the ftatute book
doubled down in dogs-ears, to defend
the caufe of liberty : if I had, I myfelf would have cited the two cafes of
Chefter and Durham. I would have
cited them, to have fhewn, that,
even under any arbitrary reigns, parliaments were afhamed of taxing a
people without their confent, and allowed them reprefentatives. Why
did the gentleman confine himfelf to
Chefter and Durham ? He might
have taken a higher example in
Wales ; Wales, that never was taxed
by parliament till it was incorporated.
I would not debate a particular point
of law with the gentleman : I know
his abilities. I have been obliged to
his diligent refearches. But, for the
defence of liberty upon a general
principle, upon a conftitutional principle, it is a ground on which I ftand
firm ; on which I dare meet any man.
The gentleman tells us of many who
are taxed, and are not reprefented.
The India company, merchants,
ftock-holders, manufacturers. Surely
many of thefe are reprefented in
other capacities, as owners of land,
or as freemen of boroughs. It is a
misfortune that more are not actually
reprefented. But they are all inhabitants, and, as fuch, are virtually
reprefented. Many have it in their
option to be actually reprefented.
They have connections with thofe
that elect, and they have influence
over them. The gentleman mentioned the ftock-holders : I hope he

does not reckon the debts of the nation as a part of the national eftate.
Since the acceffion of King William,
many minifters, fome of great, others
of more moderate abilities, have taken
the lead of government.'

He then went through the lift of
them, bringing it down till he came
to himfelf, giving a fhort fketch of
the characters of each of them.
' None of thefe, he faid, thought,
or ever dreamed, of robbing the colonies of their conftitutional rights.
That was referved to mark the æra
of the late adminiftration : not that
there were wanting fome, when I had
the honour to ferve his Majefty, to
propofe to me to burn my fingers
with an American ftamp act. With
the enemy at their back, with our
bayonets at their breafts, in the day
of their diftrefs, perhaps the Americans would have fubmitted to the impofition ; but it would have been
taking an ungenerous, and unjuft advantage. The gentleman boafts of
his bounties to America ! Are not
thofe bounties intended finally for the
benefit of this kingdom ? If they are
not, he has mifapplied the national
treafures. I am no courtier of America, I ftand up for this kingdom.
I maintain, that the parliament has
a right to bind, to reftrain America.
Our legiflative power over the colonies is fovereign and fupreme. When
it ceafes to be fovereign and fupreme,
I would advife every gentleman to
fell his lands, if he can, and embark
for that country. When two countries are connected together, like
England and her colonies, without
being incorporated, the one muft neceffarily govern ; the greater muft
rule the lefs ; but fo rule it, as not
to contradict the fundamental principles that are common to both.

' If the gentleman does not underftand the difference between internal
and external taxes, I cannot help it ;
but there is a plain diftinction between
taxes levied for the purpofes of raifing
a re-

a revenue, and duties impofed for the regulation of trade, for the accommodation of the fubject; altho', in the confequences, fome revenue might incidentally arife from the latter.

' The gentleman afks, when were the colonies emancipated? But I defire to know, when they were made flaves? But I dwell not upon words. When I had the honour of ferving his Majefty, I availed myfelf of the means of information, which I derived from my office: I fpeak therefore from knowledge. My materials were good. I was at pains to collect, to digeft, to confider them; and I will be bold to affirm, that the profits to Great-Britain from the trade of the colonies, through all its branches, is two millions a year. This is the fund that carried you triumphantly through the laft war. The eftates that were rented at two thoufand pounds a year, threefcore years ago, are at three thoufand pounds at prefent. Thofe eftates fold then from fifteen to eighteen years purchafe; the fame may be now fold for thirty. You owe this to America. This is the price that America pays you for her protection. And fhall a miferable financier come with a boaft, that he can fetch a pepper-corn into the Exchequer, to the lofs of millions to the nation! I dare not fay, how much higher thefe profits may be augmented. Omitting the immenfe increafe of people, by natural population, in the northern colonies, and the migration from every part of Europe, I am convinced the whole commercial fyftem of America may be altered to advantage. You have prohibited, where you ought to have encouraged; and you have encouraged where you ought to have prohibited. Improper reftraints have been laid on the continent, in favour of the iflands. You have but two nations to trade with in America. Would you had twenty! Let acts of parliament in confequence

of treaties remain, but let not an Englifh minifter become a cuftomhoufe officer for Spain, or for any foreign power. Much is wrong, much may be amended for the general good of the whole.

' Does the gentleman complain he has been mifreprefented in the public prints? It is a common misfortune. In the Spanifh affair of the laft war, I was abufed in all the news-papers, for having advifed his Majefty to violate the law of nations with regard to Spain. The abufe was induftrioufly circulated even in hand-bills. If adminiftration did not propagate the abufe, adminiftration never contradicted it. I will not fay what advice I did give to the King. My advice is in writing, figned by myfelf, in the poffeffion of the crown. But I will fay, what advice I did not give to the King: I did not advife him to violate any of the laws of nations.

' As to the report of the gentleman's preventing in fome way the trade for bullion with the Spaniards, it was fpoken of fo confidently, that I own I am one of thofe who did believe it to be true.

' The gentleman muft not wonder he was not contradicted, when, as the minifter, he afferted the right of parliament to tax America. I know not how it is, but there is a modefty in this houfe which does not chufe to contradict a minifter. I wifh gentlemen would get the better of this modefty. If they do not, perhaps, the collective body may begin to abate of its refpect for the reprefentative. Lord Bacon had told me, that a great queftion would not fail of being agitated at one time or another. I was willing to agitate that at the proper feafon, the German war: my German war, they called it. Every feffions I called out, has any body any objections to the German war? No body would object to it, one gentleman only excepted, fince removed to the upper houfe, by fucceffion to an

ancient

ancient barony,' (meaning Lord le Defpencer, formerly Sir Francis Dafh-wood ;) he told me, " he did not like a German war." I honoured the man for it, and was forry when he was turned out of his poft.

'A great deal has been faid without doors, of the power, of the ftrength of America. It is a topic that ought to be cautioufly meddled with. In a good caufe, on a found bottom, the force of this country can crufh America to atoms. I know the valour of your troops. I know the fkill of your of-ficers. There is not a company of foot that has ferved in America, out of which you may not pick a man of fufficient knowledge and experience, to make a governor of a colony there. But on this ground, on the ftamp-act, when fo many here will think it a crying injuftice, I am one who will lift up my hands againft it.

'In fuch a caufe, your fuccefs would be hazardous.—America, if fhe fell, would fall like the ftrong man. She would embrace the pillars of the ftate, and pull down the conftitution along with her. Is this your boafted peace ? Not to fheath the fword in its fcab-bard, but to fheath it in the bowels of your countrymen ? Will you quar-rel with yourfelves, now the whole houfe of Bourbon is united againft you ? While France difturbs your fifheries in Newfoundland, embar-raffes your flave trade to Africa, and witholds from your fubjects in Canada, their property ftipulated by treaty; while the ranfom for Manillas is de-nied by Spain, and its gallant con-queror bafely traduced into a mean plunderer, a gentleman, (Sir W. Draper) whofe noble and generous fpirit would do honour to the proudeft grandee of the country. The Ame-ricans have not acted in all things with prudence and temper. They have been wronged. They have been driven to madnefs by injuftice. Will you punifh them for the madnefs you have occafioned ? Rather let prudence and temper come firft from this fide.

I will undertake for America, that fhe will follow the example. There are two lines in a ballad of Prior's, of a man's behaviour to his wife, fo ap-plicable to you and your colonies, that I cannot help repeating them :

'Be to her faults a little blind :
'Be to her virtues very kind.

'Upon the whole, I will beg leave to tell the houfe what is really my opinion. It is, that the ftamp-act be repealed abfolutely, totally, and immediately. That the reafon for the repeal be affigned, becaufe it was founded on an erroneous principle. At the fame time, let the fovereign authority of this country over the co-lonies, be afferted in as ftrong terms as can be devifed, and be made to extend to every point of legiflation whatfoever. That we may bind their trade, confine their manufactures, and exercife every power whatfoever, ex-cept that of taking their money out of their pockets without their confent !'—

This debate determined the repeal of the ftamp-act. At the fame time a bill was brought in, and paffed, for fecuring the dependence of Ame-rica on Great Britain, in which it was afferted, " That the Parliament of Great Britain had a right to bind the Colonies in all cafes whatfoever."

When the bill to repeal the ftamp-act, was before the committee of the houfe of commons, Dr. Benjamin Franklin was examined at the bar of the houfe, on the affairs of America. The following is a copy of the exa-mination.

Q. What is your name, and place of abode ?

A. Franklin, of Philadelphia.

Q. Do the Americans pay any con-fiderable taxes among themfelves ?

A. Certainly many, and very heavy taxes.

Q. What are the prefent taxes in Pennfylvania, laid by the laws of the colony ? A. There

A. There are taxes on all estates real and personal, a poll-tax, a tax on all offices, professions, trades and businesses, according to their profits; an excise on all wine, rum, and other spirits; and a duty of ten pounds per head on all Negroes imported, with some other duties.

Q. For what purposes are those taxes laid?

A. For the support of the civil and military establishments of the country, and to discharge the heavy debt contracted in the last war.

Q. How long are those taxes to continue?

A. Those for discharging the debt are to continue till 1772, and longer, if the debt should not be then all discharged. The others must always continue.

Q. Was it not expected that the debt would have been sooner discharged?

A. It was, when the peace was made with France and Spain—But a fresh war breaking out with the Indians, a fresh load of debt was incurred, and the taxes, of course, continued longer by a new law.

Q. Are not all the people very able to pay those taxes?

A. No. The frontier counties, all along the continent, have been frequently ravaged by the enemy, and greatly impoverished, are able to pay very little tax. And therefore, in consideration of their distresses, our late tax laws do expresly favour those counties, excusing the sufferers; and I suppose the same is done in other government.

Q. Are not you concerned in the management of the post-office in America?

A. Yes. I am deputy post-master general of North-America.

Q. Don't you think the distribution of stamps, by post, to all the inhabitants, very practicable, if there was no opposition?

A. The posts only go along the sea-coasts; they do not, except in a few instances, go back into the country; and if they did, sending for stamps by post would occasion an expence of postage, amounting, in many cases, to much more than that of the stamps themselves.

Q. Are you acquainted with New-foundland?

A. I never was there.

Q. Do you know whether there are any post-roads on that island?

A. I have heard that there are no roads at all; but that the communication between one settlement and another is by sea only.

Q. Can you disperse the stamps by post in Canada?

A. There is only a post between Montreal and Quebec. The inhabitants live so scattered and remote from each other, in that vast country, that posts cannot be supported among them, and therefore they cannot get stamps per post. The English colonies too, along the frontiers, are very thinly settled.

Q. From the thinness of the back settlements, would not the stamp-act be extremely inconvenient to the inhabitants, if executed?

A. To be sure it would; as many of the inhabitants could not get stamps when they had occasion for them, without taking long journeys, and spending perhaps three or four pounds, that the crown might get six-pence.

Q. Are not the colonies, from their circumstances, very able to pay the stamp duty.

A. In my opinion, there is not gold and silver enough in the colonies to pay the stamp duty for one year.

Q. Don't you know that the money arising from the stamps was all to be laid out in America?

A. I know it is appropriated by the act to the American service; but it will be spent in the conquered colonies, where the soldiers are, not in the colonies that pay it.

Q. Is there not a balance of trade

K   due

due from the colonies where the troops are posted, that will bring back the money to the old colonies?

A. I think not. I believe very little would come back. I know of no trade likely to bring it back. I think it would come from the colonies where it was spent directly to England; for I have always observed, that in every colony the more plenty the means of remittance to England, the more goods are sent for, and the more trade with England carried on.

Q. What number of white inhabitants do you think there are in Pennsylvania?

A. I suppose there may be about 160,000.

Q. What number of them are Quakers?

A. Perhaps a third.

Q. What number of Germans?

A. Perhaps another third; but I cannot speak with certainty.

Q. Have any number of the Germans seen service, as soldiers, in Europe?

A. Yes,—many of them, both in Europe and America.

Q. Are they as much dissatisfied with the stamp-duty as the English?

A. Yes, and more; and with reason, as their stamps are, in many cases, to be double.

Q. How many white men do you suppose there are in North-America?

A. About 300,000, from sixteen to sixty years of age.

Q. What may be the amount of one year's imports into Pennsylvania from Britain?

A. I have been informed that our merchants compute the imports from Britain to be above 500,000 pounds.

Q. What may be the amount of the produce of your province exported to Britain?

A. It must be small, as we produce little that is wanted in Britain. I suppose it cannot exceed 40,000 pounds.

Q. How then do you pay the balance?

A. The balance is paid by our produce carried to the West-Indies, and sold in our own islands, or to the French, Spaniards, Danes and Dutch; by the same carried to other colonies in North-America, as to New-England, Nova-Scotia, Newfoundland, Carolina and Georgia; by the same carried to different parts of Europe, as Spain, Portugal and Italy. In all which places we receive either money, bills of exchange, or commodities that suit for remittance to Britain; which, together with all the profits on the industry of our merchants and mariners, arising in those circuitous voyages, and the freights made by their ships, center finally in Britain to discharge the balance, and pay for British manufactures continually used in the province, or sold to foreigners by our traders.

Q. Have you heard of any difficulties lately laid on the Spanish trade?

A. Yes, I have heard that it has been greatly obstructed by some new regulations, and by the English men of war and cutters stationed all along the coast in America.

Q. Do you think it right that America should be protected by this country, and pay no part of the expence?

A. That is not the case. The colonies raised, cloathed and payed, during the last war, near 25000 men, and spent many millions.

Q. Were not you reimbursed by parliament?

A. We were only reimbursed what, in your opinion, we had advanced beyond our proportion, or beyond what might reasonably be expected from us; and it was a very small part of what we spent. Pennsylvania, in particular, disbursed about 500,000 pounds, and the reimbursements in the whole, did not exceed 60,000 pounds.

Q. You

Q. You have said that you pay heavy taxes in Pennsylvania; what do they amount to in the pound?

A. The tax on all estates, real and personal, is eighteen-pence in the pound, fully rated; and the tax on the profits of trades and professions, with other taxes, do, I suppose, make full half a crown in the pound,

Q. Do you know any thing of the rate of exchange in Pennsylvania, and whether it has fallen lately?

A. It is commonly from 170 to 175. I have heard that it has fallen lately from 175 to 162 and a half, owing, I suppose, to their lessening their orders for goods; and when their debts to this country are paid, I think the exchange will probably be at par.

Q. Do not you think the people of America would submit to pay the stamp-duty, if it was moderated?

A. No, never, unless compelled by force of arms.

Q. Are not the taxes in Pennsylvania laid on unequally, in order to burthen the English trade, particularly the tax on professions and business?

A. It is not more burthensome in proportion than the tax on lands. It is intended, and supposed to take an equal proportion of profits.

Q. How is the assembly composed? Of what kind of people are the members, landholders or traders?

A. It is composed of landholders, merchants and artificers.

Q. Are not the majority landholders?

A. I believe they are.

Q. Do not they, as much as possible, shift the tax off from the land, to ease that, and lay the burthen heavier on trade?

A. I have never understood it so. I never heard such a thing suggested. And indeed an attempt of that kind could answer no purpose. The merchant or trader is always skilled in figures, and ready with his pen and ink. If unequal burthens are laid on his trade, he puts an additional price on his goods; and the consumers, who are chiefly landholders, finally pay the greatest part, if not the whole.

Q. What was the temper of America towards Great Britain before the year 1763?

A. The best in the world. They submitted willingly to the government of the crown, and paid, in all their courts, obedience to acts of parliament. Numerous as the people are in the several old provinces, they cost you nothing in forts, citadels, garrisons or armies, to keep them in subjection. They were governed by this country at the expence only of a little pen, ink and paper. They were led by a thread. They had not only a respect, but an affection for Great-Britain, for its laws, its customs and manners, and even a fondness for its fashions, that greatly increased the commerce. Natives of Britain were always treated with particular regard; to be an Old England-man was, of itself, a character of some respect, and gave a kind of rank among us.

Q. And what is their temper now.

A. O, very much altered.

Q. Did you ever hear the authority of parliament to make laws for America questioned till lately?

A. The authority of parliament was allowed to be valid in all laws, except such as should lay internal taxes. It was never disputed in laying duties to regulate commerce.

Q. In what proportion hath population increased in America?

A. I think the inhabitants of all the provinces together, taken at a medium, double in about twenty-five years. But their demand for British manufactures increases much faster, as the consumption is not merely in proportion to their numbers, but grows with the growing abilities of the same numbers to pay for them. In 1723, the whole importation from Britain to Pennsylvania, was but about 15,000

K 2　　　　　　　　　　　pound

pounds sterling; it is now near half a million.

Q. In what light did the people of America use to consider the parliament of Great-Britain?

A. They considered the parliament as the great bulwark and security of their liberties and privileges, and always spoke of it with the utmost respect and veneration. Arbitrary ministers, they thought, might possibly, at times, attempt to oppress them; but they relied on it, that the parliament, on application, would always give redress. They remembered, with gratitude, a strong instance of this, when a bill was brought into parliament, with a clause, to make royal instructions laws in the colonies, which the house of commons would not pass, and it was thrown out.

Q. And have they not still the same respect for parliament?

A. No; it is greatly lessened.

Q. To what causes is that owing?

A. To a concurrence of causes; the restraints lately laid on their trade; by which the bringing of foreign gold and silver into the colonies was prevented; the prohibition of making paper money among themselves; and then demanding a new and heavy tax by stamps; taking away, at the same time, trials by juries, and refusing to receive and hear their humble petitions.

Q. Don't you think they would submit to the stamp-act, if it was modified, the obnoxious parts taken out, and the duty reduced to some particulars, of small moment?

A. No; they will never submit to it.

Q. What do you think is the reason that the people of America increase faster than in England?

A. Because they marry younger, and more generally.

Q. Why so?

A. Because any young couple that are industrious, may easily obtain land of their own, on which they can raise a family.

Q. Are not the lower rank of people more at their ease in America than in England?

A. They may be so, if they are sober and diligent, as they are better paid for their labour.

Q. What is your opinion of a future tax, imposed on the same principle with that of the stamp-act; how would the Americans receive it?

A. Just as they do this. They would not pay it.

Q. Have not you heard of the resolutions of this house, and of the house of lords, asserting the right of parliament relating to America, including a power to tax the people there?

A. Yes, I have heard of such resolutions.

Q. What will be the opinion of the Americans on those resolutions?

A. They will think them unconstitutional and unjust.

Q. Was it an opinion in America before 1763, that the parliament had no right to lay taxes and duties there?

A. I never heard any objection to the right of laying duties to regulate commerce; but a right to lay internal taxes was never supposed to be in parliament, as we are not represented there.

Q. On what do you found your opinion, that the people in America made any such distinction?

A. I know that whenever the subject has occurred in conversation where I have been present, it has appeared to be the opinion of every one, that we could not be taxed in a parliament where we were not represented. But the payment of duties laid by act of parliament, as regulations of commerce was never disputed.

Q. But can you name any act of assembly, or public act of any of your governments, that made such distinction?

A. I do not know that there was any; I think there was never an occasion cafion to make any fuch act, till now that you have attempted to tax us; that has occasioned refolutions of affembly, declaring the diftinction, in which I think every affembly on the continent, and every member in every affembly, have been unanimous.

Q. What then could occafion converfations on that fubject before that time.

A. There was in 1754 a propofition made (I think it came from hence) that in cafe of a war, which was then apprehended, the governors of the colonies fhould meet, and order the levying of troops, building of forts, and taking every other neceffary meafure for the general defence; and fhould draw on the treafury here for the fums expended, which were afterwards to be raifed in the colonies by a general tax, to be laid on them by act of parliament. This occafioned a good deal of converfation on the fubject, and the general opinion was, that the parliament neither would nor could lay any tax on us, till we were duly reprefented in parliament, becaufe it was not juft, nor agreeable to the nature of an Englifh conftitution.

Q. Don't you know there was a time in New-York, when it was under confideration to make an application to parliament to lay taxes on that colony, upon a deficiency arifing from the affembly's refufing or neglecting to raife the neceffary fupplies for the fupport of the civil government?

A. I never heard of it.

Q. There was fuch an application under confideration in New-York; and do you apprehend they could fuppofe the right of parliament to lay a tax in America was only local, and confined to the cafe of a deficiency in a particular colony, by a refufal of its affembly to raife the neceffary fupplies?

A. They could not fuppofe fuch a cafe, as that the affembly would not raife the neceffary fupplies to fupport its own government. An affembly that would refufe it muft want common fenfe, which cannot be fuppofed. I think there never was any fuch cafe at New-York, and that it muft be a mifreprefentation, or the fact muft be mifunderftood. I know there have been fome attempts, by minifterial inftructions from hence, to oblige the affemblies to fettle permanent falaries on governors, which they wifely refufed to do; but I believe no affembly of New-York, or any other colony, ever refufed duly to fupport government by proper allowances, from time to time, to public officers.

Q. But in cafe a governor, acting by inftruction, fhould call on an affembly to raife the neceffary fupplies, and the affembly fhould refufe to do it, do you not think it would then be for the good of the people of the colony, as well as neceffary to government, that the parliament fhould tax them?

A. I do not think it would be neceffary. If an affembly could poffibly be fo abfurd as to refufe raifing the fupplies requifite for the maintenance of government among them, they could not long remain in fuch a fituation; the diforders and confufion occafioned by it muft foon bring them to reafon.

Q. If it fhould not, ought not the right to be in Great-Britain of applying a remedy?

A. A right only to be ufed in fuch a cafe, I fhould have no objection to, fuppofing it to be ufed merely for the good of the people of the colony.

Q. But who is to judge of that, Britain or the colony?

A. Thofe that feel can beft judge.

Q. You fay the colonies have always fubmitted to external taxes, and object to the right of parliament only in laying internal taxes; now can you fhew that there is any kind of difference between the two taxes to the colony on which they may be laid?

A. I

A. I think the difference is very great. An external tax is a duty laid on commodities imported; that duty is added to the first cost, and other charges on the commodity, and when it is offered to sale, makes a part of the price. If the people do not like it at that price, they refuse it; they are not obliged to pay it. But an internal tax is forced from the people without their consent, if not laid by their own representatives. The stamp act says, we shall have no commerce, make no exchange of property with each other, neither purchase nor grant, nor recover debts; we shall neither marry nor make our wills, unless we pay such and such sums, and thus it is intended to extort our money from us, or ruin us by the consequences of refusing to pay it.

Q. But supposing the internal tax or duty to be laid on the necessaries of life imported into your colony, will not that be the same thing in its effects as an internal tax?

A. I do not know a single article imported into the northern colonies, but what they can either do without, or make themselves.

Q. Don't you think cloth from England absolutely necessary to them?

A. No, by no means absolutely necessary; with industry and good management they may very well supply themselves with all they want.

Q. Will it not take a long time to establish that manufacture among them; and must they not in the mean while suffer greatly?

A. I think not. They have made a surprising progress already. And I am of opinion, that before their old clothes are worn out, they will have new ones of their own making.

Q. Can they possibly find wool enough in North-America?

A. They have taken steps to increase the wool. They entered into general combinations to eat no more lamb, and very few lambs were killed last year. This course persisted in,

will soon make a prodigious difference in the quantity of wool. And the establishing of great manufactories, like those in the clothing towns here, is not necessary, as it is where the business is to be carried on for the purposes of trade. The people will all spin, and work for themselves, in their own houses.

Q. Can there be wool and manufacture enough in one or two years?

A. In three years, I think, there may.

Q. Does not the severity of the winter, in the northern colonies, occasion the wool to be of bad quality?

A. No: the wool is very fine and good.

Q. In the more southern colonies, as in Virginia, don't you know that the wool is coarse, and only a kind of hair?

A. I don't know it. I never heard it. Yet I have been sometimes in Virginia. I cannot say I ever took particular notice of the wool there, but I believe it is good, though I cannot speak positively of it; but Virginia, and the colonies south of it, have less occasion for wool; their winters are short, and not very severe, and they can very well clothe themselves with linen and cotton of their own raising for the rest of the year.

Q. Are not the people in the more northern colonies obliged to fodder their sheep all the winter?

A. In some of the most northern colonies they may be obliged to do it some part of the winter.

Q. Considering the resolutions of parliament, as to the right, do you think, if the stamp-act is repealed, that the North-Americans will be satisfied?

A. I believe they will?

Q. Why do you think so?

A. I think the resolutions of right will give them very little concern, if they are never attempted to be carried into practice. The colonies will probably consider themselves in the same situation,

situation, in that respect, with Ireland; they know you claim the same right with regard to Ireland, but you never exercise it. And they may believe you never will exercise it in the colonies, any more than in Ireland, unless on some very extraordinary occasion.

Q. But who are to be the judges of that extraordinary occasion? Is not the parliament?

A. Though the parliament may judge of the occasion, the people will think it can never exercise such right, till representatives from the colonies are admitted into parliament, and that whenever the occasion arises, representatives will be ordered.

Q. Did you never hear that Maryland, during the last war, had refused to furnish a quota towards the common defence?

A. Maryland has been much misrepresented in that matter. Maryland, to my knowledge, never refused to contribute, or grant aids to the crown. The assemblies every year, during the war, voted considerable sums, and formed bills to raise them. The bills were, according to the constitution of that province, sent up to the council, or upper house, for concurrence, that they might be presented to the governor, in order to be enacted into laws. Unhappy disputes between the two houses arising, from the defects of that constitution principally, rendered all the bills but one or two abortive. The proprietary's council rejected them. It is true, Maryland did not contribute its proportion, but it was, in my opinion, the fault of the government, not of the people.

Q. Was it not talked of in the other provinces as a proper measure to apply to parliament to compel them?

A. I have heard such discourse; but as it was well known, that the people were not to blame, no such application was ever made, nor any step taken towards it.

Q. Was it not proposed at a public meeting?

A. Not that I know of.

Q. Do you remember the abolishing of the paper currency in New-England, by act of assembly?

A. I do remember its being abolished, in the Massachusett's-bay.

Q. Was not lieutenant-governor Hutchinson principally concerned in that transaction?

A. I have heard so.

Q. Was it not at that time a very unpopular law?

A. I believe it might, though I can say little about it, as I lived at a distance from that province.

Q. Was not the scarcity of gold and silver an argument used against abolishing the paper?

A. I suppose it was.

Q. What is the present opinion there of that law? Is it as unpopular as it was at first?

A. I think it is not.

Q. Have not instructions from hence been sometimes sent over to governors, highly oppressive and unpolitical?

A. Yes.

Q. Have not some governors dispensed with them for that reason?

A. Yes; I have heard so.

Q. Did the Americans ever dispute the controuling power of parliament to regulate the commerce?

A. No.

Q. Can any thing less than a military force carry the stamp act into execution?

A. I do not see how a military force can be applied to that purpose.

Q. Why may it not?

A. Suppose a military force sent into America, they will find nobody in arms; what are they then to do? They cannot force a man to take stamps who chuses to do without them. They will not find a rebellion; they may indeed make one. Q.

Q. If the act is not repealed, what do you think will be the consequences?

A. A total loss of the respect and affection the people of America bear to this country, and of all the commerce that depends on that respect and affection.

Q. How can the commerce be affected?

A. You will find, that if the act is not repealed, they will take very little of your manufactures in a short time.

Q. Is it in their power to do without them?

A. I think they may very well do without them.

Q. Is it their interest not to take them?

A. The goods they take from Britain are either necessaries, mere conveniences, or superfluities. The first, as cloth, &c. with a little industry they can make at home; the second they can do without, till they are able to provide them among themselves; and the last, which are much the greatest part, they will strike off immediately. They are mere articles of fashion, purchased and consumed, because the fashion in a respected country; but will now be detested and rejected. The people have already struck off, by general agreement, the use of all goods fashionable in mournings, and many thousand pounds worth are sent back as unsaleable.

Q. Is it their interest to make cloth at home?

A. I think they may at present get it cheaper from Britain, I mean of the same fineness and neatness of workmanship; but when one considers other circumstances, the restraints on their trade, and the difficulty of making remittances, it is their interest to make every thing.

Q. Suppose an act of internal regulations connected with a tax, how would they receive it?

A. I think it would be objected to.

Q. Then no regulation with a tax would be submitted to?

A. Their opinion is, that when aids to the crown are wanted, they are to be asked of the several assemblies, according to the old established usage, who will, as they always have done, grant them freely. And that their money ought not to be given away, without their consent, by persons at a distance, unacquainted with their circumstances and abilities. The granting aids to the crown, is the only means they have of recommending themselves to their sovereign, and they think it extremely hard and unjust, that a body of men, in which they have no representatives, should make a merit to itself of giving and granting what is not its own, but theirs, and deprive them of a right they esteem of the utmost value and importance, as it is the security of all their other rights.

Q. But is not the post-office, which they have long received, a tax as well as a regulation?

A. No; the money paid for the postage of a letter is not of the nature of a tax; it is merely a quantum meruit for a service done; no person is compellable to pay the money, if he does not chuse to receive the service. A man may still, as before the act, send his letter by a servant, a special messenger, or a friend, if he thinks it cheaper and safer.

Q. But do they not consider the regulations of the post-office, by the act of last year, as a tax?

A. By the regulations of last year the rate of postage was generally abated near thirty per cent. through all America; they certainly cannot consider such abatement as a tax.

Q. If an excise was laid by parliament, which they might likewise avoid paying, by not consuming the articles excised, would they then not object to it?

A. They would certainly object to it, as an excise is unconnected with

any

any service done, and is merely an aid which they think ought to be asked of them, and granted by them, if they are to pay it, and can be granted for them by no others whatsoever, whom they have not impowered for that purpose.

Q. You say they do not object to the right of parliament, in laying duties on goods to be paid on their importation ; now, is there any kind of difference between a duty on the importation of goods, and an excise on their consumption ?

A. Yes ; a very material one ; an excise, for the reasons I have just mentioned, they think you can have no right to lay within their country. But the sea is yours ; you maintain, by your fleets, the safety of navigation in it, and keep it clear of pirates ; you may have therefore a natural and equitable right to some toll or duty on merchandizes carried through that part of your dominions, towards defraying the expence you are at in ships to maintain the safety of that carriage.

Q. Does this reasoning hold in the case of a duty laid on the produce of their lands exported ? And would they not then object to such a duty ?

A. If it tended to make the produce so much dearer abroad as to lessen the demand for it, to be sure they would object to such a duty ; not to your right of laying it, but they would complain of it as a burthen, and petition you to lighten it.

Q. Is not the duty paid on the tobacco exported a duty of that kind ?

A. That, I think, is only on tobacco carried coastwise from one colony to another, and appropriated as a fund for supporting the college at Williamsburgh in Virginia.

Q. Have not the assemblies in the West-Indies the same natural rights with those in North-America ?

A. Undoubtedly.

Q. And is there not a tax laid there on their sugars exported ?

A. I am not much acquainted with the West-Indies, but the duty of four and a half per cent. on sugars exported, was, I believe, granted by their own assemblies.

Q. How much is the poll-tax in your province laid on unmarried men ?

A. It is, I think, fifteen shillings, to be paid by every single freeman, upwards of twenty-one years old.

Q. What is the annual amount of all the taxes in Pennsylvania ?

A. I suppose about 20,000 pounds sterling.

Q. Supposing the stamp act continued, and enforced, do you imagine that ill-humour will induce the Americans to give as much for worse manufactures of their own, and use them, preferably to better of ours ?

A. Yes, I think so. People will pay as freely to gratify one passion as another, their resentment as their pride.

Q. Would the people at Boston discontinue their trade ?

A. The merchants are a very small number, compared with the body of the people, and must discontinue their trade, if nobody will buy their goods.

Q. What are the body of the people in the colonies ?

A. They are farmers, husbandmen or planters.

Q. Would they suffer the produce of their lands to rot ?

A. No ; but they would not raise so much. They would manufacture more, and plough less.

Q. Would they live without the administration of justice in civil matters, and suffer all the inconveniences of such a situation for any considerable time, rather than take the stamps, supposing the stamps were protected by a sufficient force, where every one might have them ?

A. I think the supposition impracticable, that the stamps should be so protected as that every one might have them. The act requires sub-

L   distributors

diftributors to be appointed in every county town, diftrict and village, and they would be neceffary. But the principal diftributors, who were to have had a confiderable profit on the whole, have not thought it worth while to continue in the office, and I think it impoffible to find fub-diftributors fit to be trufted, who, for the trifling profit that muft come to their fhare, would incur the odium, and run the hazard that would attend it; and if they could be found, I think it impracticable to protect the ftamps in fo many diftant and remote places.

Q. But in places where they could be protected, would not the people ufe them rather than remain in fuch a fituation, unable to obtain any right, or recover, by law, any debt?

A. It is hard to fay what they would do. I can only judge what other people will think, and how they will act, by what I feel within myfelf. I have a great many debts due to me in America, and I had rather they fhould remain unrecoverable by any law, than fubmit to the ftamp act. They will be debts of honour. It is my opinion the people will either continue in that fituation, or find fome way to extricate themfelves, perhaps by generally agreeing to proceed in the courts without ftamps.

Q. What do you think a fufficient military force to protect the diftribution of the ftamps in every part of America?

A. A very great force; I can't fay what, if the difpofition of America is for a general refiftance.

Q. What is the number of men in America able to bear arms, or of difciplined militia?

A. There are, I fuppofe, at leaft—[Queftion objected to. He withdrew. Called in again.]

Q. Is the American ftamp act an equal tax on that country?

A. I think not.

Q. Why fo?

A. The greateft part of the money muft arife from law-fuits for the recovery of debts, and be paid by the lower fort of people, who were too poor eafily to pay their debts. It is therefore a heavy tax on the poor, and a tax upon them for being poor.

Q. But will not this increafe of expence be a means of leffening the number of law-fuits?

A. I think not; for as the cofts all fall upon the debtor, and are to be paid by him, they would be no difcouragement to the creditor to bring his action.

Q. Would it not have the effect of exceffive ufury?

A. Yes, as an oppreffion of the debtor.

Q. How many fhips are there laden annually in North-America with flax-feed for Ireland?

A. I cannot fpeak to the number of fhips, but I know that in 1752, 10,000 hogfheads of flax-feed, each containing feven bufhels, were exported from Philadelphia to Ireland. I fuppofe the quantity is greatly increafed fince that time; and it is underftood that the exportation from New-York is equal to that from Philadelphia.

Q. What becomes of the flax that grows with that flax-feed?

A. They manufacture fome into coarfe, and fome into a middling kind of linen.

Q. Are there any flitting-mills in America?

A. I think there are three, but I believe only one at prefent employed. I fuppofe they will all be fet to work, if the interruption of the trade continues.

Q. Are there any fulling mills there?

A. A great many.

Q. Did you never hear that a great quantity of ftockings were contracted for, for the army, during the war, and manufactured in Philadelphia?

A. I have heard fo.

Q. If

Q. If the stamp act should be repealed, would not the Americans think they could oblige the parliament to repeal every external tax-law now in force?

A. It is hard to answer questions of what people at such a distance will think.

Q. But what do you imagine they will think were the motives of repealing the act?

A. I suppose they will think that it was repealed from a conviction of its inexpediency; and they will rely upon it, that while the same inexpediency subsists, you will never attempt to make such another.

Q. What do you mean by its inexpediency?

A. I mean its inexpediency on several accounts; the poverty and inability of those who were to pay the tax; the general discontent it has occasioned; and the impracticability of enforcing it.

Q. If the act should be repealed, and the legislature should shew its resentment to the opposers of the stamp act, would the colonies acquiesce in the authority of the legislature? What is your opinion they would do?

A. I don't doubt at all, that if the legislature repeal the stamp act, the colonies will acquiesce in the authority.

Q. But if the legislature should think fit to ascertain its right to lay taxes, by any act laying a small tax, contrary to their opinion, would they submit to pay the tax?

A. The proceedings of the people in America have been considered too much together. The proceedings of the assemblies have been very different from those of the mobs, and should be distinguished, as having no connection with each other. The assemblies have only peaceably resolved what they take to be their rights; they have taken no measures for opposition by force; they have not built a fort, raised a man, or provided a grain of ammunition, in order to such opposition. The ring-leaders of riots they think ought to be punished; they would punish them themselves, if they could. Every sober, sensible man would wish to see rioters punished, as otherwise peaceable people have no security of person or estate. But as to an internal tax, how small soever, laid by the legislature here on the people there, while they have no representatives in this legislature, I think it will never be submitted to.—They will oppose it to the last:—They do not consider it as at all necessary for you to raise money on them by your taxes, because they are, and always have been, ready to raise money by taxes among themselves, and to grant large sums, equal to their abilities, upon requisition from the crown. They have not only granted equal to their abilities, but, during all the last war, they granted far beyond their abilities, and beyond their proportion with this country, you yourselves being judges, to the amount of many hundred thousand pounds, and this they did freely and readily, only on a sort of promise from the secretary of state, that it should be recommended to parliament to make them compensation. It was accordingly recommended to parliament, in the most honourable manner, for them. America has been greatly misrepresented and abused here, in papers, and pamphlets, and speeches, as ungrateful, and unreasonable, and unjust, in having put this nation to immense expence for their defence, and refusing to bear any part of that expence. The colonies raised, paid, and clothed, near 25000 men during the last war, a number equal to those sent from Britain, and far beyond their proportion; they went deeply into debt in doing this, and all their taxes and estates are mortgaged, for many years to come, for discharging

that

that debt. Government here was at that time very sensible of this. The colonies were recommended to parliament. Every year the king sent down to the house a written message to this purpose, That his Majesty, being highly sensible of the zeal and vigour with which his faithful subjects in North-America had exerted themselves, in defence of his Majesty's just rights and possessions, recommended it to the house to take the same into consideration, and enable him to give them a proper compensation. You will find those messages on your own journals every year of the war to the very last, and you did accordingly give 200,000 pounds annually to the crown, to be distributed in such compensation to the colonies. This is the strongest of all proofs that the colonies, far from being unwilling to bear a share of the burthen, did exceed their proportion; for if they had done less, or had only equalled their proportion, there would have been no room or reason for compensation. Indeed the sums reimbursed them, were by no means adequate to the expence they incurred beyond their proportion; but they never murmured at that, they esteemed their sovereign's approbation of their zeal and fidelity, and the approbation of this house, far beyond any other kind of compensation; therefore there was no occasion for this act, to force money from a willing people; they had not refused giving money for the purposes of the act; no requisition had been made; they were always willing and ready to do what could reasonably be expected from them, and in this light they wish to be considered.

Q. But suppose Great-Britain should be engaged in a war in Europe, would North-America contribute to the support of it?

A. I do think they would, as far as their circumstances would permit. They consider themselves as a part of the British empire, and as having one common interest with it; they may be looked on here as foreigners, but they do not consider themselves as such. They are zealous for the honour and prosperity of this nation, and, while they are well used, will always be ready to support it, as far as their little power goes. In 1739 they were called upon to assist in the expedition against Carthagena, and they sent 3000 men to join your army. It is true Carthagena is in America, but as remote from the Northern Colonies as if it had been in Europe. They make no distinction of wars, as to their duty of assisting in them. I know the last war is commonly spoke of here as entered into for the defence, or for the sake of the people of America. I think it is quite misunderstood. It began about the limits between Canada and Nova-Scotia, about territories to which the crown indeed laid claim, but were not claimed by any British colony; none of the lands had been granted to any colonist; we had therefore no particular concern or interest in that dispute. As to the Ohio, the contest there began about your right of trading in the Indian country, a right you had by the treaty of Utrecht, which the French infringed; they seized the traders and their goods, which were your manufactures; they took a fort which a company of your merchants, and their factors and correspondents, had erected there, to secure that trade. Braddock was sent with an army to re-take that fort (which was looked on here as another incroachment on the King's territory) and to protect your trade. It was not till after his defeat that the colonies were attacked. They were before in perfect peace with both French and Indians; the troops were not therefore sent for their defence. The trade with the Indians, though carried on in America, is not an American interest.

The

The people of America are chiefly farmers and planters; scarce any thing that they raise or produce is an article of commerce with the Indians. The Indian trade is a British interest; it is carried on with British manufactures, for the profit of British merchants and manufacturers; therefore the war, as it commenced for the defence of territories of the crown, the property of no American, and for the defence of a trade purely British, was really a British war—and yet the people of America made no scruple of contributing their utmost towards carrying it on, and bringing it to a happy conclusion.

Q. Do you think then that the taking possession of the King's territorial rights, and strengthening the frontiers, is not an American interest?

A. Not particularly, but conjointly a British and an American interest.

Q. You will not deny that the preceding war, the war with Spain, was entered into for the sake of America; was it not occasioned by captures made in the American seas?

A. Yes; captures of ships carrying on the British trade there, with British manufactures.

Q. Was not the late war with the Indians, since the peace with France, a war for America only?

A. Yes; it was more particularly for America than the former, but it was rather a consequence or remains of the former war, the Indians not having been thoroughly pacified, and the Americans bore by much the greatest share of the expence. It was put an end to by the army under General Bouquet; there were not above 300 regulars in that army, and above 1000 Pennsylvanians.

Q. Is it not necessary to send troops to America, to defend the Americans against the Indians?

A. No, by no means; it never was necessary. They defended themselves when they were but an hand-ful, and the Indians much more numerous. They continually gained ground, and have driven the Indians over the mountains, without any troops sent to their assistance from this country. And can it be thought necessary now to send troops for their defence from those diminished Indian tribes, when the colonies are become so populous, and so strong? There is not the least occasion for it; they are very able to defend themselves.

Q. Do you say there were no more than 300 regular troops employed in the late Indian war?

A. Not on the Ohio, or the frontiers of Pennsylvania, which was the chief part of the war that affected the colonies. There were garrisons at Niagara, Fort Detroit, and those remote posts kept for the sake of your trade; I did not reckon them, but I believe that on the whole the number of Americans, or provincial troops, employed in the war, was greater than that of the regulars. I am not certain, but I think so.

Q. Do you think the assemblies have a right to levy money on the subject there, to grant to the crown?

A. I certainly think so; they have always done it.

Q. Are they acquainted with the declaration of rights? And do they know that, by that statute, money is not to be raised on the subject but by consent of parliament?

A. They are very well acquainted with it.

Q. How then can they think they have a right to levy money for the crown, or for any other than local purposes?

A. They understand that clause to relate to subjects only within the realm; that no money can be levied on them for the crown, but by consent of parliament. The colonies are not supposed to be within the realm; they have assemblies of their own, which are their parliaments, and they are, in that respect, in the same situation

situation with Ireland. When money is to be raised for the crown upon the subject in Ireland, or in the colonies, the consent is given in the parliament of Ireland, or in the assemblies of the colonies. They think the parliament of Great-Britain cannot properly give that consent till it has representatives from America; for the petition of right expressly says, it is to be by common consent in parliament, and the people of America have no representatives in parliament, to make a part of that common consent.

Q. If the stamp-act should be repealed, and an act should pass, ordering the assemblies of the colonies to indemnify the sufferers by the riots, would they obey it?

A. That is a question I cannot answer.

Q. Suppose the King should require the colonies to grant a revenue, and the parliament should be against their doing it, do they think they can grant a revenue to the King, without the consent of the parliament of Great Britain?

A. That is a deep question.—As to my own opinion, I should think myself at liberty to do it, and should do it, if I liked the occasion.

Q. When money has been raised in the colonies, upon requisitions, has it not been granted to the King?

A. Yes, always; but the requisitions have generally been for some service expressed, as to raise, clothe and pay troops, and not for money only.

Q. If the act should pass, requiring the American assemblies to make compensation to the sufferers, and they should disobey it, and then the parliament should, by another act, lay an internal tax, would they then obey it?

A. The people will pay no internal tax; and I think an act to oblige the assemblies to make compensation is unnecessary, for I am of opinion, that as soon as the present heats are abated,

they will take the matter into consideration, and if it is right to be done, they will do it of themselves.

Q. Do not letters often come into the post-offices in America, directed to some inland town where no post goes?

A. Yes.

Q. Can any private person take up those letters, and carry them as directed?

A. Yes; any friend of the person may do it, paying the postage that has accrued.

Q. But must not he pay an additional postage for the distance to such inland town?

A. No.

Q. Can the post-master answer delivering the letter, without being paid such additional postage?

A. Certainly he can demand nothing, where he does no service.

Q. Suppose a person, being far from home, finds a letter in a post-office directed to him, and he lives in a place to which the post generally goes, and the letter is directed to that place, will the post-master deliver him the letter, without his paying the postage receivable at the place to which the letter is directed?

A. Yes; the office cannot demand postage for a letter that it does not carry, or farther than it does carry it.

Q. Are not ferrymen in America obliged, by act of parliament, to carry over the posts without pay?

A. Yes.

Q. Is not this a tax on the ferrymen?

A. They do not consider it as such, as they have an advantage from persons travelling with the post.

Q. If the stamp-act should be repealed, and the crown should make a requisition to the colonies for a sum of money, would they grant it?

A. I believe they would.

Q. Why do you think so?

A. I can speak for the colony I live in; I had it in instruction from the assembly affembly to affure the miniftry, that as they always had done, fo they fhould always think it their duty to grant fuch aids to the crown as were fuitable to their circumftances and abilities, whenever called upon for the purpofe, in the ufual conftitutional manner; and I had the honour of communicating this inftruction to that honourable gentleman then minifter.

Q. Would they do this for a Britifh concern; as fuppofe a war in fome part of Europe, that did not affect them?

A. Yes, for any thing that concerned the general intereft. They confider themfelves as a part of the whole.

Q. What is the ufual conftitutional manner of calling on the colonies for aids?

A. A letter from the fecretary of ftate.

Q. Is this all you mean, a letter from the fecretary of ftate?

A. I mean the ufual way of requifition, in a circular letter from the fecretary of ftate, by his Majefty's command, reciting the occafion, and recommending it to the colonies to grant fuch aids as became their loyalty, and were fuitable to their abilities.

Q. Did the fecretary of ftate ever write for money for the crown?

A. The requifitions have been to raife, clothe and pay men, which cannot be done without money.

Q. Would they grant money alone, if called on?

A. In my opinion they would, money as well as men, when they have money, or can make it.

Q. If the parliament fhould repeal the ftamp-act, will the affembly of Pennfylvania refcind their refolutions?

A. I think not.

Q. Before there was any thought of the ftamp-act, did they wifh for a reprefentation in parliament?

A. No.

Q. Don't you know that there is, in the Pennfylvania charter, an ex-

prefs refervation of the right of parliament to lay taxes there?

A. I know there is a claufe in the charter, by which the King grants that he will levy no taxes on the inhabitants, unlefs it be with the confent of the affembly, or by act of parliament.

Q. How then could the affembly of Pennfylvania affert, that laying a tax on them by the ftamp-act was an infringement of their rights?

A. They underftand it thus; by the fame charter, and otherwife, they are intitled to all the privileges and liberties of Englifhmen; they find in the great charters, and the petition and declaration of rights, that one of the privileges of Englifh fubjects is, that they are not to be taxed but by their common confent; they have therefore relied upon it, from the firft fettlement of the province, that the parliament never would, nor could, by colour of that claufe in the charter, affume a right of taxing them, till it had qualified itfelf to exercife fuch right, by admitting reprefentatives from the people to be taxed, who ought to make a part of that common confent.

Q. Are there any words in the charter that juftify that conftruction?

A. The common rights of Englifhmen, as declared by Magna Charta, and the petition of right, all juftify it.

Q. Does the diftinction between internal and external taxes exift in the words of the charter?

A. No, I believe not.

Q. Then may they not, by the fame interpretation, object to the parliament's right of external taxation?

A. They never have hitherto. Many arguments have been lately ufed here to fhew them that there is no difference, and that if you have no right to tax them internally, you have none to tax them externally, or make any other law to bind them. At prefent they do not reafon fo, but in

time

time they may poffibly be convinced by thefe arguments.

Q. Do not the refolutions of the Pennfylvania affembly fay all taxes?

A. If they do, they mean only internal taxes; the fame words have not always the fame meaning here and in the colonies. By taxes they mean internal taxes; by duties they mean cuftoms; thefe are their ideas of the language.

Q. Have you not feen the refolutions of the Maffachufet's Bay affembly?

A. I have.

Q. Do they not fay, that neither external nor internal taxes can be laid on them by parliament?

A. I don't know that they do; I believe not.

Q. If the fame colony fhould fay neither tax nor impofition could be laid, does not that province hold the power of parliament can lay neither?

A. I fuppofe that by the word impofition, they do not intend to exprefs duties to be laid on goods imported, as regulations of commerce.

Q. What can the colonies mean then by impofition as diftinct from taxes?

A. They may mean many things, as impreffing of men, or of carriages, quartering troops on private houfes, and the like; there may be great impofitions that are not properly taxes.

Q. Is not the poft-office rate an internal tax laid by act of parliament?

A. I have anfwered that.

Q. Are all parts of the colonies equally able to pay taxes?

A. No, certainly; the frontier parts, which have been ravaged by the enemy, are greatly difabled by that means, and therefore, in fuch cafes, are ufually favoured in our tax-laws.

Q. Can we, at this diftance, be competent judges of what favours are neceffary?

A. The parliament have fuppofed it, by claiming a right to make tax-laws for America? I think it impoffible.

Q. Would the repeal of the ftamp-act be any difcouragement of your manufactures? Will the people that have begun to manufacture decline it?

A. Yes, I think they will; efpecially if, at the fame time, the trade is opened again, fo the remittances can be eafily made. I have known feveral inftances that make it probable. In the war before laft, tobacco being low, and making little remittance, the people of Virginia went generally into family manufactures. Afterwards, when tobacco bore a better price, they returned to the ufe of Britifh manufactures. So fulling-mills were very much difufed in the laft war in Pennfylvania, becaufe bills were then plenty, and remittances could eafily be made to Britain for Englifh cloth and other goods.

Q. If the ftamp-act fhould be repealed, would it induce the affemblies of America to acknowledge the rights of parliament to tax them, and would they erafe their refolutions?

A. No, never.

Q. Is there no means of obliging them to erafe thofe refolutions?

A. None that I know of; they will never do it, unlefs compelled by force of arms.

Q. Is there a power on earth that can force them to erafe them?

A. No power, how great foever, can force men to change their opinions.

Q. Do they confider the poft-office as a tax, or as a regulation?

A. Not as a tax, but as a regulation and conveniency; every affembly encouraged it, and fupported it in its infancy, by grants of money, which they would not otherwife have done; and the people have always paid the poftage.

Q. When did you receive the inftructions you mentioned?

A. I brought them with me, when I came

I came to England, about fifteen months fince.

Q. When did you communicate that inftruction to the minifter?

A. Soon after my arrival, while the ftamping of America was under confideration, and before the bill was brought in.

Q. Would it be moft for the intereft of Great-Britain, to employ the hands of Virginia in tobacco, or in manufactures.

A. In tobacco, to be fure.

Q. What ufed to be the pride of the Americans?

A. To indulge in the fafhions and manufactures of Great-Britain.

Q. What is now their pride?

A. To wear their old cloaths over again, till they can make new ones.

(Withdrew.)

The bill to repeal the ftamp-act having paffed the Commons, was brought to the Lords; whofe houfe it paffed alfo. But the following protefts were entered againft it.

Die Merc. 10 Martii, 1766.

The order of the day being read for the fecond reading of the bill, entituled, "An Act to repeal an Act made in the laft feffion of Parliament, entituled, An Act for granting and applying certain Stamp-Duties and other duties in the Britifh Colonies and Plantations in America, towards further defraying the expences of defending, protecting, and fecuring the fame, and for amending fuch parts of the feveral acts of parliament relating to the Trade and Revenues of the faid Colonies and Plantations, as direct the manner of Determining and Recovering the Penalties and Forfeitures therein-mentioned." Then the faid Bill was read a fecond Time, and it being propofed to commit the Bill, the fame was objected to. After a long Debate thereupon, the Queftion was put, Whether the faid Bill fhall be committed: It was refolved in the affirmative.

Contents	73	
Proxies	32	105
Not Contents	61	
Proxies	10	71
Majority		34

Diffentient,

1ft, Becaufe, as this houfe has in this feffion by feveral refolutions moft folemnly afferted and declared, firft, " That the King's Majefty, by and with the advice and confent of the Lords Spiritual and Temporal, and Commons of Great Britain, in Parliament affembled, had, hath, and of right ought to have, full power and authority, to make laws and ftatutes of fufficient force and validity to bind the Colonies, and people of America, fubjects of the Crown of Great-Britain, in all cafes whatfoever:" Secondly, " That tumults and infurrections of the moft dangerous nature have been raifed and carried on in feveral of the North American Colonies, in open defiance of the power and dignity of his Majefty's Government, and in manifeft violation of the laws and legiflative authority of this Kingdom:" Thirdly, " That the faid tumults and infurrections have been encouraged and inflamed, by fundry votes and refolutions paffed in feveral of the Affemblies of the faid Provinces, derogatory to the honour of his Majefty's Government, and deftructive of the legal and conftitutional dependency of the faid Colonies, on the imperial Crown and Parliament of Great Britain:" Which refolutions were founded on a full examination of the papers on our table, manifefting a denial of the legiflative authority of the crown and parliament of Great Britain, to impofe duties and taxes on our North-American Colonies; and a criminal refiftance there made to the execution of the commercial and other regulations of the ftamp-act, and of other acts of parliament: we are of opinion, that the total repealing of that law, efpecially

M

especially while such resistance continues, would (as Governor Barnard says is their intention) " make the authority of Great Britain contemptible hereafter\; and that such a submission of King, Lords, and Commons, under such circumstances, in so strange and unheard of a contest, would, in effect, surrender their antient, unalienable rights of supreme jurisdiction, and give them exclusively to the subordinate provincial legislatures established by prerogative; which was never intended or thought of, and is not in the power of prerogative to bestow; as they are inferable from the three estates of the realm assembled in parliament.

2dly, Because the law, which this bill now proposes to repeal, was passed in the other house with very little opposition, and in this without one dissentient voice, during the last session of parliament, which we presume, if it had been wholly and fundamentally wrong, could not possibly have happened; as the matter of it is so important, and as the intention of bringing it in, had been communicated to the commons by the first commissioner of the treasury the year before, and a resolution, relating and preparatory to it, was then agreed to in that house, without any division.

3dly, Because, if any particular parts of that law, the principal of which has been experienced and submitted to in this country, without repining, for near a century past, had been found liable to just and reasonable objections, they might have been altered by a bill to explain and amend it, without repealing the whole. And, if any such bill had been sent to us by the commons, we should have thought it our duty to have given it a most serious consideration, with a warm desire of relieving our countrymen in America from any grievance or hardship; but with proper care to enforce their submission and obedience to the law so amended, and to the whole legislative authority of Great-Britain, without any reserve or distinction whatsoever.

4thly, Because, it appears to us, that a most essential branch of that authority, the power of taxation, cannot be properly, equitably, or impartially exercised, if it does not extend itself to all the members of the state in proportion to their respective abilities; but suffers a part to be exempt from a due share of those burthens, which the public exigencies require to be imposed upon the whole: a partiality which is directly and manifestly repugnant to the trust reposed by the people in every legislature, and destructive of that confidence on which all government is founded.

5thly, Because, the ability of our North-American Colonies, to bear without inconveniency the proportion laid on them by the stamp-act of last year, appears to us most unquestionable, for the following reasons: First, That the estimated produce of this tax, amounting to sixty thousand pounds *per annum*, if divided amongst twelve hundred thousand people (being little more than one half of the subjects of the crown in North America) would be only one shilling per head a year; which is but a third of the wages usually paid to every labourer or manufacturer there for one day's labour: Secondly, That it appears by the accounts that have been laid before this house from the commissioners of trade and plantations, that of the debt contracted by those colonies in the last war, above £.1,755,000, has already been discharged during the course of three years only, by the funds provided for that purpose in the several provinces; and the much greater part of the remaining incumbrance, which in the whole is about 760,000 pounds, will be paid in two years more: We must likewise observe, that the bounties and advantages given to them by parliament in 1764 and 1765, and the

the duties thereby loft to Great-Britain for their fervice, and in order to enable them the more eafily to pay this tax, muft neceffarily amount in a few years to a far greater fum than the produce thereof. It is alfo evident, that fuch produce being wholly appropriated to the payment of the army maintained by this kingdom in our colonies, at the vaft expence of almoft a fhilling in the pound land-tax, annually remitted by us for their fpecial defence and protection ; not only no money would have been actually drawn by it out of that country, but the eafe given by it to the people of Great Britain, who are labouring under a debt of feventy millions, contracted by them to fupport a very dangerous war, entered into for the intereft and fecurity of thofe colonies, would have redounded to the benefit of the colonies themfelves in their own immediate fafety, by contributing to deliver them from the neceffary expence, which many of them have hitherto always borne, in guarding their frontiers againft the favage Indians.

6thly, Becaufe, not only the right, but the expediency and neceffity of the fupreme legiflature's exerting its authority to lay a general tax on our American colonies, whenever the wants of the public make it fitting and reafonable that all the provinces fhould contribute in a proper proportion to the defence of the whole, appear to us undeniable, from thefe confiderations : Firft, That every province being feparate and independent on the others, and having no common council impowered by the conftitution of the colonies to act for all, or bind all, fuch a tax cannot regularly, or without infinite difficulty, be impofed upon them, at any time, even for their immediate defence or protection, by their own provincial affemblies ; but requires the intervention and fuperintending power of the parliament of Great-Britain. Se-

condly, That in looking forwards to the poffible contingency of a new war, a contingency perhaps not far remote, the profpect of the burthens, which the gentry and people of this kingdom muft then fuftain, in addition to thofe which now lie fo heavy upon them, is fo melancholy and dreadful, that we cannot but feel it, a moft indifpenfible duty, to eafe them as much as is poffible, by a due and moderate exertion of that great right, which the conftitution of this realm has vefted in the parliament, to provide for the fafety of all, by a proportionable charge upon all, equally and indifferently laid. We likewife apprehend, that a partial exemption of our colonies from any exercife of this right by the Britifh legiflature, would be thought fo invidious, and fo unjuft to the other fubjects of the crown of Great-Britain, as to alienate the hearts of thefe from their countrymen refiding in America, to the great detriment of the latter, who have on many occafions received, and may again want affiftance, from the generous warmth of their affection.

7thly, Becaufe, the reafons affigned in the public refolutions of the provincial affemblies, in the North American colonies, for their difobeying the ftamp-act, viz. " That they are not reprefented in the Parliament of Great Britain," extends to all other laws, of what nature foever, which that parliament has enacted, or fhall enact, to bind them in times to come, and muft (if admitted) fet them abfolutely free from any obedience to the power of the Britifh legiflature. We likewife obferve, that in a letter to Mr. Secretary Conway, dated the 12th of October 1765 ; the commander in chief of his Majefty's forces in North-America has declared his opinion, " That the queftion is not of the inexpediency of the ftamp-act, or of the inability of the colonies to pay the tax ; but that it is unconftitutional and contrary to their rights, fupporting the inde-

pendency

pendency of the provinces, and not subject to the legislative power of Great Britain." It is moreover affirmed, in a letter to Mr. Conway, dated 7th November, " That the people in general are averse to taxes of any kind; and that the merchants of that place think they have a right to every freedom of trade which the subjects of Great Britain now enjoy." This opinion of theirs strikes directly at the Act of Navigation, and other subsequent laws, which from time to time have been made in the wise policy of that act; and should they ever be encouraged to procure for themselves that absolute freedom of trade, which they appear to desire, our plantations would become, not only of no benefit, but in the highest degree prejudicial to the commerce and welfare of their mother-country; nor is it easy to conceive a greater encouragement, than the repealing of a law, opposed by them on such principles, and with so much contempt of the sovereignty of the British legislature.

8thly, Because, the appearance of weakness and timidity in the government and parliament of this kingdom, which a concession of this nature may too probably carry with it, has a manifest tendency to draw on further insults, and by lessening the respect of all his Majesty's subjects to the dignity of his crown, and authority of his laws, throw the whole British empire into a miserable state of confusion and anarchy, with which it seems by many symptoms to be dangerously threatened: and this is the more to be feared, as the plea of our North American colonies, that, not being represented in the parliament of Great Britain, they ought not pay taxes imposed or levied upon them by the authority thereof, may by the same reasoning be extended to all persons in this island, who do not actually vote for members of parliament; nor can we help apprehending, that the opi-

nion of some countenance being given to such notions by the legislature itself, in consenting to this bill for the repeal of the stamp-act, may greatly promote the contagion of a most dangerous doctrine, destructive to all government, which has spread itself over all our North American colonies, that the obedience of the subject is not due to the laws and legislature of the realm, farther than he in his private judgment shall think it conformable to the ideas he has formed of a free constitution.

9thly, Because, we think it no effectual guard, or security, against this danger, that the parliament has declared in the resolutions of both houses, passed during this session, and now reduced into a bill, That such notions are ill founded; as men will always look more to deeds than words, and may therefore incline to believe, that the insurrections in our colonies, excited by those notions, having so far proved successful, as to attain the very point, at which they aimed, the immediate repeal of the stamp-act, without any previous submission on the part of the colonies, the legislature has in fact submitted to them, and has only more grievously injured its own dignity and authority, by verbally asserting that right, which it substantially yields up to their opposition. The reasons assigned for this concession render it still more alarming, as they arise from an illegal and hostile combination of the people of America, to distress and starve our manufacturers, and to with-hold from our merchants the payment of their just debts: the former of which measures has only been practised in open war between two states; and the latter, we believe, not even in that situation, either by the public or by individuals, among the civilized nations of Europe, in modern times. If this unprecedented plan of intimidation shall meet with success, it is easy to foresee, that the practice of it for other and still greater objects

objects will frequently be renewed, and our manufacturers and merchants reduced to the like, and more permanent distress : we cannot therefore but wish, that some more eligible method, consistent with their future safety and our dignity, had been taken by parliament, to shew our tender concern and compassion for their sufferings, and to discourage any other such unwarrantable attempts ; which we are fully persuaded would have been very practicable, with due care and attention, and at an expence very inferior to the importance of the object.

Lastly, Because, we are convinced from the unanimous testimony of the governors, and other officers of the crown in America, that if, by a most unhappy delay and neglect to provide for the due execution of the law, and arm the government there with proper orders and powers, repeatedly called for in vain, these disturbances had not been continued and encreased, they might easily have been quieted before they had attained to any dangerous height ; and we cannot, without feeling the most lively sense of grief and indignation, hear arguments drawn from the progress of evils, which should and might have been stopped in their first and feeble beginnings, used for the still greater evil of sacrificing to a present relief the highest permanent interests, and the whole majesty, power, and reputation of government : This afflicts us the more deeply, because it appears from many letters, that this law, if properly supported by government, would from the peculiar circumstances attending the disobedience to it, execute itself without bloodshed. And it is said in one of the letters to Mr. Secretary Conway, " That the principal view is to intimidate the parliament ; but that if it be thought prudent to enforce their authority, the people dare not oppose a vigorous resolution of the parliament of Great-Britain." That

vigorous resolution has not yet been found in the parliament ; and we greatly fear, that the want of it will certainly produce one of these two fatal consequences ; either that the repeal of this law will in effect annull and abrogate all other laws and statutes relating to our colonies, and particularly the acts that restrain or limit their commerce, of which they are most impatient ; or, if we should hereafter attempt to enforce the execution of those laws against their will, and by virtue of an authority, which they have dared to insult with impunity and success, that endeavour will bring upon us all those evils and inconveniencies, to the fear of which we now sacrifice the sovereignty of the realm ; and this at a time when the strength of our colonies, as well as their desire of a total independence on the legislature and government of their mother-country, may be greatly augmented, and when the circumstances and dispositions of the other powers of Europe, may render the contest far more dangerous and formidable to this kingdom.

Bedford	Scarsdale
Coventry	Lyttelton
Bridgewater	Dunk Hallifax
Temple	Eglingtoun
Buckingham	Suffolk and Berkshire.
Wentworth	Abercorn
Sandwich	Vere
Bolingbroke	Trevor
Marlborough	Thomas Bristol
W. Gloucester	Ferrers
Ker	Grosvenor
Leigh	Townshend
Bangor	Dudley and Ward
Waldegrave	Charles Carlisle
Aylesford	Powis
Gower	Hyde.
Weymouth	

Die Lunæ, 17° *Martii,* 1766.
The Order of the Day being read for the third reading of the Bill, entituled, ' An Act to repeal an Act made in the last Session of Parliament,'

Parliament,' entituled, ' An Act for granting and applying certain Stamp Duties, and other Duties in the British Colonies and Plantations in America, towards further defraying the Expences of defending, protecting, and securing the same, and for amending such Parts of the several Acts of Parliament relating to the Trade and Revenues of the said Colonies and Plantations, as direct the Manner of determining and recovering the Penalties and Forfeitures therein mentioned.' Then the said Bill was read a third Time, and it being proposed to pass the Bill, the same was objected to. After some Debate thereupon, the Question was put, Whether the said Bill shall pass: It was resolved in the Affirmative.

Dissentient,

1st. Because we think, that the declaratory bill we past last week, cannot possibly obviate the growing mischiefs in America, where it may seem calculated only to deceive the people of Great-Britain, by holding forth a delusive and nugatory affirmance of the legislative right of this kingdom, whilst the enacting part of it does no more than abrogate the resolutions of the house of representatives in the North-American colonies, which have not in themselves the least colour of authority; and declares that, which is apparently and certainly criminal, only null and void.

2dly. Because the particular objections, which have been made to the stamp act in North-America, and which have been adopted in the course of the Debates upon this bill for repealing it, are in fact contradicted by undeniable evidence upon our table; it having been urged, first, That all the money to be collected by this tax was to be annually remitted hither, and that the North-American colonies would thereby be drained of all their specie; and secondly, That the institution of vice-admiralty courts in those colonies, for the recovery of penalties upon revenue laws without juries, is a novel practice, by means of which his Majesty's subjects in those dominions, ' would be deprived of one of their most valuable liberties, trials by juries, and in this respect distinguished from their fellow subjects in Great-Britain;' and would likewise be liable to the greatest inconvenience, vexation and injustice, through the option left to any prosecutor to call them from one end of that extensive continent to the other; and through the temptation to the judge, to condemn rather than to acquit, from his being paid by poundage of the condemnation-money: whereas, with regard to the first of these objections, it appears by the minute of the late board of treasury laid before this house, and dated on the 9th day of July last, that the fullest directions had been sent to the several officers of the revenue, ' that in order to obviate the inconvenience of bringing into this kingdom the money to be raised by the stamp duties, all the produce of the American duties arising or to arise, by virtue of any British act of parliament, should, from time to time, be paid to the deputy paymaster *in America*, to defray the subsistence of the troops, and any military expences incurred in the colonies:' and with regard to the second objection, it is manifest, from sundry acts of parliament, that a jurisdiction has been assigned to the judges of those courts, for the recovery of penalties upon the laws of revenue and of trade, without juries, for near a century past, from the consideration (as we apprehend) that in some of the colonies they are the only judges not elected by the people: and so far it is from being true, that the subjects in North-America, by being deprived in these cases of trials by by juries, were in that respect distinguished from their fellow subjects in Great-Britain; that, in this very instance of the stamp duties, the penalties, which by the American stamp act were made recoverable without a jury before a judge of the vice-admiralty court, are, by the laws now in force for collecting the stamp duties in Great-Britain, recoverable also without a jury, before two justices of the peace, with the like powers in both cases, which we earnestly wish were not still more necessary for the collection of the public revenue in America than in Great-Britain; and which we should be most desirous, if possible, to alleviate in both countries: with this view, and to take away all just occasion for discontent, we were very glad to find by the representation from the late commissioners of the treasury to his Majesty in council, dated on the 4th day of July last, that the strictest attention had been given by that board to prevent the inconvenience and injustice above-mentioned, by a plan to establish three different courts of vice-admiralty at the most convenient places, with proper districts annexed to each; and to give the judges sufficient and honourable salaries in lieu of all poundage and fees whatsoever: but we cannot observe, without the highest concern and surprize, that this representation, founded upon a clause inserted in the stamp act for this very purpose, and expressly calculated to relieve his Majesty's subjects in North-America from many unnecessary hardships and oppressions, to which they are now liable by many other laws still subsisting, should be totally disregarded for several months, and be suffered to remain unexecuted in every part of it even to this day; and that no notice whatever should be taken, in any of the dispatches from the present administration to the governors of the colonies in North-America, of the timely care

which had been employed to obviate the objections raised on both those heads: especially, as it is notorious, that the measures to be pursued, in consequence of that minute and representation, had been fully opened and approved in parliament, at the time when the stamp act was proposed; and as the total neglect of it has given occasion to great clamour and dissatisfaction in the colonies. We cannot help further observing, that as the stamp act was not to take place till the 1st of November, if the parliament had been called early, their determinations, either for enforcing or repealing that law, would probably have delivered the merchants and manufacturers here from all the difficulties and distress to which they have been for so many months exposed; nor would the disorders in America, where all government is prostrate, have risen to so great a height, or taken so deep a root.

3dly. Because the argument which has been used in favour of this bill of repeal, that the experiment of the stamp act has been tried, and has failed, is extremely ill founded; as it manifestly appears from the whole tenor of the papers laid before us, that if this experiment had been properly tried, with the same zeal for its success with which it was first proposed, it would not have failed in any of the colonies: and that this was the opinion of the greater part of the governors in North-America, and of many of the most intelligent and respectable persons in those provinces, for some time after this act was passed, is evident beyond a doubt, from the letters of the former now upon our table, and from the latter having applied for, and accepted the office of distributors of the stamps under that act, which they certainly would not have done, and thereby have exposed their lives and fortunes to the violence and outrages which they have since undergone, if they had then
thought

thought the fuccefs of this meafure in any degree precarious : nor have we heard of any impracticability attending this law in Jamaica and Barbadoes, and fome other of the Weft-India iflands, or in thofe of our colonies in North-America, where it has been executed.

4thly. Becaufe a precedent of the two houfes of parliament lending their power, from motives of fear or impatience under a prefent uneafinefs, to overturn in one month a plan of meafures, undertaken with their warmeft approbation and concurrence, after the moft mature deliberation of two years together, for the improvement of our revenue, and the relief of our people, will effectually difcourage all officers of the crown in America from doing their duty, and executing the laws of this kingdom ; and is enough to deter future minifters, in any circumftances of diftrefs or danger to their country, from oppofing their fortitude and zeal for the fervice of the public, to ftrong combinations of private and particular interefts, to the clamour of multitudes, or the malice of faction ; which muft neceffarily bring on fuch a weaknefs and pufillanimity in the adminiftration of government, as will foon end in the downfal and ruin of the ftate. .

Laftly. Becaufe the repeal of this law under the prefent circumftances, will, we fear, not only furrender the honour and effential interefts of the kingdom now and for ever, both at home and abroad, but will alfo deeply affect the fundamental principles of our conftitution ; for if we pafs this bill againft our opinion, from the threats and compulfion publicly avowed in our colonies, and enforced by the moft unjuftifiable means within Great-Britain, we difclaim that legiflative authority over the fubjects, which we own ourfelves unable to maintain. If we give our confent to it here, without a full conviction that it is right, merely becaufe it has

paffed the other houfe, by declining to do our duty on the moft important occafion which can ever prefent itfelf, and where our interpofition, for many obvious reafons, would be peculiarly proper ; we in effect annihilate this branch of the legiflature, and vote ourfelves ufelefs. Or if by paffing this bill, we mean to juftify thofe, who in America, and even in Great-Britain, have treated a feries of Britifh acts of parliament as fo many acts of tyranny and oppreffion, which it is fcarcely criminal to refift ; or thofe officers of the crown, who, under the eye, and with the knowledge of government, have taken upon themfelves, whilft the parliament was fitting, without its confent, to fufpend the execution of the ftamp act, by admitting fhips from the colonies, with unftampt clearances, to an entry, in direct violation of it, which from the papers upon our table appears to have been done ; we fhall then give our approbation to an open breach of the firft article of that great palladium of our liberties, the bill of rights ; by which it is declared, ' That the pretended power of fufpending of laws, or the execution of laws, by regal authority, without confent of parliament, is illegal.' Laftly, If we ground our proceedings upon the opinion of thofe who have contended in this houfe, that from the conftitution of our colonies they ought never to be taxed, even for their own immediate defence, we fear that fuch a declaration, by which near a fifth part of the fubjects of Great-Britain, who by the acts of parliament to reftrain the preffing of feamen in America, are already exempted from furnifhing men to our navy, are to be for ever exempted from contributing their fhare towards their own fupport in money likewife, will, from the flagrant partiality and injuftice of it, either depopulate this kingdom, or fhake the bafis of equality, and of that original compact,

upon

upon which every society is founded; and as we believe, that there is no inftance of fuch a permanent exemption of fo large a body of the fubjects of any ftate in any hiftory, antient or modern, we are extremely apprehenfive of the fatal confequences of this unhappy meafure; to which, for thefe reafons, in addition to thofe contained in the proteft of the 11th of this month, our duty to the King, and juftice to our country, oblige us to enter this our folemn diffent.

Temple	Dudley and Ward
Abercorn	Suffolk and Berkfhire
Scarfdale	Leigh
J. Bangor	Bridgewater
Trevor	Gower
Hyde	Grofvenor
Marlborough	Powis
Sandwich	Ker
Charles Carlifle	Lyttelton
Weymouth	Effex
Thomas Briftol	Ferrers
W. Gloucefter	Aylesford
Buckinghamfhire	Vere
R. Durefme	Eglintoun.

[Here the difpute feems to have ceafed—until it was revived the next feffion of parliament (1776-7), when the following letters and papers were laid upon the table; which have not been printed before.]

Copy of Mr. Secretary Conway's Circular Letter to his Majefty's Governors in America.

St. James's, March 31, 1766.

SIR,

Herewith I have the pleafure of tranfmitting to you copies of two acts of parliament juft paft, the firft for fecuring the juft dependency of the colonies on the mother-country, the fecond for the repeal of the act of the laft feffion, granting certain ftamp-duties in America; and, I expect fhortly, to fend you a third for the indemnity of fuch perfons as have incurred the penalties impofed by the act juft repealed, as fuch a bill is now depending, and has made a confiderable progrefs in the Houfe of Commons.

The moderation, the forbearance, the unexampled lenity and tendernefs of parliament towards the colonies,[*] which are fo fignally difplayed in thofe acts, cannot but difpofe the province committed to your care, to that return of chearful obedience to the laws and legiflative authority of Great Britain, and to thofe fentiments of refpectful gratitude to the mother-country,

which are the natural, and I truft will be the certain effects of fo much grace and condefcenfion fo remarkably manifefted on the part of his Majefty and of the parliament, and the future happinefs and profperity of the colonies, will very much depend on the teftimonies they fhall now give of thefe difpofitions.

For as a dutiful and affectionate return to fuch peculiar proofs of indulgence and affection, may now at this great crifis be a means of fixing the mutual interefts and inclinations of Great Britain and her colonies, on the moft firm and folid foundations, it cannot but appear vifible that the leaft coolnefs or unthankfulnefs, the leaft murmuring or diffatisfaction on any ground whatever, of former heat, or too much prevailing prejudice, may fatally endanger that union, and give the moft fevere and affecting blow to the future interefts of both countries.

You would think it fcarce poffible, I imagine, that the paternal care of his Majefty for his colonies, or the lenity and indulgence of the parliament fhould go farther than I have

The variations contained in the following notes on this letter, were the particular alterations in the letter fent to General Gage.

[* Which are fo fignally difplayed in thofe acts, cannot but difpofe the colonies to that *chearful obedience,* &c.]

N

already

already mentioned; yet so full of true magnanimity are the sentiments of both, and so free from the smallest colour of passion or prejudice, that they seem not only disposed to forgive but to forget those most unjustifiable marks of an undutiful disposition too frequent in the late transactions of the colonies, and which for the honor of those colonies it were to be wished had been more discountenanced and discouraged by those who had knowledge to conduct themselves otherwise.

A revision of the late American trade laws is going to be the immediate object of parliament, nor will the late transactions there, however provoking, I dare say, prevent the full operation of that kind and indulgent disposition prevailing in both his Majesty and parliament, to give the trade and interest of America every relief which the true state of their circumstances demanded or admits.

Nothing will tend more effectually to every conciliating purpose, and there is nothing therefore I have in command more earnestly to require of you, than that you should exert yourself * in recommending it strongly to the assembly, that full and ample compensation be made to those, who from the madness of the people have suffered for their deference to acts of the British legislature, and you will be particularly attentive that such persons be effectually secured from any further insult, and that as far as in you lies, you will take care by your example and influence, that they may be treated with that respect to their persons, and that justice in regard to all their pretensions which their merits and sufferings undoubtedly claim.—

The resolutions of the House of Commons, which by his Majesty's command † I transmit to you to be laid before the assembly, will shew you the sense of that house on those points, and am persuaded it will, as it most certainly ought to be the glory of that assembly, to adopt and imitate these sentiments of the British parliament, founded on the clearest principles of humanity and justice.

I mention one circumstance in particular that should ‡ recommend those unhappy people, whom the outrage of the populace had driven from America, to the affection of all that country, which is, that unprovoked by the injuries they had suffered, to a forgetfulness of what they owed to truth and their country, they gave their testimonies with knowledge but without passion or prejudice, and those testimonies had, I believe, great weight in persuading the repeal of the stamp-act.

I have only to add, which I do with great pleasure, that every part of your conduct has had the intire and hearty approbation of your sovereign ||, and that the judicious representations in favour of your province, which appear in your letters laid before both houses of parliament, seem to have their full weight in all those parts of the American interests to which they relate, and, as his Majesty honors you with his fullest approbation, both for the firmness and for the temperance of your conduct, so I hope your province will be sensible of their obligations to you, and will cordially feel what they owe to a governor whom no outrage could provoke to resentment, nor any insult induce to relax in his endeavour to persuade

[* In persuading *that full*, &c.]
[† I have transmitted to the several governors to be laid before the assemblies, will shew you the sense of that house on those points, and I am persuaded, need not press you to exert your utmost endeavours to excite every where a spirit of obedience and submission among the people.]
[‡ Which ought to *recommend*, &c.]
[|| This will be delivered to you by Major James, whose spirited conduct in his post at New-York, and his unprejudiced representations here must do him great

perſuade his Majeſty to ſhew indulgence and favour even to the offending part of his people. I am, &c.

H. S. Conway.

To Governor Bernard.

Like letters to the governors of New-York, New-Jerſey, Connecticut, Rhode-Iſland, Virginia, Maryland, North Carolina and Georgia, which, inſtead of the laſt paragraphs, conclude with the following one :

" Your ſituation, which has made you a witneſs of the diſtractions of that country, will enable you to form the beſt judgment of the behaviour which your province ought to uſe upon this occaſion, and of the arguments which you ought to employ to enforce the neceſſity of ſuch a behaviour as is ſuitable to their preſent circumſtances."

The three laſt paragraphs are omitted in the letters to the governors of Pennſylvania, New-Hampſhire, and South-Carolina, which conclude with the paragraph as above, with this addition to Pennſylvania :

" I am glad to find that things have remained quiet in your government: By his Majeſty's commands I tranſmit you the reſolutions of the Houſe of Commons, to be laid before your aſſembly, whom you will at the ſame time aſſure of his Majeſty's approbation of the wiſe and prudent as well as dutiful behaviour which the province of Pennſylvania has held, amidſt the too prevailing diſtractions which have ſo generally agitated the other colonies.

" This behaviour of your province reflects honor on your adminiſtration, and I have the ſatisfaction to inform you, that your own conduct meets

with his Majeſty's approbation."

And to New-Hampſhire with the following paragraph :

" By his Majeſty's commands, I tranſmit to you the reſolutions of the Houſe of Commons of Great Britain, on the occaſion of the late diſturbances in America, to be laid before the aſſembly."

The three ſaid laſt paragraphs are likewiſe omitted to the governors of Quebec, Nova-Scotia, Eaſt and Weſt-Florida, and Weſt-India Iſlands, and the following one was made uſe of:

" I am glad to find there have been no diſturbances in your * province on this occaſion, and I am confident, I need not point out to you the behaviour which it becomes the colonies to uſe at this time, or the arguments which you ought to employ to enforce the neceſſity of ſuch a behaviour in the preſent ſituation of things."

N. B. The reſolutions of the Houſe of Commons were alſo tranſmitted to them.

Copy of a circular Letter to his Majeſty's Governors in America.

Whitehall, July 10, 1766.

S I R,

I ſend you herewith incloſed, " An Act, intitled, an Act for repealing certain Duties in the Britiſh Colonies and Plantations, granted by ſeveral Acts of Parliament, &c. and for granting other Duties inſtead thereof," which I make no doubt will be received and conſidered as a further proof of the king and parliament's attention to the intereſts and proſperity of his Majeſty's American ſubjects. I am, &c.

Richmond, &c.

great credit with all honeſt men. It is by his Majeſty's commands that I recommend him not only to your protection but to your favour.

Your laſt letters of the 22d of February are juſt received : I cannot now give you a particular anſwer ; your own knowledge of things and prudence, will make any particular direction needleſs,

To Major-General Gage.   I am, &c. H. S. Conway.]

[* Government.]

Copy of a Letter from the Earl of Shelburne to Sir Henry Moore, Governor of New-York.

Whitehall, *August* 9, 1766.

SIR,

I took the firſt opportunity, after his Majeſty had been moſt graciouſly pleaſed to intruſt me with the ſeals of the ſouthern department, to lay before him your letter of the 20th of June, giving an account of the general ſatiſfaction expreſſed by all ranks and degrees of people on the repeal of the ſtamp-act, and likewiſe your reaſons for aſſenting to a bill for providing barracks, firewood, candles, bedding and utenſils for the kitchen for the king's troops as demanded, notwithſtanding the articles of ſalt, vinegar, cyder and beer, be not included, under a pretence that they are not provided for troops lodged in barracks in Europe.

I have his Majeſty's commands to acquaint you of the ſatiſfaction he feels in the happineſs of his ſubjects, ariſing from the tender care and conſideration of his parliament; but I am ordered to ſignify to you at the ſame time, that as it is the indiſpenſible duty of his ſubjects in America to obey the acts of the legiſlature of Great-Britain, the king both expects and requires a due and chearful obedience to the ſame; and it cannot be doubted that his Majeſty's province of New-York, after the lenity of Great-Britain ſo recently extended to America, will not fail duly to carry into execution the act of parliament paſſed laſt ſeſſion for quartering his Majeſty's troops, in the full extent and meaning of the act, without referring to the uſage of other parts of his Majeſty's dominions, where the legiſlature has thought proper to preſcribe different regulations, and which cannot be altered any more than in North-America, except upon a reſpectful and well-grounded repreſentation of the hardſhip or inconvenience:— Theſe conſiderations, I am convinced,

muſt of themſelves have ſo much weight with the aſſembly of New-York, not only in the preſent conjuncture, when it is natural to ſuppoſe the minds of men retain ſenſible impreſſions of what has lately paſſed, but upon other occaſions which may call for a ready obedience, that I cannot think it neceſſary for me to enlarge further upon their importance; I would only, Sir, in general, add, that I hope and believe, that a very little time, together with that temperate adminiſtration of government, which your regard to the people under it muſt make you naturally incline to, and that firmneſs which your duty to the king equally requires, will allay whatever remains of thoſe heats which have ſo unhappily for America prevailed, and which, if continued, muſt prove of the meſt fatal conſequence to whatever province they are ſuffered in. I am therefore perſuaded, that the aſſembly will loſe no occaſion that offers, of convincing his Majeſty, that the people of New-York will yield to no other part of his Majeſty's ſubjects in duty, loyalty, and obedience, to ſuch laws as the king and parliament have thought proper to enact, for their benefit and protection.

I am, &c. SHELBURNE.

Copy of a Letter from the Earl of Shelburne to Governor Bernard.

Whitehall, *Sept.* 13, 1766.

SIR,

I have had the honor to lay before the king your letters of the 29th of June and 19th of July laſt, together with the incloſures therein contained, and I have received his Majeſty's commands to communicate them to ſuch of his ſervants as he thinks proper uſually to conſult upon his moſt important affairs, as ſoon as the ſeaſon of the year will conveniently admit of their meeting for this and other purpoſes. In the mean time his Majeſty is extremely ſorry to obſerve any degree of ill temper remaining in his

colony

colony of Maffachufet's-Bay, or that points fhould be fo improperly agitated, as to tend to the revival of difputes which every friend to America muft wifh to be forgotten. They have feen the parliament of Great-Britain give due attention to all well-founded complaints of the provinces, notwithftanding they appeared to them in fome parts not fo properly urged, and though the legiflature will certainly, on all juft occafions, exercife and enforce its legiflative power over the colonies, yet it cannot be doubted but it will exert it with a due regard to the nature of their connection with the mother-country.

Upon this occafion it is proper to obferve in general, that the eafe and honor of his Majefty's government in America will greatly depend on the temper and wifdom of thofe who are intrufted with the adminiftration there, and that they ought to be perfons difdaining narrow views, private combinations, and partial attachments. It is with great pleafure, Sir, that I have obferved the manner in which you have conducted yourfelf during the difputes of the laft year, which I cannot do without highly approving your attention and watchfulnefs on the one hand to fupport the authority of government, and on the other, the tendernefs and affection which appeared in all your letters towards the people under your government.—A temperate conduct, founded on the true bafis of public good, avoiding all unneceffary referve where nothing arbitrary is thought of, and nothing unreafonable required, muft carry conviction to the hearts of the deluded, conciliate the minds of all, and infure the confidence of his Majefty's loyal and loving fubjects of America.

Upon thefe confiderations I am perfuaded that the affembly will immediately, upon their meeting, fall into meafures to terminate all local difficulties which appear by your accounts to have hitherto prevented that compliance which will be expected by parliament, with the recommendations you have been required to make, in confequence of the refolutions of both houfes.—It is impoffible to conceive, that they will fuffer any private confiderations to interfere with their defire of fhewing a proper fenfe of that paternal regard which they have experienced from his Majefty, and that attention which parliament has given to their complaints, which can never be done with more propriety than by granting, with the utmoft chearfulnefs, a juft compenfation to thofe who have fuffered by the late diforders.

I am, &c. SHELBURNE.

Extract of a Letter from Lieutenant Governor Bull to Mr. Secretary Conway.
[*Received June* 30.]
Charles-Town, May 9, 1766.

SIR,

By the Hillfborough Packet on the 15th of laft month, I received the honour of your letter (a duplicate, the original never having reached me) dated the 24th of October, 1765, fignifying his Majefty's pleafure in regard to the fuppreffion of riots in this province, and it is with no fmall fatisfaction I reflect that my behaviour in that delicate conjuncture has been regulated in the fame manner which his Majefty has gracioufly thought fit to command his governors to obferve.

I am to acquaint you, Sir, that within thefe two days we have received accounts from various parts that the ftamp-act is certainly repealed, which are attended with circumftances that leave no room to doubt the truth thereof. The joy of the people on this occafion was demonftrated by running almoft to excefs, at the thoughts of being relieved, not only from the diftrefs which the prefent ftagnation of bufinefs had brought on them, but alfo from the apprehenfions of having further burthens laid upon them; and, although I expect the arrival of Lord Charles

Charles Montague, our governor, every day, the irksomeness of the late restraint renders the people so impatient of waiting for any further confirmation of this agreeable news, that as the repeal operates from the day the king gives his royal assent to the bill, all the usual channels of business are now opened, and with them a prospect of good order, tranquility, and prosperity through the province.

Governor Sir Henry Moore's Letter to Mr. Secretary Conway.
[*Received July* 6, *by Major-General Burton.*]
Fort-George, New-York,
SIR, *May* 27, 1766.

I had the honor of receiving your letters by the hands of Major James, and at the same time dispatches for the rest of his Majesty's governors, all which were forwarded to them within a few hours after they were landed. As the general assembly of this province will meet in a few days, I shall then have an opportunity of seeing what impression has been made on their minds by the signal favours already conferred on them by his Majesty and his parliament, and what returns of gratitude they are inclined to make. Nothing, on my part, shall be wanting to bring back to their duty those who have been imposed on and misled, and I shall, in the strongest manner, recommend to the assembly the case of those persons who were sufferers in the late commotions, that they may have a full compensation made to them for the losses they sustained, by the hasty and ill-timed proceedings of the populace.

I have the honor to be, &c.
H. MOORE.

Governor Sir Henry Moore's Letter.
[*Received the* 25th *of July.*]
Fort-George, New-York,
SIR, *June* 20, 1766.
The pacquet having suffered so much in her last voyage as to stand

in need of some considerable reparations before she could venture to sea again, I am enabled, by the delay which this misfortune has occasioned, to transmit to you some accounts of our proceedings here, since I had the honor of your letter, notifying the repeal of the stamp-act. The general assembly having desired, at the close of the last session, to sit again in the spring for the dispatch of some business, their meeting was put off, by different prorogations, till the 11th day of this month, and I have here inclosed my speech at the opening of the sessions, and the addresses of the council and assembly. From the general satisfaction which was expressed here by all ranks and degrees of people, I had all the reason to expect, that the earliest opportunity would have been taken to shew their gratitude for such signal favours received; you may then easily judge, Sir, how much I was surprized to find myself disappointed in my expectations; for, upon General Gage's application to me for bedding, utensils, &c. agreeable to the act of parliament for his Majesty's troops then under orders of march for this city, the consideration of the message I sent was postponed till after the arrival of the troops, by which they were put to very great inconveniences, and afterwards such resolutions were entered into that appeared to me as evasive as they were unexpected. After informing the general with what had passed, I sent a second message, which was ordered in such a manner as to require a categorical answer, which laid them under some difficulties; for, although it appeared plainly, that they did not chooie to shew that obedience which was due to an act of parliament, it was as evident that they were too apprehensive of the ill consequences which would attend their refusing to comply with it. They have now ordered a bill to be brought in, for providing barracks, fire-wood, candles,

dles, bedding, and utensils for the kitchen as demanded, but the articles of salt, vinegar, and cyder or beer, are not to be included in the bill, being furnished with this pretence to leave them out, that they are not provided in Europe for his Majesty's troops which are in barracks; and, as the General is satisfied that nothing more can be obtained at this time, I hope that I shall be thought to act for his Majesty's service in passing the bill in its present state, for the difficulties which would arise in the other colonies upon a like application from their governors, may by this step be obviated, as I am persuaded, from what I have seen, that the example of this province, in making the provision required, will have a greater influence on the proceedings of the others than any other motive whatsoever, and it will appear on the minutes of the assembly, that I made the same demand during their last session, without being able to obtain the smallest sum for that purpose. This, Sir, is a bare relation of what has passed here, without aggravating or extenuating any one circumstance, and as matters of fact speak best for themselves, I thought it proper to lay the whole of this proceeding before you, as it will, at one view, shew the deference here paid to acts of parliament, and what may be our expectations on a future occasion; you will be pleased to observe, that my message is treated merely as a requisition made here, and that they have carefully avoided the least mention of the act on which it is founded, and it is my opinion, that every act of parliament, when not backed by a sufficient power to enforce it, will meet with the same fate here. I am, &c.

To the Right Hon.   H. MOORE.
H. S. Conway.

The Speech of his Excellency Sir Henry Moore, Bart. Captain-General and

Governor in Chief, in and over the Province of New-York, and the Territories depending thereon in America, Vice-Admiral and Chancellor of the same.

To the Council and General Assembly of the said Province.

Gentlemen of the Council, and Gentlemen of the General Assembly,

The general satisfaction which has been diffused throughout the colonies on the late favourable proceedings of the parliament of Great-Britain in the repeal of the stamp-act, and the impression made on the minds of the people on receiving such distinguishing marks of his Majesty's favour and protection, have induced me to give you the earliest opportunity of making those acknowledgements of duty and submission, which on such an occasion must arise in the breast of every individual. The misrepresentations heretofore made by artful and designing persons, have had their effect in imposing on the weak and credulous, and false hopes and fears are now conceived by those, who, from their situation, can only see and hear at a distance, and of course are easily imposed on. Let it be your concern to undeceive the deluded, and, by the powerful examples of your own conduct, bring back to a sense of their duty, those who have been misled, that nothing which can carry with it the least resemblance of former heat and prejudice may be suffered to prevail, and the minds of those who are too easily agitated, be disposed to a chearful obedience to the laws, and to sentiments of respectful gratitude to the mother-country.

Gentlemen of the General Assembly,

I must at this time recommend to your particular attention the case of those unfortunate persons, who from the licentiousness of the populace have suffered for their deference to the acts of the British legislature: I flatter myself, that they who sue to this house for justice will never sue in vain,

vain, and that it will be no ungrateful task for this province to take the lead on such an occasion, and, by making a full and ample compensation to the sufferers for their goods and effects destroyed, shew to the neighbouring provinces, by an example great as well as just, the sense which is here entertained of the benefits lately received. The resolutions of the House of Commons have, by his Majesty's commands, been transmitted to me, in order to be laid before you: these sufficiently shew the sense of that august assembly on this point, whose sentiments it should be your glory to adopt and imitate, as they are so evidently founded on the clearest principles of humanity and justice. This carries its own recommendation with it, and makes it needless for me to enforce by arguments, a measure, which at the same time it will do honour to the province, will shew yourselves not unworthy of that royal condescension and protection which have been manifested on the late interesting occasion.

Gentlemen of the Council, and Gentlemen of the General Assembly,

I have nothing more in particular to lay before you at this juncture, and shall be extremely happy to shew my ready concurrence with you in promoting every measure which can tend to the service of his Majesty, and the welfare of the people.

New-York,   H. MOORE.
June 12, 1766.

———

To his Excellency Sir Henry Moore, Bart. Captain-General and Governor in Chief in and over the Province of New-York, and the Territories depending in America, Chancellor and Vice-Admiral of the same.
The humble Address of the Council of the Province of New-York.
May it please your Excellency,

The council, impressed with the warmest sentiments of duty and gratitude to his Majesty, for the late most distinguishing mark of royal favour and protection, and filled with the highest sense of the great wisdom, justice and moderation, manifested in the proceedings of that august body the British parliament, return your Excellency their unfeigned thanks for this early communication of an event so ardently hoped for, and so highly satisfactory to these colonies.

To undeceive the deluded, and to bring back to a sense of their duty the misguided and prejudiced, have been the fixed objects of our attention, sensible that where submission to the laws is wanting, anarchy and confusion must ensue: evils the most to be dreaded, as they are the most pernicious to society. And you may be assured, Sir, that nothing shall be wanting on our part to inculcate in the minds of the people, a thorough sense of the obedience they owe, the dependence they stand in, and the benefits they receive from their most gracious sovereign, and their guardians the British parliament, confident that the colonies in general, will, by their conduct, shew themselves deserving of every mark of royal favour and indulgence.

We shall, at all times, chearfully and readily concur with your Excellency in promoting every measure which can tend to the service of his Majesty, and the happiness and prosperity of the colony. By order of the council,

New-York, DANIEL HORSMANDEN,
June 14, 1766.   Speaker.

To which his Excellency was pleased to return the following answer.

Gentlemen,

I return you many thanks for this address, as the sentiments you express therein must so manifestly tend to the establishment of the happiness and prosperity of your country.

Fort George, New-York,
June 16, 1766.

To

Addreſs of the Houſe of Aſſembly of New-York.

To his Excellency Sir *Henry Moore,* Baronet, *Captain-General and Governor in Chief, in and over the Colony of New-York, and the Territories depending thereon in America, Chancellor and Vice-Admiral of the ſame.*

The humble Addreſs of the General Aſſembly of the ſaid Colony.

May it pleaſe your Excellency,

We his Majeſty's moſt dutiful and loyal ſubjeᶜts the general aſſembly of the colony of New-York, return your Excellency our hearty thanks for your ſpeech.

The recent inſtance of his Majeſty's tender concern for the rights and liberties of his American ſubjeᶜts, and the ſignal proof of the juſtice and impartiality of the Britiſh parliament, in the repeal of the ſtamp-aᶜt, will, we doubt not, add new ardour to their affeᶜtion for his ſacred perſon and government, and augment their eſteem and veneration for his auguſt parliament.

And as we conceive it our honor and happineſs to participate in, and to the utmoſt of our power to promote and inculcate the warmeſt gratitude for every inſtance of moderation and juſtice in the grand legiſlature of the nation, ſo we ſhall negleᶜt no opportunity to diſcountenance and ſuppreſs every miſrepreſentation tending to extinguiſh or abate ſuch becoming ſentiments, and to promote by our influence and example, a chearful obedience to the laws, and a reſpeᶜtful conduᶜt to the mother-country.

The reſolutions of the honourable houſe of commons reſpeᶜting the ſufferers in the late commotions, we ſhall conſider with all the deference due to the ſentiments of that illuſtrious aſſembly, and we return your Excellency our hearty thanks for your aſſurance of your ready concurrence in promoting every meaſure which may tend to the ſervice of his Majeſty, and the welfare of the people. By order of the general aſſembly,

Aſſembly-Chamber, W. NICOLL, Sᵖʳ.
City of New-York, June 16, 1766.

To which his Excellency was pleaſed to return the following anſwer.

Gentlemen of the General Aſſembly,

I return you my thanks for this addreſs. It is hoped from the ſentiments you entertain of the benefits lately received, that thoſe who have at heart the proſperity of their country, will not negleᶜt ſo favourable an opportunity of diſtinguiſhing themſelves as that which now offers, by promoting whatever may be neceſſary towards the ſettling on a laſting foundation, the mutual intereſts of Great-Britain and her colonies.

Copies of Sir Henry Moore's two Meſſages to the Houſe of Aſſembly of New-York, and the Anſwers, in his Letter of June 20, 1776.

Copy of Sir Henry Moore's firſt Meſſage to the Houſe of Aſſembly,
June 13, 1766.

A return of his Majeſty's forces under orders of march for this city, having been ſent to me by his Excellency General Gage, I take the earlieſt opportunity of laying it before you, and hope you will give the neceſſary direᶜtions, that ſufficient quarters, bedding, utenſils, &c. may be provided for the reception of the officers and ſoldiers ſpecified in the ſaid return, agreeable to the aᶜt of parliament.

Anſwer of the Houſe of Aſſembly to the above Meſſage.

Aſſembly-Chamber, City of New-York, Die Jovis, 9 h. A. M. *the* 19th *of June,* 1766.

The houſe, according to order, reſolved itſelf into a committee of the whole houſe upon his Excellency's meſſage of the 13th inſtant, recommending the making proviſion for quarters,

O

quarters, bedding, utenfils, &c. for a number of troops mentioned in a return accompanying the faid meffage ; after fome time fpent in confidering the fame, Mr. Speaker refumed the chair, and Mr. Philip Livingfton reported the refolutions of the committee, which he read in his place, and afterwards delivered it at the table, where the fame was again read, and are as follow ; viz.

Refolved, That it is the opinion of this committee, that the general affembly of this colony have always been ready and willing to comply with every requifition made to them by order and for the fervice of his Majefty, nor can they recollect one fingle inftance wherein they have with-held the aid requefted.

Refolved, That it is the opinion of this committee, that the requifition now made by the above-mentioned meffage, is of fuch a nature and tendency, that fhould it be granted, the expence might, and probably would, very foon exceed the ability of this colony to pay, as the number of troops that may from time to time require the like provifion, are to this committee entirely unknown, and the articles required for the greateft part, as this committee is informed, unprecedented.

Refolved, That it is the opinion of this committee, that the requifition now made will amount at leaft to three-pence per day for each private man, exclufive of beds and bedding.

Refolved, That it is the opinion of this committee, that the houfe, upon a proper requifition from the crown for that purpofe, fhould be at the expence of furnifhing barracks, bedding, utenfils for dreffing victuals, and firewood, and candles, for a proportionate part of the troops with the reft of the colonies, which the committee conceives is as much as can reafonably be expected.

Refolved, That it is the opinion of this committee, that his Majefty's

fervice cannot in the leaft fuffer by the non-compliance of the houfe with this requifition, becaufe the troops have hitherto fubfifted very well without any fuch provifion, and if that was not the cafe, a fum of money to the amount of £.3990, is now remaining in the treafury of this colony, fubject to the order of the commander in chief of his Majefty's troops in North-America, which he may apply for the fervice of his Majefty's forces, as he thinks proper.

And the faid refolutions having been read a fecond time :

Refolved, That the houfe do agree with the committee in the foregoing refolutions.

Ordered, That Mr. Thomas and Colonel Livingfton wait upon his Excellency with the foregoing refolutions. By order of the general affembly, ABRAHAM LOTT, Clerk.

Copy of Sir Henry Moore's fecond Meffage to the Houfe of Affembly,
June 20, 1776.

A copy of the refolutions of the houfe of affembly, in anfwer to my meffage of the 13th inftant, recommending the making provifion for quarters, bedding, utenfils, &c. for his Majefty's troops then under orders of march for this city, having been fent to his Excellency the general, I yefterday evening received a letter from him, of which the following is an extract.

" The fum of 3990 pounds, which the houfe mentions to be remaining in the treafury of this colony, fubject to the order of the commander in chief of his Majefty's forces in North-America, I underftand was left there by Sir Jeffery Amherft, to be returned to the province, as the fervice of the public did not require it to be drawn. If the houfe means that fum as a fund to be appropriated to the ufe of quartering his Majefty's forces, it will certainly anfwer as well as any other fund they might appropriate to that ufe, uſe, as far as it will go. But I ſhould be glad to be informed, whether it is the intent and meaning of the houſe of aſſembly, that the commander in chief of his Majeſty's forces ſhould draw for the above ſum of £. 3990, or ſuch parts thereof as there may be occaſion for, to indemnify the magiſtrates for the expences they may incur in quartering his Majeſty's troops, according to the act of parliament paſſed the laſt ſeſſions of parliament for quartering his Majeſty's forces in North-America."

As by this extract it appears that a farther explication is required of that paragraph in the meſſage of yeſterday relative to the ſum of money therein mentioned to be lying in the treaſury, and at the diſpoſal of the commander in chief of his Majeſty's troops. The houſe of aſſembly is deſired to inform me, on what conditions the general is to draw for that money, and whether he is to take it on the terms mentioned in his letter or not, that no time may be loſt in furniſhing the neceſſaries for the troops.

Anſwer to Sir Henry Moore's ſecond Meſſage to the Houſe of Aſſembly, on the 20th of June, 1766.

Die Lunæ, 3 h. P. M. the 23d of June, 1766.

The houſe, according to order, reſolved itſelf into a committee of the whole houſe upon his Excellency's meſſage of the 20th inſtant, relating to the quartering of his Majeſty's forces in this colony. After ſome time ſpent therein, Mr. Speaker reſumed the chair, and Mr. Philip Livingſton reported the reſolutions of the committee, which he read in his place, and afterwards delivered in at the table, where the ſame were again read, and agreed to by the houſe, and are as follow; viz.

Reſolved, That it is the opinion of this committee, that it is impoſſible for the general aſſembly, in juſtice to their conſtituents, to raiſe or appro-

priate any fund for furniſhing his Majeſty's forces in the manner required by his Excellency, for the reaſons given in the reſolutions of the houſe of the 19th inſtant. But, as the general aſſembly have always been ready to promote his Majeſty's ſervice as far as they were able, conſiſtent with their duty to, and a due regard for the intereſt of their conſtituents, the committee are of opinion, that proviſion ſhould be made for furniſhing the barracks in the cities of New-York and Albany, with beds, bedding, fire-wood, candles, and utenſils for dreſſing of victuals for two battalions, not exceeding five hundred men each, and one company of artillery for one year.

Reſolved, That the expences to accrue by virtue of the foregoing reſolutions, be made payable out of the money now remaining in the treaſury, by virtue of an act paſſed the 20th of March, 1762, intituled, "An Act, directing the treaſurer of this colony to pay the commander in chief of all his Majeſty's forces in North-America the ſum of £. 4790 for his Majeſty's ſervice, to be repaid when his Majeſty ſhall think proper."

Ordered, That a bill be brought in purſuant to the ſaid reſolutions, and that Mr. Philip Livingſton and Mr. Douw prepare and bring in the ſame.

Ordered, That Colonel Livingſton and Mr. Ten Brock wait upon his Excellency with the foregoing reſolutions. By order of the general aſſembly,

ABRAHAM LOTT, Clerk.

Extract of a Letter from Lieutenant-Governor Colden to Mr. Secretary Conway.

[*Received July 25.*]

New-York, June 24, 1766.

The governor, in obedience to his Majeſty's command, having laid before the aſſembly of this province the reſolutions of the Houſe of Commons of Great Britain, for the payment of

loſſes

losses any person has sustained in the late riots for his deference to the acts of the British legislature; I sent in an account of things I had destroyed by the mob in the night of the first of November last, when they broke open my coach-house, and burnt my chariot, &c. The loss and value of the things lost were proved by my son's oath, amounting to the sum of one hundred and ninety-five pounds, three shillings. Major James had petitioned to have compensation for his losses sustained at that time, and his petition being referred to a committee of the whole house, my account was referred to the same committee, together with the accounts of some other persons who suffered at the same time by the mob. The method the assembly has taken of refusing any compensation to me, is by the committees passing my demand over in silence, and reporting in favour of the others, and I am assured this is their resolution.

Governor Franklin's Letter to Mr. Secretary Conway.
[*Received July 25.*]
Perth Amboy, June 19, 1766.
S I R,

I had the honour of receiving your two letters of the 1st and 31st of March with the two acts of parliament, and the resolutions of the House of Commons, which were contained in the last. I immediately summoned the council and assembly to meet at this place, when I laid those papers before them, and recommended it to them to return their thanks and acknowledgments to his Majesty and his parliament, for their great goodness and condescension in relieving this country from the difficulties occasioned by the stamp-act. This they have unanimously agreed to do, and their addresses will, I believe, be transmitted to their agent in England by this opportunity, and I have reason to think that you will

find them filled with the warmest expressions of duty and gratitude. It gives me great pleasure, that I have been able, through all the late disturbances, to preserve the tranquility of this province, notwithstanding the endeavours of some to stimulate the populace to such acts as have disgraced the colonies.

The wisdom of the present measures have already had the best effects in America, and afford the pleasing prospect of an uninterrupted harmony between the two countries.

The legislature is still sitting, and in all probability we shall have an amicable session: I send herewith a copy of my speech to the council and assembly on this occasion, and as soon as I can obtain a copy of their proceedings, I shall do myself the honour of transmitting it to you likewise. I am, &c.
To the Right Hon. W̳ᴍ. FRANKLIN.
H. S. Conway.

Extract of a Letter from Governor Bernard to Mr. Secretary Conway.
[*Received August 2.*]
Boston, June 29, 1766.

I had the honour to receive your letter of March 31st on the 31st of May, three days after the assembly was met at the usual time. I have been very desirous, that at the time I acknowledged this receipt, I should also inform you, that the assembly had complied with his Majesty's recommendation to indemnify the sufferers. But I am sorry to say, that after having waited a month for this purpose, and during that time have used all means in my power to prevail on them to give this proof of their gratitude and duty, I was obliged last evening to dismiss them, without their having done any thing towards indemnifying the sufferers, and without the least assurance that they ever intended to do it. I shall, with the first opportunity, give your honor an exact detail of this whole affair, setting

ting it in one view, and in a true light. At prefent I write only for a fhip which is to fail to-morrow, and am obliged to be fhort in what I have to write to day.

Extract of a Letter from Lieutenant-Governor Fauquier to Mr. Secretary Conway. [Received August 17.]
Williamfburgh, Virginia,
June 27, 1776.

I have been honoured within thefe few days with your favour of the 31ft of March, with the two acts of parliament and votes of the Houfe of Commons, and with their duplicates, The unexampled favours the colonies have received from the indulgence of their mother-country, and the ftill further benefits you give them reafon to hope for, furely demand the ftrongeft returns of affection, duty and obedience, which it is in their power to give.

It fhall be my part, by every means in my power, to endeavour to bring this about, and I fhall obey his Majefty's commands in laying the whole before the affembly, and make ufe of fuch arguments and meafures as fhall appear to me moft likely to produce this moft falutary and moft neceffary effect, and I have the pleafure, at prefent, to think this is in fome degree probable, though matters are not yet arrived at that maturity as to encourage me to give you any affurances of it.

I have been credibly informed, that there is a propofal now on foot to petition me to call the affembly fooner than I propofed to do, that they might have an early opportunity of teftifying their gratitude by an addrefs of loyalty, duty and obedience, with affurances of their heartily fupporting his Majefty, and the honour and dignity of his crown, againft the attacks of any of his enemies. To thofe who gave me this information, and were fent to feel my pulfe, I gave for

anfwer, that could they infure the conduct of the houfe, that it would be as they gave me reafon to hope it would, I fhould with the greateft pleafure give them the opportunity they defired, but that I muft go upon fure ground; for, if the confequence of their meeting early fhould be different from our wifhes, and any offenfive or feditious refolutions fhould be entered into, I fhould only give them a liberty effectually to cut their own throats and lofe every friend they now had, and that I had too great a regard for them to be inftrumental in what I conceived might prove their deftruction: They have undertaken to give me all the affurances I can require, if the petition fhould be prefented.

Extract of a Letter from Major General Gage to Mr. Secretary Conway. [Received August 25.]
New-York, July 15, 1766.

In my letter of the 24th of June, I had the honor to acquaint you that his Majefty's twenty-eight regiment, under the command of Major Browne, had been ordered into Dutcheffe county in this province, to affift the civil officers in putting the laws in execution, and to quell fome dangerous riots. A fmall body of the light infantry company was fired upon by the rioters, and three of them wounded: they returned the fire, wounded fome, purfued and difperfed the reft, notwithftanding their numbers. The difturbances had fpread into the county of Albany, where a fkirmifh happened between the fheriff, with about two hundred followers, and a party of the rioters. Some few were killed and wounded on both fides, but the fheriff and his people were put to flight. A great many prifoners have been taken or delivered themfelves up, and among them are feveral principals. After reftoring tranquility to the country, the regiment came to this place, leaving

leaving a captain and fifty men to guard the gaols, and brought with them the principal ringleaders of the whole confederacy. The magiſtrates commend the regiment greatly, as well for their ſpirit and readineſs in apprehending the rioters, as for their ſtrictneſs of diſcipline, not having taken the leaſt thing during their ſtay in the country, and even refuſing to plunder the houſes of ſome of the proclaimed rioters, though deſired to do it.

The aſſembly of this province has paſſed a law to provide quarters, bedding, fuel and utenſils, for two regiments and one company of artillery. There is now in this place the 28th and 46th regiments, the latter very weak, from ſome infirm and old men diſcharged, and a great number of ſoldiers whoſe times of ſervice were expiring; and the 28th regiment will alſo be ſoon very much reduced in their numbers for the ſame reaſons. Recruiting parties have been ſent home from the 46th regiment, to endeavour to compleat them; two companies of the royal regiment of artillery are incamped at the magazines, about four miles from the city, where they have a field train drawn out, and the men kept in conſtant practice in the exerciſe of the guns.

Governor Ward to Mr. Secretary Conway.

[*Received Auguſt* 26.]
Newport, Rhode-Iſland,
SIR,   *June* 25, 1766.

Having the honor of your Excellency's letter of the 31ſt of March laſt, incloſing a copy of the act of parliament, repealing the act of laſt ſeſſion for granting certain ſtampduties in America, &c. I laid it, with the incloſed copies, before the general aſſembly, at their ſeſſion on the 9th inſtant.

Upon this moſt happy occaſion, the general aſſembly, with hearts deeply impreſſed with   affection, loy-

alty and gratitude, unanimouſly reſolved upon the incloſed humble addreſs of thanks to his Majeſty, in which I moſt ſincerely concurred, and I beg leave to requeſt your Excellency to do the colony the honor to preſent it to our moſt gracious ſovereign.

Your Excellency is alſo pleaſed to inform us, that a reviſion of the American trade laws is going to be the immediate object of parliament, and that every relief which the ſtate of our circumſtances demands, or admits, will be afforded us. This freſh inſtance of the kind, and indulgent diſpoſition of the Britiſh legiſlature, is univerſally acknowledged with the moſt ſincere and reſpectful gratitude. And as nothing is more certain, than that the profits of the trade of the colonies will ultimately center in Great-Britain, I have no doubt but ſuch regulations will have the moſt happy effect upon the commerce and manufactures of the mother country.

The wiſe, upright, and benevolent meaſures of the legiſlature, in the preſent ſeſſion, have ſuppreſſed every appearance of murmuring and diſſatisfaction, and diffuſed joy, tranquility and happineſs throughout the colonies, and I can aſſure your Excellency, that the moſt dutiful, affectionate and grateful returns will be made by them, and that they are ſo firmly attached to their ſovereign and to the Britiſh conſtitution, and are ſo truly ſenſible of the parental goodneſs of the mother-country, that ſhe may rely upon every poſſible convenience and advantage from them, and I cannot but promiſe myſelf, that ſuch meaſures will continue to be purſued, as will ſo entirely conciliate the affections both of his Majeſty's European and American ſubjects, that the only future contention between them will be, which ſhall moſt effectually promote his Majeſty's ſervice, and the intereſts of all his widely extended dominions.

In

In your Excellency's letter, the making compensation to such persons as have suffered in this colony from the madness of the people, is warmly recommended, upon which I can at present only say, that if any application of that kind should be made to the assembly, I doubt not but they will take it into serious consideration, and that your Excellency may be assured of my utmost attention effectually to secure such persons from any future insult; and, that as far as my example and influence may extend, they shall receive all proper respect and regard.

Before I conclude, I must beg leave to congratulate your Excellency upon the happy success of his Majesty's councils. The nation has been often blessed with a wise and upright administration, but to relieve several millions of his Majesty's faithful subjects, plunged in the deepest anxiety, distress and confusion, and to restore them to their former tranquility, security and happiness, was an honor reserved for the present ministry. I have the honor to be, &c.

To the Right Hon. SAMUEL WARD.
H. S. Conway.

Extract of a Letter from Governor Bernard to Mr. Secretary Conway.
[*Received September* 3.]
Boston, July 19, 1766.

In my letter of June 29, I informed your honor that I would give you an exact detail of the proceedings of the house of representatives, upon the indemnification of the sufferers by the riots at Boston, setting it in one view and in a true light. For this purpose I have caused all the proceedings of the governor, council, and house of representatives to be printed together, and I have added annotations of my own upon particular passages, which will be more easily made use of than if they were dispersed in a long letter. I must desire that I may have special instructions how to conduct myself in

the further prosecution of this affair, especially if it should be thought proper to call the assembly again to move this business unto them. In the mean time, if there should be any opening for me to expect that the house will act in a different manner, I shall not fail to avail myself of it.

Copy of the Proceedings of the Governor, Council, and House of Representatives of Massachusett's Bay, on the Indemnification of the Sufferers by the Rioters in Boston, from March 31, to June 28, 1766, in Governor Bernard's Letter of July 19, 1766.
March 31, 1766.

A few days after the meeting of a a new assembly in May, 1766, his Excellency received a letter from Mr. Secretary Conway, dated St. James's, March 31, 1766, wherein he writes as follows:

" Nothing will tend more effectually to every conciliating purpose, and there is nothing therefore I have in command more earnestly to require of you, than that you should exert yourself in recommending it strongly to the assembly, that full and ample compensation be made to those who from the madness of the people, have suffered for their deference to acts of the British legislature. And you will be particularly attentive, that such persons be effectually secured from any further insult, and that as far as in you lies, you will take care, by your example and influence, that they may be treated with that respect to their persons, and that justice in regard to all their pretensions, which their merits and sufferings undoubtedly claim.

" The resolutions of the House of Commons, which by his Majesty's command I transmit to you, to lay before the assembly, will shew you the sense of that house on those points, and I am persuaded it will, as it most certainly ought, be the glory of that assembly to adopt and imitate those sentiments of the British parliament,
founded

founded on the cleareſt principles of humanity and juſtice."

The reſolutions of the Houſe of Commons relating to this buſineſs, are as follows:

Reſolved, That it is the opinion of this committee, that ſuch perſons who on account of the deſire which they have manifeſted, to comply with, or to aſſiſt in carrying into execution any acts of the legiſlature of Great-Britain relating to the Britiſh colonies in North-America, have ſuffered any injury or damage, ought to have full compenſation made to them for the ſame, by the reſpective colonies in which ſuch injuries or damages were ſuſtained.

Reſolved, That an humble addreſs be preſented to his Majeſty, humbly to deſire, that his Majeſty will be graciouſly pleaſed to give directions that the ſaid reſolutions be tranſmitted to the Governors of his Majeſty's colonies and plantations in America, to be by them communicated to the aſſemblies of their reſpective governments.

On the 3d of June his Excellency made a ſpeech to the two houſes upon the ſubject matter of Mr. Secretary Conway's letter, and having communicated to them the ſaid letter, together with the reſolutions of the Houſe of Commons, he obſerves therefrom as follows: viz

" I am alſo ordered to recommend to you, that full and ample compenſation be made to the late ſufferers by the madneſs of the people, and for that purpoſe I am directed to lay before you the votes of the Houſe of Commons, expreſſing their ſenſe upon that ſubject, whoſe humanity and juſtice it is hoped it will be your glory to imitate.

Gentlemen of the Houſe of Repreſentatives.

" The requiſition contained in this letter is of a moſt ſingular nature, and the only one of the kind that I have known ſince I have ſerved his Ma-

jeſty in America. It is founded upon a reſolution of the Houſe of Commons, formed after a full conſideration of the matter, and repreſented to his Majeſty by the addreſs of that houſe. The juſtice and humanity of this requiſition is ſo forceable, that it cannot be controverted; the authority with which it is introduced, ſhould preclude all diſputation about complying with it. I hope, therefore, you will add to the merit of your compliance, by the readineſs of it, and aſſume to yourſelves the honor which now offers itſelf, of ſetting the firſt example of gratitude and dutiful affection to the King and parliament, by giving thoſe proofs of it which are now pointed out to you. I muſt obſerve, that it is from the provincial aſſembly, that the King and parliament expect this compenſation ſhould be made to the ſufferers, without referring them to any other perſon whatſoever. Who ought finally to be charged with this expence may be a proper conſideration for you, and I ſhall readily concur with you in your reſolutions thereon, after the ſufferers have been fully ſatisfied."

The Houſe of Repreſentatives, in a meſſage, in anſwer to this ſpeech, ſay upon this head:

" The recommendation enjoined by Mr. Secretary Conway's letter, and in conſequence thereof made to us, we ſhall embrace the firſt convenient authority to conſider and act upon: In the mean time, cannot (A. *p.* 106.) *but obſerve, that it is conceived in much higher and ſtronger terms in the ſpeech than in the letter. Whether in thus exceeding, your Excellency ſpeaks by your own authority, or a higher, is not with us to determine. However, if this recommendation, which your Excellency terms a requiſition, be founded on ſo much juſtice and humanity, that it cannot be controverted. If the authority with which it is introduced ſhould preclude all diſputation about complying with*

it,

it, we should be glad to know what freedom we have in the case.

On the 25th of June, the House refuming the further confideration of this matter, fent the following meffage to the Governor:

May it pleafe your Excellency,

The Houfe of Reprefentatives have duly attended to that part of your Excellency's fpeech which had reference to a full and ample compenfation to be made to the fufferers in the late difturbances.

We are fenfibly affected with the lofs they have fuftained, and have the greateft abhorrence of the madnefs and barbarity of thofe perfons, who were the inftruments of their fufferings—Nothing fhall be omitted by us in our department to bring the perpetrators of fo horrid a fact to exemplary juftice, and if it be in their power, to a pecuniary reftitution of all damages.

But may it pleafe your Excellency, as a compliance with your Excellency's recommendation to the provincial affembly to make up thefe loffes, *appears to this houfe not as an act of juftice, but rather of generofity* (B. *p.* 106.); they are in doubt, whether they have any authority to make their conftituents chargeable with it, without their exprefs confent. The houfe, therefore, beg leave to acquaint your Excellency that they have thought it their duty to refer the confideration *of this matter to the next fitting of the general court,* (C. *p.* 107.) that the members may have the opportunity of taking the minds and inftruction of the feveral towns thereupon.

On the 27th of June the Governor fent the following meffage to the Houfe of Reprefentatives:

Gentlemen of the Houfe of Reprefentatives.

As your reafons for not complying at prefent with what has been recommended to you by order of the King with the advice of his parliament, on the behalf of the fufferers in the late difturbances, will probably be canvaffed with great precifion, it will be proper that the intendment of them fhould be as certain as may be. I fhould, therefore, be glad to know whether I muft underftand from your meffage of yefterday, that it is your opinion, that a detection of the perpetrators of the late mifchiefs is neceffary to intitle the fufferers to a compenfation for their loffes.

It appears to be the gracious intention of the King and parliament, that a veil fhould be caft over the late difturbances, provided it be covered by a general and uniform dutiful behaviour for the future; but it is certainly no lefs their firm and refolute purpofe, that the fufferers by thefe difturbances fhall have a full and ample indemnification made to them: And this bufinefs has been committed to you upon principles of humanity and juftice, rather than of meer generofity.

If you think that an inquiry into the promotion and perpetration of the late diforders, is a neceffary preliminary to determine from whence the charge of the compenfation fhall finally come, and fhall pronounce for the expediency of fuch an enquiry, you will certainly be affifted by the Governor and council in the profecution of it, and I dare fay it will be no difficult work to trace this matter to the bottom.

But in the mean time I fear the King and parliament will think their intimations difregarded, by your propofing an enquiry now, after it has been neglected for nine months paft; during all which time, the houfe have had this very bufinefs of indemnification under their confideration. They expect from you, that the fufferers fhall be indemnified at all events, whether the offenders are difcovered or not, or whether they are able to pay the damages or not, and feem to be more intent upon indemnification than punifhment.

P   I there-

I therefore wifh, for the fake of the province, whofe interefts, and efpecially thofe of its trade, are now in a very nice balance, and for the fake of this town, whofe refpectable inhabitants have already fuffered much in the opinion of the world, for having been tame fpectators of the violences committed in it, that you would remove this difgrace without the leaft delay, by ordering the indemnification immediately to be made upon the credit of thofe, whom you fhall hereafter judge to be chargeable with it— When this is done, there can be no objection to your poftponing the confideration on whom this money ought ultimately to be laid, to what time you pleafe, and there is no doubt but that any enquiry which you fhall think fit to make for this purpofe, will be as efficacious as you can defire.(D.*p*.107.)

Upon which the houfe the next day prefented to his Excellency the following addrefs :

May it pleafe your Excellency,

The houfe have duly attended to your Excellency's meffage of the 27th inftant. We are fully fenfible of the goodnefs of the King and parliament, and agree with your Excellency, that it appears to be their gracious intention that a veil fhould be drawn over the late difturbances, and we hope our behaviour will always be fuch as to merit their approbation. Sir, the houfe are ever attentive to the applications of perfons of every rank whofe cafe juftly claims their confideration : (E. *p.* 108.) *But as the fufferers, whom we apprehend your Excellency refers to, have never applied to this houfe (as we conceive) in a parliamentary way for relief, we are humbly of opinion, that we have done all at prefent that our moft gracious fovereign and his parliament can reafonably expect from us. But to fhew our regard to every thing recommended to the King and parliament, we have appointed a committee to fit in the recefs of the court, to make a thorough enquiry into the riots*

committed in the month of Auguft laft, and difcover the perfons concerned therein, as far as may be, for the effectuating which bufinefs, we doubt not but we fhall be aided by your Excellency and his Majefty's council.

And further, we would acquaint your Excellency, that the houfe have paffed a refolve to take the report of this committee under confideration at the beginning of the next feffions of this court, and act thereon what fhall appear to them to be juft and reafonable.

Your Excellency is pleafed to enforce the immediate compliance of the houfe with this requifition, by an argument drawn from a regard to the town of Bofton, the reputation of whofe inhabitants your Excellency fays, has already fuffered much, for having been tame fpectators of the violences committed, and that this difgrace would be removed thereby. We fee no reafon, why the reputation of that town fhould fuffer in the opinion of any one, from all the evidence that has fallen under the obfervation of the houfe ; nor does it appear to us, how a compliance would remove fuch difgrace, if that town had been fo unhappy as to have fallen under it.

———————

Governor Bernard's Obfervations on the Proceedings for the Indemnification of the Sufferers in the Riots at Bofton.— In his Letter of the 19th of July.

(A. *p.* 104.) He had been long ufed to term the commands of the King, requifitions, and they have been frequently fo called by the affembly, he therefore could not ufe a lower expreffion of a command of the King's, preceded by the advice of his parliament, therefore the Governor calls it a requifition of a fingular nature, and fays, that the authority of it ought to preclude all difputation.

(B. *p.* 105.) The difpute concerning the indemnification being an act of juftice, runs through the whole proceedings.

It

It has been before shewed, in support of the governors using that expression, how it is an act of justice, since that the House of Commons have declared that the sufferers *ought to have full compensation made to them*; terms very expressive of its being an act of justice; and the secretary of state, writing by the command of the King, pursuant to the address of the House of Commons, expressly says, that the sentiments of the parliament are founded *on the clearest principles of humanity and justice.* If the indemnification is to be considered as an act of justice, it ought to come from the town of Boston; if it is to be paid by the province at large, it will be an act of generosity, that is to the town of Boston, from whom it is in justice due. The people throughout the country, expect that it shall be paid by Boston only. The representatives of Boston have power enough to prevent its being charged upon Boston, but not power enough to engage the house to charge the province with it. And hence it is, that they are obliged to postpone this business, in hopes, some time or other, to prevail upon the house to charge this loss upon the province, and exempt the town of Boston from it, and so it is, that this business is put off to latter Lammas.

(C.*p.*105.) Between the foregoing message and the following answer to it, there passed a transaction which is proper to mention here. The house sent a message to the Governor verbally by a committee, to desire that he would acquaint the house with the informations he had received of the persons concerned in the riots at Boston; the Governor answered, that all his informations had been communicated by private conversations, and in such a manner, that he could not make a public use of them at present; that he had never entered into a formal enquiry, nor ever examined a single witness, although he had had offers made him of some who

would voluntarily submit to his examination, but that he declined it at first, because the government could not support itself in such a business, and since, because it appeared to him, that the King and parliament did not desire such an enquiry should be made; that he much doubted the propriety of such an enquiry, now having learnt enough to foresee, that it would go too deep and spread too wide. But if the house should determine for such an enquiry, and should be in earnest in the prosecution of it, he should think it the duty of the Governor and council to assist them in it, but he very much recommended it to the house, not to make the indemnification dependant upon, or subject to the result of the enquiry—If the house wants only to consult their constituents, they should fix upon a short day to return and desire the Governor to grant them an adjournment for that purpose, and time; but if they only postpone the consideration of it to next sessions, without giving any assurance of their intention to make an indemnification, or desiring a short day to determine upon it, it must be considered as a present refusal, and they must not expect that the Governor will move this business to them any more, without special orders for it.—This was reported to the house, and the deliberation turned upon the giving some assurance of their making an indemnification, when it was determined to avoid giving the least hint of a certain intention of making an indemnification.

(D.*p.*106.) This is quite new: to examine the force of this plea, it will be necessary to review the proceedings on this subject from the beginning.

On the day after the ruin of the Lieutenant Governor's house, or rather on the same day, the Lieutenant Governor represented the affair to the Governor in council, who thereupon appointed a committee to estimate the

P 2 damage;

damage; as his loss has been found to be above three-fourths of the whole, we may very well state the case upon his instance only. The Governor, by the advice of the council, summoned the assembly, and at the instance and on the behalf of the sufferers, recommended to the House of Representatives to make them a compensation. The house demurred upon it, but never once obj.cted to the sufferers applying through the governor's mediation, rather than immediately to the house (E. *p.* 106.). In the next session, which began the middle of January, nothing was done for indemnifying the sufferers, and not one word of objection for the sufferers not having applied to the house immediately, appears to have been urged by the house, though that session lasted near two months. In the mean time the parliament got hold of this matter, whether by petition of the sufferers, or on their own motion, *ex debito justitiæ,* does not appear. On the last day of May, being three days after the new assembly had met, the Governor received his orders from the secretary of state, and communicated them to the house on the 3d day of June. For three weeks after this matter was agitated, and there were three formal debates had upon it, and as many questions put: there were two several answers given to the governor, neither of which mentioned any objection arising from the sufferers not having petitioned the house, till after the Governor had sent his final message. This new difficulty is introduced on the last day of the session, nine months after the origination of this business, and above three weeks after it came recommended by his Majesty, at the desire of parliament, and upon the authority of this objection, the house declare that they have done all at present that the King and parliament can reasonably expect from them.

P. S. Since the writing the foregoing observations, a letter has been published in a Boston newspaper, wherein the writer endeavours to shew, that the Governor's urging the recommendation with too great authority, was the cause of its not being complied with—— Had they been disposed to have complied, they might have separated the resolutions of the House of Commons and the secretary of state's letter from the Governor's speech, and given him to understand, that it was the indulgence of the former, and not the authoritativeness of the latter, which induced them to comply with it. But the difficulty with which that business has hitherto laboured, and is ever like to labour, is, that the country thinks it most reasonable, that the charge should be borne by the town only, and the town is for flinging it upon the province in general.

Extract of a Letter from Major General Gage to the Duke of Richmond.
[*Received September 29.*]
New-York, August 25, 1766.

The first battalion of the 60th, or royal American regiment, was ordered to Quebec, to replace the 28th regiment, and the second battalion of the 60th, marched into the interior country to relieve the posts there. The 28th and 46th regiments staid in the province, and one of them destined in a little time for the province of New Jersey; but the riots in Duchess and Albany counties, occasioned their being detained in this province. The number proposed for this place, is to the amount of one regiment compleat, and a company of the royal regiment of artillery: But it is proper to acquaint your grace, that in my demand for quarters, it was necessary to manage matters so, that all the barracks here and at Albany, should be supplied with bedding and utensils, that the troops who shall march through this province, which is the route to and
from

from the province of Quebec, as well as to and from the Upper Lakes, may be hereafter comfortably lodged, instead of lying on bare boards, which they have frequently done.

Copy of a Letter from Governor Pitkin to Mr. Secretary Conway.

[*Received October* 3.]

Hartford, Connecticut, August 4, 1766.

SIR,

I have the honour of your's of the 31st of March last, directed to the Governor and company of the colony of Connecticut, in which I have the honour at present to preside, and shall take the earliest opportunity to communicate that and the several copies of acts of parliament therewith, transmitted to the general assembly of the colony.

It is impossible to express or describe the incredible joy with which the people of this country, in general, as well as of this colony in particular, received the most agreeable news of the repeal of the stamp-act, and which they have expressed by every token of gladness that they could exhibit. All America have been waiting in the most anxious suspence for the decision of this great and most interesting affair, have esteemed it the very crisis of their fate, and are now full of the warmest gratitude for the grace and goodness manifested to them. The magnanimity, moderation and condescension, the wisdom, justice, and equity so signally displayed by his Majesty and parliament, in repealing this act, have filled us with the sincerest joy, and the warmest sentiments of the most respectful gratitude to his Majesty and the parliament, and will, without doubt, confirm us in the strongest dispositions to a steady affectionate loyalty to the King, and the tenderest affection to our mother country. I am perfectly sensible of the indissoluble union that there is between Great-Britain and

her colonies respecting their interests, and that whatever prejudices the one must necessarily injure the other, and therefore earnestly hope, that no symptoms of coldness or dissatisfaction on any ground whatever, will now appear on the part of any of the colonies, which may tend to interrupt that harmony so essential to the happiness and future interests of both countries. That nothing of so disagreeable a nature appears in this colony, I can with great pleasure assure you—every thing here wears the face of decent joy and humble gratitude. Nothing could add more to the great satisfaction we feel for the indulgence already shewn to us, than the assurance you are pleased to give us, that the American Trade laws are become the immediate object of parliament, and that with equal magnanimity, clemency, and justice, they are determined to give to the trade and interests of America, every relief which our real circumstances demand or admit. This will be wisely to perfect the good work so happily begun, and to establish the union and interests of Great Britain and America upon a basis that can never be shaken. The regulations upon the importation of foreign molasses and sugars, &c. are particularly grievous to this colony, whose trade consists chiefly of articles fit only for the West-India market. These regulations have, in fact, been a principal means of our poverty and inability to discharge our debts with the American trader and the British merchant; have really, in a manner, stagnated all business among us, and compelled the people, as far as possible, to desist from the purchase and consumption of British manufactures. An alteration of the laws, in this particular, would therefore give us a most sensible relief in our present situation, and be received with the greatest gratitude and satisfaction.

I am

I am particularly happy in being able to acquaint you that no violences or outrages upon private property have been committed in this colony, for which any compensation can be expected or required.

By desire of the general assembly (who were together when the intelligence of the repeal just arrived, but are now enjoying a recess), I have signed and transmitted an humble address to his Majesty, to express the sincere joy and gratitude of this corporation upon this occasion, which I humbly hope his Majesty, of his paternal goodness and condescension, will be graciously pleased to accept; and the colony will be greatly obliged to you for giving it a regular and favourable introduction to the throne.

I have it also in charge to assure you, that the colony has the deepest sense of gratitude to you, and all other of his Majesty's ministers, for the great and good part you have taken in this most important affair: The remembrance of your wise and admirable conduct upon this occasion, and of your tenderness and concern for the colonies, will continue here to the latest posterity, and your names be blessed by millions in every generation. I have the honour to be, with the greatest esteem and respect, Sir, your most obedient and most humble servant,

(Signed) WILLIAM PITKIN,
*To the Right Hon. H. S. Conway,
one of his Majesty's Principal
Secretaries of State.*

---

*Copy of a Letter from Governor Grant
to Mr. Secretary Conway.*
[*Received October* 24, 1766.]
St. Augustine, East-Florida, August 21, 1766.

S I R,

I have had the honor to receive your letter of the 31st of March, with copies of two acts of parliament just passed; the first, for securing the just dependance of the colonies upon the mother country; the second, for the repeal of the act of last session, granting certain stamp-duties in America, and you are pleased to mention, that you expect shortly to send me a third for the indemnity of such persons as have incurred the penalties imposed by the act just repealed, as such a bill was then depending, and had made a considerable progress in the House of Commons.

Though there never was any disturbance in this province on account of the stamp-act, yet every inhabitant rejoices at the repeal of it, and all of them must have the warmest and most grateful sense of his Majesty's paternal care of his colonies, and of the lenity and indulgence of parliament, and will not, I dare say, be wanting in a dutiful and affectionate return to such peculiar proofs of indulgence and affection on the part of his Majesty and his parliament. I am, &c.

JAMES GRANT.

---

*Copy of a Letter from Governor Tryon
to the Right Hon. H. S. Conway.*
[*Received November* 4.]
Brunswick, North-Carolina, August 2, 1766.

S I R,

I had the honour of your letter of the 31st of March on the 13th of June: I got the council together the 28th of June, when I laid before them your letter, and the two acts of parliament inclosed: The one for securing the just dependency of the colony on the mother-country; the other for the repeal of the act, granting certain stamp-duties in America—as I had prorogued the general assembly to the 30th of next October before I had the honor of your dispatches, I consulted the council, if the service of his Majesty, or the circumstances of the country, required a more early meeting; they were unanimous in opinion, that considering the great heats of this season of the year, and the great scarcity of provifions in the country, moft of the members would be prevented from attending the affembly, if called earlier than it ftood prorogued, and thofe who did attend, muft fuffer great prejudice by their abfence from their plantations; and, as the country was in perfect tranquility, and the inhabitants returned to a chearful obedience to the laws, they did not fee his Majefty's fervice required a more early meeting of the affembly than the 30th of October.

I have the pleafure to inclofe you, Sir, the addrefs of the borough of Wilmington, on the fubject of the repeal of the ftamp-act, together with my anfwer; as alfo a letter fubfcribed by the mayor, and all the gentlemen of Wilmington, in confequence of my anfwer to their addrefs—my reply has wound up all jealoufies on both fides: I have reafon to believe, that the fenfe of thefe people are the fentiments of the whole province, and that we fhall meet at Newburn all in good humour. I am, &c.

WILLIAM TRYON.

――――――

Addrefs of the Borough of Wilmington to Governor Tryon. With his Anfwer. —In his Letter of Auguft 2, 1766.
North-Carolina,
To his Excellency William Tryon, Efq; Captain General, Governor, and Commander in Chief, in and over the Province of North-Carolina, &c.
The Addrefs of the Corporation of Wilmington.

SIR,

We, his Majefty's moft dutiful and loyal fubjects, the mayor, recorder, aldermen and freeholders of the borough of Wilmington, beg leave to congratulate your Excellency on the repeal of the American ftamp-act, and on the happy profpect of the union and harmony thereby eftablifhed between the colonies and their mothercountry.

Permit us alfo to exprefs our moft grateful acknowledgements to the fupreme legiflature of Great-Britain,

for their care and attention in protecting the inhabitants of his Majefty's extenfive American dominions in the enjoyment of that ineftimable blefling, Liberty, and at the fame time releafing them from a burthen they were unable to bear.

With hearts full of gratitude to the beft of Kings, we affure your Excellency, that we fhall be ready at all times to defend and protect his Majefty's perfon and government, and to evince our inviolable attachment to his illuftrious houfe, at the rifque of our lives and fortunes.

We cannot help exprefling our concern at the many reprefentations that have been made to your Excellency, of the tranfactions of the inhabitants of this borough, and feveral of the adjacent counties, fince the time of the ftamp-act taking place: Permit us to affure you, Sir, that it has ever been our conftant endeavour, as far as our influence extended, to promote the eafe and happinefs of your Excellency's adminiftration.

MOSES JOHN DE ROSSET, Mayor.
Borough of Wilmington, June 26, 1766.
His Excellency's Anfwer.
To the Mayor, Recorder, Aldermen, and Freeholders of the Borough of Wilmington.

Gentlemen,

It is with fatisfaction I receive your congratulations on the repeal of the act of parliament, granting certain ftamp-duties in America.

The grateful acknowledgments you exprefs to the fupreme legiflature of Great Britain, for their care and attention to the liberties of the inhabitants of his Majefty's American dominions, and alfo your affectionate and inviolable attachment to his Majefty's facred perfon, family, and government, as they are extremely grateful to me, I fhall, with a fenfible pleafure, tranfmit thofe warm fentiments of refpectful gratitude and duty to his Majefty's principal fecretary of ftate.

I truft

I truft that the moderation and unparalleled lenity fo remarkably manifefted by his Majefty and the parliament to the colonies, will difpofe the inhabitants to that chearful obedience to the legiflative authority of Great-Britain, on which their future profperity fo much depends ; fuch a conduct will prove the ftrongeft cement for the moft firm and happy union between the mother country and her colonies.

I profefs, gentlemen, I am at a lofs to anfwer that part of your addrefs, wherein you mention mifreprefentations having been made to me of the conduct of the inhabitants of the borough of Wilmington. I declare what impreffions I have conceived of them, arofe from a behaviour that came immediately under my own obfervation.

Brunfwick, June 26, 1766.

A true copy, taken from the original, this 2d of Auguft, 1766.

FOUNT. ELWIN, Priv. Sec.

Addrefs of the Mayor and Gentlemen of Wilmington to Governor Tryon. With his Anfwer.—In his Letter, Aug. 2.

May it pleafe your Excellency,

SIR,

It is with extreme concern we have obferved in your Excellency's letter to the addrefs of the corporation of Wilmington, expreffions which may be conftrued to charge that borough with fome marks of intentional difrefpect towards your Excellency—a conduct from the confcioufnefs of our hearts we can with the greateft juftice difclaim, and which, from a love of order and a regard to decency, we fhould fincerely condemn, not only as inconfiftent with that dutiful affection towards his Majefty's reprefentative, which we fhall always endeavour to cultivate, but with the grateful return of fentiment which your perfonal merit juftly claims.

If oppreffed by the late act, fome commotions of the country feemed to threaten a departure from moderation, your Excellency, we hope, will not impute thefe tranfactions to any other motive, than a conviction that moderation ceafes to be a virtue, when the liberty of Britifh fubjects is in danger ; but the greater the danger was, the more reafon we have to applaud the honor and juftice of the Britifh parliament, whofe prudent refolutions have relieved us from the melancholy dilemma to which we were almoft reduced.

From his Majefty, whofe heart ever rejoices in the happinefs of his people, we moft humbly and thankfully receive this mark of attention to the diftreffes of his American fubjects, and fhall always return his royal protection and regard, with all the affection and obedience of the moft loyal fubjects of a free kingdom, joined to that filial duty and conftitutional connection on which our future happinefs and exiftence entirely depends.

Amidft the variety of difagreeable events which the late commotions occafioned, we have with great indignation obferved, in the Barbadoes Gazette of the 19th of April, a paragraph as void of decency as it is of truth, well affured, that your Excellency's conduct has been always regulated by no other motive than a generous concern for the public good, and that duty which you, Sir, and we all owe to a fovereign ever intent on the welfare of his people, fupported by an ardent defire to promote the particular happinefs of a province committed to your charge. We are, &c. (Signed by nineteen perfons.)

July 28, 1766.

Brunfwick, Auguft 2, 1766.

Gentlemen,

As your letter of the 28th of laft month has removed thofe afperfions I felt you had laid on my character in your addrefs to me on the 26th of June, I am now willing to forget every impropriety of conduct any of the fubfcribers, and the town of Wilmington, have fhewn perfonally towards me in the late commotions. I thank you, gentlemen, for the teftimony

mony you give me of your approbation of my general conduct, but my acknowledgements are more expressly due for the justice you do me in such part of my conduct as has been traduced by the Barbadoes Gazette of the 19th of April last. I am, &c.

WILLIAM TRYON.

To Moses John De Rosset, Esq; Mayor, and the Gentlemen of the Borough of Wilmington.

Copy of a Letter from Horatio Sharpe, Esq; Deputy Governor of Maryland, to Mr. Secretary Conway.
[*Received November 7.*]
Annapolis, June 27, 1766.

SIR,

Having lately had the satisfaction to receive the letter you was pleased to favour me with the 31st of March last, inclosing copies of the two acts of parliament which had then passed; one for securing the just dependency of the colonies on the mother country; the other for the repeal of the act, granting certain stamp-duties in America, I now do myself the honour to acknowledge my receipt thereof, and also of the copy therewith transmitted of the resolutions of the House of Commons, which, together with your letter, I shall lay before the assembly of this province as soon as they meet, which, however, cannot be before the end of the summer. As soon as copies of the two above-mentioned acts of parliament came to my hands, I caused them to be published, and had the satisfaction to hear and see that the inhabitants of this province in general were affected with a proper sense of the moderation, forbearance and lenity of the British parliament, lately manifested with respect to the colonies; and I flatter myself they are already disposed to pay the most chearful obedience to the legislative authority of Great-Britain, and all the laws now existing. Tranquility and good order is now perfectly restored here, and the late distractions will, I

hope, soon be forgotten; the resentment some time ago expressed against the person that was appointed to distribute the stampt paper here, is intirely subsided, and he now resides and carries on business in this place to as great extent and advantage as he did before his appointment. Such a sudden alteration in the face of things, and in the behaviour of the people, encourages me to hope, that there is an end to all uneasiness, discontent and murmurings, and am inclined to think his Majesty's subjects within this province, will, for the future, be more studious than ever, to demonstrate to our most gracious sovereign their loyalty, duty and gratitude, and to the mother-country their thankfulness and affection. You may, Sir, be assured, that no endeavour of mine shall be wanting to instill and encourage such sentiments, and to effectuate what you are pleased to recommend. I am, &c.

HORATIO SHARPE.

Governor Bernard's Letter to the Earl of Shelburne.
[*Received December 29.*]
Boston, November 14, 1766.
My Lord,

By my letter, dated July 19, I informed your lordship, that if there should be any opening for me to expect that the house would act in the business of the compensation, in a different manner from what they had done, I should not fail to avail myself of it. I am, therefore, now to inform your lordship of the second trial I have made for getting this business done, with the event of it, and, in order to explain these proceedings more fully, I must beg leave to delineate to your lordship the real difficulties which have prevented this business being done, as they appear very little in the journal of the house, and pains have been taken that they should not appear, although they are

notorious

notorious to every perſon in the province who thinks upon the ſubjeɛt.

The riotous proceedings at Boſton were generally abhorred by the beſt men in the province, and by much the greater part of the common people, and therefore when a compenſation to the ſufferers was firſt talked of, it was the general opinion that it ought to be made, but that it was due from the town of Boſton only, and not from the province in general. This opinion was very prevalent when Mr. Secretary Conway's letter, dated 31ſt of March arrived here on the laſt day of May; and this was the reaſon why the members for Boſton, contrary to the real intereſt of the town, determined to oppoſe the making a compenſation even out of the treaſury. In which way, if they had at that time with their party joined the friends of government, it might have been done — But they wree apprehenſive that if the money was ordered to be paid out of the treaſury, it would be then moved that it ſhould be charged upon the town of Boſton, which, as the tax-bill was to be paſſed at that time, might have been done with the daſh of a pen — They therefore reſolving to oppoſe the granting the compenſation that ſeſſion, turned the whole buſineſs into evaſions and ſubterfuges, to give pretended reaſons for not complying, their and to conceal the true one. — The reaſons given, were, firſt, that it was a buſineſs of too much importance to tranſaɛt without conſulting their conſtituents; ſecondly, that the ſufferers had not applied to them in a parliamentary way, that is, by petitioning the houſe.

It was not long before they received repeated advices, that the general opinion in England was, that the honor of parliament was engaged to ſee the compenſation made, and they would certainly take it up where the provincial aſſembly refuſed it. And it was very obvious, that the parliament might inforce the payment of a ſum of money from a ſea-port town, or from a maritime province, without infringing any rule of right laid down by the moſt ſanguine advocate for the colonies, or even claimed by themſelves in form. The people of Boſton therefore began to be uneaſy, that this money was not paid — a town meeting was called, and inſtruɛtions were given to their members, to uſe their utmoſt endeavours to get the money paid out of the treaſury. This was a ſignal for me to call the aſſembly, which I had kept prorogued by ſhort intervals, in order to take hold of the firſt fair opportunity that offered, and I accordingly gave notice that the aſſembly would meet at the time it was then prorogued to.

In the mean time, one of the pretences which had been made uſe of the laſt ſeſſion, to excuſe the granting the compenſation, had an effeɛt contrary to what was expeɛted, or at leaſt not foreſeen. As the neceſſity of conſulting their conſtituents had been made the pretence for poſtponing the buſineſs, the members in general found themſelves obliged aɛtually to conſult their conſtituents in form, which they would not have done otherwiſe. This produced a number of inſtruɛtions againſt paying the money out of the treaſury, which prevailed very much among the repreſentatives of towns, diſtinguiſhed for their attachment to government, many of which were ſo poſitive againſt paying the money out of the treaſury, that many members ſtaid away to avoid appearing againſt government, and others were obliged to come fettered with inſtruɛtions to aɛt againſt it. Among theſe people, the general reaſoning was, that as it was notorious that the diſturbances aroſe entirely within the town of Boſton, it was not only unjuſt that the whole province ſhould be charged with the damages done by them, but if they were to conſent to the payment out of the treaſury, they ſhould thereby acknowledge

ledge themselves to be partakers of proceedings, of which they had always expressed their detestation and abhorrence. This was urged particularly at the meeting at Salem, the second town in the province, and always noted for its attachment to government, which, however, its members were not allowed to support upon this occasion only.

Upon the meeting of the assembly, I determined to say nothing that could possibly be perverted, and in general to avoid interfering with the house in any manner : I accordingly made the speech which I herewith inclose, in full confidence that it could not receive a rude answer. I was soon informed, that a majority of the house had instructions against granting the compensation out of the treasury, the only method that could be proposed with any prospect of success. The grant was strongly urged by the members for Boston, in which they were supported by some of the ablest friends of government, and opposed by only one man of ability, who in that instance seemed to be infatuated. The argument was entirely on the side of the compensation, and was much assisted by the examination of some gentlemen from England, to shew the assurances which had been given by the friends of the colonies, that this compensation would be chearfully made, and the almost certain probability that the parliament would not acquiesce in the refusal of it, but the bad weight of the instructions could not be got over, although there was a general conviction throughout the house, that the compensation ought to be made. I must again repeat, that the Boston members exerted themselves for the question in this session, as much as they did against it in the last, but they were defeated by their former machinations, otherwise I believe it would have been carried without a division.

After a litigation of a fortnight, in which the question was put in different forms two or three several times, and lost by no great majority, this expedient was hit upon : That they should bring in a bill for compensating the sufferers, in which the sums should be ascertained (the misreport of which was supposed to have hurt the cause), and also for indemnifying the rioters, and that the bill should be printed for the consideration of the constituents, and the governor should be desired to grant a recess for that purpose — This passed with little or no opposition, and a bill was accordingly brought in and printed, and a message was sent to me accordingly — Two hours after this I received your lordship's letter : I immediately communicated it to both houses, and gave the house of representatives time to consider of it, which was only spent in fruitless altercations, without any attempt to resume the business : I therefore adjourned the general court for three weeks, being the earliest day I could appoint. — I inclose copies of the message to me, and my speech upon the adjournment.

After the adjournment had passed, and before I had left the chair, it was observed in the council, that the house had not ordered your lordship's letter to be printed, as it is usual to do in cases where such publication is like to facilitate the business recommended. It was therefore moved, that the governor be desired to order the letter to be printed, as it would tend very much to conciliate the minds of the people to the compensation, and to remove the ill-humour prevailing among them. This having the unanimous voice of the council, I assented to, being fully of the same opinion. I must beg your lordship will let the occasion apologize for my taking this liberty, if there should be an impropriety in it, which at present I do not see, as these kind of publications are not uncommon in this government. I am, &c.

FRANCIS BERNARD.

Q 2

The

The Speech of the Governor of Massa-chusett's Bay, October 29, 1766—The Answer of the House, Nov. 12—The Speech of the Governor, Nov. 13—In his Letter of the 14th of November, 1766.

His Excellency's Speech to both Houses of Assembly at the opening of the Session.

Gentlemen of the Council, and Gentlemen of the House of Representatives.

I have thought proper to call you together, that you may have an opportunity to give a positive answer to what I recommended to you by order of his Majesty last session, as it will be expected of me that it will be reported to his Majesty before the opening of the business of the next year, and I heartily wish that it may be such as will answer the expectations and desires of your friends in Great-Britain. For my own part, I shall, upon this occasion, as upon all others, make the best use of the means you shall put in my hands, to promote the honor and reputation of the province.

As you are called together for this business only, when it is finished, I shall have no objection to your returning home, until the usual time of opening the winter session.

Council-Chamber. FR. BERNARD.

The following is an answer of the Honourable House of Representatives to his Excellency the Governor's speech at the opening of the session.

May it please your Excellency,

Your speech to both houses at the opening of the present session, has been repeatedly under the most deliberate consideration of the house of representatives.

It was indeed, Sir, with great reluctance, that the house found themselves under the necessity of having recourse to your former speech and message upon this occasion, but as you are pleased to refer us to them, without saying any thing to qualify them, the house cannot help observing, that the manner in which your Excellency has repeatedly proposed a compensation to the sufferers, has been derogatory to the honor of the house, and in breach of the privileges thereof:—that the terms you have made use of, have been essentially different from those dictated to you by his Majesty's express command, signified in a letter from his secretary of state—that they tended to weaken the inherent uncontroulable right of the people to dispose of their own money to such purposes as they shall judge expedient, and to no other: and that under these apprehensions, it is not improbable some of the towns may have framed their instructions to their representatives against a compensation out of the public treasury.

The house, however, with the most dutiful and profound respect, have attended to his Majesty's most gracious and mild recommendation, and observe, that it is his pious and benevolent intention, that not only a compensation should be made to the sufferers in the late times, but also that a veil be drawn over every disgraceful scene, and to forgive, and even to forget the undutiful behaviour of any of his subjects in those unhappy times.

Confirmed in the opinion that an indemnification of the offenders is of equal importance and necessity with the making compensation to the sufferers, and being ever ready with the utmost chearfulness, to unite their endeavours, in promoting the wise and most gracious purposes of their rightful sovereign, in conformity to the spirit of Mr. Secretary Conway's letter, the house have framed a bill, intitled, "An Act for granting Compensation to the Sufferers, and general Pardon, Indemnity and Oblivion, to the Offenders in the late Times."

This bill they have ordered to be published for the consideration of the several towns, and humbly pray your Excellency

Excellency would pleafe to give them a recefs for that purpofe.

His Excellency the Governor's fpeech at the adjournment of the court, *Nov.* 13, 1766
Gentlemen of the Houfe of Repre-fentatives.

In the letter of the Errl of Shelburne, which I laid before you, you have a fecond teftimony from another of his Majefty's fecretaries of ftate, of the tendernefs and affection towards the people under my government, with which I have conducted myfelf during the late difputes, and therefore, I fhall make no other anfwer to the ungenerous infinuations in your meffage of yefterday, than by referring to your own journals, from whence it will evidently appear, that it is from among yourfelves, and not from me, that the difficulties which have prevented your making a compenfation to the fufferers have arofe.

I am very forry that you have not already complied with what has been recommended to you, but it is fome fatisfaction to me, that you have laid a foundation for compleating this bufinefs, which I hope will not fail of fuccefs. The importance of the affair, and the hafty approach of the new year, will not allow the lofs of a day which can be faved, and therefore I fhall make the recefs which you defire as fhort as poffible; and that you may do the bufinefs with as much credit to yourfelves as may be, I fhall continue the feffion until you can come to a final determination.
Council-Chamber. FRAS. BERNARD.

———

Copy of a Bill for granting Compenfation to the Sufferers, &c.—In Governor Bernard's of the 14th of November, 1766.
The following bill now depending in the Houfe of Reprefentatives, is publifhed by their orders, for the confideration of the feveral towns in this province.

A bill intitled, " An Act for granting Compenfation to the Sufferers, and of free and general Pardon, Indemnity and Oblivion to the Offenders in the late Times."

Whereas the King's moft Excellent Majefty taking into his gracious and ferious confideration, the troubles, difcords, infurrections, tumults, and riots which have lately happened in America, and that divers of his fubjects have thereby fuffered greatly in their property, and others by occafion thereof, and otherwife, have fallen into, and are obnoxious to great pains and penalties, out of a hearty and pious defire that fuch fufferers be compenfated, and to put an end to all fuits, controverfies and profecutions, that by occafion of the late diftractions have arifen, or may arife between any of his Majefty's fubjects, and to the intent that a veil be drawn over the late unhappy exceffes, has been pleafed gracioufly to fignify his defire to forgive and forget them, at the fame time of his abundant clemency, recommending a compenfation to the fufferers in their property, with fuch a conduct in general, as fhall be at this great crifis the beft means of fixing the mutual intereft and inclination of Great Britain and her colonies, on the moft firm and folid foundation.

From a grateful fenfe of his Majefty's grace and clemency, in order to promote internal peace and fafety, to make compenfation to the faid fufferers, and as a means, fo far as in our power, of demonftrating to all the world, our fenfe of the happinefs we enjoy, in being a part of the Britifh empire, and intitled to the rights, liberties, and privileges of Britifh fubjects, we his Majefty's moft dutiful and loyal fubjects, the reprefentatives of the commons in this province, in the great and general court affembled, of our free and good will, have refolved to give and grant, and pray that it be enacted.

And

And be it accordingly enacted, by the Governor, council, and house of representatives, that there be granted and paid out of the public treasury of this province, to the Hon. Thomas Hutchinson, Esq; the sum of £.3194 17s. 6d.

To the Hon. Andrew Oliver, Esq; the sum of £.172 4s.

To Benjamin Hallowell, jun. Esq; the sum of £.385 6s. 10d.

To William Story, Esq; the sum of £.67 8s. 10d. in full compensation for their losses and sufferings in the late times of confusion.

And be it further enacted, that all riots and unlawful assemblies, councelled, commanded, acted, done, or made within this province between the 1st day of August, 1765, and the 1st day of May, 1766, and all burglaries, felonies, and breaches of the peace whatsoever, committed in, by, or during such riots, routs, and unlawful assemblies, be, and hereby are pardoned, released, indemnified, discharged, and put in utter oblivion, and that all and every the person or persons, acting, advising, assisting, abetting and counselling, the same be, and are hereby pardoned, released, acquitted, indemnified and discharged from the same, and of, and from all pains of death, and other pains, judgments, indictments, convictions, penalties and forfeitures, theretofore had or given, or that might accrue for the same, and that all such indictments, convictions and forfeitures, are hereby declared null and void.

And be it further enacted, that any person indicted or presented, or in any manner prosecuted, or that shall or may be hereafter indicted, presented, or in any manner prosecuted, for any of the offences by this act pardoned, may plead the general issue, and give this act in evidence, which shall be sufficient to acquit him.

Provided that nothing in this act contained, shall extend to the pardoning, or give any benefit whatever to any person who is, or may be unlawfully possessed of any goods or chattels, taken or stolen from any person, unless the possessor shall, within thirty days after the publication of this act, have surrendered and delivered them up to the owner.

Provided also, that nothing in this act shall extend to the barring any civil action of trespass for damages sustained by any person, not compensated by this act.

Extract of a Letter from Governor Ward to the Earl of Shelburne
[*Received January* 21, 1767.]
Newport, Rhode-Island, Nov. 6, 1766.

The military stores and provisions furnished by the colonies in the year 1756 for the provincial troops, were by directions from the Earl of Loudon, commander in chief of his Majesty's forces in North-America, taken into the King's magazines, and the colonies were, on the behalf of the crown, promised payment for them. The other colonies, upon presenting their accounts, received the money accordingly; but this colony unhappily neglecting to transmit their accounts (amounting to £.4211 19s. 7d.) in season, an objection arose when they were presented, to the payment of them, and they were referred to the then secretary at war and pay-master general, who proposed a deduction of £.1209 14s. -- Thus the matter rested for several years, when the agent for this colony was introduced to renew his application for payment of those accounts; upon which, they were again referred to the secretary at war and the pay-master in general, who after some further deduction, reported " that there was due and payable to the colony, £.2672 18s. 11d." which sum the colony expected the agent would soon have received, but in his last letter he informs me, that upon application for the money, he received a positive answer from the lords of the treasury, " That as a requisition was

was gone from the crown to the colony, the treasury-board thought fit to suspend the payment of the money, until an answer came from the colony relating to that requisition." The general assembly, upon receipt of this letter, requested me to lay the matter before his Majesty's principal secretary of state for this department, and I have accordingly given your lordship this short account of the affair.

I beg leave to observe to your lordship, that this colony really paid the whole sum charged for the several articles in their accounts, so that if the sum reported to be due be paid, they will suffer an actual loss of upwards of 1500 pounds, besides the damage they have sustained, by being kept out of the money ten years—interest for which, they have paid ever since at the rate of ten *per cent. per annum.*

This colony, my lord, surrounded on all sides by the Massachuset's-Bay, Connecticut, and the sea, and not exposed to the attacks of the enemy upon this continent, were animated solely by a zeal for his Majesty's service, and the honour and dignity of his crown, to exert themselves in the common cause of Britain and America, in such a manner as to merit and receive the approbation of his Majesty's Ministers and Generals, and so far beyond their ability, that they are now actually involved in a most heavy debt, for which, by reason of the scarcity of money, they have been, and for years to come, will be obliged to pay a very high interest. From these considerations, the detention of the balance reported to be due, occasions great uneasiness, and is considered as a peculiar hardship by his Majesty's loyal subjects in this colony—The more especially, as all the other colonies have long since received the monies due to them upon the same account.

I must also beg leave to submit to your lordship, whether this suspension of payment may not be considered

rather as a mode of compelling the colony to grant monies to the persons who have suffered, than as a recommendation of the sufferers, whether it will not have a manifest tendency to discourage the colonies from exerting themselves in the same vigorous manner for his Majesty's service for the future, and whether, considering his Majesty's inviolable and tender regard for the rights and privileges of all his subjects, a measure so coercive can be supposed agreeable to his royal intentions.

I am also, at the request of the general assembly, to assure your lordship, that the opinion that the rioters in this colony were countenanced in their depredations by any person of note or consequence, is so far as the members of the assembly have any knowledge or information thereof, entirely groundless, and that when the sufferers shall make a proper application to the assembly, they will consider the same, and do them all the justice the nature of their cases shall require.

Extract of a Letter from Sir Henry Moore to the Earl of Shelburne.
[*Received February 4,* 1767.]
New-York, Dec. 19, 1766.
" The letter which I had the honour of receiving from your lordship, dated the 9th of August, was laid before the house of assembly the 17th of last month, accompanied by a message.
" Yesterday the inclosed address was presented to me in answer to my message."

Copy of Governor Sir Henry Moore's Message to the General Assembly of New-York.—In his Letter of the 19th of December, 1766.
Nov. 17, 1766.
Gentlemen of the General Assembly,
In consequence of a report made to the Lords Commissioners for Trade and Plantations, of the act passed in the last sessions of assembly, for providing barracks,

barracks, fuel, &c. for his Majesty's troops quartered in this city, and my letter to the secretary of state on the same occasion, I have had the honour of the following letter from the Earl of Shelburne.

[Here follows his Lordship's Letter of the 9th of August, 1766—*sic p.* 92.]

I flatter myself, that on a due confideration of this letter, no difficulties can possibly arise, or the least objection be made to the provision for the troops, as required by the act of parliament,

Fort George,   H. MOORE.
Nov. 17, 1766.

Address of the General Assembly of New-York to Sir Henry Moore—In his Letter of December 19, 1766.

To his Excellency Sir Henry Moore, Bart. Captain-General and Governor in Chief, in and over the Colony of New-York, and the Territories depending thereon in America, Chancellor and Vice Admiral of the same.

The humble Address of the General Assembly of the said Colony.

May it please your Excellency,

We his Majesty's most dutiful and loyal subjects, the general assembly of the colony of New York, have taken your Excellency's message of the 17th of November last into our most serious consideration, and beg leave to assure your Excellency, that nothing would give us greater pleasure, than to find it in our power to comply with every requisition, tending in any manner to promote his Majesty's service—It is, therefore, with great concern, that we find it impossible to comply with what is now demanded, consistent with our obligations to our constituents. We shall always be ready to give the amplest testimony of our loyalty to his Majesty, and submission to his government, from which we humbly conceive we do not deviate, when we shew a regard to the interests of his faithful subjects in this colony, absolutely necessary for their preservation.

We hope it will be considered, that we are chosen to make such a provision for the support of his Majesty's government in this colony (as well as for other important purposes) as is most suitable to the circumstances of the people we represent, and that we should be guilty of a breach of that most sacred trust, if we should load them with burthens they are incapable of supporting.

In the provision we made last session for quartering two battalions and one company of artillery, we loaded ourselves with a burthen much greater than any of the neighbouring governments lie under for that service, and imagined, that far from being censured on that account, it would be accepted as a new instance of that loyalty and affection to his Majesty's government, of which this colony has exhibited so many proofs.

We beg leave further to represent to your Excellency, that by the act of parliament, it appears to be the intention of the legislature, to provide for the quartering soldiers only on a march:—But according to the construction put on it here, it is required that all the forces which shall at any time enter this colony, shall be quartered, during the whole year, in a very unusual and expensive manner—That by the marching several regiments into this colony, this expence would become ruinous and unsupportable, and therefore we cannot, consistent with our duty to our constituents, put it in the power of any person (whatsoever confidence we may have in his prudence and integrity) to lay such a burthen on them.

We should be very sorry to differ with your Excellency on this, or any other political subject, and therefore it is proper to offer these matters to your consideration, in hopes that they will be sufficient to demonstrate, that the objections against making the provision required, are of a nature the most

most serious and weighty imaginable, and therefore we humbly intreat your Excellency to set our conduct in the most favourable, that is, in its true light, by representing that our non-compliance on this occasion proceeds intirely from a just sense of what our duty requires. By order of the General Assembly.

Assembly-Chamber, W. NICOLL, Sp^r.
December 15, 1766.

Extract of a Letter from Governor Franklin to the Earl of Shelburne.
[*Received February* 4, 1767].
Burlington, New-Jersey,
December 18, 1766.

I should mention, however, that in the " act for supplying the several barracks erected in this colony, with furniture and other necessaries for accommodating the King's troops, in or marching through this colony," they have, instead of specifying the several articles required to be furnished by the act of parliament, empowered the barrack masters to provide " firewood, bedding, blankets, and such other necessaries, as have been heretofore usually furnished to the several barracks within this colony." I did all I could to prevail on them to insert the very words of the act of parliament, and to impower the barrack-masters to furnish, at the expence of the province, the same articles as were therein required :—But it was to no purpose ; they said they had always furnished every thing which was necessary that the officers and soldiers who had been quartered here, never complained, but, on the contrary, many of them acknowledged they were better accommodated here than they had ever been at barracks in Europe ; they added, that they looked upon the act of parliament for quartering soldiers in America, to be virtually as much an act for laying taxes on the inhabitants as the stamp-act, and that it was more partial, as the troops were kept in a few of the

colonies, whereby others were exempted from contributing any thing towards the expence. I was therefore obliged to take the act as it was tendered, or to let his Majesty's troops remain unprovided with necessaries—I have, however, the pleasure of finding the regiment stationed in this province perfectly satisfied with their quarters — No complaints whatever have been made to me, and I believe there are but few, if any articles of consequence, required by the act of parliament, but what they are furnished with here.

Copy of an Act passed in New-Jersey, appointing Commissioners for supplying the several Barracks erected in this Colony, with Furniture and other Necessaries for accommodating the King's Troops, in or marching through that Colony, &c.—In Gov. Franklin's Letter of the 18th of December, 1766.

" An Act, appointing Commissioners for supplying the several Barracks erected in this Colony, with Furniture and other Necessaries for accommodating the King's Troops, in or marching through this Colony, and for defraying other incidental Charges."

I. Whereas by an act of the legislature of this colony, passed in the fifth year of his present Majesty's reign, certain commissioners therein named, were impowered and required to sell all the perishable furniture belonging to the several barracks in this colony, and as it is requisite that the said barracks should be provided with blankets, beds, and other necessaries for the reception of the King's troops as may occasionally march through this colony ; Therefore

II. Be it enacted, by the Governor, Council, and General Assembly ; and it is hereby enacted by the authority of the same, that Daniel Ellis, Joseph Hollingshead, Abraham Hunt, Alexander Chambers, Hendrick Fisher,

R   Reuben

Reuben Runyon, Samuel Sarjant, Thomas Skinner, Robert Ogden, and John Blanchard, be, and they are hereby appointed commiſſioners for the ſeveral barracks in this colony, that is to ſay, Daniel Ellis and Joſeph Hollingſhead for the barracks at Burlington, Abraham Hunt and Alexander Chambers for the barracks at Irenton, Hendrick Fiſher and Reuben Runyon, for the barracks at New Brunſwick, Samuel Sarjant and Thomas Skinner, for the barracks at Perth Amboy, Robert Ogden and John Blanchard, for the barracks at Elizabeth Town.

III. And be it further enacted, by the authority aforeſaid, that it ſhall and may be lawful, for the ſaid commiſſioners, and the ſurvivors of them, at each reſpective place aforeſaid, for which they are appointed commiſſioners as aforeſaid, and they and the ſurvivors of them are hereby impowered to purchaſe firewood, bedding, blankets, and other neceſſaries, as have been heretofore uſually furniſhed to the ſeveral barracks within this colony, and it ſhall, and may be lawful for either of the treaſurers of this colony, to pay to the ſaid Daniel Ellis, Joſeph Hollingſhead, Abraham Hunt, Alexander Chambers, Hendrick Fiſher, Reuben Runyon, Samuel Sarjant, Thomas Skinner, Robert Ogden, and John Blanchard, or any two of them, ſuch ſums of money as may be wanted for the ſervice aforeſaid, not exceeding the ſum of one hundred pounds, for the uſe of each of the ſaid five barracks in this colony, out of the money made current for the ſervice of the late war, or now in the treaſury, and orders with a receipt thereon, or receipts ſigned by the aforeſaid commiſſioners, or any two of them, when produced by the ſaid treaſurers, or either of them, to the General Aſſembly, ſhall diſcharge the ſaid treaſurers reſpectively, their heirs, executors, and adminiſtrators, of, and

from ſo much as they ſhall have paid, by virtue of this act, and the ſaid commiſſioners, their heirs, executors, and adminiſtrators, are hereby made accountable to the General Aſſembly of this province, for all ſuch ſums of money as they ſhall reſpectively receive in purſuance of this act.

IV. And be it enacted, by the authority aforeſaid, that the commiſſioners aforeſaid, and the care of the ſeveral barracks within this colony, ſhall be under the ſame regulations as in, and by the aforeſaid recited act, is required and directed.

V. And whereas it is reaſonable that ſundry incidental charges of this colony ſhould be paid ; be it enacted, by the authority aforeſaid, that there be paid out of the public monies, now in the hands of the treaſurers of this colony, the ſums following ; viz.

To the Hon. John Stevens, Eſq; two pounds, ſeven ſhillings, and fourpence, for ſending an expreſs into this colony to inform the inhabitants of a large ſum of counterfeit Jerſey bills of credit, being arrived in a veſſel from England.

To the perſons who apprehended John Johnſon, John Fagan, and John Grimes, the ſum of thirty pounds, to be paid to Benjamin Davids and John Robins, and appropriated in manner following ; to wit : To Benjamin Davids, for his activity in taking and expences in carrying the felons to gaol, the ſum of ten pounds :—To John Robins, for his extraordinary activity, the ſum of ſix pounds—the remainder of ſaid thirty pounds to be paid to the other perſons concerned in ſearching for, and ſecuring the ſaid felons, in ſuch proportion as the ſaid Benjamin Davids and John Robins ſhall adjudge the ſame.

To Cortland Skinner, Eſq; two pounds, ten ſhillings, for an expreſs to New-York during the ſitting of this ſeſſion.

To John Allen, late barrack-maſter at Irenton, in full of his account,

thirty-

thirty-nine pounds, seventeen shillings, and nine-pence.

All which said several sums last mentioned, shall be paid to the several persons by the treasurers of this colony, or either of them, on warrants to be produced to them, or either of them, signed by the Governor, or commander in chief for the time being, in council, and the warrants so signed, with indorsements thereon, made by the persons to whom the same shall respectively be made payable, shall be sufficient vouchers to discharge them the said treasurers, or either of them, and their, or either of their heirs, executors, and administrators, of, and from so much of the said money.

June 25, 1766.

This bill having been three times read in the House of Representatives, Resolved that the same do pass. By order of the house.

CORTLAND SKINNER, Sp^r.

Council-Chamber, June 26, 1766.

This bill having been three times read in council,—Resolved that the same do pass. By order of the house.

PETER KEMBLE, Sp^r.

Perth Amboy, June 28, 1766.

I assent to this bill, enacting the same, and order it to be inrolled.

WILLIAM FRANKLIN.

Extract of a Letter from Governor Bernard to the Earl of Shelburne.
[*Received February 9, 1767.*]
Boston, December 6, 1766.

I have the honour to inform your lordship, that the act for making a compensation to the sufferers by the late riots, passed the two houses, and received my consent this day, being the fourth from their meeting, after the adjournment. The act has received very little alteration from the bill which I sent to your lordship, with my letter of the 14th of November. It passed the House of Representatives by fifty-two against

thirty-five, and in the Council, fourteen to one.

The considerable majority in the house, and the almost unanimous voice of the Council, together with the dispatch with which it has been carried through both, will, I hope, in some degree, apologize for the delay and difficulty which this business has met with heretofore.

I should not have thought myself warranted in passing an act of indemnity in a common case, without some previous instruction or order for that purpose: But this act seems to me so conformable to his Majesty's gracious intention, as it has been signified to me by your lordship, and Mr. Secretary Conway, that I think I can't have mistaken my duty, in what I have now done. However, if I have, the confirmation of the act is still in his Majesty's hands.

Copy of a Letter from Deputy Governor Sharpe to the Earl of Shelburne.
[*Received February 13, 1767.*]
Annapolis, Maryland,
Dec. 9, 1766.

My Lord,

The two letters your lordship was pleased to write to me the 9th of August last, having lately come to my hands, I now do myself the honor to acknowledge my receipt thereof, and to assure your lordship, that whatever commands your lordship may at any time communicate to me, will be punctually obeyed. In a letter I took the liberty to address to Mr. Secretary Conway last July, in answer to his of the 31st of March, I promised to lay the same, together with the resolves of the House of Commons therein transmitted, before the assembly of this province at their first meeting, which I have since done, and have now the satisfaction to inform your lordship, that upon my recommending it to them to take the letter and resolves into consideration,

and

and chearfully to comply with his Majesty's requisition thereby signified, they immediately voted a compensation to the person whose house had been pulled down by the mob that assembled in the night of the 2d of September, 1765, and also to another person who had suffered a small loss at that time, with which compensation the sufferers are, I understand, entirely satisfied. I must also, in justice to the inhabitants of this province in general, assure your lordship, that since the repeal of the stamp-act was notified to them, they have not shewed the least signs of discontent, nor have murmurings been heard amongst them; but, as far as I can judge, their behaviour has manifested the highest satisfaction at the late measures of the British legislature, while their declarations have been expressive of unfeigned loyalty and gratitude to our gracious sovereign, and of the greatest attachment to the mother-country. I am, &c.

HORATIO SHARPE.

Extract of a Letter from Lieutenant-Governor Colden to the Earl of Shelburne.
[*Received February* 18, 1767.]
New-York, December 26, 1766.
" In my letter to Mr. Secretary Conway of the 24th of June, I informed him, that the assembly, in their session in June last, would not recompense me for the losses I sustained by the mob, the 1st of November last year. They have again, in their last sessions, refused payment, with this reason annexed, that I had brought them upon myself by my misconduct."

Extract of a Letter from Major General Gage to the Earl of Shelburne.—With Copy of an Inclosure therein.
[*Received February* 18, 1767.]
January 17, 1767.
" The packet had sailed with the December mail, before I got a sight of the address from the General Assembly of this province, to their Governor, upon the subject of your lordship's letter to him, concerning the quartering of his Majesty's troops, according to the full extent and meaning of the act of parliament made in that respect. Sir Henry Moore will have transmitted your lordship a copy of the said address, and I have the honour to inclose your lordship a return of the number of troops quartered in the inhabited parts of this province.

Lieutenant Colonel Prevost has brought here one hundred and eighty-eight recruits from Hamburgh, to compleat the two battalions of the Royal American regiment, and, as they will not be able to join their respective battalions till the spring, I have wrote to the Governor of Connecticut, to desire he would provide quarters for them in his government till the month of April. As the colony of Connecticut has never erected any barracks in their country for the use of his Majesty's troops, they must be quartered there on public houses, in the same manner as in England. I have not yet received the Governor's answer to this requisition."

Return of his Majesty's Troops, quartered in the Provincial Barracks, in the Province of New-York.

Regiments.	Commissioned Officers.	Staff.	Non-Commissioned Officers.	Rank and File.
Artillery	6	3	15	63
17th Regiment	9	3	18	261
46th Ditto	10	4	19	235
Total	25	10	52	559

THOMAS GAGE,
Commander in Chief.

Copy

Copy of an Act to furnish the Barracks in the Cities of New-York and Albany with Firewood, Candles, and the other Necessaries therein-mentioned, for his Majesty's Troops.

[*Received October* 6, 1766.]

" An Act to furnish the Barracks in the Cities of New-York and Albany with Firewood and Candles, and the other Necessaries therein-mentioned, for his Majesty's Forces."

Whereas it has been represented to the General Assembly, that it is requisite for his Majesty's service, provision should be made at this time, for furnishing the barracks in the cities of New-York and Albany with sundry necessaries, for the more comfortable reception of his Majesty's troops, that now are, or soon may be quartered in the said barracks, and the General Assembly being willing to make provision for the same, pray that it may be enacted; Be it therefore enacted by his Excellency the Governor, the Council, and the General Assembly. And it is hereby enacted by the authority of the same, that the mayor, recorder, and aldermen of the cities of New-York and Albany respectively, or such person or persons as they, or the major part of them respectively shall appoint, shall, as soon as may be after the publication of this act, furnish the barracks in the said cities with the said necessaries hereafter mentioned; that is to say, " For the officers rooms, each, one pair of hand irons, one pair of tongs, one fire-shovel, one table, two chairs, and one candlestick, and for every officer, seventeen shillings sterling for one year in place of bedding—for every room for non-commissioned officers and soldiers, each room to contain fourteen men, seven cribs, seven bed-cases, seven bolsters to be filled with straw every three months, fourteen blankets, two iron posts, two trammels, one pair of tongs, one fire-shovel, one pair of hand-irons, two

cross bars, one hatchet, one iron candlestick, one table, two benches, and one bucket; and with fire-wood and candles, as follows:—for every room for officers, and for every room for non-commissioned officers and private men, to contain fourteen men each, from the 1st of October to the 1st of April, three-eights of a cord of wood per week for each room, and for five weeks preceding the 1st of October, and five weeks after the 1st of April, three-sixteenths of a cord of wood per week, and for the sixteen remaining weeks, one eighth of a cord of wood per week, one pound of candles per week for the winter only for each room, and for the guard-room in winter three candles each night, and in summer two candles each night, of ten candles to the pound," always provided, that the provision hereby made, doth not exceed the space of one year, to commence from the publication hereof; and that the whole number of troops in both cities, doth not exceed two battalions of five hundred men each, officers included, and one company of royal artillery, and also that no rooms be supplied with fire-wood and candles, or other necessaries furnished either for officers or men, but for such as actually reside in the barracks, in either of the cities of New-York and Albany. And that the said mayor, recorder, and aldermen of the said cities, or the major part of them respectively, may be enabled to furnish the several articles and things by this act directed, Be it enacted by the same authority, that the treasurer of this colony, out of the monies remaining in his hands, by virtue of an act of the Lieutenant-Governor, the Council, and the General Assembly, passed the twentieth day of March, one thousand, seven hundred, and sixty-two, intitled, " An Act, directing the Treasurer of this Colony to pay the Commander in Chief of all his Majesty's Forces in North-America, the Sum of Four
Thousand,

Thoufand, Seven Hundred and Nine-
ty-Pounds for his Majefty's Service,
to be repaid when his Majefty fhall
think proper" pay unto the mayor,
recorder, and aldermen of the faid
cities of New-York and Albany, or
the major part of them refpectively, or
to their refpective orders, from time
to time, fuch fum and fums of money
as fhall be requifite to furnifh the feveral neceffaries aforefaid, whofe refpective receipts fhall be good and fuf-
ficent vouchers to the faid treafurer,
for fuch fums of money as fhall be
therein fpecified. And be it enacted
by the fame authority, that the mayor,
recorder, and aldermen of the cities
of New-York and Albany, or the
major part of them refpectively, fhall
keep, or caufe to be kept, juft, true,
and regular accounts of the monies
by them refpectively expended in
confequence of this act, and fuch accounts fhall render on oath, to the
Governor, the Council, and the General Affembly, when by them, or
either of them, thereunto required.
Province of New-York, July 10, 1766.

This act was paffed by the General
Affembly of the faid province the
25th day of June, 1766. By the
Council on the 27th day of the fame
month of June; and on the third day
of July inftant, was affented to by his
Excellency the Governor—and the
preceding is a true copy of the original examined by me,

GEORGE BANYAN, D. Secretary.

———

*Copy of a Meffage from the Houfe of
Reprefentatives to Governor Bernard
—In Governor Bernard's of the 14th
and 18th of February,* 1767.
(No. I.)
May it pleafe your Excellency,

The Houfe of Reprefentatives beg
to be informed by your Excellency,
whether any provifion has been made
at the expence of this government,
for his Majefty's troops lately arrived
in this harbour, and by whom? And
alfo, whether your Excellency has

reafon to expect the arrival of any
more to be quartered in this province.

———

*Extract of a Letter from Governor Ber-
nard to the Earl of Shelburne.*
[*Received March* 10, 1767.]
Bofton, Dec. 24, 1766.
(No. II.)

It has been ufual in this government, to reprint fuch acts of parliament as extend to America, by order
of the Governor, with the advice of
the Council; the ftamp-act itfelf was
reprinted by the printer of the government, by fuch order. Laft fum-
mer, having received feven acts of
parliament paffed the laft feffion relating to America, I communicated
thefe to the Council, and it appearing that four of them were interefting
to this province, the Council advifed
that they fhould be printed by the
printers of the laws, and it was accordingly ordered. Among thefe acts
was the Mutiny Act, which it feems
has given as much umbrage to this
Affembly as it has done to that of a
neighbouring province, though it has
not yet fo fully fhowed itfelf. In the
interval of the adjournment of the
Affembly, a tranfport, with two companies of artillery on board, was
driven in here by ftrefs of weather;
the commanding officer applied to me
for quarters—I laid the bufinefs before
the Council: The act of parliament
was confulted, and the Council advifed me to order the commiffary to
furnifh them with what they demanded under the act. When the Affembly met, this matter was moved
in the houfe, and a committee was
appointed "to prepare a meffage to
the Council, to enquire by what authority any acts of parliament are re-
giftered among the laws of this province." This meffage was accordingly fent up by five members, and had
this queftion at the end of it, "Whether they knew of any act requiring
the regiftry of ordinances, which this
legiflature never confented to?" The
next

next morning the houſe ſent up another meſſage to the Council, to enquire " Whether the board, or the Governor and Council, had made any proviſion for his Majeſty's troops lately arrived in this harbour, and how ?" I had before, upon another occaſion, cautioned the Council againſt anſwering whilſt ſitting in their legiſlative capacity without me, for what they did as a privy council with me, and I renewed this caution at this time, and added, that application ſhould be made to me, and to me only, for an account of what was done in the privy-council. The Council, therefore, anſwered to both the meſſages : " That the orders relative to thoſe matters, were given by the Governor with the advice of Council, and therefore the houſe was referred to the Governor for the information they deſired." This anſwer was voted by the houſe to be not ſatisfactory, and a committee was appointed " to take the anſwer and matter into conſideration in the receſs, and to report what is proper to be done."

Copy of a Meſſage from Governor Bernard to the Houſe of Repreſentatives—In Governor Bernard's Letters of the 14th and 18th of February, 1767. Gentlemen of the Houſe of Repreſentatives.

In anſwer to your meſſage of this day, I ſend you a copy of the minutes of Council, by which proviſion for the artillery company at the Caſtle, in purſuance of the late act of parliament, was made.

I intended to lay the matter before you, and had given orders for an account of the preſent expence to be made out for that purpoſe, which having received ſince your meſſage came to me, I hereby communicate.

I have received no advice whatever of any other troops being to be quartered in this province, nor have I any reaſon to expect the arrival of

ſuch, except from common report, to which I gave little credit.

Copy of a Meſſage from the Houſe of Repreſentatives to Governor Bernard—In Governor Bernard's Letters of the 14th and 18th of February, 1767.
(No. III.)
May it pleaſe your Excellency,

In reply to your meſſage of the 30th of January, the Houſe of Repreſentatives beg leave to obſerve, That it is by virtue of the royal charter alone, that the Governor and Council have any authority to iſſue money out of the treaſury, and that only according to ſuch acts as are, or may be in force within the province. This clauſe was intended to ſecure to the Houſe of Repreſentatives, the privilege of originating, granting, and diſpoſing of taxes :—But we apprehend it would be of very little value and importance, if it ſhould ever become a ſettled rule, that the Houſe are obliged to impoſe and levy aſſeſſments, rates and taxes, upon the eſtates or perſons of their conſtituents, for the payment of ſuch expences as may be incurred by virtue of an order of the Governor and Council, without the knowledge and conſent of the houſe. Your Excellency, therefore, in giving orders with the advice of the Council, for making proviſion for the artillery companies at the Caſtle, acted, in an eſſential point, contrary to the plain intention of the charter of the province, wherein the powers of the ſeveral branches of the General Aſſembly, are declared and limited. If, however, there was an urgent neceſſity for this procedure in the receſs of the court, we are very much ſurprized that your Excellency ſhould ſuffer the whole of the laſt ſeſſion of the General Aſſembly to paſs over without laying this matter before us, and that it was again omitted in the preſent ſeſſion, 'till the houſe had waited upon your Excellency with their meſſage. It is the juſt expectation of
this

this houfe, founded in the principles of the conftitution, to have the earlieft notice of a matter of this nature, and we cannot but remonftrate to your Excellency, that the omiffion of it was in breach of our privilege.

But may it pleafe your Excellency, it is ftill more grievous to us, to find your Excellency making mention of a late act of parliament, in purfuance of which, your Excellency and the Council have created this expence to the province One great grievance, in regard to the ftampact, was, that it deprived us of the advantage of a fundamental and moft effential part of the Britifh conftitution, the unalienable right of freedom from all taxation, but fuch as we fhall voluntarily confent to and grant :—while we feel a fenfe of the worth and importance of this right, we cannot but exprefs a very deep concern, that an act of parliament fhould yet be in being, which appears to us to be as real a grievance, as was that which fo juftly alarmed this continent. Your Excellency, and the Council, by taking this ftep, have unwarrantably and unconftitutionally fubjected the people of this province to an expence, without giving this houfe an opportunity of paffing their judgment upon it, and have alfo put it out of our power, by an act of our own, to teftify the fame chearfulnefs which this affembly has always fhewn, in granting to his Majefty, of their free accord, fuch aids as his Majefty's fervice has, from time to time, required.

Copy of a Meffage from Governor Bernard to the Houfe of Reprefentatives, February 17, 1767 — *In Governor Bernard's Letters of the* 14*th and* 18*th of February,* 1767.
(No. IV.)
Bofton, Feb. 19.
Tuefday laft his Excellency was pleafed to fend the following Meffage

to the Hon. Houfe of Reprefentatives ; viz.
Gentlemen of the Houfe of Reprefentatives.

The charges againft me and the Council, contained in your meffage of the 4th inftant, have had a full confideration ; the refult of which is, that the proceedings in making provifion for the King's troops lately arrived here, appear to be conftitutional and warrantable, and are juftified not only by the ufage of this government, but by the authority of the General Court itfelf.

The barracks at the Caftle were built by order of the General Court, for the reception of the King's troops when they fhould arrive here, that there might be no occafion for quartering them upon the inhabitants. Fuel and candle are neceffary to the occupation of barracks—without them no troops could go in or ftay there, it being an allowance always incidental to their living in barracks. When, therefore, the General Court ordered thefe barracks to be built for troops, it muft have been implied, that the incidental neceffaries fhould be provided for the troops when they went into them—otherwife, we muft fuppofe that the General Court did not intend that the barracks fhould be applied to the ufe for which they were built.

The manner of making the provifion, and the provifion itfelf, were agreeable to the ufage of this government in the like cafes. It confifted of fuel and candle only, which are abfolutely neceffary, and always have been allowed in thofe barracks, and it did not include feveral articles prefcribed by the act of parliament, and therefore it was wholly conformable to the ufage of the government and the neceffity of the cafe, but to the act only, as it coincided with it. If there had been no fuch act, the Council would have thought themfelves

felves obliged to have advifed the ordering this provifion, as it was necef-fary to the ufe of the barracks, it being their duty, in the recefs of the General Court, to affift me in carrying into execution, by the ufual means, an eftablifhment provided for the convenience of the people.

As to your complaint againft me, for not laying this matter before you during the whole of laft feffion, and part of this feffion, I fhall only ftate the facts, and leave it there. What you call the whole of laft feffion, was only the fix laft days of it, when you met after an adjournment, to pafs upon the Compenfation Bill. As foon as you had finifhed that bufinefs, you defired me to grant you a recefs —I did fo, and told you at the fame time, that upon that account, I had poftponed all other bufinefs to the next feffion. As to the part of this feffion, it was not forty-eight hours, and within that time I had given orders for making out an account of the expence of the provifion in order to lay it before you, and I actually received it within two hours after I had your meffage. This is the whole of what you call an omiffion in breach of your privilege.

Council-Chamber. FRA'. BERNARD.

Extract from the Journals of the Upper House of Affembly — In Governor Wright's, (No. IV.) of the 6th of April, 1767.
Georgia, Die Martis, 20°. January, 1767.

Mr. Prefident informed the Houfe, that he had two Meffages from his Excellency the Governor, figned by his Excellency, which he was directed to lay before the Houfe, and he delivered them in at the Table, where the fame were read, one of which is as follows ; viz.

" *Honourable Gentlemen,*

" It is always with reluctance, that I mention any matter of expence to you, but having lately received a letter from Captain Phillips, the officer commanding the detachment of his Majefty's troops in this province, inclofing me a lift of neceffaries allowed by the Mutiny act to foldiers in America, and requefting to know where he is to procure the fame ; it is my duty to lay this matter, together with the act of parliament, before you, and to recommend it to your ferious confideration, and hope you will, as far as lies with you, enable me to comply with the direction contained in the faid act.

" *Savannah,* JAMES WRIGHT."

Extract of a Letter from Captain Lieu-tenant Phillips.

" I beg your Excellency will be pleafed to forgive the trouble I give you, by inclofing a lift of the neceffaries allowed to foldiers wherever they are lodged in barracks, and intreat your directions where I am to procure them for the garrifons in your Excellency's province."

A Lift of Neceffaries for the Soldiers on the Out-Pofts.

" Candles for the guard and hofpital—wood for the garrifons—bedding and bedfteads—rum and vinegar, &c. as ordered by the Mutiny-act—cooking utenfils, pots, platters, fpoons, &c. &c.—axes to cut their wood, and tables and forms.

" (Signed) RALPH PHILLIPS.
" *Charles-Town,* Jan. 6, 1767."

" The command at Augufta, an officer, a furgeon's mate, and twenty privates.

" The command at Frederica, a ferjeant and ten privates, but at prefent only a corporal and nine privates."

" Refolved, *Nemine Diffenfiente,* That this houfe will readily and chearfully concur with the Commons Houfe in every meafure that may be judged expedient to carry the feveral matters into execution, recommended by his Excellency in his faid meffages.

" Refolved,

S

" Refolved, That an humble addrefs be prefented to his Excellency
the Governor, acquainting his Excellency with the aforegoing refolution.

" Ordered, That Mr. Powell and
Mr. Johnfon do prefent the faid addrefs."

A true copy, examined and cer-
tified by   C. WATSON, C. G. A.

Copy of Addrefs.

Georgia, Jan. 20, 1767.
To his Excellency James Wright, Efq;
Captain-General, and Governor in
Chief of his Majefty's Province of
Georgia.
The Humble Addrefs of the Upper Houfe
of Affembly.

May it pleafe your Excellency,

This houfe having taken under confideration your Excellency's two meffages of this day, the one refpecting
the repairs requifite at Fort Hallifax,
and the other relative to fundry neceffaries allowed by the late Mutiny-
act to foldiers in America, beg leave
to affure your Excellency, that we
will readily and chearfully concur
with the Commons Houfe, in every
meafure that may be judged expedient
to carry the feveral matters therein recommended, into due execution.

By order of the Upper Houfe,
JAMES HABERSHAM, Prefident.
Examined with the original,
C. WATSON, C. G. A.

Extract of a Letter from James Wright,
Efq; Governor of Georgia, to the
Earl of Shelburne.
[Received May 21, 1767.]
Savannah, April 6, 1767.

In my letter of the 5th of January I
wrote to your lordfhip, that the Affembly begun to do bufinefs on the 2d
of December, and were to meet again
on the 13th of January, and that I
had not then obferved any improper
difpofition in them :—But, my Lord,
this did not continue to be the cafe,
for, on the 16th of January I received

a letter from Captain Lieutenant Phillips, who, by General Gage's order,
then commanded the detachment of
his Majefty's Royal American regiment, doing duty in this province and
South Carolina, defiring me to let
him know where he was to apply for
the barrack-neceffaries directed by the
Mutiny act, and on the 20th of January I fent a meffage to the Council
and Affembly on that fubject, together with the Mutiny act, it being
the ufe and cuftom here, to fend a
meffage to the Council, as well as to
the Affembly, in fuch cafes—copies
of which I now inclofe to your lordfhip (No. I.) ; alfo a copy of the addrefs of the Council as an Upper
Houfe, in anfwer to my meffage of
the fame date (No. II.)—but the Affembly delayed fending any anfwer
for a confiderable time, and finding
no anfwer came, I fent for two of the
members, and let them know, that if
I did not receive an anfwer forthwith,
I fhould be obliged to fend a fecond
meffage, in which poffibly I might
mention fomething that would not be
pleafing, as I had underftood they did
not intend to comply with the act of
parliament ; and that day I was informed, by direction of the houfe,
that I might depend on an anfwer in
a day, or two, at fartheft, and on
the 18th of February I received the
inclofed addrefs. (No. II)

Extract of a Letter from Major General
Gage to the Earl of Shelburne.
[Received March 25.]
New-York, Feb. 20, 1767.
(No. IV.)

Your Lordfhip has been informed of
the arrival of a number of German
recruits in this port for the Royal
American regiment, and of my intention to quarter them in the colony
of Connecticut, 'till the feafon fhould
allow them to join their corps.   I
wrote two letters to Governor Pitkin
on the fubject of quartering thefe recruits by the authority of the act of
parliament

parliament folely, but the Governor would do nothing in the affair, 'till authorized fo to do by his Provincial Affembly. I have the honor to tranfmit your Lordfhip copies of faid letters, with the Governor's anfwers thereto. The men are now quartered in the towns, where the Governor told me provifion would be made for their reception.

Copy of a Letter from Governor Pitkin, of the Colony of Connecticut, to General Gage—In Major General Gage's Letters, (No. IV.) of the 20th of February, 1767.

Hartford, *Jan.* 31, 1767.

SIR,

Your letter of the 25th inftant I received; notwithftanding your furprize at the delay of his Majefty's fervice, I can affure your Excellency, that this colony have nothing more at heart, than to forward his Majefty's fervice, and promote his intereft by every part of their conduct. I have now the pleafure to inform your Excellency, that the needful provifion is made for quartering the number of troops mentioned in your firft letter.

The towns referred to in your requifition, have lately been greatly burthened with a large number of his Majefty's regular troops, and had encouragement that for the future they fhould be excufed, which induced the Affembly to provide quarters for the faid troops in the towns of New Haven, Wallingford, and Brandford —am therefore defired to requeft this favour of your Excellency, if it can be without prejudice to his Majefty's fervice, otherwife, provifion is made in the towns of Stamford, Norwalk, and Fairfield.

I am further defired to requeft your Excellency, that orders be given that the foldiers may not carry their arms, except when called upon duty, which may prevent their difturbing the peace of his Majefty's fubjects, which the people here have fearful apprehenfions of, from their former experience.

I am, &c.

(Signed) WM. PITKIN.

Copy of a Letter from General Gage to Governor Pitkin, of the Colony of Connecticut—In Major Gen. Gage's Letter (No. IV.) of the 20th of February, 1767.

New-York, *Jan.* 25, 1767.

SIR,

Captain Kemble has delivered me your letter of the 20th inftant, and I can't help expreffing my furprize at the contents of it, and the delays given to his Majefty's fervice—I had the honor to make application to you as the executive part of government, for the due execution of a law in your colony, in the fame manner as the faid law is daily put in execution by every juftice of the peace, conftable, headborough, or tythingman, throughout the kingdom of England. I cannot comprehend that your colony is affected by my requifition in any fhape, as to expence, there being no barracks in the colony, therefore there is no expence to be incurred for bedding, fuel, utenfils, &c. but the troops to be quartered in public houfes, in the fame manner as in England; and as the public houfes in the places mentioned in my letter of the 8th inftant, are more than fufficient to quarter the few troops that are to be fent into them, the further provifion required by the law, of fitting up out-houfes, barns, &c. in cafe there fhould not be fufficient room in the faid public houfes to quarter the troops, is out of the queftion: I can't, therefore, fee by what means the colony is to be involved in confiderable expences, or that it is neceffary to raife a fingle fhilling on this account. The King's fervice requires that I fhould be at a certainty in this bufinefs, and I am once more obliged to trouble you on the fubject of my

firft

firſt letter, and to deſire your anſwer, whether you will give the proper directions to the inferior magiſtrates to obey the law, by billeting the ſoldiers in ſuch houſes as are particularly ſpecified in the act of parliament, made and provided in this reſpect.

I am, &c.   THOˢ. GAGE.

Copy of a Letter from Governor Pitkin, of the Colony of Connecticut, to General Gage—In Major Gen. Gage's Letter (No. IV.) of the 20th of February, 1767.

Hartford, Jan. 20, 1767,
SIR,

I received yours of the 8th inſtant, by Captain Kemble, requeſting quarters for one hundred and thirty-four of his Majeſty's troops, in the towns of Stamford, Norwalk, and Fairfield, in this colony. It would have given me pleaſure to have returned an immediate anſwer, but as it was neceſſary for me to call the Council of this colony to meet, and adviſe on the ſubject matter of your Excellency's letter, I immediately gave them notice, but as they live ſcattered in the various parts of the colony, and the ſeaſon being ſo extraordinary, rendered it impracticable to convene them 'till this day, which I truſt will appear a ſufficient reaſon to your Excellency for the delay I have been obliged to give Captain Kemble. I am ſorry it is not in my power, at this time, to give ſuch immediate and ſpecific orders as your Excellency ſeemed to expect. As the requiſition was unexpected, no barracks, or other proviſions, are made for quartering ſoldiers here—A compliance therewith, would involve the colony in conſiderable expence, which cannot be provided for, otherwiſe than by their repreſentatives in General Aſſembly, which makes it neceſſary to call the ſame on this occaſion. I have accordingly ſent out orders for convening the Aſſembly on Thurſday the 29th inſtant, which is as ſoon as they poſ-

ſibly can meet. I ſhall then lay the matter before them, and doubt not but they will give the utmoſt attention and diſpatch the nature of the affair will admit. I ſhall not fail to give your Excellency the earlieſt notice of their concluſion thereon. I am, &c.
(Signed)   WM. PITKIN.

Copy of a Letter from General Gage to Governor Pitkin, of the Colony of Connecticut—In Major Gen. Gage's Letter (No. IV.) of the 20th of February, 1767.

New-York, Jan. 8, 1767.
SIR,

I have the honour to acquaint you, that a veſſel is juſt arrived here, with one hundred and eighty-eight recruits from Germany, for his Majeſty's two battalions of the Royal American regiment. As both theſe battalions are ſo ſituated (the one being quartered at Quebec, the other garriſoning the forts in the Upper country) as to render it impracticable for theſe recruits to join them this winter, and the quarters in the provinces of Pennſylvania, New Jerſeys, and New-York, being occupied by other corps, and two companies of the Royal regiment of Artillery being quartered at Boſton, I have no choice left but the province of Connecticut—I, therefore, ſend to you, by Captain Kemble, one of my aid de camps, to requeſt that you will be ſo good as to order quarters to be provided at Stamford, Norwalk, and Fairfield, or which you ſhall judge beſt of thoſe towns, for two officers, and one hundred and thirty-four of his Majeſty's troops—the other fifty-four being deſtined to recruit the three companies of the firſt battalion of the Royal American regiment ſtationed in South-Carolina, will be immediately ſent thither. I have no doubt but you will give ſuch immediate and ſpecifick orders upon this head, as that this detachment of his Majeſty's forces may be ſupplied
with

with quarters, &c. according to the act of parliament.

You will be so good to return me an answer to this requisition, by Captain Kemble, acquainting me of the number of men you think best to be severally quartered in the towns before-mentioned. I am, &c.

THOMAS GAGE.

Extract of a Letter from Governor Bernard to the Earl of Shelburne.
[*Received March* 28.]
Boston, 14*th and* 18*th of Feb.* 1767.
(No. V.)

In my letter (No. II.) I informed your lordship, that the house had, at the end of last session, taken umbrage at the Governor, with the advice of Council, having ordered provision for two companies of artillery (which were drove in here), pursuant to act of parliament, and had appointed a committee thereupon—so that this subject was to be worked up as a cause of liberty. The third day of this session, the house sent me a message, desiring to know, "Whether any provision had been made at the expence of this government, for his Majesty's troops lately arrived in this harbour, and by whom?" To this I returned an answer, inclosing a copy of the minutes of Council, by which such provision was made, in which it is said to be in pursuance of the act of parliament. I also added an account of the expence, which in more than two months amounted to £60 sterling. In reply to this, they sent me a message, wherein they say, that " I and the Council, in making such provision, acted unwarrantably and unconstitutionally, and it is the more grievous to them, for that it is mentioned to be in pursuance of an act of parliament, which act appears to them as real a grievance as the stampact." They also say, " that my not laying this matter before them for the whole of the last session, and part of this session, until they sent their mes-

sage, was in breach of their priviledge." What they call the whole of the last session, was only the six last days, when they met, after an adjournment, to pass the Indemnification bill, and for no other purpose —after which, they desired I would dismiss them, and I told them in so doing, that I had postponed all other business to the next session, on that account. The part of this session was not forty-eight hours, in which I had given orders for making out an account of the expence, to be laid before them —when they hurried their message so, that it came to me two hours before I received the account. I mention this only, to shew upon what trifling pretences, a charge of a breach of this privilege is formed.

In the business itself, the Governor and Council acted precisely according to the constant usage of this government, both in the manner of providing, and the things provided, and in regard to the latter, not quite conformably to the act of parliament, for there was no beer, vinegar, &c. provided, the officer not requiring them. The entry in the minute of the Council, " in pursuance of the act of parliament" was made at the desire of some of the Council, thinking, I suppose, that it would protect them from being called to an account for doing, what, in other times, would have passed as a common act of government, and even these words are more properly applicable to the request of the officer, than the order—But the reverse has happened. The act of parliament, instead of protecting them, has been the cause of their being arraigned. Political measures are very catching in this country. When the matter was first agitated, advice had been received of the Assembly of New-York having refused to comply specifically with the act of parliament; and it was mentioned in the house, and then (last session) it was said that this act was worse than the stamp-act.
And

And when it was revived in the house this session, a member opposite to government, said that the Governor and Council were not to blame, the act under which they had acted was what was to be condemned. And indeed this trifling business, which in the whole expence won't cost above £.150 sterling, seems to be laid hold of, only to make a public declaration against the act of parliament—All papers of this kind, which used formerly to be seen no where but in the votes, being now printed in all the news-papers; and, from some particular expressions, it has the air of a manifesto much more than of a message to a Governor, who is the last person to whom a claim to an exemption from acts of parliament should be made, as it is impossible for him to concede to it.

This letter still remaining with me, I have an opportunity to add, that for above a week past, I had endeavoured to prevail with the Council, to join with me in a justification of our proceedings, in making provision for the King's troops, but at the same time I protested against their answering without me, as it was a business of Privy Council, in which they could not act separately from me. This distinction was made use of to introduce a squabble about privileges, which prevented any resolution being taken. To put an end to this, yesterday I introduced the inclosed answer in my own name only, which I told them I would send if they would advise to it, which, after some debate, they did; and I sent it to the house. Your Lordship will observe, that in this answer there is a careful avoidance, though no denial of this provision being made, in pursuance of the act of parliament: I was obliged to frame it thus to obtain the Council's concurrence. For, though the greater part of them have, I believe, a due respect for an act of parliament,

not one of them would dare to avow it in this instance, and at this time.

Copy of an Act for granting Compensation to the Sufferers, and of free and general Pardon, Indemnity and Oblivion to the Offenders in the late Times, passed in the Province of the Massachusett's Bay, Dec. 6, 1766.
(No. I.)

" An Act for granting Compensation to the Sufferers, and of free and general Pardon, Indemnity and Oblivion, to the Offenders in the late Times."

Whereas the King's most Excellent Majesty, taking into his gracious and most serious consideration, the troubles, discords, tumults and riots which have lately happened in America, and that divers of his subjects have thereby greatly suffered in their property, and others have fallen into, and are obnoxious to great pains and penalties, out of a hearty and pious desire that such sufferers be compensated, and to put an end to all suits and controversies, and prosecutions, that by occasion of the late distractions have arisen, or may arise between any of his Majesty's subjects, and to the intent that a veil be drawn over the late unhappy excesses, has been graciously pleased to signify his desire to forgive and forget them, at the same time, of his abundant clemency, recommending a compensation to the sufferers in their property, with such a conduct in general, as shall be, at this great crisis, the best means of fixing the mutual interest and inclination of Great Britain and her colonies, on the most firm and solid foundation.

From a grateful sense of his Majesty's grace and clemency, in order to promote internal peace and safety, to make compensation to said sufferers, and as a means, so far as it is in our power, of demonstrating to all the world, our sense of the happiness we enjoy, in being a part of the British empire,

empire, and being intitled to the rights, liberties, and privileges of British subjects, We, his Majesty's most dutiful and loyal subjects, the Representatives of the Commons of this province, in the Great and General Court, assembled of our free and good will, have resolved to give and grant, and pray that it may be enacted.

And be it accordingly enacted, by the Governor, Council, and House of Representatives, that there be granted and paid out of the public treasury of this province, to the Hon. Thomas Hutchinson, Esq; the sum of £.3194 17s. 6d. in full compensation for the losses and sufferings that he, and the several persons in his family, sustained in the late times of confusion.

To the Hon. Andrew Oliver, Esq; the sum of £.172 4s.

To Benjamin Hallowell, jun. Esq; the sum of £.385 6s. 10d.

To William Story, Esq; the sum of £.67 8s. 10d. in full compensation for their losses and sufferings, in the late times of confusion.

And be it further enacted, that all riots, routs, and unlawful assemblies, councelled, commanded, acted, done, or made within this province, between the 1st day of September, 1765, and the 1st day of May, 1766, and all burglaries, felonies, rescues, and breaches of the peace whatsoever, committed in, by, or during such riots, routs, or unlawful assemblies, be, and hereby are pardoned, released, indemnified, discharged, and put in utter oblivion, and that all and every the person or persons, acting, advising, assisting, abetting, and counselling the same, be, and are hereby pardoned, released, acquitted, indemnified and discharged from the same, and of, and from all pains of death, and other pains, judgments, indictments, convictions, penalties, and forfeitures, are hereby declared null and void.

And be it further enacted, that any person indicted or presented, or in any manner prosecuted, or that shall, or may be hereafter indicted, presented, or in any manner prosecuted, or that shall, or may be hereafter indicted, presented, or in any manner prosecuted for any of the offences by this act pardoned, may plead the general issue, and give this act in evidence, which shall be sufficient to acquit him.

Provided, that nothing in this act contained, shall extend to the pardoning, or give any benefit whatever to any person who is, or may be unlawfully possessed of any goods or chattels, taken or stolen from any person, unless the possessor shall, within thirty days after the publication of this act, have surrendered and delivered them up to the province treasurer, for the use of the province.

Provided also, that nothing in this act shall extend to the carrying any civil action of trespass for damages sustained by any person, not by this act compensated, nor to the pardoning any of the crimes or offences above-named, wherein any burglaries, arsons, or thefts were committed against the properties of any persons, not compensated by this act.

Extract of the Minutes of the Proceedings of the Commissioners for Trade and Plantations, so far as relates to the Act passed in the Province of the Massachusett's Bay, in December, 1766, intituled,
" An Act for granting Compensation to the Sufferers, and of free and general Pardon, Indemnity, and Oblivion, to the Offenders in the late Times." From the Time of the Receipt of the said Act.

(No. II.)

At a meeting of his Majesty's Commissioners for Trade and Plantations, on Tuesday, March 10, 1767.

Present—Lord Clare, Mr. Jenyns, Mr. Roberts, Mr. Fitzherbert, Mr. Rice, Mr. Dyson, Mr. Robinson.

The

The Secretary laid before the Board the following papers, which were this day received from the Secretary of the Province of Massachuset't's Bay; viz. Two Acts passed in 1766.

Ordered, That the Secretary do forthwith communicate to the Secretary to the Earl of Shelburne, for his Lordship's information, the act of compensation to the sufferers by the disturbances at Boston, in August, 1765, and for indemnity to those concerned in the said disturbances.

CLARE.

At a meeting of his Majesty's Commissioners for Trade and Plantations, on Tuesday, March 12, 1767.

Present—Lord Clare, Mr. Jenyns, Mr. Dyson, Mr. Roberts, Mr. Fitzherbert.

The Secretary acquainted the Board that he had, pursuant to their order, communicated to the Earl of Shelburne's Secretary, the Act passed in Massachuset't's Bay, in December, 1766, for Compensation and Indemnity.

Their Lordships took into consideration the law passed in the province of Massachuset't's Bay, in December, 1766, for Compensation to the Sufferers by the Disturbances at Boston in 1765, and for Indemnity, &c. and the said law appearing to be of a new and extraordinary nature and importance, it was ordered that it should be referred to his Majesty's Attorney and Solicitor-General, for their opinion upon it.

CLARE.

At a meeting of his Majesty's Commissioners for Trade and Plantations, on Monday, April 13, 1767.

Present—Lord Clare, Mr. Jenyns, Mr. Dyson, Mr. Rice, Mr. Fitzherbert, Mr. Robinson.

The Secretary laid before the Board a report of his Majesty's Attorney and Solicitor-General, dated the 10th instant, upon the act passed in the province of the Massachuset't's Bay in December last, intituled, An Act for Compensation to the Sufferers by the

Disturbances at Boston in 1765, and for Indemnity, &c. Their Lordships took the said act and report into consideration, and having agreed upon a representation to his Majesty thereupon, a draught of such representation was prepared, approved, transcribed, and signed.

CLARE.

Copy of a Letter from John Pownall, Esq; to his Majesty's Attorney and Sollicitor-General, dated Whitehall, March 13, 1767, desiring their Opinion upon an Act passed in the Massachuset't's Bay, in December, 1766, intituled,

"An Act for granting Compensation to the Sufferers, and of free and general Pardon, Indemnity, and Oblivion, to the Offenders in the late Times."

(No. III.)

Whitehall, March 13, 1767.

Gentlemen,

As the law herewith inclosed, passed in the province of the Massachuset't's Bay, in December, 1766, appears to the Lords Commissioners for Trade and Plantations, to be of a new and extraordinary nature and importance, I am directed by their lordships to desire you will be pleased to take it into consideration, and to favour them with your opinion, whether the legislature of that province have, by their constitution, a power to enact a law of general pardon, indemnity, and oblivion, in the case to which it refers, without the previous consent of the crown. I am, with great respect, Gentlemen, your most obedient, humble servant, J. POWNALL.

To William de Grey and Edward Willes, Esqrs. his Majesty's Attorney and Sollicitor Generals.

Copy of a Report of his Majesty's Attorney and Sollicitor-General, dated April 10, 1767, on an Act passed in the Province of the Massachuset't's Bay, on the 6th of December, 1766, intituled, "An Act for granting Compensation

Compensation to the Sufferers, and of free and general Pardon, Indemnity, and Oblivion, to the Offenders in the late Times."

(No. IV.)

To the Right Hon. the Lords Commiffioners for Trade and Plantations.

May it pleaſe your Lordſhips,

In obedience to your lordſhips commands fignified to us by Mr. Pownal's letter of the 13th of March laſt, incloſing to us a law paffed in the province of Maffachufett's Bay, in December, 1766, appearing to your lordſhips to be of a new and extraordinary nature and importance, and defiring us to take it into our confideration, and report our opinion, whether the legiſlature of that province have, by their conftitution, a power to enact a law of general pardon, indemnity and oblivion, in the cafe to which it refers, without the previous confent of the crown. We have taken the fame into our confideration, and are of opinion, that the Governor, Council, and Affembly of the Maffachufett's Bay, have not, by the conftitution of that province, any original power to enact a law of general pardon, indemnity, and oblivion, in the cafe referred to, without the previous communication of the grace and pleaſure of the crown.

All which is humbly fubmitted to your Lordſhips' confideration.

W. DE GREY,

•E. WILLES.

Whitehall, April 13, 1767.

Copy of a Repreſentation of the Commiſſioners for Trade and Plantations, to his Majeſty, dated Whitehall, April 13, 1767, *on an Act paffed in the Maffachufett's Bay, in December,* 1766, *intitled,* " An Act for granting Compenſation to the Sufferers, and of free and general Pardon, Indemnity, and Oblivion, to the Offenders in the late Times."

(No. V.)

To the King's Moſt Excellent Majeſty.

May it pleaſe your Majeſty,

We have had under our confideration an act paffed in your Majeſty's province of Maffachufett's Bay, in New-England, on the 6th of December, 1766, intituled, " An Act for granting Compenſation to the Sufferers, and of free and general Pardon, Indemnity, and Oblivion, to the Offenders in the late Times."

As this act appeared to us to be of an extraordinary nature and importance, we thought it our duty immediately, to refer it to the confideration of your Majeſty's Attorney and Sollicitor General, defiring their opinion, whether the legiſlature of that province have, by their conftitution, a power to enact a law of general pardon, indemnity, and oblivion, in the cafe to which this act refers, without the previous confent of the crown; and your Majeſty's Attorney and Sollicitor General, having, on the 10th inftant, reported to us their opinion, " That the Governor, Council, and Affembly of the Maffachufett's Bay, have not, by the conftitution of that province, any original power to enact a law of general Pardon, Indemnity, and Oblivion, in the cafe refered to, without the previous communication of the grace and pleaſure of the crown." We do, upon a confideration of this report, agree in opinion with them, and humbly beg leave to lay the faid act before your Majeſty, fubmitting it to your Majeſty to take fuch meafures thereupon, as your Majeſty, in your great wifdom, and with the advice of your Council, fhall think moſt proper.

Which is moſt humbly fubmitted.

Clare   Wm. Fitzherbert

Soame Jenyns   Thoˢ. Robinſon.

George Rice

Copy of a Repreſentation of the Lords Commiſſioners for Trade and Plantations, dated the 13th *of April,* 1767, *upon the Maffachufett's Act,*

T   *for*

for granting Compensation to the Sufferers, &c.

(No. I.)

To the King's Most Excellent Majesty.

May it please your Majesty,

We have had under our consideration an act passed in your Majesty's province of the Massachusett's Bay, in New England, on the 6th of December, 1766, intituled,

" An Act for granting Compensation to the Sufferers, and of free and general Pardon, Indemnity, and Oblivion, to the Offenders in the late Times."

As this act appeared to us to be of an extraordinary nature and importance, we thought it our duty immediately to refer it to the consideration of your Majesty's Attorney and Sollicitor General, desiring their opinion, whether the legislature of that province, have, by their constitution, a power to enact a law of general Pardon, Indemnity, and Oblivion, in the case to which this act refers, without the previous consent of the crown? And your Majesty's Attorney and Sollicitor-General, having, on the 10th instant, reported to us their opinion, " That the Governor, Council, and Assembly of the Massachusett's Bay, have not, by the constitution of that province, any original power to enact a law of general Pardon, Indemnity, and Oblivion, in the case referred to, without the previous communication of the grace and pleasure of the crown." We do, upon a consideration of this report, agree in opinion with them, and humbly beg leave to lay the said act before your Majesty, submitting it to your Majesty, to take such measures thereupon, as your Majesty, in your great wisdom, and with the advice of your Council, shall think most proper.

Which is most humbly submitted.

Clare   Wm. Fitzherbert
Soame Jenyns   Tho⁵. Robinson.
George Rice

Whitehall, April 13, 1767.

L. S.

Fr⁵. Bernard.

By his Excellency Francis Bernard, Esq; Captain General and Governor in Chief, in, and over his Majesty's Province of the Massachusett's Bay, in New-England, and Vice-Admiral of the same.

I do hereby certify, that the Great and General Court, or Assembly of his Majesty's province of the Massachusett's Bay, abovesaid, did at their session begun and held at Boston, upon Wednesday the 28th day of May, 1766, and continued by sundry prorogations to Wednesday the 29th day of October following, and then met, make, and pass an act, intituled, " An Act for granting Compensation to the Sufferers, and of free and general Pardon, Indemnity, and Oblivion, to the Offenders in the late Times." Passed by the Representatives, December 6, 1766.

Passed by the Council, ditto.

Signed by the Governor, ditto.

And I do further certify, that the paper annexed is a true and authentic copy of the act, or law aforementioned.

In testimony whereof, I have caused the public seal of the province of Massachusett's Bay aforesaid, to be hereunto affixed, dated at Boston the 27th day of December, 1766, in the 7th year of his Majesty's reign. By his Excellency's command,

A. OLIVER, Secretary.

Copy of the Act mentioned in the aforegoing Representation (No. I.) *passed in Massachusett's Bay, Dec.* 6, 1766.

(No. II.)

An Act passed by the Great and General Court, or Assembly, of his Majesty's Province of the Massachusett's Bay, in New-England, begun and held at Boston, upon Wednesday the 28th Day of May, 1766, and from thence continued by several Prorogations, to Wednesday the 29th Day of October following, and then met.

" An

" An Act for granting Compensation to the Sufferers, and of free and general Pardon, Indemnity, and Oblivion, to the Offenders in the late Times."

Whereas the King's most Excellent Majesty, taking into his gracious and serious consideration, the troubles, discords, tumults, and riots that have lately happened in America, and that divers of his subjects have thereby greatly suffered in their property, and others have fallen into, and are obnoxious to great pains and penalties, out of a hearty and pious desire that such sufferers be compensated, and to put an end to all suits, controversies, and prosecutions, that by occasion of the late distractions have arisen, or may arise between any of his Majesty's subjects, and to the intent that a veil may be drawn over the late unhappy excesses, has been graciously pleased to signify his desire to forgive and forget them, at the same time, of his abundant clemency, recommending a compensation to the sufferers in their property, with such a conduct in general, as shall be at this general crisis, the best means of fixing the mutual interest and inclination of Great Britain and her Colonies, on the most firm and solid foundations.

From a grateful sense of his Majesty's grace and clemency, in order to promote internal peace and safety, to make compensation to said sufferers, and as a means, so far as it is in our power, of demonstrating to all the world our sense of the happiness we enjoy, in being a part of the British empire, and being intitled to the rights, liberties, and privileges of British subjects. We his Majesty's most dutiful and loyal subjects, the Representatives of the Commons of this Province, in the Great and General Court assembled, of our free and good will, have resolved to give and grant, and pray that it be enacted.

And be it accordingly enacted, by the Governor, Council, and House of Representatives, that there be granted and paid out of the public treasury of this Province, to the Hon. Thomas Hutchinson, Esq; the sum of £.3194 17s. 6d. in full compensation for the losses and sufferings that he, and the several persons in his family sustained, in the late times of confusion.

To the Hon. Andrew Oliver, Esq; the sum of £.172 4s.

To Benjamin Hallowell, jun. the sum of £.385 6s. 10d.

To William Story, Esq; the sum of £.67 8s. 10d. in full compensation for their losses and sufferings, in the late times of confusion.

And be it further enacted, that all riots, routs, and unlawful assemblies, councelled, commanded, acted, done, or made within this province, between the 1st day of August, 1765, and the 1st day of May, 1766, and all burglaries, felonies, rescues, and breaches of the peace whatsoever, committed in, by, or during such riots, routs, and unlawful assemblies, be, and are hereby pardoned, released, indemnified, discharged, and put in utter oblivion, and that all and every the person or persons, acting, advising, assisting, abetting, and councelling the same, be, and are hereby pardoned, released, acquitted, indemnified, and discharged from the same, and of, and from all pains of death, and other pains, judgments, indictments, convictions, penalties, and forfeitures, therefore had or given, or that might accrue for the same, and that such indictments, convictions, and forfeitures, are hereby declared null and void.

And be it further enacted, that any person indicted or presented, or in any manner prosecuted, or that shall, or may be hereafter indicted, presented, or in any manner prosecuted for any of the offences by this act pardoned, may plead the general issue, and give this act in evidence, which shall be sufficient to acquit him.

Provided,

Provided, that nothing in this act contained, shall extend to the pardoning, or give any benefit whatever to any person who is, or may be unlawfully possessed of any goods or chattels, taken or stolen from any person, unless the possessor shall, within thirty days after the publication of this act, have surrendered and delivered them up to the Province treasurer, for the use of the province.

Provided also, that nothing in this act contained, shall extend to the barring any civil action of trespass for damages sustained by any person not by this act compensated, nor to the pardoning any of the crimes or offences above-named, wherein any burglaries, arsons, or thefts were committed against the properties of any persons not compensated by this act.

Copy of his Majesty's Order in Council, dated April 13, 1767, referring to the Lords of the Committee of Council, the aforegoing Representation and Act.
(No. III.)
At the Court at St. James, April 13, 1767.
P R E S E N T,
The King's Most Excellent Majesty in Council.

Upon reading at the Board, a representation from the Lords Commissioners for Trade and Plantations, dated this day, upon an act passed in his Majesty's Province of the Massachusett's Bay, in New-England, on the 6th of December, 1766, intitled, " An Act for granting Compensation to the Sufferers, and of free and general Pardon, Indemnity, and Oblivion, to the Offenders in the late Times."

Which act had not, till this day, been laid before the Council Board—It is ordered by his Majesty in Council, that the said representation and act be, and they are hereby referred to the Right Hon. the Lords of the Committee of Council for Plantation Affairs, to consider the same, and

report their opinion thereupon to his Majesty at this Board.

Copy of the Report of the Lords of the Committee of Council, dated May 9, 1767, upon considering the aforegoing Representation and Act.
(No. IV.)
At the Council-Chamber, Whitehall, May 9, 1767.
By the Right Hon. the Lords of the Committee of Council for Plantation Affairs.
P R E S E N T,

Lord Chancellor	Visc. Barrington
Lord President	Viscount Clare
Duke of Grafton	Lord North
Duke of Bolton	Lord Sandys
Duke of Ancaster	Mr. Speaker
Lord Steward	J. Stuart Mackenzie, Esq;
Earl of Denbigh	
Earl of Cholmondeley	Mr. Sec. Conway
E. of Marchmont	Mr. Chancellor of the Exchequer
Earl of Bristol	Welb. Ellis, Esq;
Earl of Harcourt	Hans Stanley, Esq;
E. of Hillsborough	L. C. J. Wilmot
Earl of Shelburne	Isaac Barré, Esq;
Viscount Howe	

Your Majesty having been pleased by your order in Council, of the 13th of last month, to refer unto this committee a representation of the Lords Commissioners for Trade and Plantations, touching and concerning an act passed by the Great and General Court, or Assembly of your Majesty's Province of the Massachusett's Bay, in New-England, on the 6th day of December, 1766, intituled,

" An Act for granting Compensation to the Sufferers, and of free and general Pardon, Indemnity, and Oblivion, to the Offenders in the late Times."

The Lords of the Committee, in obedience to your Majesty's said order of reference, did on the 1st and 4th of this instant, and again upon this day, meet, and take the said representation and act into their consideration, fideration, together with the charter granted to the said Province, by your Majefty's royal predeceffors, King William and Queen Mary, and alfo your Majefty's commiffion and inftruction to the prefent Governor of that Province, and upon a due deliberation had thereupon, and after a diligent enquiry into the precedents of the conduct of the Council Board, in fimilar cafes, their Lordfhips are humbly of opinion, that it may be advifeable for your Majefty (if in your royal wifdom you fhall think fit) to difallow and reject the faid act, the faid Affembly having therein unwarrantably incorporated an act of Pardon with an act of Compenfation, without having obtained your Majefty's previous confent to fuch act of Pardon— And that it may likewife be advifeable for your Majefty to direct your Governor of the Maffachufett's Bay, forthwith to require the faid act of Affembly to pafs a particular and effectual act for compenfating all or any of the fufferers, unmixed with any other matter whatfoever, in cafe fuch compenfation fhall not have been already made--And the Committee fubmit this opinion to your Majefty, without prejudice to the confideration of any queftion touching the nullity of the act now under confideration, *ab initio*, whenever the fame may judicially come into queftion.

Copy of his Majefty's Order in Council, dated May 13, 1767, approving of the aforegoing Report of the Lords of the Committee of Council.
(No. V.)
At the Court at St. James's, the 13th of May, 1767.
PRESENT,
The King's Moft Excellent Majefty.
His R. H. the D. of York
A. of Canterbury
Lord Prefident
Duke of Bolton
D. of Queenfbury
E. of Hillfborough
Earl of Shelburne
Vifc. Falmouth
Vifc. Barrington
Vifc. Clare
Bifhop of London

Duke of Argyle
Marq. of Granby
Lord Steward
L. Chamberlain
Earl of Denbigh
E. of Shaftefbury
Earl of Litchfield
E. of Marchmont
Earl of Briftol
Earl of Harcourt
Earl of Ilchefter
Earl of Befborough
L. Berkley of Stratton
Lord Bathurft
Lord Sandys
Mr. Treafurer of the Houfehold
J. Stewart Mackenzie, Efq.
Wellb. Ellis, Efq.
Sir Gilbert Elliot
Mafter of the Rolls.

Upon reading at the Board a report of the Right Hon. the Lords of the Committee of Council for Plantation Affairs, dated the 9th of this inftant, in the words following, viz.
At the Council-Chamber, Whitehall, May 9, 1767.
By the Right Honourable the Lords of the Committee of Council for Plantation Affairs.
PRESENT,
Lord Chancellor
Lord Prefident
D. of Grafton
Duke of Bolton
Duke of Ancafter
Lord Steward
Earl of Denbigh
E of Cholmondeley
E. of Marchmont
E. of Briftol
Earl of Harcourt
E. of Hillfborough
E. of Shelburne
Vifc. Howe
Vifc. Barrington
Vifcount Clare
Lord North
Lord Sandys
Mr, Speaker
J. Stuart Mackenzie, Efq;
Mr. Secr. Conway
Mr. Chancellor of the Exchequer
Wellb. Ellis, Efq;
Hans Stanley, Efq;
L. C. J. Wilmot
Ifaac Barré.

Your Majefty having been pleafed, by your order in Council of the 13th of laft month, to refer unto this Committee a reprefentation of the Lords Commiffioners for Trade and Plantations, touching, and concerning an act paffed by the Great and General Court, or Affembly of your Majefty's Province of the Maffachufett's Bay, in New-England, on the 6th of December, 1766, intituled,
" An Act for granting Compenfation to the Sufferers, and of free and general Pardon, Indemnity,

demnity, and Oblivion to the Offenders in the late Times.''

The Lords of the Committee, in obedience to your Majesty's said order of reference, did on the 1st and 4th of this instant, and again, upon this day meet and take the said representation and act into their consideration, together with the charter granted to the said Province, by your Majesty's royal predecessors, King William and Queen Mary, and also your Majesty's commission and instructions to the present Governor of that Province, and upon due deliberation had thereupon, and after a diligent enquiry into the precedents of the conduct of the Council Board, in similar cases, their Lordships are humbly of opinion, that it may be adviseable for your Majesty (if in your royal wisdom you shall think fit) to disallow and reject the said act, the said Assembly having therein unwarrantably incorporated an act of Pardon with an act of Compensation, without having obtained your Majesty's previous consent to such act of Pardon:—And that it may likewise be adviseable for your Majesty to direct your Governor of the Massachusett's Bay forthwith, to require the said Assembly to pass a particular and effectual act for compensating all, or any of the Sufferers, unmixed with any other matter whatsoever, in case such compensation shall not have been already made—And the Committee submit this opinion to your Majesty, without any prejudice to the consideration of any question touching the nullity of the act now under consideration, *ab initio,* whenever the same may judicially come into question.

His Majesty this day took the said report into consideration, and was pleased, with the advice of his Privy Council, to approve thereof, and accordingly to order that the said act be, and it is hereby disallowed and rejected, and his Majesty doth hereby further order, that the Governor,

Lieutenant-Governor, or Commander in Chief of the Province of the Massachusett's Bay, do forthwith require the said Assembly to pass a particular and effectual act for compensating all or any of the sufferers, unmixed with any other matter whatsoever, in case such compensation shall have been already made.

Copy of Major General Gage's Letter to the Secretary at War.
New-York, Oct. 11, 1766.
(No. V.*)

My Lord,

I have used all endeavours to transmit to you the estimates of North-America by the present opportunity, and have the honor to send herewith sixteen different estimates of the ordinary contingent military expences, and three of extraordinary contingent expences, with an abstract of the whole. There yet remains to be sent the estimates of West-Florida, and that of the Quarter-master's department in the district of Albany—both have been wrote for frequently, and will be forwarded to your Lordship as soon as they can be obtained. The engineers are not yet come in from the out-posts, nor the naval people from the Lakes; if any thing shall appear farther necessary to be done in repairs, or to strengthen ourselves in those parts, particular estimates thereof will be transmitted hereafter.

For a long time past I have been examining and curtailing expences as much as could be, in every part under my command, and the estimates now transmitted, I believe to be as exact as they can be made at an average, to ascertain the annual contingent military expences of North America, wanting only to complete the whole of the estimates already mentioned, from West-Florida and Albany.

There appears in the estimate from Hallifax, a great number of store-houses to be repaired; I have wrote to the officer commanding, to dispose

of

of any that fhall not be abfolutely wanted for the fervice.

In the Quarter-Mafter General's department, the article of building boats at Fort Pitt is heavy, but that bufinefs was examined and enquired into before it was undertaken, and the crown pays the fame prices as every trader upon the Ohio; but the moft weighty article, is the tranf-portation of provifions and ftores from Fort Pitt to Fort Chartres. This is put down to fhew the expence that will be incurred, if the neceffity of the fervice fhall oblige me to forward provifions, fufficient for the feeding of a regiment for twelve months, with their cloathing, &c. and that no af-fiftance can be got from the country in the article of provifion. This year a large quantity of provifions has been procured there; if their harveft has been good, a further fupply will be got next year, by which confiderable tranfportations will be faved; and opportunities have offered this year, which has enabled me to make further favings. The recruits which arrived for the 34th regiment have been em-ployed in the tranfportation, in lieu of batteau men, and though to be allowed fome gratuity for the wear of their neceffaries, it will be far fhort of the wages of the others. Upon the whole, this article muft be un-certain, but the fupplying a regiment at the Ilinois is fo very expenfive, that I muft ufe every means in my power that can reduce it.

The payment of the two troops of Rangers in Georgia, is included in the contingent expences, as I don't know whether provifion is made for them with the reft of the army, or not. They are not paid out of the contingencies, but by warrants on the Deputy Pay-mafter General, as the other troops are paid.

It was remarked with the eftimates fent laft year, that the Superinten-dants of the Northern and Southern Indians, drew upon the Commander in Chief for their falaries, as well as for the falaries of all the officers in their refpective departments, and their other contingent expences; but that I could not fend their eftimates, as they were tranfmitted to the Board of Trade. I have, however, defired Sir William Johnfon and Mr. Steuart, to fend me a lift of all their deputies, commiffaries, interpreters, fmiths, &c. with their annual pay. As foon as I fhall be able to procure thefe lifts, they will be forwarded to your Lord-fhip.

Your Lordfhip will pardon my errors from the hurry I write in, to be in time for the mail; which being very near clofing, will not permit me to make further obfervations at pre-fent. If any occur hereafter, I fhall have the honor to mention them by another opportunity. I have the honor to be with great truth, refpect, and efteem, my Lord, your Lord-fhip's moft obedient, and moft hum-ble fervant,

THOMAS GAGE.

Extract of a Letter from Major General Gage to Lord Barrington.
New-York, October 28, 1766.
(No. VI.*)

I take the opportunity of a private fhip, to tranfmit your Lordfhip the eftimates of the Deputy Quarter-Mafter General's department in the diftricts of Albany, and of the ex-pences for the repairs and contin-gencies of Fort Amherft, in the ifland of St. John's, both which arrived too late for the laft packet; and I had omitted to take notice of the laft in my letter, with the other eftimates fent by that opportunity. The efti-mate of Weft Florida, I hope, may be tranfmitted to your Lordfhip di-rectly from thence, which I directed to fave time, as alfo that a duplicate might be fent here.

Some

Some expences will probably be incurred at the Ilinois, the estimates of which have been wrote for long ago, but I can't expect any clear account of that post, 'till the chief engineers, whom I sent there, and down the Mississippi, in the spring, shall return to me.

In the estimate of the Barrack-Master General, the yearly sum to be allowed contractors, for keeping up and repairing the furniture of the Barracks for twenty years, is inserted, though no contract has as yet been entered into. As soon as any proposals shall be made on this head, they will be transmitted to the Lords Commissioners of his Majesty's Treasury. A sum is likewise charged in the above estimate, for a compleat new set of furniture for the whole barracks in North-America, which in general, was much wanted. From comparing these two sums, the Board of Treasury will be able to form a judgment of the contract, according to the proposals on this head already sent by the Barrack-Master General.

I likewise herewith inclose a list of the superintendants, deputies, commissaries, interpreters, and Smiths, for the managements of Indians in the northern district of North-America, according to what is there called the new plan, which I presume to be a plan settled with the Board of Trade, and may be properly called the Indian Staff for the northern district. As soon as Mr. Steuart, the Superintendant of the southern Indians, sends me the staff of his district, it will be transmitted to your Lordship;—both the Superintendants draw upon the Commander in Chief for their salaries of all their staff, as well as their other expences, estimates of which I have already acquainted your Lordship, are ordered, as I am informed, to be transmitted to the Board of Trade.

An estimate of the expence of provisions is making out in the best manner it can be done, but I fear it will not be finished in time for the present conveyance.

Extract of a Letter from Major General Gage to Lord Barrington.
New-York, Nov. 9, 1766.
(No. VII.*)

I have the honour to transmit your Lordship the estimate of the expence of provisions consumed annually in North-America, calculated for every part except West-Florida, from whence the returns were forbid to be sent to the Commissary General, as his deputy informs him; but as I afterwards sent particular directions to Colonel Taylor, acting Brigadier-General, concerning this matter, since his arrival at Pensacola, I am to hope they will at length be procured. When the returns shall be received, the expence arising from the provisions in that province, will be added to the inclosed estimate. As your Lordship pressed so strongly for the estimates, I send off without delay, all that I can procure, as they come in.

Extracts from the Manuscript Journal of the General Assembly of New-York, laid before Parliament.
Assembly-Chamber, City-Hall, in the City of New-York, Die Lunæ, 11 ho. A. M. the 10th of November, 1766.

The General Assembly having on the 3d of July last, been prorogued to Tuesday the 7th of October next following, and his Excellency the Governor having, by several proclamations since published, farther prorogued them to this day, to meet upon business.

Fifteen members pursuant thereto, appearing in the Assembly-Chamber, Mr. Speaker took the chair.

Ordered, That Mr. Bayard and Colonel Livingston wait upon his Excellency the Governor, and acquaint him that a sufficient number of members are met to proceed upon business, fines, and that they attend his directions.

Mr. Bayard reported, that Colonel Livingston and himself, had waited on his Excellency the Governor, and delivered their message, and that his Excellency had been pleased to say he would come up to the Council-Chamber in the City-Hall immediately, and send a message for the house.

A message from his Excellency the Governor, by Mr. Banyar, Deputy Secretary.

Mr. Speaker, His Excellency the Governor requires the immediate attendance of this house in the Council-Chamber, in the City-Hall.

Mr. Speaker left the chair, and the whole house attended accordingly, and being returned, he resumed the chair, and reported that his Excellency had been pleased to make a speech to the house, of which, to prevent mistakes, he had obtained a copy, which being read, is in the words following ; viz.

Gentlemen of the Council, and Gentlemen of the General Assembly,

" The meeting of the General Assembly has been delayed beyond the usual time, as I was in daily expectation of receiving his Majesty's commands, in regard to an humble representation made of the distress in which this colony would shortly be involved, through the want of a sufficient paper currency. And it is with the greatest satisfaction, that I can open this session with a fresh instance of his Majesty's paternal regard and protection extended to this Province, who has been graciously pleased, under certain restrictions, to revoke that instruction, by which the Commander in Chief here was precluded from giving his consent to any act which should be framed for striking bills of credit, and issuing the same in lieu of money. The royal attention, so constantly paid to the sufferings of the people, and the late examples given of it, are such signal instances of his Majesty's condescension and tenderness

for their interests, as cannot fail of exciting the warmest sentiments of gratitude in the minds of every subject, and be productive of the highest returns of duty and submission.

Gentlemen of the General Assembly,

" The great expence in which this colony has been engaged for some time past, and the difficulties which still subsist in regard to limits, between this and the neighbouring Provinces of Massachusett's and the Jerseys, have engaged me to ascertain as soon as possible, the line which his Majesty has been pleased to fix by his royal proclamation, for the boundary between this Province and Quebec, and after the necessary supplies of government are raised, I must recommend it to the General Assembly to make provision for the farther opening and continuing this line, in which I flatter myself, that the province of Quebec, equally interested in it, will readily contribute, as a mutual benefit will be derived from it. I must at the same time, earnestly request that proper measures may be taken to settle the boundaries between the different counties in this Province, and fix them by authority :—The want of a due attention to so necessary a service, has already given rise to many inconveniences, and the continual scenes of litigation and disorder, occasioned by vague and undetermined limits, call for redress in the strongest terms.

Gentlemen of the Council, and Gentlemen of the General Assembly,

" I shall, during the course of your session, take opportunities of laying before you some matters which have occurred to me during the late tour I made, and recommending to your consideration whatever may be conducive to the public service ; as I am fully persuaded, that the legislative bodies will chearfully co-operate with me in whatever can be proposed for his Majesty's service, and the good of their country.   H. MOORE."

New-York, Nov. 10, 1766.

U   Resolved,

Refolved, That his Excellency's fpeech be taken into confideration, to-morrow, by the houfe.

Affembly - Chamber, at the Houfe of Matthew Erneft, in the Out-Ward of the City of New-York, Die Martis, 10 ho. A. M. the 11th of November, 1766.

To his Excellency Sir Henry Moore, Bart. Captain-General, and Governor in Chief, in, and over the Colony of New-York, and the Territories depending thereon in America, Chancellor and Vice-Admiral of the fame.

The humble Addrefs of the General Affembly of the faid Colony.

May it pleafe your Excellency,

We his Majefty's moft dutiful fubjects, the General Affembly of the Colony of New-York, return your Excellency our moft hearty thanks for your fpeech.

The fatisfaction your Excellency expreffes in being permitted to relieve the diftrefs this colony is fallen into, through the want of a medium of trade, cannot but be extremely agreeable to us, as it affords a further proof of your attention to, and concern for our interefts.

We are deeply fenfible of his Majefty's paternal care and tender regard for all his fubjects, and we are confident we fhall ever be ready to make fuch returns of duty and fubmiffion, as may be expected from the moft loyal fubjects to the beft of fovereigns.

Had your Excellency been permitted, by the inftructions you have received, to have paffed a bill for the iffuing of paper money in the ufual manner, we fhould have been fo cautious in the exercife of that power, that no perfon, either at home or abroad, would have been in the leaft danger of being injured in his property, and the public credit of this Colony would have been, as it ever has been, the object of our peculiar care and attention. But, fince we fear that no bill for that purpofe can be paffed without a fufpending claufe, are determined to bear our diftreffes

as well as we are able, except your Excellency will be pleafed, confidering the preffing neceffities we lay under, to pafs a bill without fuch an unufual claufe.

Your Excellency's care to fettle the boundaries between this Colony and Quebec, will probably prevent many mifchievous confequences which might otherwife arife from the neglect of a thing of that importance, and, for like reafons, we fhall be ready to contribute all the affiftance in our power, to enable your Excellency to fettle, at leaft, a temporary line of jurifdiction between this Colony and the Province of the Maffachufett's Bay.

The fettlement of the boundaries of the feveral counties in this Colony, where they are in a manner uncertain, we look upon as an object deferving the moft ferious attention of the legiflature, and abfolutely neceffary to peace, order, and the due execution of the powers of government. We fhall pay a due regard, therefore, to what your Excellency recommends on that fubject, as well as to whatever elfe you fhall think proper to lay before us during the courfe of this feffion, in which we fhall be ambitious of demonftrating, that your Excellency has done us no more than ftrict juftice, in fuppofing that we will chearfully co-operate with you, in whatever can be propofed for his Majefty's fervice, and the good of this country. By order of the General Affembly, W. NICOLL, Speaker.

Affembly-Chamber, in the Out-Ward of the City of New-York, the 13th of November, 1766.

His Excellency's Anfwer.

Gentlemen of the General Affembly,

I return you my hearty thanks for this addrefs, and for the fentiments you exprefs of my attention to the public welfare. The affurances you give of acting chearfully with me, in fo good a caufe, cannot fail of being productive of the greateft advantage to this Colony.

Mr.

Mr. Banyar, Deputy Secretary, brought to the House, from his Excellency the Governor, an additional instruction from his Majesty to him, which his Excellency desired might be communicated to the House, and being read, is in the words following:

Additional Instructions to our Trusty and Well-beloved Sir H. Moore, Bart. our Captain-General, and Governor in Chief of our Province of New-York, and the Territories depending thereon in America. Given at our Court at St. James's, the 15th Day of July, 1766, in the Sixth Year of our Reign.

George R.

L. S.

Whereas by the 20th Article of our General Instructions to you, given at our Court at St. James's, the day of   , in the sixth year of our reign, you are strictly forbid to give your assent to any act within our Province of New-York, under your government, whereby paper bills may be struck or issued in lieu of money, unless upon sudden and extraordinary emergencies of government, in case of war, or invasion, and upon no other occasion whatever. And whereas it hath been represented unto us, that the currency of all the paper bills of credit now in circulation within our said Province of New-York, will, by the limitation of the laws by which they were respectively issued, cease and determine in the year 1768, by means whereof the commerce of our said Province, as well as the ordinary services of government there, will be exposed to great difficulty and inconvenience. It is, therefore, our will and pleasure, that the 20th Article of our said General Instructions to you, relative to the issue of paper bills of credit,

be, and it is hereby revoked and annulled. And it is our further will and pleasure, and you are hereby permitted and allowed to give your assent to any act or acts of Assembly of the said Province, for creating and issuing paper bills of credit, in lieu of, and for securing any sum or sums of money, not exceeding in the whole the sum of £260000 currency of that Province, provided that in such act or acts of Assembly, whereby such paper bills, or bills of credit, shall be created or issued, due care be taken to ascertain the real value of such paper bills, or bills of credit, and that an ample and sufficient fund be provided for calling in, sinking, and discharging the said bills within a reasonable time, not exceeding five years, and provided, that you do take care, in the passing of any act, or acts of Assembly for the purposes above-mentioned, that there be a clause, or clauses inserted, therein suspending and deferring the execution thereof, until our pleasure shall be known concerning the same.

G. R.

The House then resolved itself into a committee of the whole House, upon his Excellency's speech—after some time spent therein, Mr. Speaker resumed the chair, and Mr. Philip Livingston reported from the said committee, that they had made some progress therein, and had directed him to move that they may have leave to sit again.

Resolved, That his Excellency's speech be taken into further consideration to-morrow—and then the House adjourned till nine o'clock to-morrow morning.

Die Mercurii, 9 ho. A. M. the 12th of November, 1766.

Ordered, That the Treasurer of the Colony, do, by Tuesday the 25th instant, lay before this House, the several following accounts on oath, viz. " An account of the amount of the duty, laid by virtue of an act for

granting

granting to his Majefty the feveral duties and impofitions on goods, wares, and merchandizes imported into this Colony therein-mentioned, together with an account how much had been paid out of the fame, from the 1ft day of September, 1765, to the firft day of September, 1766.

" An account of the amount of licences to hawkers and pedlars, from the 1ft day of September, 1765, to the 1ft day of September, 1766.

" An account of the amount of his receipts, from the feveral and refpective loan-officers, diftinguifhing how much, on account of the principal, and how much for intereft, fince his laft account thereof delivered.

" An account of his receipts on the excife fund fince his laft account thereof delivered—An account of his payments out of the £5000, lodged in his hands, by an act paffed in the year 1765, for refrefhing, &c. fuch of his Majefty's troops as may pafs through this Colony, fince his laft account thereof delivered—An account of his receipts from the feveral and refpective collectors and county Treafurers, on account of the feveral and refpective taxes, and arrears of taxes due to this Colony, from the time that his laft accounts thereof was delivered, until the day he delivered his accounts, diftinguifhing particularly, how much paid by each refpective city and county, on what tax, and on what arrears of taxes.

" An account how much hath arifen by virtue of an act, intitled, An Act for laying a Duty of Tonnage on the Veffels, and for the Time therein-mentioned, from the 1ft day of September, 1765, to the firft day of September, 1766.

" An account of his receipts, by virtue of the feveral acts, enabling him to draw bills of exchange on Sir William Baker, Knt. and Robert Charles, Efq; for money allotted to this Colony by his Majefty, out of the parliamentary grants, towards re-

imburfing the Colonies the expence of the war, fince his laft account thereof delivered.

" An account of his receipts, by virtue of an act paffed the 20th of October, 1764, intitled, An Act, appropriating the fum of £59250 of the monies therein-mentioned, for calling in, finking, and cancelling bills of credit, to the amount of the miffions therein-mentioned, together with an account of the bills of credit cancelled in confequence of the faid act, fince his laft account thereof delivered.

" An account how much he hath received, purfuant to an act paffed the 20th of December, 1763, intitled, An Act to impower John Cruger, Robert R. Livingfton, Philip Livingfton, Leonard Lifpenard, and William Bayard, Efqrs. to receive from the Colony of Pennfylvania, the fum of £4368 2s. 6d. fterling, overpaid to the faid Colony out of the parliamentary grant, for the fervice of the year 1760, fince his laft account thereof delivered.

" An account of his payments, purfuant to an act paffed the 20th of October, 1764."

Die Martis, 9 *ho. A. M. the* 18th *of November*, 1766.

A meffage from his Excellency the Governor, by Mr. Banyar, Deputy-Secretary, which being read, is in the words following ; viz.

Gentlemen of the General Affembly,

In confequence of a report made to the Lords Commiffioners for Trade and Plantations, of the act paffed in the laft feffion of Affembly, for providing barracks, fuel, &c. for his Majefty's troops quartered in this city, and my letter to the Secretary of State on the fame occafion, I have had the honor of the following letter from the Earl of Shelburne.

S I R, *Whitehall, Aug.* 9, 1766.

I took the firft opportunity, after his Majefty had been moft gracioufly pleafed to entruft me with the feals of the fouthern department, to lay before

fore him your letter of the 20th of June, giving an account of the general fatisfaction expreffed by all ranks and degrees of people, on the repeal of the Stamp-act, and likewife your reafons for affenting to a bill for providing barracks, firewood, candles, bedding, and utenfils for the kitchen, for the King's troops, as demanded, notwithftanding the articles of falt, vinegar, cyder, and beer, be not included, under a pretence that they are not provided for the troops lodged in the barracks in Europe.

I have his Majefty's commands to acquaint you of the fatisfaction he feels in the happinefs of his fubjects, arifing from the tender care and confideration of his Parliament. But I am ordered to fignify to you, at the fame time, that as it is the indifpenfible duty of his fubjects in America to obey the acts of the legiflature of Great Britain, the King both expects and requires a due and chearful obedience to the fame, and it cannot be doubted that his Majefty's Province of New-York, after the lenity of Great Britain fo recently extended to America, will not fail duly to carry into execution the act of parliament paffed laft feffion, for quartering his Majefty's troops, in the full extent and meaning of the act, without referring to the ufage of other parts of his Majefty's dominions, where the legiflature has thought fit to prefcribe different regulations, and which cannot be altered any more than in North America, except upon a refpectful and well-grounded reprefentation of the hardfhip or inconvenience. Thefe confiderations, I am convinced muft, of themfelves, have fo much weight with the Affembly of New-York, not only in the prefent conjuncture, when it is natural to fuppofe the minds of men retain fenfible impreffions of what has lately paffed, but upon other occafions which may call for a ready obedience, that I cannot think it necef-

fary for me to enlarge further upon their importance—I muft only, Sir, in general, add, that I hope and believe, that a very little time, together with that temporal adminiftration of government, which your regard to the people under it, muft make you naturally incline to, and that firmnefs which your duty to the King equally requires, will allay whatever remains of thofe heats, which have fo unhappily for America prevailed, and which if continued, muft prove of the moft fatal confequence to whatever Province they are fuffered in. I am, therefore, perfuaded that the Affembly will lofe no occafion that offers, of convincing his Majefty, that the people of New-York will yield to no other part of his fubjects, in duty, loyalty, and obedience to fuch laws as the King and Parliament have thought proper to enact, for their benefit and protection.

(Signed)   SHELBURNE.

I flatter myfelf, that on a due confideration of this letter, no difficulties can poffibly arife, or the leaft objection be made to the provifion for the troops, as required by the act of parliament.   H. MOORE.
Fort-George, Nov. 17, 1766.

Ordered, That the faid meffage be referred to the confideration of the committee, to whom his Excellency's fpeech is committed.

Die Mercurii, 9 ho. A. M. the 19th *of November,* 1766.

The Houfe (according to order) refolved itfelf into a committee of the whole Houfe upon his Excellency's fpeech—after fome time fpent therein, Mr. Speaker refumed the chair, and Mr. Philip Livingfton reported the refolutions of the committee, which he read in his place, and afterwards delivered in at the table, where the fame were again read and agreed to by the Houfe, and are as follow, viz.

" Refolved, That it is the opinion of this committee, that there be allowed unto his Excellency Sir Henry Moore,

Moore, Bart. for adminiftring the government of this Colony, from the 1ft day of September, 1766, to the 1ft day of September, which will be in the year 1767, after the rate of £2000 *per annum*.

" Refolved, That it is the opinion of this committee, that there be allowed unto his faid Excellency, for providing firewood and candles for his Majefty's Fort George, in the city of New-York, from the 1ft day of September, 1766, to the 1ft day of September, 1767, the fum of £400.

" Refolved, That it is the opinion of this committee, that there be allowed unto the Hon. Daniel Horfemanden, Efq; as Chief Juftice of the Supreme Court of this Colony, and for going the circuits from the 1ft day of September, 1766, to the 1ft day of September, 1767, after the rate of £300 *per Annum*.

" That it is the opinion of this committee, that there be allowed unto the Hon. David Jones, Efq; as Second Juftice of the Supreme Court of this Colony, and for going the circuits from and to the time aforefaid, after the rate of £200 *per annum*.

" Refolved, That it is the opinion of this committee, that there be allowed unto the Hon. William Smith, Efq; as Third Juftice of the Supreme Court of this Colony, and for going the circuits from and to the time aforefaid, after the rate of £200 *per annum*.

" Refolved, That it is the opinion of this committee, that there be allowed unto the Hon. Robert R. Livingfton, Efq; as Fourth Juftice of the Supreme Court of this Colony, and for going the circuits from and to the time aforefaid, after the rate of £200 *per annum*.

" That it is the opinion of this committee, that there be allowed unto William Weyman, as public Printer of this Colony, for his fervices in that ftation, from and to the time aforefaid, after the rate of £50 *per annum*.

" Refolved, That it is the opinion of this committee, that there be allowed unto Abraham de Peyfter, Efq; Treafurer of this Colony, for his fervices in that ftation, from and to the time aforefaid, after the rate of £200 *per annum*.

" Refolved, That it is the opinion of this committee, that there be allowed unto the faid Treafurer, for the extraordinary fervices which he is now obliged to perform beyond the ufual duty of his office, after the rate of the further fum of £100 *per annum*.

" Refolved, That it is the opinion of this committee, that there be allowed unto Robert Charles, Efq; Agent for this Colony in Great-Britain, as a reward for his care, trouble, and diligence, in attending upon his Majefty, and his minifters of ftate, in that ftation, from and to the time aforefaid, after the rate of £500 *per annum*.

" Refolved, That it is the opinion of this committee, that there be allowed unto John Tabor Kempe, Efq; his Majefty's Attorney-General of this Colony, for feveral extraordinary fervices by him performed in that ftation, the fum of £150.

" Refolved, That it is the opinion of this committee, that there be allowed unto Abraham Lott, Efq; Clerk of the General Affembly, for his fervices in that ftation, from the 1ft day of September, 1766, to the 1ft day of September, 1767, twenty fhillings *per diem*, payable upon a certificate from the General Affembly, figned by the Speaker, for the number of days he has ferved, or may ferve the General Affembly.

" Refolved, That it is the opinion of this committee, that there be allowed for anfwering fuch neceffary and contingent charges as may arife or happen for the fervice of this Colony, from the 1ft day of September, 1766, to the 1ft day of September, 1767, the fum of £100.

" Refolved,

" Refolved, That the foregoing feveral allowances be made payable out of the monies arifen, or which may arife by virtue of the following acts ; viz.

" An act for granting to his Majefty the feveral duties and impofitions on goods, wares, and merchandizes imported into this Colony therein-mention. And

" An Act to reftrain hawkers and pedlars within this Colony, from felling without licence.

" Ordered, That a bill be brought in, purfuant to the faid refolutions, and that Colonel Seaman and Mr. Schenk prepare and bring in the fame."

Die Martis, 9 ho. A. M. the 25th of November, 1766.

A meffage from his Excellency the Governor by Mr. Banyar, Deputy Secretary, which being read, is in the words following ; viz. ·

Gentlemen of the General Affembly,

" Inclofed, is an account of what money has been paid to the officers of his Majefty's 28th regiment in quarters here, who were lodged in the town, as there was not fufficient room for them in the barracks provided for the two battalions and company of artillery, by act paffed in the laft feffion of Affembly. This fum has been advanced by the Mayor and corporation of this city, and agreeable to their requeft, it is now recommended to the Houfe of Affembly, that they may be re-imburfed. No money has been paid as yet, either to the officers of his Majefty's 46th regiment, or to the officers of the artillery. H. MOORE. " *Fort-George, Nov. 24, 1766.*"

Ordered, That the faid meffage and account mentioned therein, be referred to the confideration of a committee of the whole Houfe.

Abraham de Peyfter, Treafurer of this Colony (according to order) attending at the door, was called in, and laid before the Houfe the feveral accounts on oath ; viz.

" An account of the produce of the tonnage fund, from the 1ft day of September, 1765, to the 1ft day of September, 1766, amounting to the fum of £406 18s. 4d. $\frac{1}{4}$.

" An account that he has received from the feveral and refpective loan-officers, fince his laft account thereof delivered ; viz.

For intereft   -   -   £. 1375
On account of the principal £11375

" An account that he has received from the feveral collectors and county Treafurers, on account of the feveral taxes laid by feveral laws of this Colony, amounting from the 5th of December, 1765, to the 25th of November, 1766, to the fum of £17829 6s. 2d. $\frac{1}{2}$.

" An account that he has paid, purfuant to an act paffed the 3d of July, 1766, intitled, An Act to furnifh the Barracks in the Cities of New-York and Albany, with Firewood and Candles, and the other Neceffaries therein-mentioned, for his Majefty's Forces, the fum of £3200.

" An account that he has received from John Cruger, Philip Livingfton, Robert R. Livingfton, Leonard Lifpenard, and William Bayard, Efqrs. on account of the £4368 2s. 6d. fterling, they were impowered by law to receive from the Colony of Pennfylvania, fince his laft account thereof delivered, the fum of £456 0s. 2d.

" An account that he has received for feveral bills of exchange drawn on Sir William Baker, Knt. and Robert Charles, Efq; fince his laft account thereof delivered, the fum of £4608.

" A general account of the amount of the feveral duties, &c. for fupporting the government of this Colony, together with an account of the payments out of the fame, from the 1ft day of September, 1765, to the 1ft day of September, 1766, wherein he charges himfelf with the balance due to this Colony on account of the faid duties, &c. on the 1ft day of

September,

	£.	s.	d.
September, 1765, of the fum of	2460	3	5¾

With the fum of £4811 8s. 11d. ¾ received for the duty on rum, wine, brandy, &c. during the abovefaid time. — 4811   8   11¾

And with the fum of £135 received for licence to hawkers and pedlars, during the abovefaid time — 135

£7406   12   5½

And charges the Colony with fundry fums paid out of the faid fund, amounting to the fum of — £7111   4   6

And makes a balance due to the Colony on the 1ft day of September, 1766, of the fum of £ 295   7   11½

Die Martis, 9 ho. A. M. the 2d of December, 1766.

Mr. Speaker communicated to the Houfe the following letter and accounts ; viz.

" A letter from his Honor the Lieutenant-Governor, dated the 1ft inftant, demanding payment for arrears of falary due to him, from the 1ft of September to the 13th of November, 1765, and alfo for damages by him fuftained on the 1ft day of November, 1765.

" An account of Alexander Gordon, Efq; for a fingle fleigh loft on the faid 1ft day of November, 1765.

" An account of Dr. Jonathan Mallet, of a fingle horfe-chaife, and part of harnefs, loft on the faid 1ft day of November, 1765.

" And an account of Andrew Gautier, for repairing the damages done to the houfe of Samuel Francis,

on the faid 1ft day of November, 1765.

" Ordered, That the faid letter and accounts be referred to the confideration of a committee."

Die Veneris, 9 ho. A. M. 5th of December, 1766.

The Houfe taking into confideration the many grievances refulting from the act of parliament, reftraining the iffuing paper bills of credit to the inhabitants of this Colony, for want of a proper medium of trade.

" Refolved, Than an humble addrefs be prepared, in order to be prefented to the parliament of Great-Britain, reprefenting the hardfhips and inconveniencies the inhabitants of this Colony lay under, for the want of a competent medium of trade, and praying relief.

" Ordered, That a committee be appointed to prepare the faid addrefs, and a committee was appointed accordingly."

Die Martis, 9 ho. A. M. the 9th of December, 1766.

A meffage from his Excellency the Governor, by Mr. Banyar, Deputy-Secretary, which being read, is in the words following ; viz.

Gentlemen,

" The inclofed accounts duly attefted, of the workmen employed in the reparations and alterations of the houfe at the Fort, are now laid before the Houfe of Affembly, and recommended for payment.   H. MOORE.

" *Fort-George, Dec.* 8, 1766."

Ordered, That the faid meffage and accounts be referred to the confideration of a committee, and that it be an inftruction to them to add a proper claufe, or claufes to the bill now in committee, for paying Major James his loffes, for paying fo much of the faid accounts as fhall be found to be really and truly due thereon.

A meffage from his Excellency the Governor, by Mr. Banyar, Deputy-Secretary, which being read, is in the words following ; viz.

Gentlemen,

Gentlemen,

" His Majesty's 28th and 46th regiments having been employed for some time in quelling the riots and disorders which had broke out in the counties of Duchess and Albany, I now recommend it to the House of Assembly, that a compensation be made to them for the extraordinary necessaries expended by them in the service of the government.

H. MOORE.

" *Fort George, Dec.* 8, 1766."

A petition of Henry Van Shaack, of the city of Albany, merchant, was presented to the House, and read, praying an allowance for damages by him sustained on the 6th of January last, by disorders occasioned by the late Stamp-act, amounting, as by the account annexed to the said petition, to the sum of £103 1s. 6d.

Ordered, That the said petition and account be referred to the same committee.

The House resolved itself into a committee of the whole House, upon the bill, intitled, " An Act for paying Major Thomas James, the Losses by him sustained on the 1st of November, 1765," and the several other accounts referred to the committee on the said bill :—after some time spent therein, Mr. Speaker resumed the chair, and Mr. Bayard reported the proceedings of the committee to have been in manner following ; viz. " That they had resolved to make the following allowances, and added proper clauses to the said bill, for paying unto Andrew Gautier, for repairing the house of Samuel Francis, for damages done thereto, on the 1st of November, 1765, the sum of £404 6s. 5d.

Unto Jonathan Mallet, for damages by him sustained on the said 1st day of November, 1765, the sum of ——— £36 0s. 0d.

And unto Henry Van Shaack,

of Albany for damages by him sustained on the 6th day of January, 1766, the sum of - £103 1s. 6d.

" That a letter from his Honor the Lieutenant-Governor to Mr. Speaker, of the 1st instant, demanding payment for arrears of salary, due to him from the 1st of September to the 13th of November, 1765, also for damages by him sustained on the 1st of November, 1765, was then read, and the same being maturely considered, the committee came to the following resolutions thereon ; viz.

" Resolved, That it is the opinion of this committee, that the loss sustained by Lieutenant - Governor Colden, on the 1st day of November, 1765, was occasioned by his own misconduct, and that therefore no provision ought to be made for paying him the same.

" Resolved, That it is the opinion of this committee, that that part of the Lieutenant Governor's letter relating to the arrears of salary due to him, be referred to the consideration of the committee to whom his Excellency's speech is committed.

" Resolved, That the message of his Excellency the Governor, relating to the repairs done to the house in the Fort, with the accounts accompanying the same, be referred to the consideration of the committee to whom his Excellency's speech is committed."

Die Veneris, 9 *ho. A. M. the* 12*th of December,* 1766.

The House (according to order) resolved itself into a committee of the whole House, upon the message of his Excellency the Governor, of the 17th of November last, relating to the provision required for his Majesty's troops quartered in this colony :—after some time spent therein, Mr. Speaker resumed the chair, and Mr. Philip Livingston reported the resolution of the committee thereon, which he read in

X his

his place, and afterwards delivered it in at the table, where the same was again read, and is as follows; viz.

" Refolved, That it is the opinion of this committee, that an humble addrefs be prefented to his Excellency the Governor, in anfwer to the faid meffage, fhewing that the General Affembly cannot, confiftent with the truft repofed in them by their conftituents, comply with the requifition made by the faid meffage, and that the reafons thereof be fet forth in the faid addrefs.

" Refolved, *(Nemine Contradicente)* That the Houfe do agree with the committee in the faid refolution."

The Houfe (according to order) refolved itfelf into a committee of the whole Houfe upon his Excellency's fpeech, and the feveral other papers referred thereto :—after fome time fpent therein, Mr. Speaker refumed the chair, and Colonel Seaman, in behalf of Mr. Philip Livingfton, reported the proceeding of the committee, which he read in his place, and afterwards delivered in at the table, where the fame were again read and agreed to by the Houfe, and are as follows ; viz.

" That upon reading of the meffage from his Excellency the Governor, of the 8th inftant, recommending a compenfation to be made to the detachments of his Majefty's 28th and 46th regiments that were employed in quieting the diforders in the counties of Duchefs and Albany, Mr. Juftice Livingfton moved, that there be allowed to each private man of the 46th regiment the fum of twenty fhillings, and to each private man of the 28th the fum of ten fhillings, as a gratuitity for their fervices."

And a debate arifing, and the queftion being put upon the faid motion, it was carried in the negative, in the manner following ; viz.

For the Affirmative	For the Negative
Col. Livingfton	Mr. Speaker
Mr. Cruger	Mr. Kiffam
Mr. Bayard	Mr. Boerum
Col. Philipfe	Mr. Schenk
Mr. Holland	Mr. Thomas
Mr. de Lancey	Col. Haring
Mr. Juftice Livingfton	Mr. Philip Livingfton
Mr. Miller	Capt. Seaman
	Col. Seaman.

[Upon all divifions, the names of the gentlemen, *for* and *againft*, are entered upon the journals.]

Die Sabbati, 9 *ho. A. M. the* 13*th of December,* 1766.

The engroffed bill, intituled, " An Act for paying the Salaries and Services of the feveral Officers of the Government, from the 1ft Day of September, One Thoufand Seven Hundred and Sixty-Six, to the 1ft Day of September, One Thoufand Seven Hundred and Sixty-Seven, inclufive, and other Services thereinmentioned," was read the third time.

Refolved, That the bill do pafs.

Ordered, That Mr. Cruger and Mr. Bayard do carry the bill to the Council, and defire their concurrence thereto.

A petition of Jacob Dyckman, junior, Benjamin Palmer, and John Vermillie, was prefented to the Houfe and read, praying a reimburfement of the expence they have been at in building a free bridge over Harlem River, nigh King's Bridge.

Ordered, That the faid petition be referred to the confideration of the committee to whom the memorial of Col. Philipfe is committed.

The Houfe then refolved itfelf into a committee of the whole Houfe upon the faid memorial and petition :— after fome time fpent therein, Mr. Speaker refumed the chair, and Mr. Kiffam reported the refolution of the committee, which he read in his place,

place, and afterwards delivered in at the table, and is as follows; viz.

"Resolved, That it is the opinion of this committee, that the further consideration of the said memorial and petition be postponed until the second Tuesday next, after the first meeting of this House, after the 1st day of May next."

And the said resolution being again read,

"Resolved, That the House do agree with the committee in the said resolution."

Die Lunæ, 3 ho. P. M. the 15th of December, 1766.

The engrossed address to his Excellency the Governor was read, and approved of by the House.

Ordered, That Mr. Speaker sign the said address in behalf of the House, which is in the following words; viz.

To his Excellency Sir Henry Moore, Bart. Captain-General and Governor in Chief in and over the Colony of New-York, and the Territories depending thereon in America, Chancellor, and Vice Admiral of the same.

The Humble Address of the General Assembly of the said Colony.

May it please your Excellency,

We his Majesty's most dutiful and loyal subjects the General Assembly of the Colony of New-York, have taken your Excellency's message of the 17th of November last into our most serious consideration, and beg leave to assure your Excellency, that nothing would give us greater pleasure, than to find it in our power to comply with every requisition tending in any manner to promote his Majesty's service. It is, therefore, with great concern, that we find it impossible to comply with what is now demanded, consistent with our obligations to our constituents. We shall always be ready to give the amplest testimonies of our loyalty to his Majesty, and submission to his government, from which we humbly conceive we do not deviate,

when we shew a regard to the interests of his faithful subjects in this Colony, absolutely necessary to their preservation.

We hope it will be considered, that we are chosen to make such a provision for the support of his Majesty's government in this Colony (as well as for other important purposes) as is most suitable to the circumstances of the people we represent, and that we should be guilty of a breach of that most sacred trust, if we should load them with burthens we are incapable of supporting.

In the provision we made last session for quartering two battalions and one company of artillery, we loaded ourselves with a burthen much greater than any of the neighbouring governments lie under for that service, and imagined, that far from being censured on that account, it would be accepted as a new instance of that loyalty and affection to his Majesty's government, of which this Colony has exhibited so many proofs.

We beg leave further to represent to your Excellency, that by the act of parliament it appears to be the intention of the legislature to provide for the quartering soldiers only on a march, but according to the construction put on it here, it required that all the forces which shall at any time enter this Colony, shall be quartered during the whole year in a very unusual and expensive manner. That by the marching several regiments into this Colony, this expence would become ruinous and insupportable. And, therefore, we cannot, consistent with our duty to our constituents, put it in the power of any person (whatsoever confidence we may have in his prudence and integrity) to lay such a burthen on them.

We should be very sorry to differ from your Excellency on this or any other political subject, and therefore it is proper to offer these matters to your consideration, in hopes that they will be sufficient to demonstrate, that

X 2   the

the objections against making the provision required, are of a nature the most serious and weighty imaginable. And, therefore, we humbly intreat your Excellency to set our conduct in the most favourable, that is in its true light, by representing that our non-compliance on this occasion proceeds entirely from a just sense of what our duty requires. By order of the General Assembly.

W NICOLL, Speaker.

Assembly-Chamber, Dec. 15, 1766.

Resolved, That the said address be presented to his Excellency by the whole House.

Die Jovis, 9 *ho. A. M. the* 18th *of December,* 1766.

Mr. Speaker reported, that the House had attended his Excellency the Governor with their humble address, according to his appointment, and that his Excellency had been pleased to return the following answer thereto ; viz.

Gentlemen of the General Assembly,

It is with no small concern, that I find the sentiments of this House differing so much from mine, in regard to the subject matter of the address now presented to me, which shall by the first opportunity be transmitted to the Secretary of State, in order to be laid before his Majesty."

Die Veneris, 9 *ho. A. M. the* 19th *of December,* 1766.

A message from his Excellency the Governor, by Mr. Banyar, Deputy-Secretary.

Mr. Speaker, His Excellency the Governor requires the immediate attendance of this House in the Council Chamber, at the house of Mr. Matthew Ernest.

Mr. Speaker left the chair, and with the House attended accordingly, where his Excellency, in the presence of the Council, was pleased to give his assent to twenty acts passed this session.

And after the same was published in the usual manner, his Excellency was pleased to prorogue the General Assembly till Tuesday the 10th day of March, 1767.

In page 5, it is noticed that the Assemblies of Massachusett's Bay and New-York, petitioned in 1764 against the resolution to charge stamp-duties in America ; and that these petitions were suppressed. *(See* Prior Documents, *p.* 5, *first column.)*

[The Editor having been favoured with copies of these Petitions, inserts them as soon as possible.]

Copy of an Address to the King, from the Council and House of Burgesses of the Province of Virginia

To the King's Most Excellent Majesty.

Most Gracious Sovereign,

We your Majesty's dutiful and loyal subjects, the Council and Burgesses of your ancient colony and dominion of Virginia, now met in General Assembly, beg leave to assure your Majesty of our firm and inviolable attachment to your sacred person and government : And as your faithful subjects here have at all times been zealous to demonstrate this truth, by a ready compliance with the royal requisitions during the late war, by which a heavy and oppressive debt of near half a million hath been incurred ; so at this time they implore permission to approach the throne with humble confidence, and to entreat that your Majesty will be graciously pleased to protect your people of this Colony in the enjoyment of their ancient and inestimable right of being governed by such laws, respecting their internal polity and taxation, as are derived from their own consent, with the approbation of their sovereign or his substitute :—a right, which as men and the descendants of Britons, they have ever quietly possessed, since first by royal permission and encouragement they left the mother kingdom to extend its commerce and dominion.

Your

Your Majefty's dutiful fubjects of
Virginia moft humbly and unanimoufly hope, that this invaluable
birth-right, defcended to them from
their anceftors, and in which they
have been protected by your royal
predeceffors, will not be fuffered to
receive injury under the reign of your
facred Majefty, already fo illuftrioufly
diftinguifhed by your gracious attention to the liberties of the people.

That your Majefty may long live
to make nations happy, is the ardent
prayer of your faithful fubjects the
Council and Burgeffes of Virginia.

*To the Right Honourable the Lords
Spiritual and Temporal, in Parliament affembled.*

*The Memorial of the Council and Bur-
geffes of Virginia, now met in General
Affembly,*

Humbly Reprefents,

That your Memorialifts hope an
application to your Lordfhips, the
fixed and hereditary guardians of
Britifh liberty, will not be thought
improper at this time, when meafures
are propofed fubverfive, as they conceive, of that freedom which all men,
efpecially thofe who derive their conftitution from Britain, have a right
to enjoy: and they flatter themfelves
that your Lordfhips will not look upon
them as objects fo unworthy your attention, as to regard any impropriety
in the form or manner of their application, for your Lordfhip's protection
of their juft and undoubted rights as
Britons.

It cannot be prefumption in your
memorialifts, to call themfelves by
this diftinguifhed name, fince they are
defcended from Britons, who left their
native country to extend it's territory
and dominion, and who happily for
Britain, and, as your Memorialifts
once thought for themfelves too, effected this purpofe. As our anceftors
brought with them every right and
privilege they could with juftice claim,
in their mother kingdom, their de-
fcendants may conclude they cannot

be deprived of thofe rights without
injuftice.

Your Memorialifts conceive it to be
a fundamental principle of the Britifh
conftitution, without which freedom
can no where exift; that the people
are not fubject to any taxes, but fuch
as are laid on them by their own confent, or by thofe who are legally appointed to reprefent them: Property
muft become too precarious for the ge-
nius of a free people, which can be
taken from them at the will of others,
who cannot know what taxes fuch people can bear, or the eafieft mode of
raifing them; and who are not under
that reftraint, which is the greateft fecurity againft a burthenfome taxation,
when the reprefentatives themfelves
muft be affected by every tax impofed
on the people.

Your Memorialifts are therefore led
into an humble confidence, that your
lordfhips will not think any reafon fufficient to fupport fuch a power in the
Britifh parliament, where the colonies
cannot be reprefented; a power never
before conftitutionally affumed, and
which if they have a right to exercife
on any occafion, muft neceffarily eftablifh this melancholy truth, That the
inhabitants of the colonies are the
flaves of Britons, from whom they
are defcended, and from whom they
might expect every indulgence, that
the obligations of intereft and affection
can entitle them to.

Your Memorialifts have been invefted with the right of taxing their
own people, from the firft eftablifhment of a regular government in the
colony; and requifitions have been
conftantly made to them by their Sovereigns, on all occafions, when the
affiftance of the colony was thought
neceffary, to preferve the Britifh intereft in America, from whence they
muft conclude they cannot now be deprived of a right they have fo long
enjoyed, and which they have never
forfeited.

The expences incurred during the
laft

laſt war, in compliance with the demands on this colony, by our late and
preſent moſt gracious Sovereigns, have
involved us in a debt of near half a
million : a debt not likely to decreaſe
under the continued expence we are at
in providing for the ſecurity of the
people againſt the incurſions of our
ſavage neighbours, at a time when
the low ſtate of our ſtaple commodity,
the total want of ſpecie, and the late
reſtrictions upon the trade of the colonies, render the circumſtances of the
people extremely diſtreſsful, and which,
if taxes are accumulated upon them by
the Britiſh Parliament, will make them
truly deplorable.

Your Memorialiſts cannot ſuggeſt to
themſelves any reaſon why they ſhould
not ſtill be truſted with the property of
their people, with whoſe abilities, and
the leaſt burthenſome mode of taxing,
(with great deference to the ſuperior
wiſdom of Parliament) they muſt be
beſt acquainted.

Your Memorialiſts hope they ſhall
not be ſuſpected of being actuated on
this occaſion by any principles but
thoſe of the pureſt loyalty and affection, as they always endeavoured,
by their conduct, to demonſtrate that
they conſider their connections with
Great-Britain, the ſeat of Liberty, as
their greateſt happineſs.

The duty they owe to themſelves
and their poſterity, lays your Memorialiſts under the neceſſity of endeavouring to eſtabliſh their conſtitution
upon its proper foundation. And
they do moſt humbly pray your Lordſhips to take this ſubject into your
conſideration, with the attention that
is due to the well-being of the colonies, on which the proſperity of
Great Britain does in a great meaſure
depend.

To the Right Honourable the Knights,
Citizens, and Burgeſſes of Great-
Britain, in Parliament aſſembled.
The Remonſtrance of the Council and
Burgeſſes of Virginia.

It appearing by the printed votes
of the Houſe of Commons of Great-
Britain in parliament aſſembled, that
in a committee of the whole Houſe
the 17th day of March laſt, it was
reſolved, That towards defending,
protecting and ſecuring the Britiſh
colonies and plantations in America,
it may be proper to charge certain
ſtamp duties in the ſaid colonies and
plantations ; and it being apprehended that the ſame ſubject which
was then declined, may be reſumed
and further purſued in a ſucceeding
ſeſſion, the Council and Burgeſſes of
Virginia met in General Aſſembly,
judge it their indiſpenſable duty in a
reſpectful manner, but with decent
firmneſs, to remonſtrate againſt ſuch
a meaſure ; that at leaſt a cenſion of
thoſe rights, which in their opinion
muſt be infringed by that procedure, may not be inferred from
their ſilence at ſo important a
criſis.

They conceive it is eſſential to Britiſh liberty that laws impoſing taxes
on the people ought not to be made
without the conſent of repreſentatives
choſen by themſelves ; who, at the
ſame time that they are acquainted
with the circumſtances of their conſtituents, ſuſtain a proportion of the
burthen laid on them, This privilege inherent in the perſons who diſcovered and ſettled theſe regions,
could not be renounced, or forfeited
by their removal hither, not as vaga-
bonds and fugitives, but licenſed and
encouraged by their Prince, and animated with a laudable deſire of enlarging the Britiſh dominion, and
extending its commerce ; on the contrary it was ſecured to them and their
deſcendants, with all other rights and
immunities of Britiſh ſubjects, by a
royal charter, which hath been invariably recognized and confirmed by
His Majeſty and his predeceſſors in
their commiſſions to the ſeveral Governors, granting a power, and pre-
ſcribing a form of legiſlation : according to which, laws for the adminiſtration of juſtice, and for the welfare
and

and good government of the colony, have been enacted by the Governor, Council and General Affembly; and to them requifitions and applications for fupplies have been directed by the crown. As an inftance of the opinion which former fovereigns entertained of thefe rights and privileges, we beg leave to refer to three acts of the General Affembly, paffed in the thirty-fecond year of the reign of King Charles the Second (one of which is intitled, *An act for raifing a publick revenue for the better fupport of the government of His Majefty's Colony of* Virginia, impofing feveral duties for that purpofe) which being thought abfolutely neceffary, were prepared in England, and fent over by their then Governor, the Lord Culpepper, to be paffed by the General Affembly, with a full power to give the royal affent thereto; and which were accordingly paffed after feveral amendments were made to them here. Thus tender was His Majefty of the rights of his American fubjects: and the remonftrants do not difcern by what diftinction they can be deprived of that facred birthright and moft valuable inheritance, by their fellow-fubjects; nor with what propriety the can be taxed or affected in their eftates by the parliament, wherein they are not, and indeed cannot, conftitutionally be reprefented.

And if it were proper for the parliament to impofe taxes on the colonies at all, which the remonftrants take leave to think would be inconfiftent with the fundamental principles of the conftitution, the exercife of that power at this time would be ruinous to Virginia, who exerted herfelf in the late war it is feared beyond her ftrength; infomuch that to redeem the money granted for that exigence, her people are taxed for feveral years to come: this, with the large expences incurred for defending the frontiers againft the reftlefs In-

dians, who have infefted her as much fince the peace as before, is fo grievous that an increafe of the burthen will be intolerable; efpecially as the people are very greatly diftreffed already from the fcarcity of circulating cafh amongft them, and from the little value of their ftaple at the Britifh markets.

And it is prefumed, that adding to that load which the colony now labours under, will not be more oppreffive to her people than deftructive of the intereft of Great-Britain: for the plantation trade, confined as it is to the mother-country, hath been a principal means of multiplying and inriching her inhabitants; and if not too much difcouraged, may prove an inexhauftible fource of treafure to the nation. For fatisfaction in this point, let the prefent ftate of the Britifh fleet and trade be compared with what they were before the fettlement of the colonies; and let it be confidered, that whilft property in land may be acquired on very eafy terms, in the vaft uncultivated territory of North America, the colonifts will be moftly, if not wholly employed in agriculture; whereby the exportation of their commodities to Great-Britain, and the confumption of their manufactures fupplied from thence, will be daily increafing. But this moft defirable connection between Great-Britain and her colonies, fupported by fuch an happy intercourfe of reciprocal benefits as is continually advancing the profperity of both, muft be interrupted, if the people of the latter, reduced to extreme poverty, fhould be compelled to manufacture thofe articles they have been hitherto furnifhed with from the former.

From thefe confiderations it is hoped that the Honourable Houfe of Commons will not profecute a meafure, which thofe who may fuffer it cannot but look upon as fitter for exiles driven from their native country

try after ignominiously forfeiting her favours and protection, than for the posterity of Britons, who have at all times been forward to demonstrate all due reverence to the mother-kingdom, and are so instrumental in promoting her glory and felicity; and that British patriots will never consent to the exercise of anti-constitutional power; which even in this remote corner may be dangerous in its example to the interior parts of the British empire, and will certainly be detrimental to its commerce.

To the Honourable the Commons of Great-Britain in Parliament assembled.

The Petition of the Council and House of Representatives of his Majesty's Province of Massachusets Bay,

Most humbly sheweth,

That the act passed in the last session of parliament entitled, *An act granting certain duties in the British colonies and plantations in America, &c.* must necessarily bring many burdens on the inhabitants of those colonies and plantations, which your petitioners conceive, would not have been imposed, if a full representation of the state of the colonies had been made to this honourable house.

That the duties laid upon foreign sugars and molasses by a former act of parliament, entitled, *An act for the better securing and encouraging the trade of his Majesty's sugar colonies in America:* if the act had been executed with rigor, must have had the effect of an absolute prohibition.

That the duties laid on those articles by the present act still remain so great, that, however otherwise intended, they must undoubtedly have the same effect.

That the importation of foreign molasses into this province in particular, is of the greatest importance, and a prohibition will be prejudicial to many branches of its trade, and will lessen the consumption of the manufactures of Great-Britain,

That this importance does not arise merely nor principally from the necessity of foreign molasses, in order to its being consumed or distilled within this province.

That if the trade for many years carried on for foreign molasses can no longer be continued, a vent cannot be found for more than one half the fish of inferior quality, which is caught and cured by the inhabitants of this province; the French permitting no fish to be carried by foreigners to any of their islands, unless it be bartered or exchanged for molasses.

That if there be no sale of fish of inferior quality, it will be impossible to continue the fishery; the fish usually sent to Europe will then cost so dear, that the French will be able to undersell the English at all the European markets, and by this means one of the most valuable returns to Great-Britain will be utterly lost, and that great nursery of seamen destroyed.

That the restraints laid upon the exportation of timber, boards, staves, and other lumber from the colonies to Ireland and other parts of Europe, except Great-Britain, must greatly affect the trade of this province, and discourage the clearing and improving the lands which are yet uncultivated.

That the powers given by the late act to the court of vice-admiralty constituted over all America, are so expressed, as to leave it doubtful, whether goods seized for illicit importation in any of the colonies, may not be removed to any other colony where the judge may reside, although at many hundred miles distance from the place of seizure.

That, if this construction should be admitted, many persons, however legally their goods may have been imported, must lose their property, merely from an inability of following after it, and making that defence which they might do, if the trial had been

been in the colony where the goods were seized; that this construction would be so much the more grievous, seeing that in America, the officers by this act are indemnified in case of seizure, whensoever the judge of admiralty shall certify that there was probable cause; and the claimant can neither have costs, nor maintain an action against the persons seizing, how much soever he may have expended in defence of his property.

That the extension of the powers of courts of vice-admiralty, have, so far as the jurisdiction of the said courts have been extended, deprived the colonies of one of the most valuable of English liberties, trials by juries.

That every act of parliament, which in this respect distinguishes his Majesty's subjects in the colonies, from their fellow-subjects in Great-Britain, must create a very sensible concern and grief.

That there have been communicated to your petitioners sundry resolutions of the House of Commons in their last session, for imposing stamp duties or taxes upon the inhabitants of the colonies, consideration whereof was referred to the next session.

That your petitioners acknowledge with all gratitude, the tenderness of the legislature of Great-Britain, of the liberties and privileges of the subjects in the colonies, who have always judged by their representatives, both of the way and manner in which internal taxes should be raised within the respective governments.

That they humbly hope the colonies in general have so demeaned themselves, more especially during the late war, as still to deserve the continuance of all those liberties and privileges which they have hitherto enjoyed.

That although during the war the taxes upon the colonies were greater than they have been since the conclusion of it, yet the sources by which the inhabitants were enabled to pay their taxes having ceased, and their trade being decayed, they are not so able to pay the taxes they are subjected to in time of peace, as they were the greater taxes in time of war.

That one principal difficulty which has ever attended the trade of the colonies proceeds from the scarcity of money, which scarcity is caused by the balance of trade with Great-Britain, which has been continually against the colonies.

That the drawing sums of money from the colonies from time to time, must distress the trade to that degree, that eventually Great-Britain must lose more by the diminution of the consumption of her manufactures, than all the sums which it is possible for the colonies thus to pay can countervail.

That they humbly conceive, if the taxes which the inhabitants of this province are obliged annually to pay towards the support of the internal government, the restraint they are under in their trade, for the benefit of Great-Britain, and the consumption thereby occasioned of British manufactures be all considered, and have their due weight, it must appear, that the subjects in this province, are as fully burthened as their fellow-subjects in Britain, and that they are, whilst in America, more beneficial to the nation than they could be if they should be removed to Britain, and there held to a full proportion of the national taxes and duties of every kind.

Your petitioners therefore most humbly pray, that they may be relieved from the burdens, which they have humbly represented to have been brought upon them by the late act of parliament, as to the wisdom of the
V   honour-

honourable houfe fhall feem meet; that the privileges of the colonies, relative to their internal taxes, which they have fo long enjoyed, may ftill be continued to them, or that the confideration of fuch taxes upon the colonies may be referred until your petitioners, in conjunction with the other governments, can have opportunity to make a more full reprefentation of the ftate and condition of the colonies, and the intereft of Great-Britain with regard to them.

*** *The Petitions and Reprefentations from New-York, Rhode-Ifland, &c. are to the fame effect.*

On Friday the 15th of May, 1767, Mr. Fuller having reported to the Houfe of Commons from the committee of the whole houfe, to whom it was referred, to confider of the feveral papers which had been prefented to the houfe this feffion of parliament, relating to the North American colonies—feveral refolutions, importing, That it appeared to the committee, that the Houfe of Reprefentatives of his Majefty's province of New-York, have, in direct difobedience of the authority of the legiflature of Great-Britain, refufed to make provifion for fupplying with neceffaries his Majefty's troops, in fuch manner as is required by an act of parliament, made in the 5th year of his Majefty's reign, intituled, ' An ' act to amend and render more ef- ' fectual, in his Majefty's dominions ' in America, an act paffed in this pre- ' fent feffions of parliment, entitled, ' An act for punifhing mutiny and ' defertion, and for the better pay- ' ment of the army and their quar- ' ters.'

Alfo that it appeared to the committee, that an act of affembly hath been paffed in the faid province, for furnifhing the barracks in the cities of New-York and Albany, with fire-wood and candles, and other neceffaries therein mentioned, for his Majefty's forces, inconfiftent with the provifions, and in oppofition to the directions of the faid act of parliament.

Alfo, that it is the opinion of the committee, that until provifion fhall have been made by the faid Affembly, for furnifhing the King's troops, with all the neceffaries required by the faid act of parliament, the governor, council, and affembly, be refpectively reftrained and prohibited from paffing or affenting to any act of Affembly, for any other purpofe whatever;— and in confequence of thefe refolutions, a bill was brought in, and paffed.

In the debate on this bill Gov. Pownall faid, Are you determined from hence to direct and regulate the quartering of the King's troops in North America ?—Do it in a way that brings it home to the executive power there, to carry your directions and regulations into execution; explain and amend your act: make it practicable; make it effective; and then you may fairly decide whether they deny your fovereignty or not. You will find they do not. If you think your way of making an adequate and certain provifion for the charge of this fervice, is *by the parliament's impofing a tax* upon the people for that purpofe; and that you have power, and it is advifeable to exert that power, to effectuate fuch fupply, by fuch tax, you need not hefitate to avow it openly and directly ; for the people of the colonies, from one end of the continent to the other, do invariably confider the claufe in the act of parliament, directing *how* that charge fhall be fupplied, as an *internal tax impofed upon them.*— It is from this idea, that every act of obedience, as well as of difobedience to your act of parliament, muft be conftrued and explained ed. Those whom you are willing to understand as having obeyed your act, have contrived to do it *in a mode* which neither recognizes the act of parliament, nor submits to the taxation—as such. And although you represent the assembly of the province of New-York *alone*, as having revolted against this power—believe me, *there is not a province, a colony, or a plantation, that will submit to a tax thus imposed*, more than New-York will. All have shewn their readiness to execute this service of quartering as an act of their own—all have, in their zeal to provide for it, by a grant of their own, provided a supply to answer the expence ;—but not one single assembly has or ever will, act under the powers and provisions of this act, as acknowledging, and, in consequence thereof apportioning, assessing, and levying, the supply, as a tax imposed by parliament. They have either acted without taking notice at all of this act of parliament, or have contrived some way or other to vary in some particulars, sufficient to make the execution and the tax an act of their own.—Try the conduct of every province and colony through by this rule, and you will find nothing particular in the case of New-York— *Don't fancy that you can divide the people upon this point*, and that you need only divide to govern—*you will by this conduct only unite them the more* inseparably—you will make the cause of New-York a common cause and will call up every other province and colony to stand forth in their justification—while New-York, learning from the complexion of your measure, how to avoid or evade the purport of your *enforcing bill*, will *suspend the force* of it, instead of it *suspending the assembly* of that province, against whom it is brought forward.

The clause in the quartering act, directing that the supply for reim-

burfing the expence of quartering the troops *shall be raised* by the respective assemblies of the provinces or colonies—which is by all the people of America, considered as (and is indeed) a tax imposed by parliament, *has brought in fact, into discussion, that question of the right of taxation*, which the cautious and (what I think) imprudent wisdom of many have endeavoured to keep wrapped up and suspended in theory,—Those things which schemes of policy wished to hold in question—acts and deeds will bring into decision. You have, on one hand, by your declaratory law, asserted your right and power of taxation over the colonies, and so far as this act goes, you have exerted that power. On the other hand, it is a fact which the House ought to be apprized of in all its extent, THAT THE PEOPLE OF AMERICA, UNIVERSALLY, UNITEDLY, AND UNALTERABLY, ARE RESOLVED NOT TO SUBMIT TO ANY INTERNAL TAX IMPOSED UPON THEM BY ANY LEGISLATURE, IN WHICH THEY HAVE NOT A SHARE BY REPRESENTATIVES OF THEIR OWN ELECTION.

" This claim must not be understood, as though it were only the pretences of party-leaders and demagogues; as though it were only the visions of speculative enthusiasts; as though it were the mere ebullition of a faction which must subside; as though it were only temporary or partial—it is the cool, deliberate, principled maxim of every man of business in the country."

The following Petition from the Merchants of New-York, was presented to the House of Commons in this session.

This petition set forth, ' That the commerce of the North American colonies is so severely clogged and restricted by the statutes of the 4th and

6th of his prefent Majefty's reign, as to afford a melancholy prefage of its deftruction, the fatal effects of which, though firft felt there, muft be finally transferred to Great Britain, and center with her merchants and manufacturers: that an evil fo extenfive, could not fail of alarming the petitioners, whofe fituation expofes them to the firft impreffion of this calamity; whence they think it their duty to implore the houfe to refume the confideration of the plantation trade, for effectual redrefs. It is the fingular difadvantage of the Northern Britifh colonies, that, while they ftand in need of vaft quantities of the manufactures of Great Britain, the country produces very little that affords a direct remittance thither in payment, and therefore from neceffity they have been driven to feek a market for their produce, and by a courfe of traffic, to acquire either money or fuch merchandize, as would anfwer the purpofe of a remittance, and enable them to fuftain their credit with their mother country: as the nature of the petitioners commerce, when free from the late reftraints, ought to be underftood, they beg leave to obferve, that their produce then fent to our own and the foreign iflands, was chiefly bartered for fugar, rum, melaffes, cotton, and indigo; that the fugar, cotton, and indigo, ferved as remittance to Great Britain, which the rum and melaffes conftituted effential branches of their commerce, and enabled them to barter with our own colonies for fifh and rice, and by that means to purfue a valuable trade with Spain, Portugal and Italy, where they chiefly obtained money, or bills of exchange in return, and likewife qualified them for adventures to Africa, where they had the advantage of putting off great quantities of Britifh manufactures, and of receiving in exchange gold, ivory, and flaves, which

laft being difpofed of in the Weft India iflands, commanded money or bills: rum was indifpenfable in their Indian trade, and with Britifh manufactures, procured furs and fkins, which both ferved for confiderable returns to Great Britain, and encreafed its revenue. The trade to the bay of Honduras was alfo of great importance, it being managed with fmall cargoes of provifions, rum, and Britifh manufactures, which, while they were at liberty to fend foreign logwood to the different ports in Europe furnifhed them with another valuable remittance. From this view, it is evident that fugar, rum, melaffes and logwood, with cotton and indigo, are the effentials of their return cargoes, and the chief fources, from which, in a courfe of trade they have maintained their credit with Great-Britain. That confidering the prodigious confumption of the produce of the Weft Indies in Great Britain, Ireland, and the colonies on the continent of America; the rapid increafe of thofe colonies; the vaft acceffion of fubjects by the late conquefts; the utter incapacity of our own ifland to fupply fo great a demand, will, the petitioners prefume, be out of all queftion; on the other hand, the lumber produced from clearing this immenfe territory, and the provifions extracted from a fertile foil, muft raife a fupply for exportation much greater than all our iflands can confume; it feems therefore confiftent with found policy, to indulge thofe colonies both in the free and unreftrained exportation of all the lumber and produce they can fpare, and an ample importation of fugar, rum and melaffes, to fupply the various branches of their trade; fince without the one the clearing of lands will be difcouraged; and provifions, for want of vent, become of little profit to the farmer; without the other, the petitioners fitioners muſt be plunged into a total incapacity of making good their payments of Britiſh debts; their credit muſt ſink, and their imports from Great Britain gradually diminiſh, till they are contracted to the narrow compaſs of remittances, in articles of their own produce; ·whence the colonies muſt, from inevitable neceſſity, betake themſelves to manufactures of their own, which will be attended with conſequences very detrimental to thoſe of Great Britain.

The petitioners having thus repreſented the nature of their commerce, humbly beg leave to point out the ſeveral grievances under which it labours, from the regulations preſcribed by the two before-mentioned acts, The heavy embarraſſments, which attend the article of ſugar, is a capital ſubject of complaint; and, beſides the abſolute neceſſity of a great importation to ſuſtain their trade, it often happens, that at the foreign iſlands a ſufficient return-cargo independent of ſugar, cannot be procured, which renders trade precarious and diſcouraging; beſides, the high duty of 5s. ſterling a hundred, is found by experience to be ſo exceſſive, that it has induced the fair trader to decline that branch of buſineſs, while, to people leſs ſcrupulous, it preſents an irreſiſtible temptation to ſmuggling. That the preſſure of this duty is not aggravated, the petitioners appeal to the officers of the cuſtoms of their port, who muſt confeſs that there have not been wanting inſtances where merchants have been driven to the diſagreeable neceſſity of bringing their very plate into the cuſtom-houſe to diſcharge it. The petitioners therefore moſt humbly intreat that a more moderate duty be laid on foreign ſugars, which, they are aſſured, would not only greatly promote the proſperity both of thoſe colonies and their mother country, but encreaſe the

royal revenue far beyond what can be expected under the preſent reſtraints. The compelling merchants to land and ſtore foreign ſugars in Great Britain, before they are exported to other parts of Europe, is another expenſive and dilatory reſtriction, without being of any material advantage to the revenue of Great Britain; for it puts it out of the petitioners power to meet foreigners at market upon an equal footing. That Britiſh plantation ſugar exported from North America, ſhould be declared French on being landed in England, the petitioners conceive may be juſtly claſſed among the number of hardſhips inflicted by thoſe regulations, as in effect it deprives them of making a remittance in that article, by expoſing them to the payment of the foreign duty in Great Britain, which appears the moſt ſevere, as their fellow-ſubjects of the iſlands are left at liberty to export thoſe ſugars for what they really are, and a diſtinction is formed which the petitioners cannot but regard with uneaſineſs. That foreign rum, French excepted, is the next article which the petitioners moſt humbly propoſe for conſideration, as its importation, on a moderate duty, would add conſiderably to the revenue, prevent ſmuggling, encreaſe the ſale of Britiſh manufactures, and enable the petitioners to bring back the full value of their cargoes, more eſpecially from the Daniſh iſlands of St. Thomas and St. Croix, where they can only receive half the value in ſugar and cotton, and conſequently rum alone can be expected for the other half, thoſe iſlands having no ſpice but of a baſe kind. That it is with the greateſt concern the petitioners obſerve, that foreign logwood is alſo made ſubject to the delay, hazard, and expence of being landed in Great Britain; which with its low price, its bulk, and the duty
with

with which it is now burthened, muſt totally deſtroy that valuable branch of the petitioners commerce, and throw it into the hands of foreigners unfettered with thoſe heavy embarraſſments. That their lumber and pot-aſh, even when ſhipped for Ireland, where the latter is ſo neceſſary for the progreſs of their linen manufacture, and even proviſions, though intended to relieve that kingdom from a famine, are ſubject to the ſame diſtreſſing impediments; nor is flax-feed on the timely importation of which the very exiſtence of the linen manufacture immediately depends, exempted: yet both flax-feed, lumber, and pot-aſh, may all be imported into Ireland directly from the Baltic, where they are purchaſed from foreigners under the national diſadvantage of being paid for with money inſtead of manufactures; the petitioners, therefore, humbly beg leave to expreſs their hopes, that an evil ſo highly prejudicial to them, to the ſtaple of Ireland, and to the trade and manufactures of Great Britain, will not fail of obtaining the attention of the Houſe, and an immediate and effectual redreſs. The petitioners beg leave further to repreſent, that the wines from the iſlands, in exchange for wheat, flour, fiſh and lumber, would conſiderably augment the important article of remittance, was the American duty withdrawn on exportation to Great Britain: it is therefore humbly ſubmitted to the Houſe, whether ſuch an expedient, calculated at once to attach the inhabitants to huſbandry, by encreaſing the conſumption of American produce, to encourage Britiſh manufactures by enabling the petitioners to make good their payments, and to encreaſe the royal revenue by an additional import of wines into Great Britain, will not be conſiſtent with the united intereſts both of the mother country and her colonies. The petitioners alſo conceive that the North American fiſhery is of the higheſt national importance, ſince, by annually employing ſo great a number of ſhipping, it conſtitutes a reſpectable nurſery for ſeamen, and is ſo advantageous in remittances in payment for Britiſh manufactures; whence the petitioners humbly preſume it will be cheriſhed by the Houſe, and every impediment removed that tends to check its progreſs. The enlarging the juriſdiction of the admiralty is another part of the fourth of his Majeſty's reign, very grievous to the trade and navigation of the colonies, and oppreſſive to the ſubjects. The petitioners beg leave to expreſs their warmeſt ſentiments of gratitude for the advantages intended by parliament in the opening free ports in the iſlands of Jamaica and Dominica; yet, at the ſame time, cannot but lament their being ſo unhappy as to be unable to reap the benefits, which, it was imagined, would flow from ſo wiſe a policy. The collecting great quantities of the produce of Martinico, Guadaloupe, &c. at the iſland of Dominica, would be of real advantage to the colonies, were they permitted to take them in return for their lumber and proviſions; but as they are now prohibited from taking any thing but melaſſes, the petitioners think it evident, that they can derive no ſubſtantial advantage under ſuch a reſtraint, and are unable to diſcern the principle on which the prohibition is founded; for ſince ſugar may be imported directly from the foreign iſlands, it ſeems much more reaſonable to ſuffer it from a free port belonging to Great Britain. The petitioners, therefore humbly hope, that the Houſe will think it equitable to adapt this trade to their circumſtances, by granting them liberty to import into the colonies all Weſt India productions, in exchange for

for their commodities; and that, upon the whole, the petitioners, with the greatest anxiety, find themselves obliged to inform the House, that although, at the last seffion, the necessity of relieving the trade of those colonies seems to have been universally admitted, and the tender regard of parliament for their happiness highly distinguished; neverthelefs, experience has evinced, that the commercial regulations then enacted, instead of remedying, have encreased the heavy burthen under which it already laboured. Hence, upon due consideration, nothing can be more manifest, than that the ability of those colonies to purchase the manufactures of Great Britain, immediately depends upon, and is infeparably connected with the progrefs of their commerce; and that ability, by removing the necessity of home manufactures, would leave them at liberty to pursue agriculture, in which their interest consists. The petitioners, therefore, pray the house to take the above into consideration, and to grant such relief therein as shall be thought consistent with good policy, and the mutual interests of Great Britain and her colonies.

The petition was ordered to lie upon the table: no other notice was taken of it.

A Letter to Dennis De Berdt, Esq; Agent for the House of Representatives.
Province of the Massachusetts-Bay,
January 12, 1768.
S I R,
Since the last fitting of the general court, divers acts of parliament relating to the colonies have arrived here: and as the people of this province had no share in the framing those laws, in which they are so deeply interested, the House of Representatives, who are constitutionally entrusted by them as the guardians of their rights and liberties, have

thought it their indispensable duty carefully to perufe them; and having so done, to point out such matters in them as appear to be grievous to their constituents, and to feek redrefs.

The fundamental rules of the constitution are the grand security of all British subjects; and it is a fecurity which they are all equally entitled to in all parts of his Majesty's extended dominions. The supreme legiflative, in every free state, derives its power from the constitution, by the fundamental rules of which it is bounded and circumfcribed. As a legislative power is effentially requisite, where any powers of government are exercised, it is conceived, the several legislative bodies in America were erected, becaufe their existence, and the free exercise of their power within their several limits, are effentially important and necessary, to preferve to his Majesty's subjects in America the advantages of the fundamental laws of the constitution.

When we mention the rights of the subjects in America, and the interest we have in the British constitution, in common with all other British subjects, we cannot justly be sufpected of the most distant thought of an independency on Great Britain. Some, we know, have imagined this of the colonists; and others may perhaps have industriously propagated it, to raife groundless and unreasonable jealousies of them: but it is so far from the truth, that we apprehend the colonies would refuse it if offered to them, and would even deem it the greatest misfortune to be obliged to accept it. They are far from being infensible of their happiness in being connected with the mother country, and of the mutual benefits derived from it to both: it is therefore the indispensible duty of all, to cultivate and establish a mutual harmony, and to promote the intercourse of good offices

fices betwee them: and while both have the free enjoyment of the rights of our happy conftitution, there will be no grounds of envy and difcontent in the one, nor of jealoufy and miftruft in the other.

It is the glory of the Britifh conftitution, that it hath its foundation in the law of God and nature: It is an effential natural right, that a man fhall quietly enjoy, and have the fole difpofal of his own property: this right is adopted into the conftitution: this natural and conftitutional right is fo familiar to the American fubjects, that it would be difficult, if poffible, to convince them, that any neceffity can render it juft, equitable, and reafonable, in the nature of things, that the parliament fhould impofe duties, fubfidies, talliages, and taxes, upon them, internal or external, for the fole purpofe of raifing a revenue. The reafon is obvious; becaufe they cannot be reprefented, and therefore their confent cannot be conftitutionally had in parliament.

When the parliament, foon after the repeal of the ftamp-act, thought proper to pafs another act, declaring the authority, power, and right of parliament to make laws that fhould be binding on the colonies in all cafes whatever, it is probable, that acts for levying taxes on the colonies, external and internal, were included: for the act made the laft year, impofing duties on paper, glafs, &c. as well as the fugar-acts and the ftamp-act, are, to all intents and purpofes, in form as well as in fubftance, as much revenue acts as thofe for the land-tax, cuftoms and excifes in England. The neceffity of eftablifhing a revenue in America is exprefsly mentioned in the preambles: they were originated in the honourable Houfe of Commons, as all other money and revenue bills are; and the property of the colonies, with the

fame form, ceremony and expreffions of loyalty and duty, is thereby given and granted to his Majefty, as they ufually give and grant their own. But we humbly conceive that objections to acts of this kind may be fafely, if decently made, if they are of dangerous tendency in point of commerce, policy, and the true and real intereft of the whole empire. It may, and if it can, it ought to be made to appear, that fuch acts are grievous to the fubject, burthenfome to trade, ruinous to the nation, and tending on the whole to injure the revenue of the crown. And furely, if fuch mighty inconveniencies, evils and mifchiefs can be pointed out with decency and perfpicuity, there will be the higheft reafon not only to hope for, but fully to expect redrefs.

It is obfervable, that though many have difregarded life and contemned liberty, yet there are few men who do not agree that property is a valuable acquifition, which ought to be held facred. Many have fought, and bled, and died for this, who have been infenfible to all other obligations. Thofe who ridicule the ideas of right and juftice, faith and truth among men, will put a high value upon money: property is admitted to have an exiftence even in the favage ftate of nature: the bow, the arrow, and the tomahawk: the hunting and the fifhing ground, are fpecies of property as important to an American favage, as pearls, rubies and diamonds are to the Mogul or a Nabob in the Eaft, or the lands, tenements, hereditaments, meffuages, gold and filver of the Europeans. And if property is neceffary for the fupport of favage life, it is by no means lefs fo in civil fociety. The Utopian fchemes of levelling, and a community of goods, are as vifionary and impracticable, as thofe which veft all property, in the crown, are arbitrary, defpotick,

fpotick, and in our government unconftitutional. Now, what property can the colonifts be conceived to have, if their money may be granted away by others without their confent? This moft certainly is the prefent cafe: for they were in no fenfe reprefented in parliament when this act for raifing a revenue in America was made. The ftamp-act was grievoufly complained of by all the colonies: and is there any real difference between this and the ftamp-act? They were both defigned to raife a revenue in America, and in the fame manner, viz. by duties on certain commodities: the payment of the duties impofed by the ftamp-act might have been eluded by a total difufe of the ftamped paper; and fo may the payment of thefe duties, by the total difufe of the articles on which they are laid: but in neither cafe without difficulty. Therefore the fubjects here are reduced to the hard alternative, either of being obliged totally to difufe articles of the greateft neceffity in common life, or to pay a tax without their confent.

The fecurity of right and property is the great end of government: furely then, fuch meafures as tend to render right and property precarious, tend to deftroy both property and government; for thefe muft ftand and fall together. It would be difficult, if poffible, to fhew, that the prefent plan of taxing the colonies is more favourable to them, than that put in ufe here before the revolution. It feems, by the event, that our anceftors were in one refpect, not in fo melancholy a fituation as we their pofterity are. In thofe times, the crown and the minifters of the crown, without the intervention of the parliament, demolifhed charters, and levied taxes on the colonies at pleafure. Governor Androfs, in the time of James the fecond, declared, that wherever an Englifhman fets his foot, all he hath is the king's: and Dudley

declared at the council board, and even on the facred feat of juftice, that the privilege of Englifhmen, not to be taxed without their confent, and the laws of England, would not follow them to the ends of the earth. It was alfo, in thofe days, declared in council, that the king's fubjects in New-England did not differ much from flaves; and that the only difference was, that they were not bought and fold: but there was, even in thofe times, an excellent Attorney-General, Sir William Jones, who was of another mind; and told King James, that he could no more grant a commiffion to levy money on his fubjects in Jamaica, though a conquered ifland, without their confent by an affembly, than they could difcharge themfelves from their allegiance to the Englifh crown. But the misfortune of the colonifts at prefent is, that they are taxed by parliament without their confent: this, while the parliament continues refolved to tax us, will ever render our cafe, in one refpect, more deplorable and remedilefs, under the beft of kings, than that of our anceftors was, under the worft. They found relief by the interpofition of parliament: but by the intervention of that very power, we are taxed, and can appeal for relief from their final decifion to no power on earth; for there is no power on earth above them.

The original contract between the King and the firft planters here, was a royal promife in behalf of the nation, and which till very lately it was never queftioned but the King had a power to make; namely, that if the adventurers would, at their own coft and charge, and at the hazard of their lives and every thing dear to them, purchafe a new world, fubdue a wildernefs, and thereby enlarge the king's dominions, they and their pofterity fhould enjoy fuch rights and privileges as in their refpective char-

Z   ters

ters are expressed; which are in general all the rights, liberties and privileges of his Majesty's natural born subjects within the realm. The principal privilege implied, and in some of their charters expressed, is a freedom from all taxes but such as they shall consent to in person, or by representatives of their own free choice and election. The late king James broke the original contract of the settlement and government of these colonies: but it proved happy for our ancestors in the end that he had also broken the original compact with his three kingdoms. This left them some gleam of hope: this very thing, finally, was the cause of deliverance to the nation and the colonies, nearly at the same time: it was the parliament, the supreme legislative and constitutional check on the supreme executive, that in time operated effects worthy of itself: the nation and her colonies have since been happy, and our princes patriot kings. The law and reason teaches that the King can do no wrong; and that neither king nor parliament are otherwise inclined than to justice, equity and truth: but the law does not presume that the King may not be deceived, nor that the parliament may not be misinformed: if therefore any thing is wrong, it must be imputed to such causes: how far such causes have taken place and operated against the colonies, is humbly submitted to the revision and reconsideration of all.

By the common law, the colonists are adjudged to be natural-born subjects! So they are declared by royal charter; and they are so, by the spirit of the law of nature and nations: no jurist, who has the least regard to his reputation in the republic of letters, will deny that they are entitled to all the essential rights, liberties, privileges and immunities of his Majesty's natural subjects, born within the realm. The children of his Majesty's natural

born subjects, born passing and repassing the seas, have by sundry acts of parliament, from Edward the third to this time, been declared natural-born subjects: and even foreigners, residing a certain time in the colonies, are by acts of parliament entitled to all the rights and privileges of natural-born subjects. And it is remarkable that the act of 13 Geo. II. chap. 7. presupposes that the colonists are natural-born subjects; and that they are entitled to all the privileges of such; as appears by the preamble, which we shall now recite: " Whereas the increase of people is a means of advancing the wealth and strength of any nation or country: and whereas many foreigners and strangers, from the lenity of our government and purity of our religion, the benefit of our laws, the advantages of our trade, and the security of our property, might be induced to come and settle in some of his Majesty's colonies in America, if they were made partakers of the advantages and privileges which natural-born subjects of this realm do enjoy: " which plainly shows it to be the sense of the nation that the colonies were entitled to, and did actually enjoy the advantages and privileges of natural-born subjects. But if it could be admitted as clearly consistent with the constitution, for the parliament of Great-Britain to tax the property of the colonies, we presume, it can be made to appear to be utterly inconsistent with the rules of equity that they should, at least at present. It must be considered, that by acts of parliament, the colonies are prohibited from importing commodities of the growth or manufacture of Europe, except from Great-Britain, saving a few articles. This gives the advantage to Great-Britain of raising the price of her commodities, and is equal to a tax. It is too obvious to be doubted, that by the extraordinary demands, from the colonies, of the manufactures of

Britain,

Britain, occafioned by this policy, fhe reaps an advantage of at leaft twenty per cent. in the price of them, beyond what the colonies might purchafe them for at foreign markets : the lofs therefore to the colonifts is equal to the gain which is made in Britain. This in reality is a tax, though not a direct one : and admitting, that they take annually from Great-Britain manufactures to the value of two millions fterling, as is generally fuppofed, they then pay an annual tax of four hundred thoufand pounds, befides the taxes which are directly paid on thofe manufactures in England. The fame reafoning will hold good with refpect to the many enumerated articles of their produce, which the colonies are reftrained by act of parliament from fending to any foreign port : by this reftraint, the market is glutted, and confequently the produce fold, is cheaper; which is an advantage to Great-Britain, and an equal lofs to, or tax upon the colonifts. Is it reafonable, then, that the colonies fhould be taxed on the Britifh commodities here? efpecially when it is confidered, that the moft of them fettled a wildernefs, and till very lately defended their fettlements without a farthing's expence to the nation. They bore their full portion of the charges of fecuring and maintaining his Majefty's rights in America, in every war from their firft fettlement, without any confideration; for the grants of parliament in the laft war were compenfations for an overplus of expence on their part: many of them, and this province in particular, have always maintained their own frontiers at their own expence; and have alfo frequently defended his Majefty's garrifon at Annapolis, when it muft otherwife have been unavoidably loft. The nation, in the late war, acquired lands equal in value to all the expence fhe has been

at in America, from its fettlement ; while the trade of the colonies has been only " fecured and reftricted : " it has not been enlarged, though new avenues of beneficial commerce have been opened to the mother country. The colonies have reaped no fhare in the lands which they helped to conquer, while millions of acres of thofe very lands have been granted, and ftill are granting to people, who, in all probability, will never fee, if they fettle, them.

The appropriation of the monies to arife by thefe duties is an objection of great weight. It is in the firft place, to be applied for the payment of the neceffary charges of the adminiftration of juftice, and the fupport of civil government in fuch colonies where it fhall be judged neceffary. This houfe apprehend, it would be grievous and of dangerous tendency, if the crown fhould not only appoint governors over the feveral colonies, but allow them fuch ftipends as it fhall judge proper, at the expence of the people and without their confent. Such a power under a corrupt adminiftration, it is to be feared, would introduce an abfolute government in America; at beft it would leave the people in a ftate of utter uncertainty of their fecurity, which is far from being a ftate of civil liberty. The judges in the feveral colonies do not hold their commiffions during good behaviour; if then they are to have falaries independent of the people, how eafy will it be for a corrupt governor to have a fet of judges to his mind, to deprive a bench of juftice of its glory, and the people of their fecurity. If the judges of England have independent livings, it muft be remembered, that the tenure of their commiffion is during good behaviour, which is a fafeguard to the people, and befides, they are near the throne, the fountain of right and juftice :

Z 2 whereas

whereas American judges, as well as governors, are at a diſtance from it: moreover, it is worth particular notice, that in all diſputes between power and liberty in America, there is danger that the greateſt credit will always be given to the officers of the crown, who are the men in power. This we have ſometimes found by experience; and it is much to be feared, that the nation will fall into ſome dangerous miſtake, if ſhe has not already, by too great attention to the repreſentations of particular perſons, and a diſregard to others.

But the reſidue of theſe monies is to be applied by parliament, from time to time, for defending, protecting and ſecuring the colonies. If the government at home is apprehenſive that the coloniſts will be backward in defending themſelves and ſecuring his Majeſty's territories in America, it muſt have been egregiouſly miſinformed. We need look back no further than the laſt war for evidence of a contrary diſpoſition: they always diſcovered the moſt chearful compliance with his Majeſty's requiſitions of men and money for this purpoſe. They were then treated as free Britiſh ſubjects, and never failed to grant aid to his Majeſty of their own free accord, to the extent of their ability, and even beyond it; of which, the parliament were then ſo ſenſible, that they made them grants, from year to year, by way of compenſation for extra ſervices. It is not at all to be doubted, but if they are ſtill conſidered upon the footing of ſubjects, they will always diſcover the ſame diſpoſition to exert themſelves for his Majeſty's ſervice and their own defence; which renders a ſtanding army in the colonies a needleſs expence. Or, if it be admitted that there may be ſome neceſſity for them in the conquered province of Canada, where the exerciſe of the Romiſh re-

ligion, ſo deſtructive to civil ſociety, is allowed, ſurely there can be no need of them in the bowels of the old colonies, and even in cities where there is not the leaſt danger of a foreign enemy, and where the inhabitants are as ſtrongly attached to his Majeſty's perſon, family and government, as in Great Britain itſelf. There is an Engliſh affection in the coloniſts towards the mother country, which will for ever keep them connected with her, to every valuable purpoſe, unleſs it ſhall be eraſed by repeated unkind uſage on her part: as Engliſhmen, as well as Britiſh ſubjects, they have an averſion to an unneceſſary ſtanding army, which they look upon as dangerous to their civil liberties; and conſidering the examples of ancient times, it ſeems a little ſurprizing, that a mother ſtate ſhould truſt large bodies of mercenary troops in her colonies, at ſo great a diſtance from her, leſt, in proceſs of time, when the ſpirits of the people ſhall be depreſſed by the military power, another Cæſar ſhould ariſe and uſurp the authority of his maſter.

The act enabling his Majeſty to appoint commiſſioners of the cuſtoms to reſide in America, has alſo been read in the houſe. It declares an intention to facilitate the trade of America, of which we cannot have any great hopes from the tenor of the commiſſion. In general, innovations are dangerous: the unneceſſary increaſe of crown officers is moſt certainly ſo. Theſe gentlemen are authorized to appoint as many as they ſhall think proper, without limitation: this will probably be attended with undeſirable effects: an hoſt of penſioners, by the arts they may uſe, may in time become as dangerous to the liberties of the people as an army of ſoldiers; for there is a way of ſubduing a people by art as well as by arms: we are happy and ſafe under

his

his prefent Majefty's mild and gracious adminiftration; but the time may come, when the united body of penfioners and foldiers may ruin the liberties of America. The trade ef the colonies, we apprehend, may be as eafily carried on, and the acts of trade as duly enforced without this commiffion; and if fo, it muft be a very needlefs expence, at a time when the nation and her colonies are groaning under debts contracted in the late war, and how far diftant another may be, God only knows.

There is another act which this houfe apprehend muft be alarming to all the colonies; which is the act for fufpending the legiflative power of the affembly of New-York on a certain condition. A legiflative body without the free exercife of the powers of legiflation is to us incomprehenfible: there can be no material difference between fuch a legiflative and none at all. It cannot be faid that the affembly of New York hath the free exercife of legiflative power, while their very exiftence is fufpended upon their acting in conformity to the will of another body. Such a reftriction throughout the colonies would be a fhort and eafy method of an-nihilating the legiflative powers in America, and by confequence, of depriving the people of a fundamental right of the conftitution, namely, that every man fhall be prefent in the body which legiflates for him.

It may not be amifs to confider the tendency of a fufpenfion of colony legiflation for non-compliance with acts of parliament requiring a provincial affembly to give and grant away their own and their conftituent's money for the fupport of a ftanding army. We cannot but think it hard enough to have our property granted away without our confent: without being order-ed to deal it out ourfelves, as in the cafe of the mutiny act. It muft be

fufficiently humiliating to part with our property in either of thofe ways, much more in both; whereby, as loyal fubjects as any under his Majefty's government, and as true lovers of their country as any people whatever, are deprived of the honour and merit of voluntarily contributing to the fervice of both. What is the plain language of fuch a fufpenfion? We can difcover no more nor lefs in it than this; if the American affemblies refufe to grant as much of their own and their conftituents money, as fhall from time to time be enjoined and prefcribed by the parliament, befides what the parliament directly taxes them, they fhall no longer have any legiflative authority; but if they comply with what is prefcribed, they may ftill be allowed to legiflate under their charter reftrictions. Does not political death and annihilation ftare us in the face as ftrongly on one fuppofition as the other? Equally in cafe of compliance as of non-compliance.

But let us fuppofe, for a moment, a feries of events taking place, the moft favourable in the opinion of thofe who are fo fond of thefe new regulations: that all difficulties and fcruples of confcience were removed, and that every reprefentative in America fhould acknowledge a juft and equitable right in the commons of Great-Britain to make an unlimited grant of his and his conftituents property: that they have a clear right to inveft the crown with all the lands in the colonies, as effectually as if they had been forfeited; would it be poffible for them to conciliate their conftituents to fuch meafures? Would not the attempt fuddenly cut afunder all confidence and communication between the reprefentative body and the people? What then would be the confequence? Could any thing be reafonably expected but difcontent, defpair, and rage againft their reprefentatives,

fentatives, on the fide of the people, and on the part of government, the rigorous exertion of civil and military power? The confufion and mifery after fuch a fatal crifis cannot be conceived, much lefs defcribed.

The prefent regulations and proceedings, with refpect to the colonies, we apprehend to be oppofite to every principle of good and found policy. A ftanding army, in the time of profound peace, is naturally productive of uneafinefs and difcontent among the people: and yet the colonies, by the mutiny act, are ordered and directed to provide certain enumerated articles: and the pains and penalties in cafe of non-compliance are evident in the precedent of New-York. It alfo appears that revenue officers are multiplying in the colonies with vaft powers: the board of commiffioners lately appointed to refide here, have ample difcretionary powers given them to make what appointments they pleafe, and to pay the appointees what fums they pleafe: the eftablifhment of a proteftant epifcopate in America is alfo very zealoufly contended for: and it is very alarming to a people, whofe fathers, from the hardfhips they fuffered under fuch an eftablifhment, were obliged to fly their native country into a wildernefs, in order peaceably to enjoy their privileges, civil and religious: their being threatened with the lofs of both at once, muft throw them into a very difagreeable fituation. We hope in God fuch an eftablifhment will never take place in America, and we defire you will ftrenuoufly oppofe it. The revenue raifed in America, for ought we can tell, may be as conftitutionally applied towards the fupport of prelacy as of foldiers and penfioners: if the property of the fubject is taken from him without his confent, it is immaterial, whether it be done by one man or five hundred; or whether it be applied for the fupport of ecclefiaftic or military power, or both. It may be well worth the confideration of the beft politician in Great-Britain or America, what the natural tendency is of a vigorous purfuit of thefe meafures. We are not infenfible that fome eminent men, on both fides the water, are lefs friendly to American charters and affemblies than could be wifhed: it feems to be growing fafhionable, to treat them in common converfation, as well as in popular publications, with contempt: but if we look back a few reigns, we fhall find that even the auguft affembly, the parliament, was in every refpect the object of a courtier's reproach: it was even an aphorifm with King James I. that the Lords and Commons were two very bad copartners with a monarch; and he and his fucceffors broke the copartnerfhip as faft as poffible. It is certainly unnatural for a Britifh politician to expect, that ever the fupreme executive of the nation can long exift, after the fupreme legiflative fhall be depreffed and deftroyed, which may God forbid. If the fupreme executive cannot exift long in Britain, without the fupport of the fupreme legiflative, it fhould feem very reafonable, in order to fupport the fame fupreme executive, at the diftance of a thoufand tranfmarine leagues from the metropolis, there fhould be, in fo remote dominions, a free legiflative, within their charter limitations, as well as an entirely free reprefentative of the fupreme executive of his Majefty, in the perfons of governors, judges, juftices, and other executive officers; otherwife ftrange effects are to be apprehended. For the laws of God and nature are invariable: a politician may apply or mifapply thefe to a multiplicity of purpofes, good or bad; but thefe laws were never made for politicians to alter. Should the

the time ever come, when the legiflative affemblies of North America fhall
be diffolved and annihilated, no more
to exift again, a ftrange political phe-
nomenon will probably appear. All
laws both of police and revenue muft
then be made by a legiflative at fuch
a diftance, that without immediate
infpiration, the local and other circumftances of the governed cannot
poffibly be known to thofe who give
and grant to the crown, what part of
the property of their fellow-fubjects
they pleafe. There will then be no
affemblies to fupport the execution of
fuch laws: and indeed, while exifting,
by what rule of law or reafon are the
members pf the colony-affemblies executive officers? They have, as reprefentatives, no commiffion but from
their conftituents: and it muft be difficult to fhow, why they are more
obliged to execute acts of parliament
than fuch of their conftituents as hold
no commiffions from the crown. The
moft that can be expected from either,
is fubmiffion to acts of parliament;
or to aid the officers as individuals,
or part of the poffe comitatus if required. It would feem ftrange to call
on the representative, in any other
way, to execute laws againft their
conftituents and themfelves, which
both have been fo far from confenting
to, that neither were confulted in
framing them. Yet it was objected
by fome to the American affemblies,
that they neglected to execute the ftamp
act: and that their refolves tended to
raife commotions; which certainly
was not the cafe here: for all the diforders in Bofton, in which any damage
was done to property, happened long
before the refolves of the houfe of reprefentatives here were paffed.

We have reafon to believe, that the
nation has been grofsly mifinformed
with refpect to the temper and behaviour of the colonifts, and it is to
be feared that fome men will not
ceafe to fow the feeds of jealoufy and

difcord, till they fhall have done irre-
parable mifchief. You will do a fingular fervice to both countries, if
poffible, in detecting them. In the
mean time, we defire you would make
known to his Majefty's minifters the
fentiments of this houfe contained in
this letter, and implore a favourable
confideration of America.
Signed by the Speaker.

Agreeable to a Vote of the Houfe of Re-
prefentatives of Maffachufett's-Bay,
the following Petition to the King,
was figned by the Speaker, by their
order of the 20th Jan. 1768.
An humble Petition to the King's moft
Excellent Majefty.
Moft Gracious Sovereign,

Your Majefty's faithful fubjects, the
reprefentatives of your province of the
Maffachufetts-Bay, with the warmeft
fentiments of loyalty, duty, and affection, beg leave to approach the
throne, and to lay at your Majefty's
feet their humble fupplications, in
behalf of your diftreffed fubjects the
people of the province.

Our anceftors, the firft fettlers of
this country, having with the royal
confent, which we humbly apprehend
involves the confent of the nation,
and at their own great expence, migrated from their mother kingdom,
took poffeffion of this land, at that
time a wildernefs, the right whereof
they had purchafed for a valuable
confideration of the council eftablifhed at Plimouth, to whom it had been
granted by your Majefty's royal pre-
deceffor King James the firft.

From the principles of loyalty to
their fovereign which will ever warm
the breaft of a true fubject, though
remote, they acknowledged their allegiance to the Englifh crown: and
your Majefty will allow us with all
humility to fay, that they and their
pofterity, even to this time, have afforded frequent and fignal proofs of
their zeal for the honour and fervice
of

of their prince, and their firm attachment to the parent country.

With toil and fatigue, perhaps not to be conceived by their brethren and fellow-subjects at home, and with the constant peril of their lives, from a numerous, savage, and warlike race of men, they began their settlement, and God prospered them.

They obtained a charter from King Charles the first; wherein his Majesty was pleased to grant to them and their heirs and assigns for ever, all the lands therein described, to hold of him and his royal successors in free and common soccage; which we humbly conceive is as absolute an estate as the subject can hold under the crown. And in the same charter were granted to them, and their posterity, all the rights, liberties, privileges, and immunities of natural subjects, born within the realm.

This charter they enjoyed, having, as we most humbly conceive, punctually complied with all the conditions of it, till in an unhappy time it was vacated.—But after the revolution, when King William and Queen Mary, of glorious and blessed memory, were established on the throne: in that happy reign, when to the joy of the nation and its dependencies, the crown was settled in your Majesty's illustrious family, the inhabitants of this province shared in the common blessing. Then they were indulged with another charter; in which their Majesties were pleased for themselves, their heirs and successors, to grant and confirm to them as ample estate in the lands or territories as was granted by the former charter, together with other the most essential rights and liberties contained therein: the principal of which, is that which your Majesty's subjects within the realm have ever held a most sacred right, of being taxed only by representatives of their own free election.

Thus blessed with the rights of Englishmen, through the indulgent smiles of Heaven, and under the auspicious government of your Majesty and your royal predecessors, your people of this province have been happy, and your Majesty has acquired a numerous increase of loyal subjects, a large extent of dominion, and a new and inexhaustible source of commerce, wealth and glory.

With great sincerity permit us to assure your Majesty, that your subjects of this province, ever have, and still continue to acknowledge your Majesty's high court of parliament the supreme legislative power of the whole empire. The superintending authority of which is clearly admitted in all cases, that can consist with the fundamental rights of nature and the constitution, to which your Majesty's happy subjects in all parts of your empire conceive they have a just and equitable claim.

It is with the deepest concern that your humble suppliants would represent to your Majesty, that your parliament, the rectitude of whose intentions is never to be questioned, has thought proper to pass divers acts imposing taxes on your Majesty's subjects in America, with the sole and express purpose of raising a revenue. If your Majesty's subjects here shall be deprived of the honour and privilege of voluntarily contributing their aid to your Majesty, in supporting your government and authority in the province, and defending and securing your rights and territories in America, which they have always hitherto done with the utmost chearfulness: if these acts of parliament shall remain in force, and your Majesty's commons in Great Britain shall continue to exercise the power of granting the property of their fellow subjects in this province, your
people

people muſt then regret their unhappy fate in having only the name left of free ſubjects.

With all humility we conceive that a repreſentation of your Majeſty's ſubjects of this province in the parliament, conſidering their local circumſtances, is utterly impracticable: your Majeſty has heretofore been graciouſly pleaſed to order your requiſitions to be laid before the repreſentatives of your people in the general aſſembly, who have never failed to afford the neceſſary aid to the extent of their ability, and ſometimes beyond it; and it would be ever grievous to your Majeſty's faithful ſubjects to be called upon in a way, that ſhould appear to them to imply a diſtruſt of their moſt ready and willing compliance.

Under the moſt ſenſible impreſſions of your Majeſty's wiſe and paternal care for the remoteſt of your faithful ſubjects, and in full dependence on the royal declarations in the charter of this province, we moſt humbly beſeech your Majeſty to take our preſent unhappy circumſtances under your royal conſideration, and afford us relief in ſuch manner as in your Majeſty's great wiſdom and clemency ſhall ſeem meet.

A letter to the Right Hon. the Earl of Shelburne, one of his Majeſty's principal Secretaries of State.
Province of the Maſſachuſetts-Bay, Jan. 15, 1768.

My Lord,

The Houſe of Repreſentatives of this his Majeſty's province, having had experience of your Lordſhip's generous ſentiments of his Majeſty's moſt loyal though remote ſubjects in America, and of your noble exertions in their behalf in the late time of their diſtreſs, beg leave to lay before your Lordſhip's view, the new ſcenes of difficulty, which are again opened upon us, and to implore your repeated interpoſition.

Your Lordſhip is not inſenſible, that our forefathers were in an unhappy reign driven into this wilderneſs by the hand of power; at their own expence they croſſed an ocean of three thouſand miles; and purchaſed an inheritance for themſelves and their poſterity, with the view of propagating the chriſtian religion, and enlarging the Engliſh dominion in this diſtant part of the earth. Through the indulgent ſmiles of Heaven upon them, though not without hardſhip and fatigue unexperienced and perhaps hardly to be conceived by their brethren and fellowſubjects in their native land; and with the conſtant peril of their lives from a numerous race of men, as barbarous and cruel, and yet as warlike as any people upon the face of the earth, they increaſed in their numbers and enlarged their ſettlement.--They obtained a charter from King Charles the firſt, wherein his Majeſty was pleaſed to recognize to them, a liberty to worſhip God according to the dictates of their conſcience; a bleſſing which in thoſe unhappy times was denied to them in their own country: and the rights, liberties, privileges, and immunities of his natural born ſubjects within the realm. This charter they enjoyed, having punctually fulfilled the conditions of it, till it was vacated, as we conceive arbitrarily, in the reign of King Charles the ſecond. After the revolution, that grand æra of Britiſh liberty, when King William and Queen Mary, of glorious and bleſſed memory, were eſtabliſhed on the throne, the inhabitants of this province obtained another charter; in which the moſt eſſential rights and privileges contained in the former were reſtored to them. Thus bleſſed with the liberties of Engliſhmen, they continued to increaſe and multiply, till, as your Lordſhip knows, a dreary
A 2   wilder-

wilderness is become a fruitful field, and a grand source of national wealth and glory.

By the common law, my Lord, as well as sundry acts of parliament from the reign of Edward the third, the children of his Majesty's natural born subjects, born passing and repassing the seas, are intitled to all the rights and privileges of his natural subjects born within the realm. From hence the conclusion appears to be indisputable, that the descendants of his Majesty's subjects in the realm, who migrated with the consent of the nation, and purchased a settlement with their own treasure and blood, without any aid from the nation; who early acknowledged their allegiance to the Crown of England; and have always approved themselves faithful subjects, and in many instances given signal proofs of their loyalty to their King, and their firm attachment and affection to their mother country :— The conclusion is strong, that exclusive of any consideration of their charter, they are intitled to the rights and privileges of the British constitution in common with their fellow subjects in Britain. And it is very remarkably the sense of the British nation that they are so; as appears by an Act of Parliament made in the 13th of his late Majesty King George the second. The preamble of that act plainly presupposes it; and the purview of the same act enables and directs the superior court of judicature of this province, a court erected by the authority of the general court, to naturalize foreigners under certain conditions; which it is presumed the wisdom of the Parliament would not have empowered any people to do, who were not *themselves* deemed natural born subjects.

The spirit of the law of nature and nations supposes that all the free subjects of any kingdom, are entitled equally to all the rights of the consti-

tution; for it appears unnatural and unreasonable to affirm, that local or any other circumstances can justly deprive any part of the subjects of the same Prince, of the full enjoyments of the rights of that constitution, upon which the government itself is formed, and by which sovereignty and allegiance are ascertained and limited. But your Lordship is so thoroughly acquainted with the extent of the rights of men and subjects, as to render it altogether improper to take up any more of your time on this head.

There are, my Lord, fundamental rules of the constitution, which it is humbly presumed, neither the supreme legislative nor the supreme executive can alter. In all free states the constitution is fixed: it is from thence the legislative derives its authority; therefore it cannot change the constitution without destroying its own foundation. If then the constitution of Great-Britain is the common rights of all British subjects, it is humbly referred to your Lordship's judgment, whether the supreme legislative of the empire may rightly leap the bounds of it in the exercise of power over the subjects in America, any more than those in Britain.

When mention is made of the rights of American subjects and the interest they have in the British constitution in common with all other British subjects, your Lordship is too candid and just in your sentiments to suppose that the House have the most distant thought of an independency on Great-Britain.—They are not insensible of their security and happiness in their connection with and dependance on the mother-state. These, my Lord, are the sentiments of the House and of their constituents; and they have reason to believe they are the sentiments of all the colonies: those who are industriously propagating in the nation a different opinion of the colonists, are not only doing the

greatest

greateſt injuſtice to them, but an ir-
reparable injury to the nation itſelf.

It is the glory of the Britiſh conſtitution that it has its foundation in the
law of God and nature : it is eſſenti-
ally a natural right that a man ſhall
quietly enjoy, and have the ſole diſpoſal of his own property : this right
is ingrafted into the Britiſh conſtitution and is familiar to the American
ſubjeȼts : and your Lordſhip will
judge whether any neceſſity can render it juſt and equitable in the nature
of things, that the ſupreme legiſlative
of the empire, ſhould impoſe duties,
ſubſidies, talliages and taxes, internal or external, for the ſole purpoſe
of raiſing a revenue, upon ſubjeȼts
that are not, and cannot, conſidering
their local circumſtances, by any poſ-
ſibility be equally repreſented, and
conſequently, whoſe conſent cannot
be had in Parliament.

The ſecurity of right and property
is the great end of government. Surely then ſuch meaſures as tend to render right and property precarious,
tend to deſtroy both property and government, for theſe muſt ſtand or fall
together.— Property is admitted to
have an exiſtence in the ſavage ſtate
of nature : and if it is neceſſary for
the ſupport of ſavage life, it by no
means becomes leſs ſo in civil ſociety,
The Houſe intreats your Lordſhip to
conſider, whether a coloniſt can be
conceived to have any property which
he may call his own, if it may be
granted away by any other body without his conſent : and they ſubmit to
your Lordſhip's judgment whether
this was not aȼtually done, when the
aȼt for granting to his Majeſty certain
duties on paper, glaſs, and other articles, for the ſole and expreſs purpoſe of raiſing a revenue in America,
was made. It is the judgment of
Lord Coke that the Parliament of
Great Britain cannot tax Ireland
*"quia milites ad Parliamentum non mit-
tant."* And Sir William Jones, an

eminent juriſt, declared it as his
opinion, to King Charles the Second,
that he could no more grant a commiſſion to levy money on his ſubjeȼts
in Jamaica, without their conſent by
an aſſembly, than they could diſcharge
themſelves from their allegiance to
the crown.

Your Lordſhip will be pleaſed to
conſider that Ireland and Jamaica
were both conquered ; which cannot
be ſaid of any of the colonies, Canada excepted ; the argument therefore
is ſtronger in favour of the colonies.

Our anceſtors, when oppreſſed in
the unfortunate reign of James the
Second, found relief by the interpoſition of the Parliament : but it is the
misfortune of the colonies at preſent,
that by the intervention of that power they are taxed ; and they can appeal for relief from their final deciſion
to no power on earth, for there is no
power on earth above them. — Your
Lordſhip will indulge the Houſe in
expreſſing a deep concern upon this
occaſion ; for it is the language of
reaſon, and it is the opinion of the
greateſt writers on the law of nature and nations, that if the Parliament ſhould make any conſiderable
change in the conſtitution, and the
nation ſhould be voluntarily ſilent upon it, this would be conſidered as an
approbation of the aȼt.

But the Houſe beg leave to repreſent to your Lordſhip, that although
the right of the Parliament to impoſe
taxes on the colonies without a repreſentation there were indiſputable, we
humbly conceive it may be made fully
to appear to be unequal that they
ſhould, at leaſt at preſent. Your
Lordſhip will be pleaſed to remember
that by aȼt of Parliament, the coloniſts are prohibited from importing
commodities and manufaȼtures of the
growth of Europe, ſaving a few articles, except from Great Britain.
This prohibition not only occaſions a
much greater demand upon the mo-

ther-

ther-country for her manufactures, but gives the manufacturers there the advantage of their own price; and can it be questioned, my Lord, but the colonists are obliged by means of this policy, to purchase the British manufactures at a much dearer rate, than the like manufactures would be purchased at, if they are allowed to go to foreign markets. It is a loss to the colonists and an equal gain to Great Britain. The same reasoning holds good with respect to the many articles of their produce, which the colonies are restrained by act of Parliament from sending to foreign ports.— This is in reality a tax though an indirect one on the colonies, besides the duties of excise and customs, laid on the manufactures in Great Britain. A celebrated British writer on trade, computes the artificial value arising from these duties, to be not less than fifty per cent. Your Lordship will then form an estimate of the part that is paid by the colonies upon the importation into America, which is generally said to be at least the value of two millions sterling.

The House is not at this time complaining of this policy of the mother state; but beg your Lordship's impartial and candid consideration, whether it is not grievous to the colonies to be additionally taxed upon the commodities of Great Britain here — and to be solely charged with the defending and securing his Majesty's colonies, after they have chearfully borne their full proportion of maintaining his Majesty's rights in this part of his dominions, and reducing his enemies to terms of peace.

Your Lordship will allow the House to express their fears that the colonies have been misrepresented to his Majesty's ministers and the Parliament, as having an undutiful disposition towards his Majesty, and a disaffection to the mother-kingdom. It has till a few years past been the usage for his

Majesty's requisitions to be lain before the representatives of his people in America. And we may venture to appeal to your Lordship, that the people of this province have been ready to afford their utmost aid for his Majesty's service. It would be grievous to his most faithful subjects, to be called upon for aid in a manner which implies a mistrust of a free and chearful compliance: and the House intreat your Lordship's consideration, whether our enemies at least, would not infer a want of duty and loyalty in us, when the Parliament have judged it necessary to compel us by laws for that purpose; as by the late acts for raising a revenue in America, and the act for preventing mutiny and desertion; in the latter of which the governor and council are directed to supply the King's troops with enumerated articles, and the people are required to pay the expence. But besides, your Lordship will judge whether the execution of this act can comport with the existence of a free legislative in America.

It is unnatural to expect, that the supreme executive power can long exist, if the supreme legislative should be distressed and destroyed. In order, therefore, to support the supreme executive of his Majesty, at so great a distance, in the person of his governor, judges, and other executive officers, it seems necessary that there should be a legislative in America as perfectly free, as can consist with a subordination to the supreme legislative of the whole empire.

Such a legislative is constituted by the royal charter of this province: in this charter, my Lord, the King, for himself, his heirs and successors, grants to the general assembly, full power and authority to impose and levy proportionable and reasonable assessments, rates and taxes upon the estates and persons of the inhabitants, to be issued and disposed of, by warrant

rant under the hand of the governor, with the advice and confent of the council, for the fervice of his Majefty, in the neceffary defence and fupport of his government of the province, and the protection and prefervation of the inhabitants, according to fuch acts, as are or fhall be in force in the province. And the Houfe are humbly of opinion, that the legiflative powers in the feveral colonies in America were originally erected upon a conviction, that the fubjects there, could not be reprefented in the fupreme legiflative, and confequently that there was a neceffity that fuch powers fhould be erected.

It is by no means, my Lord, a difpofition in the Houfe to difpute the juft authority of the fupreme legiflative of the nation, that induces them thus to addrefs your Lordfhip; but a warm fenfe of loyalty to their prince, and, they humbly apprehend, a juft concern for their natural and conftitutional rights. They beg your Lordfhip would excufe their trefpaffing upon your time and attention to the great affairs of the ftate: they apply to you as a friend to the rights of mankind and of Britifh fubjects. As Americans they implore your Lordfhip's patronage, and befeech you to reprefent their grievances to the King our fovereign, and employ your happy influence for their relief.

Signed by the Speaker.

A Letter to the Right Hon. Henry Seymour Conway, Efq; one of his Majefty's principal Secretaries of State. Province of the Maffachufetts-Bay, February 13, 1768.

SIR,

The Houfe of reprefentatives of this his Majefty's province have ftill the fenfible impreffions of gratitude upon their minds, for the fignal and fuccefsful exertions you were pleafed to make for them when the liberties of the colonies were in danger. And although they do not fall immediately

under your care in that department, to which his Majefty has been gracioufly pleafed to appoint you; yet your known attachment to the rights of fubjects, in their juft extent, the conftitutional authority of the fupreme legiflative and the prerogative of the fovereign, is a ftrong inducement to the Houfe, when new grievances happen, to implore your repeated aid. Confcious of their own difpofition, they rely upon that candour which is a diftinguifhed mark of your character. And however they may have been reprefented to his Majefty's minifters as undutiful, turbulent and factious, your fentiments are too generous, to impute the expreffions of uneafinefs under the operation of any particular acts of the Britifh parliament to a peevifh or difcontented habit, much lefs to the want of a due veneration for that auguft affembly.

This Houfe is at all times ready to recognize his Majefty's high court of parliament, the fupreme legiflative power over the whole empire; its fuperintending authority, in all cafes confiftent with the fundamental rules of the conftitution, is as clearly admitted by his Majefty's fubjects in this province as by thofe within the realm: fince the conftitution of the ftate, as it ought to be, is fixed; it is humbly prefumed, that the fubjects, in every part of the empire, however remote, have an equitable claim to all the advantages of it.

It is the glory of the Britifh Prince, and the happinefs of all his fubjects, that their conftitution hath its foundation in the immutable laws of nature: and as the fupreme legiflative, as well as the fupreme executive derives its authority from that conftitution, it fhould feem that no laws can be made or executed, that are regugnant to any effential law in nature. Hence a Britifh fubject is happily diftinguifhed from the fubjects of many

many other ſtates, in a juſt and well grounded opinion of his own ſafety, which is the perfection of political liberty.

It is acknowledged to be an unalterable law in nature, that a man ſhould have the free uſe and ſole diſpoſal of the fruit of his honeſt induſtry, ſubject to no controul. The equity of this principle ſeems to have been too obvious to be miſunderſtood by thoſe who framed the conſtitution; into which it is ingrafted as an eſtabliſhed law. It is conceived that this principle gave riſe in early time to a repreſentation in parliament; where every individual in the realm has ſince been, and is ſtill conſidered by acts of parliament as preſent by himſelf, or by his repreſentative of his own free election: conſequently, the aid afforded there to the ſovereign is not of the nature of a tribute, but the free and voluntary gift of all.

The Houſe ſubmit to your conſideration, whether his Majeſty's ſubjects of this province, or any of them, can be conſidered as having been preſent in parliament, when an act of the fourth of his preſent Majeſty's reign, and another paſſed the laſt ſeſſion, were made. If not, it ſeems to be concluſive, that, as thoſe acts were made with the ſole and expreſs purpoſe of raiſing a revenue out of America, the ſubjects here are in thoſe inſtances unfortunately deprived of the ſole diſpoſal of their property, and the honour and privilege of contributing to the aid of their ſovereign by a free and voluntary gift.

The people of this province would by no means be inclined to petition the parliament for a repreſentation. Separated from the mother-country by a mighty ocean, and at the diſtance of three thouſand miles, they apprehend it is, and ever will be, utterly impracticable that they ſhould be equally repreſented there: they

have always been conſidered by the nation as ſubjects remote: and his Majeſty's royal predeceſſors were graciouſly pleaſed to conſtitute by charter a ſubordinate legiſlative in the province, as it is conceived, with a view of preſerving to their remote ſubjects the unalienable right of a repreſentation. By this charter the lands therein deſcribed are granted to the inhabitants in free and common ſoccage; and the general aſſembly is inveſted with the power of impoſing and levying proportionable and reaſonable aſſeſſments, rates and taxes, upon the eſtates and perſons of the inhabitants, for his Majeſty's ſervice, in the neceſſary defence and ſupport of his government of the province, and the protection and preſervation of the inhabitants; and of ordaining and eſtabliſhing all manner of wholeſome and reaſonable orders, laws, ſtatutes and ordinances, directions and inſtructions, either with or without penalties, as they ſhall judge to be for the good and welfare of the province: and as a ſufficient check upon this ſubordinate power, which ſecures its dependance on the ſupreme legiſlative, no law can be made repugnant to the laws of England; and all laws that are made, are laid before his Majeſty, who at any time during three years after, diſannulls them at his royal pleaſure.

All that is deſired by the people of this province, is, that they may be reſtored to their original ſtanding: they may venture to appeal to the nation, that they have never failed to afford their utmoſt aid to his Majeſty whenever he hath required it; and they may ſay it without vanity, that in many inſtances from their ſettlement, they have given ſtriking proofs of their zeal for the honour of their ſovereign, and their affection for the mother-ſtate. Muſt it not then be grievous to free and loyal ſubjects,

subjects, to be called upon in a manner which appears to them, to divest them of their freedom, and so far to impeach their loyalty as to imply a mistrust of their chearful compliance with his Majesty's royal requisitions.

The House also beg leave to submit, whether the people can continue free, while the crown in addition to its uncontroverted right of appointing a governor, may appoint him such stipends as it shall judge fit, at the expence of the people, and without their consent : and whether, while the judges of the land, at so great a distance from the throne, the fountain of justice, may be altogether independent on the people for their support, it may not probably happen, that in some future time, the principles of equity may be subverted even on the bench of justice, and the people deprived of their happiness and security.

The House could add, that by restraints laid upon the American trade by acts of parliament, which operate equally to the advantage of Great-Britain and the disadvantage of this and the other colonies, and the taxes which the inhabitants here eventually pay as the consumers of the British manufactures, it should seem to be beyond all the rules of equity, that these additional burdens should be laid on them. But they would not trespass upon your time and attention to the great affairs of the nation. They beg your candid consideration of the unhappy circumstances of the province, and hope, that your great interest in the national councils, so far as shall appear to you to be just, will be employed on their behalf.

Signed by the Speaker.

A Letter to the Right Hon. the Marquis of Rockingham.
Province of the Massachusetts-Bay,
January 22, 1768.

My Lord,

The House of representatives of this his Majesty's province have had the honour of your letter of the 7th of May last, communicated to them by their speaker, and thank your Lordship for your condescension, in the kind sentiments you are pleased to express of his Majesty's good subjects of America and of this province. The establishing the harmony between Great Britain and her colonies, is a subject which your Lordship has judged worthy of your particular attention : and the exertions which you have made for this very important purpose, claim the most grateful acknowledgements of the House. Your sentiments are so nobly extended beyond the most distant partial considerations, as must distinguish you as a patron of the colonies, a friend to the British constitution, and the rights of mankind.

Your Lordship is pleased to say, that you will not adopt a system of arbitrary rule over the colonies ; nor do otherwise, than strenuously resist where attempts shall be made to throw off that dependency to which the colonies ought to submit. And your Lordship with great impartiality adds " not only for the advantage of Great " Britain but for their own real hap- " piness and safety."

This House, my Lord, have the honour heartily to join with you in sentiment ; and they speak the language of their constituents. So sensible are they of their happiness and safety, in their union with and dependance upon the mother country, that they could by no means be inclined to accept of an independency if offered to them. But, my Lord, they intreat your consideration, whether the colonies have not reason to fear some danger of arbitrary rule over them, when the supreme power of the nation, have thought proper to impose impofe taxes on his Majefty's American fubjects, with the fole and exprefs purpofe of raifing a revenue, and without their confent.

My Lord, the fuperintending power of that high court over all his Majefty's fubjects in the empire, and in all cafes which can confift with the fundamental rules of the conftitution, was never queftioned in this province, nor, as the Houfe conceive, in any other. But in all free ftates the conftitution is fixed: it is from thence that the fupreme legiflative as well as the fupreme executive derives its authority: neither, then, can break through the fundamental rules of the conftitution, without deftroying their own foundation.

It is humbly conceived, that all his Majefty's happy fubjects, in every part of his wide extended dominions, have a juft and equitable claim to the rights of that conftitution, upon which government itfelf is formed, and by which fovereignty and allegiance is afcertained and limited. Your Lordfhip will allow us to fay, that it is an effential right of a Britifh fubject, ingrafted into the conftitution, or if your Lordfhip will admit the expreffion, a facred and unalienable natural right, quietly to enjoy and have the fole difpofal of his own property. In conformity to this, the acts of the Britifh Parliament declare, that every individual in the realm, is prefent in his Majefty's high court of Parliament, by himfelf or his reprefentative of his own free election. But, my Lord, it is apprehended, that a juft and equal reprefentation of the fubjects, at the diftance of a thoufand tranfmarine leagues from the metropolis is utterly impracticable. Upon this opinion, this Houfe humbly conceive, his Majefty's royal predeceffors, thought it equitable to form fubordinate legiflative powers in America, as perfectly free as the nature of things would ad-

mit, that fo, their remote fubjects might enjoy a right, which thofe within the realm have ever held facred, of being taxed only by reprefentatives of their own free election.

The Houfe beg leave to obferve to your Lordfhip, that the monies that fhall arife by the act for granting to his Majefty certain duties on paper, glafs, and other articles, paffed in the laft feffion of Parliament, are to be applied, in the firft place, for the payment of the neceffary charges of the adminiftration of juftice, and the fupport of civil government, in fuch colonies where it fhall be judged neceffary; and the refidue for defending, protecting and fecuring the colonies. They intreat your Lordfhip's confideration, what may be the confequence, in fome future time, if the crown, in addition to its right of appointing governors over the colonies, which the Houfe chearfully recognize, fhould appoint them fuch ftipends, as it fhall judge fit, without the confent of the people, and at their expence. And as the judges of the land here do not hold their commiffions during good behaviour, your Lordfhip will judge, whether it may not hereafter happen, that at fo great a diftance from the throne, the fountain of juftice, for want of an adequate check, corrupt and arbitrary rule may take place, even within the colonies, which may deprive a bench of juftice of its glory, and the people of their happinefs and fafety.

Your Lordfhip's juftice and candor will induce you to believe, that what our enemies may have taken occafion to reprefent to his Majefty's minifters and the Parliament, as an undutiful difpofition in the colonies, is nothing more than a juft and firm attachment to their natural and conftitutional rights. It is humbly fubmitted to your Lordfhip whether thefe ideas are well founded. And while this

pro-

province and the colonies shall continue in your Lordship's judgment to be faithful and loyal subjects to his Majesty, they rely upon it, that your happy influence will ever be employed, to promote the sentiments of tenderness as well as justice in the parent country.

Signed by the Speaker.

A letter to the Right Hon. Lord Camden, Lord High Chancellor of Great Britain.

Province of the Massachusetts-Bay, Jan. 29, 1768.

My Lord,

Your great knowledge of the constitution and laws of the nation, of the just extent of parliamentary authority, and the rights of British subjects, is a prevailing inducement to the House of Representatives of this his Majesty's province, to address your Lordship, at a time when your attention to the British colonies, their connection with and dependance upon the mother state, and their rights as subjects, seems to be necessary and important, not to them alone, but to the whole empire.

This House can speak only for the people of one province: but no assembly on this continent, it is presumed, can long be silent, under an apprehension, that without the aid of some powerful advocate, the liberties of America will soon be no more.

It is a cause which the House is assured your Lordship has at heart: and the past experience of your patronage, and the noble exertions you were pleased to make for them in a late time of distress, affords the strongest reason to hope that your happy influence will still be employed in their behalf, as far as your Lordship shall judge to be right.

If in all free states, the constitution is fixed, and the supreme legislative power of the nation, from thence derives its authority; can that

power overleap the bounds of the constitution, without subverting its own foundation? If the remotest subjects are bound by the ties of allegiance, which this people and their forefathers have ever acknowledged; are they not by the rules of equity, intitled to all the rights of that constitution, which ascertains and limits both sovereignty and allegiance? If it is an essential unalterable right in nature, ingrafted into the British constitution as a fundamental law, and ever held sacred and irrevocable by the subjects within the realm, that what is a man's own is absolutely his own; and that no man hath a right to take it from him without his consent; may not the subjects of this province, with a decent firmness, which has always distinguished the happy subjects of Britain, plead and maintain this natural constitutional right?

The superintending authority of his Majesty's high court of parliament over the whole empire, in all cases which can consist with the fundamental rights of the constitution, was never questioned in this province, nor, as this House conceive, in any other: but they intreat your Lordship's reflection one moment, on an act of parliament passed the last session; and another in the fourth of his present Majesty's reign; both imposing duties on his subjects in America, which as they are imposed with the sole and express purpose of raising a revenue, are, in effect, taxes. The position, that taxation and representation are inseparable, is founded on the immutable laws of nature: but the Americans had no representation in the parliament, when they were taxed: are they not then unfortunate in these instances, in having that separated, which God and nature had joined? Such are the local circumstances of the colonies, at the

B b distance

diſtance of a thouſand leagues from the metropolis, and ſeparated by a wide ocean, as will for ever render a juſt and equal repreſentation in the ſupreme legiſlative, utterly impracticable. Upon this conſideration, it is conceived, that his Majeſty's royal predeceſſors thought it equitable to form legiſlative bodies in America, as perfectly free as a ſubordination to the ſupreme legiſlative would admit of, that the ineſtimable right of being taxed only by repreſentatives of their own free election, might be preſerved and ſecured to their ſubjects here. The Americans have ever been conſidered by the nation as ſubjects remote; and ſucceeding kings, even to the preſent happy reign, and until theſe acts were made, have always directed their requiſitions, to be laid before the repreſentatives of their people in America, with which this province, and it is preſumed, all the other colonies, have with the utmoſt chearfulneſs complied. Muſt it not then be grievous to ſubjects, who have in many repeated inſtances afforded the ſtrongeſt marks of loyalty and zeal for the honour and ſervice of their ſovereign, to be now called upon, in a manner, which implies a diſtruſt of a free and willing compliance ? Such is the misfortune of the coloniſts, not only in the inſtances before-mentioned, but alſo in the caſe of the act for preventing mutiny and deſertion; which requires the governor and council to provide enumerated articles for the King's marching troops, and the people to pay the expence.

This is a great change; and in its nature delicate and important. Your Lordſhip will form your own judgement of the wiſdom of making ſuch a change, without the moſt preſſing reaſon, or an abſolute neceſſity. There can be no neceſſity, my Lord, as this Houſe humbly conceive: the ſubjects in this province, and undoubtedly in all the colonies, however they may have been otherwiſe repreſented to his Majeſty's miniſters, are loyal : they are firmly attached to the mother ſtate : they always conſider her intereſt and their own as inſeparably interwoven, and it is their fervent wiſh that it may ever ſo remain : all they deſire is, to be reſtored to the ſtanding upon which they were originally put ; to have the honour and privilege of voluntarily contributing to the aid of their ſovereign, when required : they are free ſubjects; and it is hoped the nation will never conſider them as in a tributary ſtate.

It is humbly ſubmitted to your Lordſhip, whether ſubjects can be ſaid to enjoy any degree of freedom, if the crown in addition to its undoubted authority of conſtituting governors, ſhould be authorized to appoint ſuch ſtipends for them, as it ſhall judge proper, at their expence, and without their conſent. This is the unhappy ſtate to which his Majeſty's ſubjects in the colonies are reduced, by the act for granting certain duties on paper, and other articles. A power without a check is always unſafe; and in ſome future time may introduce an abſolute government into America. The judges of the land here do not hold their commiſſions during good behaviour: is it not then juſtly to be apprehended, that at ſo great a diſtance from the throne, the fountain of national juſtice, with ſalaries altogether independent of the people, an arbitrary rule may take effect, which ſhall deprive a bench of juſtice of its glory, and the people of their ſecurity.

When a queſtion ariſes on the public adminiſtration, the nation will judge and determine in conformity to its political conſtitution : the great end of the Britiſh conſtitution is univerſal liberty ; and this Houſe reſts aſſured,

assured, that your Lordship's great interest in the national councils will always be engaged on the side of liberty and truth.

Signed by the Speaker.

A letter to the Right Hon. the Earl of Chatham.

Province of the Massachusetts-Bay, Feb. 2, 1768.

My Lord,

The particular attention you were pleased to give to the interest of the American subjects when their rights were in danger, and your noble and successful efforts in support of them, have left in the breasts of all, the indelible marks of gratitude. The House of Representatives of this his Majesty's province, having reason to be assured, that in every instance of your public conduct, you are influenced by the principles of virtue and a disinterested public affection, beg leave to manifest to your Lordship, a testimony of their full confidence in you, by imploring your repeated aid and patronage at this time when the cloud again gathers thick over them.

It must afford the utmost satisfaction to the distressed colonists, to find your Lordship so explicitly declaring your sentiments in that grand principle in nature, " that what a man hath honestly acquired is absolutely and uncontroulably his own." This principle is established as a fundamental rule in the British constitution, which eminently hath its foundation in the laws of nature; and consequently it is the indisputable right of all men, more especially of a British subject, to be present in person, or by representation, in the body where he is taxed.

But however fixed your Lordship and some others may be in this cardinal point, it is truly mortifying to many of his Majesty's free and loyal sub-

jects, that even in the British parliament, that sanctuary of liberty and justice, a different sentiment seems of late to have prevailed.

Unwilling to intrude upon your attention to the great affairs of state, the House would only refer your Lordship to an act passed in the fourth year of the present reign, and another in the last session of parliament; both imposing duties on the Americans, who were not represented, with the sole and express purpose of raising a revenue. What, my Lord, have the colonists done to forfeit the character and privilege of subjects, and to be reduced in effect to a tributary state? This House may appeal to the nation, that the utmost aid of the people has been chearfully given when his Majesty required it: often, on their own motion, and when almost ready to succumb under the expence of defending their own borders, their zeal has carried them abroad for the honour of their sovereign, and the defence of his rights: of this, my Lord, not to mention any more, the reduction of Louisburgh in the year 1745, and the defence of his Majesty's garrison at Annapolis, and of all Nova Scotia, will be standing monuments. Can there then be a necessity for so great a change, and in its nature so delicate and important, that instead of having the honour of his Majesty's requisitions laid before their representatives here, as has been invariably the usage, the parliament should now tax them without their consent?

The enemies of the colonists, for such they unfortunately have, may have represented them to his Majesty's ministers, and the parliament, as factious, undutiful, disloyal: they, my Lord, are equally the enemies of Britain: such is your extensive knowledge of mankind, and the sentiments and disposition of the colonies in general, that this house would freely venture to rest the character of their

B b 2 con-

conftituents in your Lordfhip's judgment: furely it is no ill difpofition in the loyal fubjects of a patriot king, with a decency and firmnefs adapted to their character, to affert their freedom.

The colonies, as this Houfe humbly conceive, cannot be reprefented in the Britifh parliament: their local circumftances, at the diftance of a thoufand leagues beyond the feas, forbids, and will for ever render it impracticable: this they apprehend, was the reafon that his Majefty's royal predeceffors faw fit to erect fubordinate legiflative bodies in America as perfectly free as the nature of things would admit, that their remote fubjects might enjoy that ineftimable right, a reprefentation. Such a legiflative is conftituted by the royal charter of this province. In this charter, the King, for himfelf, his heirs and fucceffors, grants to the inhabitants all the lands and territories therein defcribed, in free and common foccage; as ample eftate as the fubjects can hold under the crown; together with all the rights, liberties, privileges, and immunities of his natural fubjects born within the realm; of which the moft effential is a power invefted in the general affembly to levy proportionable and reafonable taxes on the eftates and perfons of the inhabitants, for the fervice of his Majefty, and the neceffary defence and fupport of his government of the province, and the protection and prefervation of the inhabitants. But though they were originally, and always, fince their fettlement, have been confidered as fubjects remote, they have ever cherifhed a warm affection for the mother ftate, and a regard for the intereft and happinefs of their fellow fubjects in Britain. If then the colonies are charged with the moft diftant thought of an independency, your Lordfhip may be affured, that, with refpect to the people of this province, and it is prefumed, of all the colonies, the charge is unjuft.

Nothing would have prevailed upon the Houfe to have given your Lordfhip this trouble, but the neceffity of a powerful advocate, when their liberty is in danger: fuch they have more than once found you to be; and as they humbly hope they have never forfeited your patronage, they intreat that your great intereft in the national councils may ftill be employed in their behalf, that they may be reftored to the ftanding of free fubjects.

That your Lordfhip may enjoy a firm ftate of health, and long be continued a great bleffing to the nation and her colonies, is the ardent wifh of this Houfe.

Signed by the Speaker.

A Letter to the Right Hon. the Lords Commiffioners of the Treafury.
Province of the Maffachufetts-Bay, February 17, 1768.

My Lords,

The Houfe of Reprefentatives of this his Majefty's province beg leave to lay before your Lordfhips the great difficulties to which they are reduced, by the operation of divers acts of Parliament, impofing duties to be levied on the fubjects of the American colonies, and made with the fole and exprefs purpofe of raifing a revenue: and beg the favour of your candid judgment and great intereft in the national councils for their redrefs.

As their conftituents are not in any manner reprefented in the Parliament, they cannot fo much wonder, that taxes and burdens are laid upon them, which they humbly apprehend could have been made to appear to be beyond all bounds of equity and proportion; and this confideration they are fure would have had its due weight in the Britifh houfe of commons.

By act of Parliament, your Lord-ships are fensible, that the colonies are reftrained from importing commodities, the growth or manufacture of Europe, faving a few articles, except from Great Britain: by this policy, the demand of Britifh manufactures from the colonies is greatly increafed; and the manufacturers have the advantage of their own price. Hence it appears, that what is gained by the fubjects in Great Britain, is a lofs to thofe in America; for there can be no doubt, as this Houfe conceive, but that if the colonifts were allowed to purchafe fuch commodities at foreign markets, they might have them at a cheaper rate; or, which is the fame thing to them, the Britifh manufacturers would be neceffitated to reduce their price. Thus alfo, with regard to the many articles of their produce, which the colonies are by act of Parliament reftrained from fending to foreign ports: this occafioned a great plenty of American exports, and oftentimes a glut at the Britifh markets, which always diminifhes the price, and makes a lofs to the American, and an equal gain to the fubject in Britain. This regulation, evidently defigned in favour of thofe of his Majefty's fubjects inhabiting in Great Britain, the houfe is not at this time complaining of: but they beg your Lordfhips confideration, whether, in addition to thefe burdens, it is not grievous to their conftituents, to be obliged to pay duties on Britifh manufactures here: efpecially confidering, that, as the confumers of thofe manufactures, they pay a great proportion of the duties and taxes laid upon them in Britain. It is computed by a late celebrated Britifh writer, that the artificial value arifing from thefe duties are not lefs than fifty per cent. Your Lordfhips will then form an eftimate of the part that is paid annually upon the impor

tation into America, which is generally allowed to be at leaft two millions fterling.—So great are the advantages arifing yearly to Great Britain from the colonies, moft of which, it is faid, were fettled, and have been maintained and defended, till within a very few years, folely at their own expence: this Houfe can affirm for one province only.

But the bearing an unequal fhare of the public burthens, though a real grievance, is of but fmall confideration, when compared with another, in the mentioning of which, the Houfe begs your Lordfhip's indulgence. The duties levied in America, by virtue of the aforementioned acts, were impofed with the fole and exprefs purpofe of raifing a revenue; and are to be applied, in the firft place, for making a more certain and adequate provifion for the charge of the adminiftration of juftice, and the fupport of civil government, in fuch colonies where it fhall be found neceffary; and the refidue is from time to time to be difpofed of by Parliament, towards defraying the neceffary expences of defending, protecting, and fecuring the colonies. It is humbly fubmitted, whether his Majefty's commons in Britain have not, by thefe acts, granted the property of their fellow fubjects in America, without their confent in Parliament. Your Lordfhips will allow, that it is an unalterable rule in equity, that a man fhall have the free ufe and the fole difpofal of his property. This original principle, to the lafting honour of our Britifh anceftors, was in early time ingrafted into the Britifh conftitution, and is the greateft fecurity, as well as the brighteft ornament of a Britifh fubject. It adds to the real grandeur of the Britifh monarch, whofe happy fubjects have an unfha-, ken opinion of their own fafety, which is the perfection of political liberty:

liberty: such a constitution shall in future ages be admired, when the names of tyrants and their vassals shall be alike forgot. This constitution, my Lords, is fixed: it is from thence that all power in the state derives its authority: therefore, no power can exceed the bounds of it without destroying its own foundation. It is conceived, that even the remotest and most inconsiderable subject hath an equitable claim to the benefit of the fundamental rules of the constitution; for all British subjects are alike free. The blessings of the British constitution will for ever keep the subjects in this province united to the mother state, as long as the sentiments of liberty are preserved: but what liberty can remain to them, when their property, the fruit of their toil and industry, and the prop of all their future hopes in life, may be taken from them at the discretion of others? They have never been backward in affording their aid to his Majesty, to the extent of their ability: they can say without vanity, and they may be allowed to boast, that from the days of their ancestors, no subjects have given more signal proofs of zeal for the service and honour of their sovereign, and affection for the parent country: It has still of late been the invariable usage for his Majesty's requisitions to be laid before their own representatives; and their aid has not been tributary, but the free and voluntary gift of all: the change is in its nature delicate and important; your Lordships will judge whether there be any necessity or pressing reasons of it: the House are not insensible that the colonies have their enemies, who may have represented them to his Majesty's ministers and the Parliament as seditious, disloyal, and disposed to set up an independency on Great Britain: but they rely upon the candour of your Lord-

ships judgment: they can affirm, that with regard to this province, and, they presume, all the colonies, the charge is injurious and unjust; the superintending authority of his Majesty's high court of Parliament, the supreme legislative over the whole empire, is as clearly admitted here as in Britain; so far as is consistent with the fundamental rules of the constitution: and, it is presumed, it is not further admissable there.

The House are humbly in opinion, that a representation of their constituents in that high court, by reason of local circumstances, will for ever be impracticable: and that his Majesty's royal predecessors were graciously pleased, by charter, to erect a legislative in the province, as perfectly free as a subordination would admit, that the subjects here might enjoy the unalienable right of a representation; and further, that the nation hath ever since considered them as subjects, though remote, and conceded to the acts of the subordinate legislation. Their charter is a check upon them, and effectually secures their dependance on Great Britain; for no acts can be in force till the King's governor has given his assent, and all laws that are made are laid before his Majesty, who at any time, during three years after they are made, may disannul them at his royal pleasure: under this check the House humbly conceive a representation in Parliament cannot be necessary for the nation, and for many reasons it cannot be eligible to them: all they desire is, to be placed on their original standing, that they may still be happy in the enjoyment of their invaluable privileges, and the nation may still reap the advantage of their growth and prosperity.

The House intreat your Lordships patience one moment longer, while they just mention the danger they
                                                                appre-

apprehend to their liberties, if the crown, in addition to its uncontroverted right of appointing a governor, fhould alfo appoint him a ftipend at the expence of the people, and without their confent. And alfo, whether, as the judges and other civil officers of the province do not hold commiffions during good behaviour, there is not a probability that arbitrary rule may in fome time take effect, to the fubverfion of the principles of equity and juftice, and the ruin of liberty and virtue.

It is humbly hoped, that your Lordfhips will conceive a favourable opinion of the people of the province; and that you will patronize their liberties, fo far as in your great wifdom and candour you fhall judge to be right.

Signed by the Speaker.

The following is a genuine copy of the circulatory letter which was fent from the Houfe of Reprefentatives of the province of Maffachufetts-Bay, to the Speakers of the refpective Houfes and Burgeffes on the Continent of North America.
Province of the Maffachufetts-Bay, Feb. 11, 1768.

SIR,

The Houfe of Reprefentatives of this province have taken into their ferious confideration the great difficulties that muft accrue to themfelves and their conftituents, by the operation of the feveral Acts of Parliament impofing duties and taxes on the American colonies.

As it is a fubject in which every colony is deeply interefted, they have no reafon to doubt but your Houfe is duly impreffed with its importance; and that fuch conftitutional meafures will be come into as are proper. It feems to be neceffary, that all poffible care fhould be taken that the reprefentations of the feveral affemblies,

upon fo delicate a point, fhould harmonize with each other: the Houfe therefore hope that this letter will be candidly confidered in no other light than as expreffing a difpofition freely to communicate their mind to a fifter colony, upon a common concern, in the fame manner as they would be glad to receive the fentiments of your, or any other Houfe of Affembly on the continent.

The Houfe have humbly reprefented to the Miniftry their own fentiments: that his Majefty's High Court of Parliament is the fupreme legiflative power over the whole empire: that in all free ftates the conftitution is fixed: and as the fupreme legiflative derives its power and authority from the conftitution, it cannot overleap the bounds of it, without deftroying its foundation: that the conftitution afcertains and limits both fovereignty and allegiance: and therefore his Majefty's American fubjects who acknowledge themfelves bound by the ties of allegiance, have an equitable claim to the full enjoyment of the fundamental rules of the Britifh conftitution: that it is an effential unalterable right in nature, ingrafted into the Britifh conftitution as a fundamental law, and ever held facred and irrevocable by the fubjects within the realm, that what a man hath honeftly acquired is abfolutely his own, which he may freely give, but cannot be taken from him without his confent: that the American fubjects may therefore, exclufive of any confideration of charter rights, with a decent firmnefs adapted to the character of freemen and fubjects, affert this natural conftitutional right.

It is moreover their humble opinion, which they exprefs with the greateft deference to the wifdom of the parliament; that the acts made there, impofing duties on the people of this province, with the fole and exprefs purpofe purpose of raising a revenue, are infringements of their natural and constitutional rights; because, as they are not represented in the British parliament, his Majesty's commons in Britain by those acts grant their property without their consent.

This House further are of opinion, that their constituents, considering their local circumstances, cannot by any possibility be represented in the Parliament; and that it will for ever be impracticable that they should be equally represented there, and consequently not at all; being separated by an ocean of a thousand leagues: that his Majesty's royal predecessors, for this reason, were graciously pleased to form a subordinate legislative here, that their subjects might enjoy the unalienable right of a representation. Also that considering the utter impracticability of their ever being fully and equally represented in parliament, and the great expence that must unavoidably attend even a partial representation there, this House think, that a taxation of their constituents, even without their consent, grievous as it is, would be preferable to any representation that could be admitted for them there.

Upon these principles, and also considering that were the right in the parliament ever so clear, yet for obvious reasons it would be beyond the rule of equity, that their constituents should be taxed on the manufactures of Great Britain here, in addition to the duties they pay for them in England, and other advantages arising to Great Britain from the acts of trade; this House have preferred a humble, dutiful, and loyal petition to our most gracious sovereign, and made such representation to his Majesty's ministers, as they apprehend would tend to obtain redress.

They have also submitted to consideration, whether any people can be said to enjoy any degree of freedom, if the crown, in addition to its undoubted authority of constituting a governor, should appoint him such a stipend as it shall judge proper, without the consent of the people, and at their expence: and whether, while the judges of the land, and other civil officers, hold not their commissions during good behaviour, their having salaries appointed for them by the crown, independant of the people, hath not a tendency to subvert the principles of equity, and endanger the happiness and security of the subject.

In addition to these measures, the House have wrote a letter to their agent, Mr. De Berdt, the sentiments of which he is directed to lay before the ministry; wherein they take notice of the hardship of the act for preventing mutiny and desertion; which requires the governor and council to provide enumerated articles for the King's marching troops, and the people to pay the expence: and also the commission of the gentlemen appointed commissioners of the customs to reside in America, which authorizes them to make as many appointments as they think fit, and to pay the appointees what sums they please, for whose mal-conduct they are not accountable: from whence it may happen, that officers of the crown may be multiplied to such a degree, as to become dangerous to the liberty of the people, by virtue of a commission which doth not appear to this House to derive any such advantages to trade as many have been led to expect.

These are the sentiments and proceedings of this house: and as they have too much reason to believe, that the enemies of the colonies have represented them to his Majesty's ministers and the parliament as factious, disloyal, and having a disposition to make

make themfelves independent of the mother country, they have taken occafion, in the moft humble terms, to affure his Majefty and his minifters, that with regard to the people of this province, and, as they doubt not, of all the colonies, that the charge is unjuft.

The Houfe is fully fatisfied, that your affembly is too generous and enlarged in fentiment to believe, that this letter proceeds from an ambition of taking the lead, or dictating to the other affemblies: they freely fubmit their opinion to the judgment of others; and fhall take it kind in your Houfe to point out to them any thing further that may be thought neceffary.

This Houfe cannot conclude without expreffing their firm confidence in the King, our common head, and father, that the united and dutiful fupplications of his diftreffed American fubjects will meet with his royal and favourable acceptance.

Signed by the Speaker.

A copy of the above letter was alfo by order of the Houfe, fent to Dennis De Berdt, Efq; agent to the province in London; that he might make ufe of it, if neceffary, to prevent any mifreprefentation of it in England.

In the Houfe of Reprefentatives, Feb. 13, 1768.

Whereas this Houfe hath directed that a letter be fent to the feveral Houfes of Reprefentatives and Burgeffes of the Britifh colonies on the continent, fetting forth the fentiments of the Houfe, with regard to the great difficulties that muft accrue by the operation of divers acts of parliament, for levying duties and taxes on the colonies for the fole and exprefs purpofe of raifing a revenue, and their proceedings thereon, in an humble, loyal and dutiful petition to the King, and fuch reprefentations to his Majefty's minifters as they apprehended might have a tendency to their obtaining relief: and whereas it is the opinion of this Houfe, that all effectual methods fhould be taken to cultivate a harmony between the feveral branches of this government, as being neceffary to promote the profperity of his Majefty's government in the province:

Refolved, That Mr. Otis, Col. Preble, Mr. Spooner, Mr. Sayward, and Mr. Hall, be a committee to wait on his Excellency the Governor, and acquaint him that a copy of the letter aforefaid will be laid before him as foon as it can be drafted, as well as of all the proceedings of the Houfe relative to faid affair, if he fhall defire it; and that the faid committee humbly requeft that his Excellency would be pleafed to favour the Houfe with a copy of the letter from the Right Hon. the Earl of Shelburne, lately read to the Houfe by order of his Excellency, and his own fevera letters to which it refers.

T. CUSHING, Speaker.

His Excellency's Anfwer.

Gentlemen of the Houfe of Reprefentatives.

In anfwer to your meffage of the 13th inftant, I find it neceffary to inform you, that foon after the letter of the Earl of Shelburne was read in your Houfe, I ordered a copy of it to be given to the Speaker, to be ufed as he fhould think fit, upon condition that no other copy fhould be taken thereof: I am very willing that the copy in the Speaker's hands fhould be communicated to you in any manner which is confiftent with that reftriction.

I know of no letters of my own which I think can be of any ufe to you upon this occafion.

I quite agree with you in opinion that all effectual methods fhould be taken to cultivate an harmony between

C c   the

the feveral branches of the legiflature of this government, as being necef-fary to promote the profperity of the province; and I fhall chearfully join with you in all proper meafures for fo falutary a purpofe.

Council-Chamber, FRA. BERNARD. *Feb.* 16, 1768.

In the Houfe of Reprefentatives, Feb. 18, 1768.

Ordered, that Mr. Hancock, Major Frye, Colonel Richmond, Colonel Noyes, and Col. Stoddard, be a committee to wait upon his Excellency the Governor, and prefent to him the following anfwer to his meffage of the 16th inftant.

T. CUSHING, Speaker.

May it pleafe your Excellency,

Your meffage of the 16th inftant has been read and duly confidered in the Houfe of Reprefentatives. The manner, in which your Excellency was pleafed to introduce into this houfe the letter from the Right Hon. the Earl of Shelburne, by giving orders to the fecretary to read it without leaving a copy, appeared to be unprecedented and unparliamentary; but this made but a light impreffion on the houfe, when the members re-collected, as far as they could, the unfavourable fentiments his lordfhip thought himfelf neceffitated to entertain of the two houfes of this affembly, and of fome particular members in this houfe, whofe characters in the opinion of the houfe ftand unimpeach-able. Under this apprehenfion they thought it neceffary for their vindica-tion humbly to requeft your Excellency to favour them with a copy of his lordfhip's letter; and as it appeared to them that his lordfhip had formed his fentiments of the two houfes, and their members, from your own letters to which he referred, the houfe thought they could not do themfelves and their members juftice, unlefs they could be favoured with a fight of them alfo,

and accordingly requefted it of your Excellency.

You are pleafed to fay that you know of no letters of your " own that you think can be of any ufe to the houfe upon this occafion."--The houfe did not in their vote or meffage fay what occafion they had to requeft them. But when his lordfhip exprefs-ly fays, that it appears from your feveral letters, that your negativing counfellors in the late elections was done with due deliberation and judg-ment, it is natural for the houfe to conclude, that your Excellency had thought it convenient, to give his lordfhip, the particular reafons you had, for a meafure fo rare and extra-ordinary.——Thefe reafons feem to have prevailed to juftify your Excel-lency; for his lordfhip acquaints you, that his Majefty is gracioufly pleafed to approve of your having exerted the power lodged in you by the con-ftitution of the province: but unfor-tunately for the two houfes his lord-fhip paffes a different judgment upon their conduct, and takes occafion to applaud the wifdom of thofe who framed the charter, in providing that a power fhould be placed in the Go-vernor as an occafional check upon any indifcreet ufe of the right of electing counfellors. It evidently ap-pears from this paffage, that his Ma-jefty's minifter has conceived an opi-nion of the two houfes, as having made an indifcreet ufe of a charter right. The houfe were willing to be convinced that this opinion and other fentiments expreffed in his lordfhip's letter, which imply an high cenfure upon the two houfes, and upon par-ticular members of this houfe, were rather inferences drawn from your letters, in which his lordfhip might be liable to miftake, than the direct expreffions of it: had your Excellen-cy been pleafed, to have favoured them with the copies, they might have

have been of ufe on this occafion, and fatisfactory to the houfe: but as you have thought proper to refufe them, they are left to conjecture with all poffible candour, and appeal to the world.

His Lordfhip is induced to believe, that the affembly have made an indifcreet ufe of their right of chufing counfellors, to the exclufion of the principal officers of government from the board, whofe prefence there as counfellors fo manifeftly tends to facilitate the courfe of public bufinefs, and who have therefore been before this period ufually elected; and, that they have thus exerted their right, with a far different intention from that, of promoting the re-eftablifhment of tranquility, and evincing the duty and attachment of the colony towards Great-Britain.—The houfe would be glad to juftify this conftruction of his Lordfhip's letter, which is nearly in the words of it, by publifhing it in their journals, but that is inconfiftent with your Excellency's reftrictions.—This is not the firft time that his Majefty's minifters, and even his Majefty himfelf, after having had before him your Excellency's letters, and the inclofures, has thought it neceffary to form an opinion of his loyal fubjects of this province, as having a degree of ill temper prevailing among them: and your Excellency cannot be infenfible, that the prefent houfe have heretofore, for the fake of conciliating the minds of the people, and reftoring an unanimity to this general court, requefted your Excellency to give them the opportunity of making it evident to their conftituents, that your letters had no tendency to induce fuch an opinion: and the houfe ftill think that nothing would tend more to promote the falutary purpofe of cultivating an harmony between the feveral branches of this legiflature, in which your Ex-

cellency exprefies a difpofition chearfully to join with the houfe, than an open and unreferved explanation to each other: for this purpofe, the houfe in their meffage affured you, that they were ready to lay before you their humble petition to his Majefty, and their reprefentations to his minifters, with all their other proceedings upon the important matters that have been before them, at the fame time that they made their reafonable requeft of your Excellency's letters.

After having recited a great part of the fentiment of his Lordfhip's letter, no one can be aftonifhed at the conclufion he is pleafed to make, that under fuch circumftances it cannot be furprifing, that his Majefty's governor exerts the right entrufted to him by the fame conftitution, to the purpofe of excluding thofe from the council, whofe miftaken zeal may have led them into improper exceffes, and whofe private refentments (and his lordfhip adds, he fhould be forry to afcribe to them motives ftill more blameable) may in your opinion further lead them to embarrafs the adminiftration and endanger the quiet of the province.—Surely his lordfhip would never have paffed fuch a cenfure upon the two houfes of affembly, nor upon particular gentlemen altogether ftrangers to him, but upon what he thought to be the beft authority: it is far beneath his character and dignity to give credit, or even to hearken to any account fo prejudicial to the reputation of the province, and of particular perfons, but what he receives from gentlemen in the higheft ftations in it.—Your Excellency then muft allow the houfe to believe, until they fhall be convinced to the contrary, that your feveral letters, to which his lordfhip refers, are fo fully expreffed as to have left his lordfhip no room to fufpect that he could be miftaken.

In

In such a case your Excellency cannot think that the house can remain in silence: they recommend to their injured members a becoming calmness and fortitude; and take this occasion to bear a testimony to their zeal for the honour of their king and the rights of their constituents: but the character of the people whom this house represent, as well as their own honour is at stake, and requires them to take every prudent measure for their own vindication. The house are truly sorry that this new occasion of mistrust and jealousy has happened, but they can never be so wanting to themselves, as to omit the opportunity of removing from his lordship's mind the unfavourable impressions which appear by his letters, and what is of much greater importance to them, of standing before their sovereign in their own just character of loyal subjects.

February 23, 1768.
The Secretary went down to the House of Representatives with the following message from his Excellency the Governor, which to prevent mistakes was reduced to writing, and a copy thereof delivered to the Speaker.

Mr. Speaker,

I am ordered by his Excellency to inform you that as this House has thought fit to permit their message of Feb. 18th, containing extracts from the Secretary of State's letter with observations upon it to be printed in a common news-paper, it is to no purpose to continue the restriction against granting copies of such letter: he therefore consents that it may be entered upon the journal of the house.

Copy of a letter from the Right Hon. the Earl of Shelburne, to his Excellency Gov. Bernard, dated White-hall, 17th Sept. 1767, which was read to the House by order of his Excellency, and occasioned the letter to his Lordship inserted p. 198.

I have the pleasure to signify to you his Majesty's approbation of your conduct, and to acquaint you, that he is graciously pleased to approve of your having exerted the power lodged in you by the constitution of the province of Massachusetts-Bay, of negativing counsellors in the late election, which appears from your several letters to have been done with due deliberation and judgment.

Those who framed the present charter very wisely provided that this power should be placed in the governor as an occasional check upon any indiscreet use of the right of electing counsellors, which was given by charter to the assembly, which might at certain periods, by an improper exercise, have a tendency to disturb the deliberations of that part of the legislature, from whom the greatest gravity and moderation is more peculiarly expected. As long therefore as the assembly shall exert their right of election to the exclusion of the principal officers of government, from council, whose presence there, as counsellors, so manifestly tends to facilitate the course of public business, and who have therefore been before this period usually elected, and whilst, in particular, they exclude men of such unexceptionable characters as both the present lieutenant governor and secretary undoubtedly are, and that too, at a time when it is more peculiarly the duty of all parts of the constitution to promote the re-establishment of tranquility, and not forego the least occasion of evincing the duty and attachment of the colony towards Great-Britain; it cannot, under such circumstances, be surprizing that his Majesty's governor exerts the right entrusted to him by the same constitution, to the purpose of excluding

cluding those from the council whose mistaken zeal may have led them into improper excesses, and whose private resentments (and I should be sorry to ascribe to them motives still more blameable) may in your opinion further lead them to embarrass the administration and endanger the quiet of the province.

The dispute which has arisen concerning the lieutenant-governor's being present without a voice, at the deliberations of the council, is no otherwise important, than as it tends to shew a warmth in the House of Representatives which I am extremely sorry for.—There is no pretence of danger to be apprehended from the presence of the lieutenant governor in council, there is no novelty in the practice, and there is an apparent utility and propriety in admitting *him* to be present at the deliberations of the council, who may be suddenly called to the administration of the province. If this opposition to the lieutenant governor's sitting in council, is to be considered as personal, it must appear here very extraordinary, that a person of his very respectable character, and whose learning and ability have been exerted in the service of America, should yet meet with so much animosity and ill-will in a province, which seems to owe him particular obligations. But the question concerning his admission seems to lie after all in the breast of the council only, as being the proper judges of their own privileges, and as having the best right to determine whom they will admit to be present at their deliberations.

As to what concerns the agency of the province, it is doubtless a point that merits attention: but as matters of this nature from other provinces have been heretofore under the consideration of the lords of trade, his Majesty has been pleased to refer the whole matter to their lordships for their report, before any determination shall be taken thereupon.

I am to inform you, Sir, that it is his Majesty's determined resolution to extend to you his countenance and protection in every constitutional measure that shall be found necessary for the support of his government in the Massachusetts-Bay: and it will be your care and your duty to avail yourself of such protection in those cases only, where the honour and dignity of his Majesty's government is really either mediately or immediately concerned.

It is unnecessary to observe that the nature of the English constitution is such as to furnish no real ground of jealousy to the colonies, and where there is so large a foundation of confidence, it cannot be, but that accidental jealousies must subside, and things again return to their proper and national course; the extremes even of legal right, on either side, though sometimes necessary, are always inconvenient, and men of real property, who must be sensible that their own prosperity is connected with the tranquility of the province, will not long be inactive, suffer their quiet to be disturbed, and the peace and safety of the state endangered by the indiscretion or resentment of any.

I am, with great truth and regard,
  Sir, your most obedient
   humble servant,
    SHELBURNE.

———————

A Letter to the Right Hon. the Earl of Shelburne, occasioned by his Lordship's Letter to his Excellency Governor Bernard, read to the House by the Secretary, by his Excellency's Order.

Province of the Massachusetts-Bay, January 22, 1768.

My

My Lord,

His Excellency Governor Bernard has been pleased to give orders to the secretary of this province to read to the House of Representatives a letter he had received from your Lordship, dated Whitehall the 17th of September, 1767; which having done, the secretary withdrew, without leaving a copy as usual.

The House were both grieved and astonished to find your Lordship under a necessity of expressing such unfavourable sentiments of the two Houses of the general assembly, as well as of some particular members of this House, altogether strangers to you, with regard to the election of counsellors in May last. They observed, that your Lordship's letter had a reference to several of his Excellency's letters, upon which your sentiments seemed to be formed: and as his Excellency had intimated to the Speaker of the House his desire of having a copy of a certain letter which the House had directed to be sent to the Speakers of the several Houses of Assembly in the other colonies, a copy of which it is presumed will be laid before your Lordship; the House appointed a committee to wait on his Excellency, and acquaint him, that they were ready to lay before him the said letter, and their whole proceedings, relating to an important affair then before them, if he should desire it. And the same committee was directed humbly to request his Excellency to favour the House with a copy of your Lordship's letter, together with his own letters to which it referred. Whereupon messages passed between the Governor and House, which the House begs leave to inclose to your Lordship.

As the House think they have just grounds of suspicion, that his Excellency's letters to your Lordship contain, at least, an implication of charge and accusation against them, which they are kept in ignorance of, they rely upon your known candour and justice, that upon this their humble request, you will be pleased to give orders, that copies be laid before the House of Representatives; that they may have the opportunity of vindicating themselves and their constituents, and of happily removing from your mind an opinion of them, grounded, as your Lordship might then reasonably judge, upon good information, as having behaved in a manner unbecoming the character of loyal subjects. They hope you will be so favourable as to suspend your farther judgment of them, till they can be made acquainted with the matters that may have been alledged against them, and can make their defence. In the mean time they beg leave just to mention to your Lordship, that the elections of the last May, so far as this House had a part in them, were made with a freedom and deliberation suitable to the importance of them; that they were influenced by no motives but the prosperity of his Majesty's government, and the happiness of his subjects: that the non-election of several gentlemen of distinguished character and station, was by no means the effect of party prejudice, private resentment, or motives still more blameable; but the result of calm reflection upon the danger that might accrue to our excellent constitution, and the liberties of the people, from too great an opinion of the legislative, executive and judiciary powers of government, which, in the opinion of the greatest writers, ought always to be kept separate: nor was this a new opinion, formed at a certain period; but it has been the prevailing sentiment of many of the most sensible and unexceptionable gentlemen in the province for many years past; upon principles, which your Lordship's thorough

rough knowledge of the conftitution, and the juft balance of the feveral powers of government, this Houfe is affured, will juftify. And although his Excellency was pleafed to exercife his undoubted right of negativing fome of the gentlemen elected, the Houfe have had no reafon to alter their opinion of them, as being unexceptionable in point of ability, fortune, and character. They beg pardon for this further trouble given to your Lordfhip, which they could not avoid; being folicitous to fet their conduct in its true point of light before you: and they rely upon your known juftice, that you will intercede with the throne for this province. They are affured, that your Lordfhip will not fuffer a province to be mifreprefented, even by perfons of ftation here: and if there be any fuch, they flatter themfelves, that their removal will render this people happy in the efteem of the parent country, and much more fo in the fmiles of the beft of Kings.

Signed by the Speaker.

Papers relating to a fuppofed libel on the Governor of the Province of the Maffachufetts-Bay.
The following was publifhed in the Bofton Gazette, of February 29. Meffrs. Edes and Gill.
Pleafe to infert the following.

May it pleafe your ———, We have for a long time known your enmity to this province. We have full proof of your cruelty to a loyal people. No age has perhaps furnifhed a more glaring inftance of obftinate perfeverance in the path of malice, than is now exhibited in your ———. Could you have reaped any advantage from injuring this people, there would have been fome excufe for the manifold abufes with which you have loaded them. But when a diabolical thirft for mifchief is the alone motive of your conduct, you muft not wonder if you are treated with open diflike; for it is impoffible, how much foever we endeavour it, to feel any efteem for a man like you—Bad as the world may be, there is yet in every breaft fomething which points out the good man as an object worthy of refpect, and marks the guileful treacherous man-hater for difguft and infamy——

Nothing has ever been more intolerable than your infolence upon a late occafion, when you had by your judicial infinuations, induced a worthy minifter of ftate, to form a moft unfavourable opinion of the province in general, and fome of the moft refpectable inhabitants in particular; you had the effrontery to produce a letter from his Lordfhip, as proof of your fuccefs in calumniating us.— Surely you muft fuppofe we have loft all feeling, or you would not dare thus tauntingly to difplay the trophies of your flanders, and upbraidingly, to make us fenfible of the inexpreffible misfortunes which you have brought upon us. ——But I refrain, left a full reprefentation of the hardfhips fuffered by this too long infulted people fhould lead them to an unwarrantable revenge. We never can treat good and patriotic rulers with too great reverence——But it is certain that men totally abandoned to wickednefs, can never merit our regard, be their ftations ever fo high.

" *If fuch men are by God appointed,*
" *The Devil may be the Lord's anointed.*"*

A TRUE PATRIOT.

* Thefe two Lines are taken from Rochefter's Satires.

Bofton, March 3,
Tuefday laft his Excellency the Governor was pleafed to fend the following Meffage to the Hon. his Majefty's Council.

Gentlemen of the Council,
I have been ufed to treat the publications in the Bofton Gazette with the

the contempt they deferve, but when they are carried to a length, which, if unnoticed, muft endanger the very being of government, I cannot confiftently with the regard to this province which I profefs and really have, excufe myfelf from taking notice of a publication in the Bofton Gazette of yefterday, beginning at the top of the fecond column of the fecond page of the fupplement. I therefore confult you in council thereupon, and have received your unanimous advice, that I fhould lay the faid libellous paper before the Houfe of Reprefentatives.

In purfuance of which advice, I have ordered the Secretary to communicate to you the faid libellous paper, that you may take the fame, together with all the circumftances attending it, into your ferious confideration, and do therein as the Majefty of the King, and the dignity of his government, the honour of this general court, and the true intereft of this province, fhall require.

Council Chamber,   FRA. BERNARD,
    March 1, 1768.

In anfwer to which, there being the full number of the council prefent, excepting three gentlemen, the board unanimoufly voted the following addrefs to his Excellency.

The board have taken into ferious confideration your Excellency's meffage of the firft inftant, with the Bofton Gazette communicated therewith.

The article in faid Gazette, referred to by your Excellency, gave the board a real concern, not only as it is mifchievous in its tendency, but as it is a falfe, fcandalous, and impudent libel upon your Excellency.

Although the author of it may endeavour to fcreen himfelf by the omiffion of a name, yet as it refers particularly to a tranfaction fo lately had in the general court, there is the higheft prefumption, the intention of it could be no otherwife than to place your Excellency in the moft odious light.

Such an infolent and licentious attack on the chief magiftrate (the King's reprefentative in the province) involves in it an attack on government itfelf; as it is fubverfive of all order and decorum, and manifeftly tends to deftroy the fubordination, that is abfolutely neceffary to good government, and the well-being of fociety. It would have been flagitious at any time, but being perpetrated while the general court is fitting, and a tranfaction in the court the alledged occafion of it, it becomes from thefe and other circumftances, in the higheft degree flagitious; and may juftly be deemed, not only an infult on the general court; not only an infult on the King's authority, and the dignity of his government; but, as it concludes with the moft unwarrantable profanenefs, an infult upon the King of Kings.

The board therefore cannot but look upon the faid libel with the utmoft abhorrence and deteftation: and they are firmly perfuaded the province in general view it in the fame light: the threats therefore implied in the faid libel cannot be the threats of the province, but of the libeller.

The board take this opportunity with one voice to affure your Excellency, that, to the utmoft of their power, they will always defend and fupport the honour and dignity of the King's governor: and will be ever ready to do, in this affair, as in every other, whatever the majefty of the King, the honour of the general court, and the true intereft of this province, fhall require.

His Excellency was pleafed to return the following anfwer.

Gentlemen,

I thank you moft heartily for this addrefs, in which you exprefs fo full
and

and unanimous a fenfe of your duty to the King, and your refolution to fupport his government in this province. For myfelf, I am fo fortified in a confcioufnefs of my own integrity, which has hitherto defied the utmoft malice to impeach it publickly, that I am not to be moved by the impotent attacks of an anonymous libeller. I fhould not have taken notice of the libel in queftion, if I had not apprehended it pregnant with danger to the government. As you are of the fame opinion, I have only to affure you, that I will at all times moft readily join with you in all proper meafures to maintain the authority of the King, and to promote the welfare of the people, within the province, committed by his Majefty to my charge.

Council-Chamber, FRA. BERNARD. March 3, 1768.

His Excellency fent the like meffage to the Houfe of Reprefentatives, as the preceeding to the Council, mutatis mutandis ; to which the Houfe made the following anfwer.

In the Houfe of Reprefentatives, March 3, 1768.

Ordered, That Mr. Hancock, Mr. Otis, Col. Ward, Mr. Spooner, and Capt. Bradford, be a committee to wait on his Excellency the Governor, with the following anfwer to his meffage of the 1ft inftant.

May it pleafe your Excellency,

In duty and great refpect to his Majefty's reprefentative and governor of the province, this houfe have given all due attention to your meffage of the firft inftant. You are pleafed to recommend to their ferious confideration, a publication in the Bofton Gazette of Monday laft as " being carried to a length, which if unnoticed, muft endanger the very being of government." In this view, your Excellency, in the notice you have taken of it, without doubt, acted

" confiftently with the regard to this province, which you profefs."

We are very forry that any publication in the news-paper, or any other caufe, fhould give your Excellency an apprehenfion of danger to the being or dignity of his Majefty's government here. But this houfe, after examination into the nature and importance of the paper referred to, cannot fee reafon to admit of fuch conclufion as your Excellency has formed. No particular perfon public or private is named in it : and as it doth not appear to the houfe, that any thing contained in it can affect " the majefty of the King, the dignity of the government, the honour of the general court, or the true intereft of the province," they think they may be fully juftified in their determination to take no further notice of it.†

The liberty of the prefs is a great bulwark of the liberty of the people : it is therefore the incumbent duty of thofe who are conftituted the guardians of the people's right, to defend and maintain it. This houfe, however, as one branch of the legiflature, in which capacity alone they have any authority, are ready to difcountenance an abufe of this privilege, whenever there fhall be occafion for it : fhould the proper bounds of it be at any time tranfgreffed, to the prejudice of individuals, or the public, it is their opinion at prefent, that provifion is already made for the punifhment of offenders in the common courfe of the law. This provifion, the houfe apprehend, in the prefent ftate of tranquility in the province, is fufficient, without the interpofition of the general affembly; which,

† The divifion upon this queftion was 56 to 18.—It was afterwards given in charge to the Grand Jury to prefent the piece as a libel. They refufed to find the bill. And thus the matter ftood when the laft advices came from Bofton.

D d

which, however it is hoped, will at all times be both ready and willing to support the executive power in the due administration of justice, whenever any extraordinary aid shall become needful.

The division in the House upon this message was 39 to 30.

Boston, (Friday) March 4, 1768.
This day his Excellency the Governor prorogued the great and general court unto Wednesday the 13th of April next, after making the following speech.
Gentlemen of the House of Representatives,

The moderation and good temper, which appeared to regulate your conduct at the opening this session, so flattered me that I promised myself that the like disposition would have continued to the end of it. But I am sorry to find that the lovers of contention, have shewed themselves not so intent upon preventing it, as upon waiting for a fit opportunity to revive it. The extraordinary and indecent observations which have been made upon the Secretary of State's letter, wrote, as I may say in the presence of the King himself, will fully justify this suggestion. The causes of the censure therein contained, have been specifically assigned and set forth in the letter itself. These causes are facts universally known, and no where to be denied; they are considered in the letter as the sole causes of the censure consequent thereto; and there was no occasion to resort to my letters, or any other letters, for other reasons for it. If you think that this censure is singular, you deceive yourselves; and you are not so well informed of what passes at Westminster as you ought to be, if you do not know that it is as general and extensive as the knowledge of the proceeding to which it is applied: and therefore all your

infinuations against me, upon false suppositions of my having misrepresented you, are vain and groundless, when every effect is to be accounted for from plain narrative of facts which must have appeared to the Secretary of State from your own journals. It is not therefore me, gentlemen, that you call to account: it is the noble writer of the letter himself, the King's minister of state, who has taken the liberty to find fault with the conduct of a party in your assembly.

Nor am I less innocent of the making this letter a subject of public resentment. When upon the best advice, I found myself obliged to communicate it to you, I did it in such a manner, that it might not, and would not, if you had been pleased, have transpired out of the general court. Prudent men, moderate men would have considered it as an admonition rather than a censure, and have made use of it as a means of reconciliation, rather than of further distraction: but there are men to whose being (I mean the being of their importance) everlasting contention is necessary. And by these has this letter been dragged into public, and has been the subject of declamatory observations; which together with large extracts of the letter itself, have immediately after been carried to the press of the publishers of an infamous news-paper; notwithstanding the letter had been communicated in a confidence that no copy of it should be permitted to be taken. So little have availed the noble Lord's intentions of pointing out the means of restoring peace and harmony to this government, and my desire to pursue such salutary purpose to the utmost of my power.

Having said thus much to vindicate myself, which every honest man has a right to do, I must add, that I have done nothing on my part to occasion a difa dispute between me and your house; it has been forced upon me by particular persons for their own purposes. I never will have any dispute with the representatives of this good people which I can prevent, and will always treat them with due regard, and render them real service when it is in my power. Time and experience will soon pull the masks off those false patriots, who are sacrificing their country to the gratification of their own passions. In the mean while, I shall with more firmness than ever, if it is possible, pursue that steady conduct, which the service of the King and the preservation of this government so forcibly demand of me. And I shall, above all, endeavour to defend this injured country from the imputations which are cast upon it, and the evils which threaten it, arising from the machinations of a few, very few, discontented men, and by no means to be charged on the generality of the people.

Gentlemen of the Council,

I return you thanks for your steady, uniform and patriotic conduct during this whole session, which has shewn you impressed with a full sense of your duty both to your king and to your country. The unanimous example of men of your respectable characters, cannot fail of having great weight to engage the people in general, to unite in proper means to put an end to the dissention, which has so long harrassed this province in its internal policy, and disgraced it in its reputation abroad. I shall not fail to make a faithful representation to his Majesty of your merit upon this occasion.

Council-Chamber, March 4, 1768.

On the 21st of June, the members of the assembly of Massachusetts-bay received the following message from Governor Bernard.

Gentlemen of the House of Representatives,

I have his Majesty's orders to make a requisition to you, which I communicate in the very words in which I have received it. I must desire you to take it into immediate consideration, and I assure you that your resolution thereon will have most important consequences to the province. I am myself merely ministerial in this business, having received his Majesty's instruction for all I have to do in it. I heartily wish that you may see how forcible the expediency of your giving this testimonial of your duty and submission is at this time. If you should think otherwise, I must nevertheless do my duty.

Council-Chamber, FRA. BERNARD. *June 21, 1768.*

The following was the extract of the letter from the Earl of Hillsborough, referred to in Governor Bernard's message, dated Whitehall, April 22d, 1768.

It gives great concern to his Majesty to find that the same moderation which appeared by your letter to have been adopted at the beginning of the session in a full assembly, had not continued, and that, instead of that spirit of prudence and respect to the constitution, which seemed at that time to influence the conduct of a large majority of the members, a thin house at the end of the session should have presumed to revert to, and resolve upon a measure of so inflammatory a nature as that of writing to the other colonies on the subject of their intended representations against some late acts of parliament.

His Majesty considers this step as evidently tending to create unwarrantable combinations, to excite an unjustifiable opposition to the constitutional authority of Parliament, and to revive those unhappy divisions and distractions which have operated so

D d 2 preju-

prejudicially to the true interefts of Great Britain and the colonies.

After what paffed in the former part of the feffion, and after the declared fenfe of fo large a majority when the houfe was full, his Majefty cannot but confider this as a very unfair proceeding, and the refolutions taken thereupon to be contrary to the real fenfe of the affembly, and procured by furprize : and therefore it is the King's pleafure, that fo foon as the general court is again affembled at the time prefcribed by the charter, you fhould require of the Houfe of Reprefentatives, in his Majefty's name, to refcind the refolution which gave birth to the circular letter from the Speaker, and to declare their difapprobation of, and diffent to, that rafh and hafty proceeding.

His Majefty has the fulleft reliance upon the affection of his good fubjects in the Maffachufetts-Bay, and has obferved, with fatisfaction, that fpirit of decency, and love of order, which has difcovered itfelf in the conduct of the moft confiderable of its inhabitants ; and therefore his Majefty has the better ground to hope, that the attempts made by a defperate faction to difturb the public tranquility, will be difcountenanced, and that the execution of the meafure recommended to you will not meet with any difficulty.

Governor of the Maffachufetts-Bay.

Two days after, the Houfe of Affembly fent this meffage to Governor Bernard.

May it pleafe your Excellency,

The Houfe of Reprefentatives humbly requeft your Excellency to lay before them a copy of his Majefty's inftructions referred to in your meffage of the 21ft inftant ; a copy of the letter to your Excellency from the Right Hon. the Earl of Hillfborough of April 22, 1768 ; a copy of a letter to his lordfhip, communicated lately

to the Honourable Board ; and copies of letters wrote by your Excellency to his lordfhip, relating to the fubject of the aforefaid meffage.

June 23, 1768.
The Governor replied to this meffage next day as follows :
Gentlemen of the Houfe of Reprefentatives.

I fhould have communicated the whole of the Earl of Hillfborough's letter relating to the bufinefs which I laid before you on the 21ft inftant, if I had not been defirous that your compliance with his Majefty's requifition might have its fulleft merit, by its appearing to be entirely dictated by a fenfe of your duty.

But fince you defire to know what my further orders are, I hereby fend you a copy of the other part of the letter relative to this bufinefs, which contains all my inftructions thereupon: and as I know you will not expect that I fhould difobey the King's pofitive commands, I muft defire that if you fhould refolve to oblige me to execute them, you will previoufly to your giving your final anfwer, prevent the inconveniencies which muft fall upon the people for want of the annual tax bill, which I underftand is not as yet fent up to the board; for if I am obliged to diffolve the general court, I fhall not think myfelf at liberty to call another, till I receive his Majefty's commands for that purpofe, which will be too late to prevent the treafurer iffuing his warrants for the whole tax granted by the act of laft year.

As to the letter of the Earl of Hillfborough, which I communicated to the council, I muft beg leave to be the proper judge of the time and occafion of communicating any papers I receive, to the council or the houfe. If I had then thought it expedient to lay it before the houfe, I fhould have then done it; when I fhall think it fo, I fhall do it.　　　　　　As

As to your request of copies of my letters to the Secretary of State, you may assure yourselves that I shall never make public my letters to his Majesty's ministers, but upon my own motion, and for my own reasons.
Council-Chamber, FRA. BERNARD.
June 24, 1768.

Remainder of Lord Hillsborough's letter to the Governor of the Massachusetts-Bay, dated April 22, 1768.
—If it should, and if, notwithstanding the apprehensions which may justly be entertained of the ill consequence of a continuance of this factious spirit, which seems to have influenced the resolutions of the assembly at the conclusion of the last session, the new assembly should refuse to comply with his Majesty's reasonable expectation, it is the King's pleasure that you should immediately dissolve them, and transmit to me, to be laid before his Majesty, an account of their proceedings thereupon, to the end that his Majesty may, if he thinks fit, lay the whole matter before his Parliament, that such provisions as shall be found necessary may be made, to prevent for the future a conduct of so extraordinary and unconstitutional a nature.

As it is not his Majesty's intention that a faithful discharge of your duty should operate to your own prejudice, or to the discontinuance of any necessary establishments, proper care will be taken for the support of the dignity of government.
I am, with great truth and regard,
Sir, your most obedient
humble servant,
HILLSBOROUGH.
On the 28th of June, 1768, the House of Representatives received a message from the Governor in these words :
Gentlemen of the House of Representatives,
It is now a full week since I laid

before you his Majesty's requisition, signified by his Secretary of State : I must therefore desire you to come to a resolution upon it, for I cannot admit of a much longer delay, without considering it as an answer in the negative.
Council-Chamber, FRA. BERNARD.
June 28, 1768.
To this message the House returned the following answer the next day :
May it please your Excellency,
In answer to your Excellency's message of the 28th instant, the House of Representatives request, that your Excellency would favour this general court with a recess, that *they* may consult their constituents respecting the requisition contained in your message of the 21st inst. in consequence of the Earl of Hillsborough's letter to your Excellency.
The Governor immediately sent his reply to this request of the House of Assembly, as follows :
Gentlemen of the House of Representatives,
I cannot consistently with my sense of my duty prorogue or adjourn the general court, until I have received your answer to his Majesty's requisition ; I must therefore repeat my request to you to bring this matter to a conclusion.
Council-Chamber, FRA. BERNARD.
June 29, 1768.
The next day, being Thursday the 30th of June, a committee of the House reported a letter to the Right Honourable the Earl of Hillsborough, which was distinctly read to the members several times, and afterwards accepted by a majority of *ninety-three* out of *one hundred and five.* A fair copy was ordered to be directly taken for the Speaker to sign and transmit to his lordship as soon as possible. This letter was in the following words :

Pro-

Province of the Massachusetts-Bay,
  June 30, 1768.

My Lord,

His Excellency the governor of this province has been pleased to communicate to the House of Representatives extracts of a letter he had received from your lordship, dated Whitehall, 22d of April, 1768; wherein it is declared to be the royal pleasure, that he should require of them, in his Majesty's name, to rescind the resolution, which gave birth to a circular letter from the Speaker of the last House, and to declare their disapprobation of, and dissent to, that rash and hasty proceeding.

The House are humbly of opinion, that a requisition from the throne of this nature, to a British House of Commons has been very unusual: perhaps there has been no such precedent since the revolution. If this be the case, some very aggravated representations of this measure must have been made to his Majesty, to induce him to require of this House to rescind a resolution of a former House, upon pain of forfeiting their existence; for, my Lord, the House of Representatives, duly elected, are constituted by the royal charter, the representative body of his Majesty's faithful commons of this province in the general assembly.—Your Lordship is pleased to say, that his Majesty considers this step " as evidently tending to create unwarrantable combinations, and to excite an unjustifiable opposition to the constitutional authority of Parliament:" the House, therefore, thought it their indispensible duty immediately to revise the letter referred to, and carefully to recollect, as far as they were able, the sentiments which prevailed in that House, to induce them to revert to and resolve on the measure.

It may be necessary to observe, that the people in this province have attended, with a deep concern, to the several acts of the British Parliament, which impose duties and taxes on the colonies; not for the purpose of regulating the trade, but with the sole intention of raising a revenue. This concern, my Lord, so far from being limited within the circle of a few inconsiderate persons, is become universal: the most respectable for fortune, rank, and station, as well as probity and understanding, in the province, with very few exceptions, are alarmed with apprehensions of the fatal consequences of a power exercised in any one part of the British Empire, to command and apply the property of their fellow-subjects at discretion. This consideration prevailed on the last House of Representatives to resolve on an humble, dutiful, and loyal petition to the King, the common head and father of all his people, for his gracious interposition in favour of his subjects of this province.—If your Lordship, whom his Majesty has honoured with the American department, has been instrumental in presenting a petition so interesting to the well-being of his loyal subjects here, this House beg leave to make their most grateful acknowledgements, and to implore your continued aid and patronage.

As all his Majesty's North American subjects are alike affected by these Parliamentary revenue acts, the former House very justly supposed, that each of the assemblies on the continent would take such methods of obtaining redress as should be thought by them respectively to be regular and proper; and being desirous that the several applications should harmonize with each other, they resolved on their circular letter, wherein their only view seems to be to advertise their sister colonies of the measures they had taken upon a common and important concern, without once calling

       ling

ling upon them to adopt thofe meafures, or any other.

Your Lordfhip, furely, will not think it a crime in that Houfe, to have taken a ftep which was perfectly confiftent with the conftitution, and had a natural tendency to compofe the minds of his Majefty's fubjects of this and his other colonies, until in his royal clemency he fhould afford them relief—at a time when it feemed to be the evident defign of a party to prevent calm, deliberate, rational, and conftitutional meafures from being purfued, or to ftop the diftreffes of the people from reaching his Majefty's ear, and confequently to precipitate them into a ftate of defperation and melancholy extremity.—Thus, my Lord, it appears to this Houfe; and your Lordfhip will impartially judge, whether a reprefentation of it to his Majefty as a meafure " of an inflammatory nature "—as a ftep evidently tending " to create unwarrantable combinations," and " to excite an unjuftifiable opinion to the conftitutional authority of the Parliament," be not injurious to the reprefentatives of this people, and an affront to his Majefty himfelf.

An attempt, my Lord, to imprefs the royal mind with a jealoufy of his faithful fubjects, for which there are no juft grounds, is a crime of the moft malignant nature, as it tends to difturb and deftroy that mutual confidence between the Prince and the fubjects, which is the only true bafis of public happinefs and fecurity: your Lordfhip, upon enquiry, may find that fuch bafe and wicked attempts have been made.

It is an inexpreffible grief to the people of this province, to find repeated cenfurers calling upon them, not from minifters of ftate alone, but from Majefty itfelf, grounded on letters and accufations from the governor, a fight of which tho' repeatedly requefted of his Excellency, is refufed. —There is no evil of this life which they fo fenfibly feel as the difpleafure of their fovereign; it is a punifhment which they are affured his Majefty would never inflict, but upon a reprefentation of the juftice of it from his fervants whom he confides in.—Your Lordfhip will allow the Houfe to appeal to your own candor upon the hardfhip of their being made to fuffer fo fevere a misfortune, without ever being called to anfwer for themfelves, or even made acquainted with the matters of charge alledged againft them; a right which, by the common rules of fociety, founded in the eternal laws of reafon and equity, they are juftly entitled to. The Houfe is not willing to trefpafs upon your patience; they could recite numbers of inftances fince Governor Bernard has been honoured by his Majefty to prefide over this province, of their fuffering the King's difpleafure through the inftrumentality of the Governor, intimated by the Secretary of State, without the leaft previous notice that they had ever deviated from the path of their duty. This they humbly conceive, is juft matter of complaint, and it may ferve to convince your Lordfhip, that his Excellency has not that tender feeling for his Majefty's fubjects which is characteriftic of a good Governor, and of which the fovereign affords an illuftrious example.

It is the good fortune of the Houfe to be able to fhew that the meafures of the laft Houfe, referred to in your Lordfhip's letter to the governor, have been grofly mifreprefented in all its circumftances; and it is matter of aftonifhment, that a tranfaction of the Houfe, the bufinefs of which is conftantly done in the open view of the world, could be thus coloured; a tranfaction which, by fpecial order of the Houfe, was laid before his Excellency,

lency, whose duty to his Majesty is, at least, not to misinform him.

His Excellency could not but acknowledge, in justice to that House, that moderation took place in the beginning of the session. This is a truth, my Lord. It was a principle with the House to conduct the affairs of government in their department so as to avoid the least occasion of offence. As an instance of their pacific disposition, they granted a further establishment for one of his Majesty's garrisons in the province, rather to gratify his Excellency, who had requested it, than from a full conviction of its necessity. But your Lordship is informed, that this moderation "did not continue," and that "instead of a spirit of prudence and respect of the constitution, which seemed at that time to influence the conduct of a large majority of the members, a thin House, at the end of the session, presumed to revert to, and resolve on a measure of an inflammatory nature," —"contrary to the real sense of the House,"—and "procured by surprize."—My Lord, the journal and minutes of the House will prove the contrary of all this: and to convince your Lordship, the House beg leave to lay before you the several resolutions relating to these matters as they stand recorded.

The House having finished their petition to the King, and their letters to divers of his Majesty's ministers; a motion was regularly made, on the 21st of January, which was the middle of the session, and a resolution was then taken, to appoint a time to consider the expediency of writing to the assemblies of the other colonies on this continent, with respect to the importance of their joining with them in petitioning his Majesty at this time. Accordingly, on the day assigned, there being eighty-two members present, a number always allowed to be sufficient to make a full House, the question was debated; in consequence of which a motion took place, that letters be wrote to the several assemblies of the provinces and colonies on the continent, acquainting them that the House had taken into consideration the difficulties to which they are, and must be reduced, by the operation of the late acts of Parliament, for levying duties and taxes on the colonies; and have resolved on an humble, dutiful, and loyal petition to his Majesty for redress, and also upon proper representations to his Majesty's ministers on the subject. And to desire that they would severally take such constitutional measures thereupon, as they should judge most proper. And the question upon the motion passed in the negative — On Thursday the 4th of February, it was moved in the House, that the foregoing question be reconsidered, so far as to leave it at large; and, conformable to a standing rule of the House, that no vote or order shall be reconsidered at any time, unless the House be as full as when such vote or order was passed; the number in the House was called for, and it appearing that eighty-two members were present*, the question was put, and passed in the affirmative by a large majority: and by an immediately subsequent resolve, the first vote was ordered to be erased.—The same day the resolution which gave birth to the circular letter took place; a question being regularly moved and fairly debated, whether the House would appoint a committee to prepare a letter to be sent to each of the Houses of

* The same number as before: it is to be observed that the House at that time consisted of about 110 members: by the royal charter 40 makes a quorum; hence it appears that 82 members are more than double the number sufficient legally to transact business, and were then three quarters of the whole House.

Representatives

Representatives and Burgesses on the continent, to inform them of the measures which this House has taken with regard to the difficulties arising from the acts of Parliament for levying duties and taxes on the American colonies, and report to the House, which passed in the affirmative; and a committee was appointed accordingly: This committee, after deliberating a week, reported the letter, which was read in the House and accepted almost unanimously; and fair copies of the same were ordered to be taken for the Speaker to sign and forward as soon as might be: and this day there were eighty-three members in the House.

The day following an order passed, that a fair copy of this letter be transmitted to Dennis De Berdt, Esq; in London. The design of which was, that he might be able to produce it, as necessity might require, to prevent any misrepresentation of its true spirit and design.

On Saturday the 13th of February, in order that no possible occasion might be taken by the governor, to think that the debates and resolutions were designed to be kept a secret from his Excellency, the House came into the following resolution, viz.—Whereas this House hath directed, that a letter be sent to the several Houses of Representatives and Burgesses of the British colonies on the continent, setting forth the sentiments of the House, with regard to the great difficulties that must accrue by the operation of divers acts of Parliament, for levying duties and taxes on the colonies, with the sole and express purpose of raising a revenue; and their proceedings thereon, in an humble, dutiful, and loyal petition to the King, and such representations to his Majesty's ministers, as they apprehend may have a tendency to obtain redress: and whereas it is the opinion of this House, that all effectual methods

should be taken, to cultivate an harmony between the several branches of this government, as being necessary to promote the prosperity of his Majesty's government in this province: Resolved, that a committee wait on his Excellency the governor, and acquaint him a copy of the letter aforesaid will be laid before him as soon as it can be drafted, as well as of all the proceedings of this House relative to the said affair, if he shall desire it. And a committee was appointed, who waited on his Excellency accordingly. —On Monday following, the House resolved on the establishment already mentioned, which is observed, only to shew your Lordship, that there was at this time, no disposition in the House, " to revive unhappy divisions and distractions, so prejudicial to the true interest of Great-Britain and the colonies."

The House beg leave to apologize to your Lordship for the trouble given you in so particular a narration of facts; which they thought necessary to satisfy your Lordship;—that the resolution of the last House referred to by your Lordship, was not an unfair proceeding, procured by surprize in a thin House, as his Majesty has been informed; but the declared sense of a large majority, when the House was full: that the governor of the province was made fully acquainted with the measure; and never signified his disapprobation of it to the House, which it is presumed he would have done, in duty to his Majesty, if he had thought it was of evil tendency: and, that therefore, that House had abundant reason to be confirmed in their own opinion of the measure, as being the production of moderation and prudence. And the House humbly rely on the royal clemency, that to petition his Majesty, will not be deemed by him to be inconsistent with a respect to the British constitution as settled at the revolution by

E e   William

William the Third: that to acquaint their fellow-subjects, involved in the same distress, of their having so done, in full hopes of success, even if they had invited the union of all America in one joint supplication, would not be discountenanced by our gracious sovereign, as a measure of an inflammatory nature: that when your Lordship shall in justice lay a true state of these matters before his Majesty, he will no longer consider them as tending to create unwarrantable combinations, or excite an unjustifiable opposition to the constitutional authority of the Parliament: that he will then clearly discern, who are of that desperate faction, which is continually disturbing the public tranquility; and, that while his arm is extended, for the protection of his distressed and injured subjects, he will frown upon all those, who, to gratify their own passions, have dared even to attempt to deceive him!

The House of Representatives of this province, have more than once, during the administration of Governor Bernard, been under the necessity of intreating his Majesty's ministers to suspend their further judgment, upon such representations of the temper of the people, and the conduct of the assembly, as they were able to make appear to be injurious: the same indulgence this House now beg of your Lordship: and beseech your Lordship to patronize them so far as to make a favourable representation of their conduct to the King our sovereign: it being the highest ambition of this House, and the people whom they represent, to stand before his Majesty in their just character of affectionate and loyal subjects.

Signed by the Speaker.

Then it was moved that the question be put, whether the House will rescind the resolution of the last House, which gave birth to their circular letter to the several Houses of Representatives and Burgesses of the other colonies on the continent? and passed in the negative by a division of *ninety-two* to *seventeen.*

Hereupon the committee reported an answer to the Governor's messages of the 21st and 24th of June, which was accepted by a large majority, and is as follows.

A Message from the Assembly to the Governor, June 30, 1768.

May it please your Excellency,

The House of Representatives of this his Majesty's ancient and loyal province of the Massachusetts Bay, have, with the greatest deliberation, considered your messages of the 21st and 24th instant, with the several extracts from the letter of the Right Honourable the Earl of Hillsborough, his Majesty's principal Secretary of State for North American affairs, dated the 22d of April last, which your Excellency has thought fit to communicate. We have also received the written answer which your Excellency was pleased to give the committee of this House, directed to wait on you the 29th instant with a message humbly requesting a recess, that the members might be favoured with an opportunity to consult their constituents at this important crisis, when a direct and peremptory requisition is made of a new and strange construction, and so strenuously urged, viz. That we should immediately rescind the resolution of the last House to transmit circular letters to the other British colonies on the continent of North America, barely intimating a desire that they would join in similar dutiful and loyal petitions to our most gracious sovereign, for the redress of the grievances, occasioned by sundry late acts of Parliament calculated for the sole purpose of raising a revenue in America. We have most diligently revised not only the said resolution, but also the circular letter written and sent in consequence thereof,

thereof, and after all; they both appear to us, to be conceived in terms not only prudent and moderate in themselves, but respectful to the authority of that truly august body the Parliament of Great-Britain, and very dutiful and loyal in regard to his Majesty's sacred person, crown, and dignity; of all which we entertain sentiments of the highest reverence and most ardent affection; and should we ever depart from these sentiments, we must stand self-condemned, as unworthy the name of British subjects descended from British ancestors, intimately allied and connected in interests and inclination with our fellow subjects the Commons of Great-Britain. We cannot but express our deep concern, that a measure of the late House, in all respects so innocent, in most so virtuous and laudable, and as we conceive so truly patriotic, should have been represented to administration in the odious light of a party and factious measure, and that pushed through by reverting in a thin House to, and re-considering, what in a full assembly had been rejected. It was and is a matter of notoriety, that more than eighty members were present at the reconsideration of that vote against application to the other colonies. The vote of re-consideration was obtained by a large majority; it is, or ought to be well known, that the presence of eighty members makes a full House, this number being just double to that by the royal charter of the province required to constitute the third branch of our colony legislature.

Your Excellency might have been very easily informed, if you was not, that the measures of the late House in regard to sundry acts of the late Parliament for the sole purpose of raising a North American revenue, were generally carried by *three* to *one*; and we dare appeal to your Excellency for the truth of this assertion, namely, that there were many persons in the majority, in all views, as respectable as the very best of the minority. Nay, so far from any sinister views, were the committee of the late House, appointed and directed to take into their most serious consideration the then present state of the province, from going into any rash or precipitate measures, that they for some days actually delayed their first report, which was a letter to Mr. agent De Berdt, on this candid and generous principle, that those who were reasonably presupposed to be most warmly attached to all your Excellency's measures, especially those for furthering, and by all means enforcing the acts for levying a North American revenue, might be present, and a more equal contest ensue. It would be incredible should any one assert, that your Excellency wanted a true information of all these things, which were not done, or desired to be hid in a corner, but were notoriously transacted in the open light at noon-day. It is to us altogether incomprehensible that we should be required, on the peril of a dissolution of the great and general court or assembly of this province, to rescind a resolution of a former House of Representatives, when it is evident that resolution has no existence but as a mere historical fact.

Your Excellency must know that the resolution referred to, is, to speak in the language of the common law, not now, " executory," but to all intents and purposes, " executed." The circular letters have been sent, and many of them have been answered: these answers are now in the public papers; the public, the world, must and will judge of the proposals, purposes, and the answers. We could as well rescind those letters as the resolves, and both would be equally fruitless; if by *rescinding*, as the word properly imports, is meant a repeal and nullifying of the resolution referred to: but, if, as is

most

moft probable, by the word *refcinding* is intended the paffing a vote of this Houfe in direct and exprefs difapprobation of the meafures abovementioned as " illegal, inflammatory, and tending to promote unjuftifiable combinations" againft his Majefty's peace, crown, and dignity, we muft take the liberty to teftify, and publickly to declare, that we take it to be the native, inherent, and indefeafible right of the fubject, jointly or feverally to petition the King for the redrefs of grievances: provided always, that the fame be done in a decent, dutiful, loyal, and conftitutional way, without tumult, diforder, or confufion. We are alfo humbly, but clearly and very firmly of opinion, that the petition of the late dutiful and loyal Houfe to his Majefty, and their other very orderly applications for the redrefs of grievances, have had the moft defirable tendencies and effects to keep mens minds in eafe and quiet. We muft be excufed in thinking that the people were in truth patiently waiting for the meeting of the new Parliament, their meafures, and his Majefty's pleafure: and it is probable that they would every where have thus waited for the great event, had it not been revealed here that the late provincial applications for redrefs of grievances were fome-how ftrangely obftructed, and the province, in confequence of mifinformation and mifreprefentation, moft unfortunately fallen under the royal difpleafure: and to compleat this misfortune, it was not only difguifed to the other colonies, but fome of them actually received the information before it was made known here, that the houfe had been accufed to his Majefty, or his miniftry, or fallen under the difpleafure of the one, or the cenfure of the other.

On the whole, Sir, we will confider his moft facred Majefty, under God, as our King, and beft protected and common Father: and fhall ever bear him true and faithful allegiance. We alfo regard your Excellency as the reprefentative of the greateft potentate on earth, and at all times have, fo far as could confift with the important purpofes of preferving life, liberty, and property, been moft ready and willing to treat you with all that refpect juftly due to your high rank and ftation. But we are conftrained to fay, that we are difagreeably convinced that your Excellency entertains not that parental regard for the welfare of the good people of this province, which you have fome times been pleafed to profefs, and which they have at all times an irrefragable right to expect from their governor. Your Excellency has thought fit not only to deny us a recefs to confult our conftituents, in regard to the prefent requifition, but has affured us, in effect, that you fhall take filence, at leaft a delay, not as ufual for a confent, but for a denial. You have alfo thought fit to inform us that you cannot think yourfelf at liberty, in cafe of the diffolution of this, to call another affembly, without the exprefs orders of his Majefty for that purpofe: at the fame time your Excellency has been pleafed to affure us that you have communicated the whole of Lord Hillfborough's letter, and your inftructions, fo far as relates to the requifition.—In all this, however, we cannot find that your Excellency is more than directed to diffolve the prefent affembly, in cafe of a non-compliance on the part of the Houfe. If the votes of the Houfe are to be controuled by the direction of a Minifter, we have left us but a vain femblance of liberty. We know it to be the juft prerogative of the Crown, at pleafure, to diffolve a Parliament: we are alfo fenfible, that confiftently with the

the great charter of this province, your Excellency when you shall think fit, with or without the intervention of the minister, can dissolve the great and general court of this colony, and that without the least obligation to convene another within the year. But should it ever grow in use for any ill-disposed governor of the province, by means of a mistaken or willfully wrong state of facts, to procure orders for a dissolution, that same charter will be of no value.

We take this opportunity faithfully and firmly to represent to your Excellency, that the new revenue acts and measures are not only disagreeable to, but in every view are deemed an insupportable burthen and grievance, with a very few exceptions, by all the freeholders and other inhabitants of this jurisdiction; and we beg leave, once for all, to assure your Excellency, that those of this opinion are of no "party or expiring faction." They have at all times been ready to devote their lives and fortunes to his Majesty's service. Of loyalty this majority could as reasonably boast as any who may happen to enjoy your Excellency's smiles: their reputation, rank, and fortune, are at least equal to those who may have been sometimes considered as the only friends to good government, while some of the best blood of the colony, even in two Houses of Assembly lawfully convened, and duly acting, have been openly charged with the unpardonable crime of oppugnation against the royal authority. We have now only to inform your Excellency, that this House have voted not to rescind, as required, the resolution of the last House, and that, on a division on the question, there were 92 *Nays* and 17 *Yeas*. In all this we have been actuated by a conscientious, and finally, a clear and determined sense of duty to God, to our King, our coun-try, and to our latest posterity: and we most ardently wish, and humbly pray, that in your future conduct your Excellency may be influenced by the same principles.

His Excellency after having received the last foregoing message from the House, directed their attendance in the Council-Chamber; when, after giving his assent to several bills, he was pleased to prorogue the great and general court, to Wednesday the third day of August next; but the next day the assembly was *dissolved* by proclamation.

The following letters from several Houses of Representatives of the other Colonies, were received by the House of Representatives of the Province of Massachusetts-Bay, in answer to their circular letter of the 11th of February last.

To the Honourable the Speaker of the Honourable House of Representatives of the Province of the Massachusetts-Bay.

Virginia, May 9, 1768.

SIR,

The House of Burgesses of this colony proceeded very soon after they met to the consideration of your important letter of the 11th of February, 1768, written in the name and by the order of the House of Representatives of your province; and I have received their particular direction to desire you to inform that honourable House, that they applaud them for their attention to American liberty, and that the steps they have taken thereon, will convince them of their opinion of the fatal tendency of the acts of parliament complained of, and of their fixed resolution to concur with the other colonies in their application for redress.

After the most deliberate consultation, they thought it their duty to represent to the Parliament of Great-Britain, that they are truly sensible

of

of the happiness and security they derive from their connexions with, and dependance on Great Britain, and are under the greatest concern that any unlucky incident should interrupt that salutary harmony, which they wish ever to subsist. They lament that the remoteness of their situation often exposes them to such misrepresentations, as are apt to involve them in censures of disloyalty to their sovereign, and the want of a proper respect to the British Parliament, whereas they have indulged themselves in the agreeable persuasion, that they ought to be considered as inferior to none of their fellow-subjects in loyalty and affection.

That they do not affect an independency of their parent kingdom, the prosperity of which they are bound to the utmost of their abilities to promote, but cheerfully acquiesce in the authority of parliament to make laws for preserving a necessary dependance and for regulating the trade of the colonies. Yet they cannot conceive, and humbly insist, it is not essential to support a proper relation between a mother-country and colonies transplanted from her, that she should have a right to raise money from them without their consent, and presume they do not aspire to more than the natural rights of British subjects, when they assert that no power on earth has a right to impose taxes on the people, or take the smallest portion of their property, without their consent, given by their representatives in parliament. This has ever been considered as the chief pillar of the constitution; without this support no man can be said to have the least shadow of liberty, since they can have no property in that, which another can by right take from them when he pleases, without their consent.

That their ancestors brought over with them intire, and transmitted to their descendants, the natural and constitutional rights they had enjoyed in their native country; and the first principles of the British constitution were early engrafted into the constitution of the colonies. Hence a legislative authority, ever essential in all free states, was derived, and assimilated as nearly as might be to that in England; the executive power and the right of assenting or dissenting to all laws reserved to the crown, and the privilege of choosing their own representatives continued to the people, and confirmed to them by repeated and express stipulations. The government thus established, they enjoyed the fruits of their own labour with a serenity which liberty only can impart. Upon pressing occasions they applied to his Majesty for relief, and gratefully acknowledge they have frequently received it from their mother-country; whenever their assistance was necessary, requisitions have constantly been made from the crown to the representatives of the people, who have complied with them to the utmost extent of their abilities. The ample provision made for the support of civil government, in the reign of King Charles the second, and at his request, and the large supplies voted during the last war upon requisitions from his Majesty and his royal grandfather, afford early and late instances of the dispositions of the assemblies of this colony, and are sufficient proofs that the parliament of Great Britain did not till lately, assume a power of imposing taxes on the people, for the purpose of raising a revenue.

To say that the Commons of Great Britain have a right to impose internal taxes on the inhabitants of this continent, who are not and cannot
be

be reprefented, is in effect to bid them prepare for a ftate of flavery. What muft be their fituation, fhould fuch a right be eftablifhed? The colonies have no conftitutional check on their liberality in giving away their money, cannot have an opportunity of explaining their grievances, or of pointing out the eafieft method of taxation, for their doom will generally be determined before they are acquainted that the fubject has been agitated in parliament, and the commons bear no proportion of the taxes they lay upon them. The notion of a virtual reprefentation, which would render all our rights merely ideal, has been fo often and fo clearly refuted, that nothing need be faid on that head.

The oppreffive ftamp-act confeffedly impofed internal taxes, and the late acts of Parliament, giving and granting certain duties in the Britifh colonies, plainly tend to the fame point. Duties have been impofed to reftrain the commerce of one part of the empire that was likely to prove injurious to another, and by this means the welfare of the whole promoted; but duties impofed on fuch of the Britifh exports as are neceffaries of life, to be paid by the colonifts on importation, without any view to the interefts of commerce, but merely to raife a revenue, or in other words to compel the colonifts to part with their money againft their inclinations, they conceive to be tax internal to all intents and purpofes. And can it be thought juft or reafonable, reftricted as they are in their trade, confined as they are in their exports, obliged to purchafe thefe very neceffaries at the Britifh Market, that they fhould now be told they fhall not have them without paying a duty for them?

The act fufpending the legiflative power of New-York, they confider as ftill more alarming to the colonies, though it has that fingle province in view. If the Parliament can compel them to furnifh a fingle article to the troops fent over, they may, by the fame rule, oblige them to furnifh cloaths, arms, and every other neceffary, even the pay of the officers and foldiers—a doctrine replete with every mifchief, and utterly fubverfive of all that's dear and valuable:—for what advantage can the people of the colonies derive from their right of choofing their own reprefentatives, if thofe reprefentatives when chofen, not permitted to exercife their own judgments, were under a neceffity (on pain of being deprived of their legiflative authority) of inforcing the mandates of a Britifh Parliament.

This, Sir, is a fketch of their fentiments, as they are expreffed in a petition to his Majefty, a Memorial to the Right Honourable the Lords Spiritual and Temporal, and in a Remonftrance to the Knights, Citizens and Burgeffes of Great Britain in Parliament affembled. In all their proceedings the council of this colony have concurred, and have directed their agent, James Abercromby, Efq; to join Edward Montague, Efq; the agent for this colony, in applying for redrefs of the grievances they fo juftly complain of. Copies were delivered to the Prefident of the Council, now Commander in Chief, who is defired to tranfmit them to the Secretary of State appointed by his Majefty to manage the affairs of North America, and Mr. Montague is enjoined to confult the agents of the other colonies, and to co-operate with them in every meafure that fhall be thought neceffary to be taken on this critical point.

They truft they have expreffed themfelves with a firmnefs that becomes freemen pleading for effential rights, and with a decency that will take off every imputation of faction

or

or disloyalty. They repose entire confidence in his Majesty, who is ever attentive to the complaints of his subjects, and is ever ready to relieve their distress; and they are not without hopes that the colonies united in a decent and regular opposition, may prevail on a new House of Commons to put a stop to measures so directly repugnant to the interests both of the mother country, and her colonies. In the name and by order of the House of Burgesses, I am, with the greatest respect, your most obedient humble servant,

PEYTON RANDOLPH, Speaker.

Colony of New Jersey, May 9, 1768.
S I R,

As soon as the House of Representatives of this colony met, which was on the 12th of April, I laid your letter of the 11th of February before them.

Sensible that the law you complain of, is a subject in which every colony is interested, the House of Representatives readily perceived the necessity of an immediate application to the King, and that it should correspond with those of the other colonies; but as they have not had an opportunity of knowing the sentiments of any other colonies but that of the Massachusetts-Bay, they have endeavoured to conform themselves to the mode adopted by you.

They have therefore given instructions to their agent, and enjoined his attention to the subject of their petition.

The freedom with which the House of Representatives of the Massachusetts-Bay have communicated their sentiments upon a matter of so great concern to all the colonies, hath been received by this House, with that candor, the spirit and design of your letter merits.—And at the same time, that they acknowledge themselves ob-

liged to you for communicating your sentiments to them, they have directed me to assure you, that they are desirous to keep up a correspondence with you, and to unite with the colonies, if necessary, in further supplications to his Majesty to relieve his distressed American subjects. In the name and by order of the House of Representatives, I am, Sir, your most obedient humble servant,

CORTLAND SKINNER, Speaker.

Colony of Connecticut, 11th June, 1768.
S I R,

By order of the House of Representatives of this colony, I am to acknowledge the receipt of your letter of the 11th February last, communicating the sense which the representative body of your province have of the great difficulties to which they and their constituents must be subjected by the operation of the several acts of the British Parliament by you referred to, and the measures they have gone into for obtaining redress of those grievances.

Your letter was laid before this House of Representatives early in the session which is now just closed. They consider the said acts of parliament in their nature, tendency, and operation as matters of serious concern, and of very interesting importance, to this and all the English American colonies, and are of opinion that no constitutional measures proper for obtaining relief ought to be neglected by any, and that it is of importance their measures for that end should harmonize with each other, as their success may in a great degree depend on their union in sentiment and practice, on this critical and interesting occasion.

The House therefore very kindly accepted your letter, and are persuaded from the importance of the cause, the laudable zeal, and the gene-

rous

rous exertions of the province of the Maſſachuſetts-Bay, from time to time, in favour of her conſtitutional freedom, that it proceeded only from a hearty concern for the juſt rights, the common intereſt and welfare of theſe colonies.

This Houſe are deſirous ever to cultivate the ſtricteſt friendſhip and harmony with the neighbouring colonies, and with none more than your's, and will be always ready to receive, with the utmoſt candor, their opinion in any matters of general concern, and equally willing on all proper occaſions to communicate their own ſentiment on any ſubjects of our common welfare, in full confidence they would meet with the ſame friendly and candid acceptance.

This Houſe have alſo taken into their ſerious conſideration the operation of the ſaid acts of parliament, and are deeply ſenſible that this, in common with her ſiſter colonies, muſt thereby be involved in great difficulties, which are perhaps a prelude to ſtill greater, and have purſued meaſures for obtaining redreſs, ſimilar to thoſe adopted by the Houſe of Repreſentatives of your province.

We cannot but entertain with you, the ſtrongeſt confidence in the King's royal clemency, juſtice, and goodneſs, that the united, dutiful ſupplications of his faithful, diſtreſſed ſubjects in America, will meet with a kind and gracious acceptance.

In the name and by order of the Houſe of Repreſentatives, I am, Sir, with great eſteem and reſpect, your moſt obedient humble ſervant,

ZEBULON WEST, Speaker.

To the Honourable the Speaker of the Houſe of Repreſentatives in the Province of the Maſſachuſetts-Bay.

Province of Georgia, 15th June, 1768.

S I R,

Your reſpected favour of the 11th February came to my hand only a few days ſince. I am ſorry it is not in my power to give you ſo full and ſatisfactory an anſwer thereto, as the importance of the ſubject requires: the members of the preſent aſſembly of this province have but lately been elected, and though the writs were returnable, and the Houſe required to meet the firſt of this month, yet our Governor thought proper, prior thereto, to prorogue the aſſembly until November; for this reaſon, Sir, I can only for the preſent, reply to your favour as a private perſon, or late Speaker, and inform you, that before the diſſolution of the laſt aſſembly, the Houſe took under conſideration the ſeveral late acts of parliament for impoſing taxes and duties on the American colonies, and being ſenſibly affected thereby, ordered the committee of correſpondence to inſtruct our provincial agent, (Mr. Benjamin Franklin) to join earneſtly with the other colonies agents in ſolliciting a repeal of thoſe acts, and in remonſtrating againſt any acts of the like nature for the future : this inſtruction hath been tranſmitted to Mr. Franklin, and I have no doubt but he will punctually obſerve it. When the aſſembly meet I will lay your favour before the Houſe; and I am aſſured ſuch meaſures will be purſued in conſequence thereof as will manifeſt their regard for conſtitutional liberty, and their reſpect for the Houſe of Repreſentatives of the province of Maſſachuſetts-Bay, whoſe wiſe and ſpirited conduct is ſo juſtly admired.

I am Sir, with the utmoſt reſpect, Your moſt obedient ſervant,

ALEXANDER WYLLY.

The Speaker of the Houſe of Repreſentatives of Maſſachuſetts-Bay alſo received the following letter from the Speaker of the Houſe of Repreſentatives of the Province of Maryland, relating to the circular letter.

F f

Pro-

Province of Maryland, June 24th,
1768.

SIR,

I had the honour to receive your favour of the 11th of February laft, and on a meeting of our affembly I communicated it to our Houfe, and I am defired to affure you they acknowledge themfelves obliged by a candid and free communication of fentiments of a fifter colony on a point fo interefting to the whole; and that their opinion of the confequences to the colonies of the operation of the feveral acts of parliament you allude to, coincide exactly with yours, and that they are perfuaded of the neceffity of harmonizing as much as poffible in proper meafures for redrefs.

This Houfe, upon confidering the acts of parliament, prepared an humble, dutiful, and loyal petition to his Majefty, fetting forth, That it is a fixed and unalterable principle in the nature of things, and a part of the very idea of property, that whatever a man hath honeftly acquired cannot be taken from him without his confent; that this immutable principle is ingrafted as a fundamental into the Englifh conftitution, and is declared by Magna Charta, and the petition and bill of rights, and from thence every Britifh fubject, the moft diftant, is juftly intitled to all the rights of Englifhmen; that this right is further declared and confirmed by our charter; under the confidence whereof our forefathers encountered ever difficulty, to fettle this colony, which under providence has increafed his Majefty's fubjects, extended the trade, and added to the wealth of the mother country: that we have always been permitted to enjoy this right until lately; that we are not, nor can we ever be effectually reprefented in the Britifh parliament; and that thefe ftatutes do, in our apprehenfion, in-

fringe the great fundamental principle, that no man can be taxed but with his own confent given by himfelf or his Reprefentative. This, Sir, is the fubftance of our petition, and I am ordered to tranfmit it to Charles Garth, Efq; fpecial agent for our Houfe of Delegates, to be prefented, and we fhall requeft him to co-operate with yours and the other colony agents in endeavouring to procure us relief, and hope with you his Majefty's great goodnefs of heart will incline him to receive the dutiful fupplications of his remote fubjects with favour and attention.

Juft before the clofe of our feffion we received a meffage from our Governor, a copy of which you have herewith; and alfo a copy of the addrefs by our Houfe in anfwer thereto, which fully convey to you their fentiments on the fubject.

I am, in the name and by order of the Houfe of Reprefentatives, Sir, with very great refpect, your moft humble and obedient fervant,

ROBERT LLOYD, Speaker.

To the Honourable Thomas Cufhing, Efq; Speaker of the Honourable Houfe of Reprefentatives of Maffachufetts-Bay.

Copy of the meffage from Governor Sharpe to the Houfe of Reprefentatives of the Province of Maryland.

Gentlemen of the Lower Houfe of Affembly.

The King our moft gracious fovereign having been informed that a circular letter, a copy of which hath been communicated to his minifters, was in February laft fent by the Speaker of the Houfe of Reprefentatives of the colony of Maffachufetts to the Speakers of other Houfes of Affembly in North America, hath been pleafed to order it to be fignified to me, that he confiders fuch meafure to be of a moft dangerous and

and factious tendency, calculated to inflame the minds of his good subjects in the colonies, to promote an unwarrantable combination, to excite and encourage an open opposition to and denial of the authority of Parliament, and to subvert the true principles of the constitution; but while I notify to you his Majesty's sentiments with respect to this matter, I am also to tell you that the repeated proofs which have been given by the assembly of this province of their reverence and respect for the laws, and of their faithful attachment to the constitution, leave little room for his Majesty to doubt of their shewing a proper resentment of such unjustifiable attempt to revive those distractions which have operated so fatally to the prejudice of both the colonies and the mother-country, and I flatter myself that in case such a letter has been addressed to the Speaker of your House, you will confirm the favourable opinion his Majesty at present entertains of his Maryland subjects, by taking no notice of such letter, which will be treating it with the contempt it deserves.

HORATIO SHARPE.

20th *June*, 1768.

Copy of the Address of the House of Delegates to Governor Sharpe, occasioned by the above Message.

To his Excellency Horatio Sharpe, Esq; Governor and Commander in Chief in and over the Province of Maryland.

May it please your Excellency,

In answer to your Excellency's message of the 29th we must observe, that if the letter from the Speaker of the House of Representatives of the colony of Massachusetts-Bay, addressed to and communicated by our Speaker to this House, be the same with the letter, a copy of which you are pleased to intimate, hath been communicated to the King's ministers, it is very alarming to find that at a time when the people of America think themselves aggrieved by the late acts of Parliament imposing taxes on them for the sole and express purpose of raising a revenue, and in the most dutiful manner are seeking redress from the Throne, any endeavours to unite in laying before their sovereign what is apprehended to be their just complaint, should be looked upon ' as a measure of most dangerous and ' factious tendency, calculated to in- ' flame the minds of his Majesty's ' good subjects, in the colonies, to ' promote an unwarrantable combina- ' tion, to excite and encourage an ' open opposition to, and denial of ' the authority of Parliament, and ' to subvert the true principles of ' the constitution.' We cannot but view this as an attempt in some of his Majesty's ministers to suppress all communication of sentiments between the colonies, and to prevent the united supplications of America from reaching the royal ear. We hope the conduct of this House will ever evince their reverence and respect for the laws and faithful attachment to the constitution; but we cannot be brought to resent an exertion of the most undoubted constitutional right of petitioning the throne, or any endeavours to procure and preserve an union of the colonies as an unjustifiable attempt to revive those distractions which it is said have operated so fatally to the prejudice of both the colonies and the mother country. We have the warmest and most affectionate attachment to our most gracious sovereign, and shall ever pay the readiest and most respectful regard to the just and constitutional power of the British Parliament; but we shall not be intimidated by a few founding expressions from doing what we think is right. The House of Representatives of the colony of Massachusetts-Bay in their letter to us, have intimated that they have preferred an humble, dutiful and loyal petition to the

F f 2

the King, and expressed their confidence that the united and dutiful supplications of his distressed American subjects will meet with his royal and favourable acceptance; and we think they have asserted their rights with a decent respect to their sovereign, and a due submission to the authority of Parliament. What we shall do upon this occasion, or whether in consequence of that letter we shall do any thing, it is not our present business to communicate to your Excellency: but of this be pleased to be assured, that we cannot be prevailed on to take no notice of, or to treat with the least degree of contempt, a letter so expressive of duty and loyalty to the sovereign, and so replete with just principles of liberty; and your Excellency may depend that whenever we apprehend the rights of the people to be affected, we shall not fail boldly to assert and steadily endeavour to maintain and support them, always remembering, what we could wish never to be forgot, that by the Bill of Rights it is declared, ' that it is ' the right of the subject to petition ' the King, and all commitments and ' prosecutions for such petitioning are ' illegal.' By order of the Lower House of Assembly,

ROBERT LLOYD. Speaker. *
June 23d, 1768.

The following is a Copy of a Letter communicated to the House of Assembly of the Colony of Rhode-Island, on Saturday the 18th of June, by the Governor of that Colony.

Whitehall, *April* 21, 1768.
Gentlemen,
I have his Majesty's commands to transmit to you the inclosed copy of a

* The answer of Governor Sharpe to this address, imported his disappointment in the effect of his message; and his having instructions to put an end to the session (whether to dissolve or prorogue it, he did not say) if the House proceeded to any measures in favour of liberty.

letter from the Speaker of the House of Representatives of the colony of the Massachusetts-Bay, addressed by order of that House to the Speaker of the assembly of each colony upon the continent of North-America; as his Majesty considers this measure to be of a most dangerous and factious tendency, calculated to enflame the minds of his good subjects in the colonies; to promote an unwarrantable combination, and to excite and encourage an open opposition to and denial of the authority of Parliament, and to subvert the true principles of the constitution.—It is his Majesty's pleasure that you should, immediately upon the receipt hereof, exert your utmost influence to defeat this flagitious attempt to disturb the public peace, by prevailing upon the assembly of your province to take no notice of it, which will be treating it with the contempt it deserves.

The repeated proofs which have been given by the assembly of Rhode-Island of their reverence and respect for the laws, and of their faithful attachments to the constitution, leave little room in his Majesty's breast to doubt of their shewing a proper resentment of this unjustifiable attempt to revive those distractions which have operated so fatally to the prejudice of this kingdom and the colonies: and accordingly his Majesty has the fullest confidence in their affection, and expects they will give him the strongest proofs of them on this and every other occasion.

I am, with great truth and regard, Gentlemen, your most obedient humble servant,

HILLSBOROUGH.

In the Providence Gazette, July 9, was published the following Letter to the Printer from Roger Martyn, Esq;
If the design of the Earl of Hillsborough's letter, of the 21st of April last,

laft, to the colony of Rhode Iſland, was to detach and divert them from uniting with the continent, in all legal endeavours, for a removal of general grievances, he hath miſſed of his aim. This colony is but the more confirmed of the neceſſity of a general union, when the oppreſſion is common. This I think I may ſay, after having heard no one, even during the Seſſion of Aſſembly in which that letter was read, expreſs the leaſt cenſure of the colony of the Maſſachuſetts Bay, for writing the circular letter complained of; but, on the contrary, that proceeding is univerſally approved of. If it be the privilege of every ſubject to petition to the King, it is undoubtedly the right of a whole country to unite in a ſupplication for redreſs of grievances, which equally affect them all, This colony have adopted the meaſures recommended to them by their brethren of the Maſſachuſetts-Bay, and a committee hath been appointed to prepare a draft of a petition on the ſubject recommended, who will ſoon report to the Aſſembly, notwithſtanding the Earl's letter; and there cannot be the leaſt doubt, but that ſuch petition will be forwarded as ſoon as may be, as at the time when his ſurprizing letter was received, the aſſembly were addreſſed by the Speaker of the Houſe of Burgeſſes in Virginia, on the ſubject contained in the circular letter from Boſton, wherein the ſentiments of that ancient and reſpectable government appear to coincide with thoſe of the Maſſachuſſetts-Bay, to which addreſs the Houſe directed their Speaker to ſend an anſwer, and ſignify their full approbation of the ſentiments therein contained, and to aſſure him, that meaſures ſimilar to thoſe taken in that dominion ſhould be purſued. And I am authorized to ſay, that an anſwer from our Houſe of Commons, in this colony, to the letter from Boſton, would have been ſent, and made public, had it not been for the intervention of ſome ſpecial buſineſs, which engroſſed the attention of the Houſe ſo much, during their ſeſſion of only three or four days continuance, that they omitted to give any particular direction to their Speaker in that behalf, many of the Houſe ſuppoſing he would have written an anſwer ex officio, as the Houſe had entered into the meaſures recommended.

Upon a re-examination of the circular letter from the Maſſachuſetts-Bay (with all due ſubmiſſion to the ſagacity of his Lordſhip) nobody amongſt us can diſcover any dangerous or factious tendency therein, or conceive it to be calculated to inflame the minds of the King's ſubjects in the colonies, or to promote any unwarrantable combinations, or to ſubvert any principles of the conſtitution: we rather think it a meaſure of the higheſt expediency—that the principles therein held forth are right, and in which all the colonies on the continent are unanimous in ſentiment. A receſſion of one jot from the principles contained in that letter, would be dangerous to the general ſafety: and from the reception it hath met with, we hope that the colony of the Maſſachuſetts-Bay will have the fortitude to endure all extremities, rather than reſcind any reſolutions that gave birth to it.

One would think, that a joint ſupplication would meet with a more gracious reception than ſeparate and different prayers. In public and joint worſhip of the ſupreme being a ſpecial promiſe of bleſſing is annexed. Is it not very ſtrange, then, that the miniſter ſhould attempt to make us believe, that the recommendation from the principal government to the ſeveral legiſlatures in this remote part
of

of the world, to join in befeeching our gracious fovereign to confider and remove our griefs, is dangerous or factious? He might as well perfuade us, that in a time of peftilence or famine, an united fupplication to heaven to remove the calamity was an unwarrantable combination.

Unlefs the colonies are for tamely yielding up every valuable privilege, the minifter ought to be plainly told, that let his fingle opinion be what it may, they fo far underftand their own liberties, that they will at all times, when they fee fit, confer together, and correfpond about their joint concernments, without afking his leave, and that they have a lawful right fo to do.

If our petitions are prevented from reaching the royal ear—if the moft dutiful fupplications are called unwarrantable combinations—and, in fine, if legiflation in this country is fufpended, becaufe we decently declare our rights, and pray for a continuance of them, of what ufe are agents at the court of Great Britain? If I might advife in this matter, I would propofe a general revocation of their powers, and a difcontinuance of any further commerce or bufinefs with the inhabitants of a country, who, being only fellow-fubjects, would tyrannize over us.

Colony of Rhode-Ifland,　*Roger Martyn.*
July 5, 1768.

A Memorial in behalf of the Inhabitants of Bofton.
　Sheweth,

That they bear the fame fentiments of loyalty and duty towards our gracious King; and the fame reverence for the great council of the nation, the Britifh Parliament, as ever; and therefore are not willing their conduct fhould appear in an odious light to the miniftry.—The principal occafion of the late tumults arofe from the haughty conduct of the commiffioners, and other officers appointed by

them.—The Romney man of war, having moored before the town, intimidated the coafting veffels bringing provifions, firewood, &c. committed many acts of violence and outrage; and in particular, by cutting away a veffel from Mr. Hancock's Wharf, detaining her feveral days, without any legal procefs being filed againft her, &c. This irritated the people; who patrolled the ftreets in a tumultuous manner, broke feveral windows to the value of about 5l. fterling, burnt a pleafure boat belonging to the collector, and then difperfed at about 11 o'clock at night.—All which will more fully appear by twelve affidavits, of different perfons, who were eye witneffes of the proceedings, hereunto annexed.—Three days after this, the commiffioners made a voluntary abdication of their office, and went on board the Romney man of war. And from all the affidavits it does appear, that the caufe of fuch tumult was entirely from the impudent and violent proceedings of the officers, particularly from the mafter of the Romney, who frequently ordered the marines to fire, and abufed every body who advifed a cooler conduct.

The above Memorial was prefented to Adminiftration with the twelve Affidavits, (immediately upon hearing the Reports which were fo prejudicial to the Town) by Dennis De Berdt, Efq; Agent for the Affembly.

SIR,　*Bofton, July 13, 1768.*
It is very furprifing to people here, that the circular letter, tranfmitted from this government to the other colonies, could be reprefented and confidered by the miniftry in fo odious a light as it appears it has been, by the late letter from the Earl of Hillborough. It is amazing, that a meafure fo innocent, fo prudent, and that had fuch a tendency to quiet the minds of the people, fhould be fo mifconftrued.
　　　　　　　　However

However, it seems the letter from the Earl of Hillsborough, respecting this affair, has had quite a different effect from what was designed and expected: instead of preventing the colonies from uniting in their applications to the throne for relief, it has served to make them more solicitous than ever of an union in sentiment and measures. This you will perceive, upon perusing the inclosed news paper, where you will find what has been done by the House of Delegates at Maryland. The colony of Rhode Island has immediately upon the reception of the letter abovementioned, prepared an address to his Majesty, which will soon be forwarded. Many of the other colonies have also forwarded their petitions and representations. The people through the continent are greatly alarmed, and will never be easy till the late acts are repealed, and things return to their old course. The merchants find they cannot vend your manufactures, the country people are so disgusted, and are determined not to continue their importations of English goods. We have now in the harbour five or six vessels of war, and are threatened with troops. If they should be sent here to enforce acts of Parliament, God only knows what will be the event. This we are sure of, that be the number of the troops ever so great, they cannot force us either to import, buy, or consume English goods. The mercantile interest on your side of the water is, and will be, greatly affected by these measures. It behoves them to bestir themselves upon this occasion, if they design to preserve their trade. It is the opinion of men of discernment and good judgment, that the people through the continent are much more alarmed at the late acts, than they were at the stamp act; and it would be vastly more difficult to reconcile the people

to them. God grant that the union between the mother country and the colonies may not be interrupted; and that those at the helm may be endowed with all that wisdom which may be needful to direct at such a critical day! I doubt not your good wishes for America.

Your most humble Servant,
T. CUSHING.
To Dennis De Berdt, Esq;

An Address read at a numerous meeting of the Merchants in Philadelphia on the 25th of April, 1768.
(Written by Mr. Dickenson, author of the Farmer's Letters.)

Gentlemen, Friends, and Fellow Citizens,

You are called together to give your advice and opinion, what answer shall be returned to our brethren of Boston and New-York, who desire to know whether we will unite with them, in stopping the importation of goods from Great Britain, until certain acts of Parliament are repealed, which are thought to be injurious to our rights, as freemen and British subjects.

Before you come to any resolution, it may be necessary to explain the matter more fully.

When our forefathers came into this country, they considered themselves as freemen, and that their coming and settling these colonies did not divest them of any of the rights inherent in freemen; that, therefore, what they possessed, and what they or their posterity should acquire, was and would be so much their own, that no power on earth could lawfully, or of right, deprive them of it without their consent. The governments, which they, with the consent of the crown, established in the respective colonies, they considered as political governments, "where (as Mr. Locke expresses it) men

men have property in their own difposal." And therefore (according to the conclusion drawn by the same author in another place) " No taxes ought or could be raised on their property without their consent given by themselves or their deputies," or chosen representatives.

As they were members of one great empire, united under one head or crown, they tacitly acquiesced in the superintending authority of the Parliament of Great Britain, and admitted a power in it, to make regulations to preserve the connection of the whole entire. Though under colour of this, sundry regulations were made that bore hard on the colonies; yet, with filial respect and regard for Great Britain their mother country, the colonies submitted to them.

It will be sufficient here just to enumerate some of the most grievous.

1. The law against making steel, or erecting steel furnaces, though there are not above five or six persons in England engaged in that branch of business, who are so far from being able to supply what is wanted, that great quantities of steel are yearly imported from Germany.

2. Against plating and slitting mills and tilt hammers; though iron is the produce of our country, and from our manner of building, planting, and living, we are under a necessity of using vast quantities of nails and plated iron, as hoes, stove-pipes, plates, &c. all which are loaded with double freight, commissions, &c.

3. The restraint laid on hatters, and the prohibition of exporting hats.

4. The prohibition of carrying wool or any kind of woollen goods manufactured here, from one colony to another. A single fleece of wool or a dozen of home-made hose carried from one colony to another is

not only forfeited, but subjects the vessel, if conveyed by water, or the waggon and horses, if carried by land, to a seizure, and the owner to a heavy fine.

5. Though the Spaniards may cut and carry logwood directly to what market they please, yet the Americans cannot send to any foreign market, even what the demand in England cannot take off, without first carrying it to some British port, and there landing and re-shipping it at a great expence and loss of time.

6. Obliging us to carry Portugal and Spanish wines, fruit, &c. to England, there to unload, pay a heavy duty and re-ship it, thus subjecting us to a great expence, and our vessels to an unnecessary voyage of 1000 miles in a dangerous sea.

7. Imposing a duty on Madeira wines, which, if re-shipped to England, are subjected to the payment of the full duties there without any drawback for what was paid here.

8. The emptying their jails upon us, and making the colonies a receptacle for their rogues and villains; an insult and indignity not to be thought of, much less borne without indignation and resentment.

Not to mention the restrictions attempted in the fisheries, the duties laid on foreign sugar, molasses, &c. I will just mention the necessity they have laid us under of supplying ourselves wholly from Great-Britain with European and East-India goods at an advance of 20, and as to some articles, even of 40 per cent. higher than we might be supplied with them from other places.

But as if all these were not enough, a party has lately arisen in England, who, under colour of superintending authority of parliament, are labouring to erect a new sovereignty over the colonies, with power inconsistent with liberty or freedom.

The

The firſt exertion of this power was diſplayed in the odious Stamp-Act. As the authors and promoters of this act were ſenſible of the oppoſition it muſt neceſſarily meet with, from men, who had the leaſt ſpark of liberty remaining, they accompanied it with a bill ſtill more odious, wherein they attempted to empower officers to quarter ſoldiers on private houſes, with a view no doubt, to dragoon us into a compliance with the former act.

By the interpoſition of the American agents, and of the London merchants who traded to the colonies, this clauſe was dropt, but the act was carried, wherein the aſſemblies of the reſpective colonies were ordered, at the expence of the ſeveral provinces, to furniſh the troops with a number of articles, ſome of them never allowed in Britain. Beſides, a power is therein granted to every officer, upon obtaining a warrant from any juſtice, (which warrant the Juſtice is thereby empowered and ordered to grant, without any previous oath) to break into any houſe by day or by night, under pretence (theſe are the words of the act) of ſearching for deſerters.

By the ſpirited oppoſition of the colonies, the firſt act was repealed: but the latter continued, which, in its ſpirit, differs nothing from the other. For thereby the liberty of the colonies is invaded, and their property diſpoſed of without their conſent, no leſs than by the Stamp-Act. It was rather the more dangerous of the two, as the appearance of the conſtitution was preſerved while the ſpirit of it was deſtroyed, and thus a tyranny introduced under the forms of liberty. The aſſemblies were not at liberty to refuſe their aſſent, but were to be forced to a literal compliance with the act. Thus, becauſe the aſſembly of New-York heſitated to comply, their legiſlative power was immedi-

ately ſuſpended by another act of parliament.

That the repeal of the Stamp-act might not invalidate the claims of ſovereignty now ſet up, an act was paſſed, aſſerting the power of Parliament to bind us with their laws in every reſpect whatever. And to aſcertain the extent of this power, in the very next ſeſſion they proceeded to a direct taxation; and in the very words in which they diſpoſe of their own property, they gave and granted that of the coloniſts, impoſing duties on paper, glaſs, &c. imported into America, to be paid by the coloniſts for the purpoſe of raiſing a revenue.

This revenue, when raiſed, they ordered to be diſpoſed of in ſuch a manner as to render our aſſemblies or legiſlative bodies altogether uſeleſs, and to make Governors and Judges, who hold their commiſſions during pleaſure, and the whole executive powers of government, nay, the defence of the country, independent of the people, as has been fully explain'd in the Farmer's Letters.

Thus with a conſiſtency of conduct having diveſted us of property, they are proceeding to erect over us a deſpotic government, and to rule us as ſlaves. For "a deſpotical power, ſays Mr. Locke, is over ſuch as have no property at all." If, indeed, to be ſubject in our lives and property to the arbitrary will of others, whom we have never choſen, nor ever entruſted with ſuch power, be not ſlavery, I wiſh any perſon would tell me what ſlavery is.

Such then being the ſtate of the caſe, you are now, my fellow-citizens, to deliberate, not, whether you will tamely ſubmit to this ſyſtem of government.—That I am ſure your love of freedom and regard for yourſelves and your poſterity will never ſuffer you to think of—But by what means you may defend your rights

G g
and

and liberties, and obtain a repeal of these acts.

In England, when the prerogative has been strained too high, or the people oppressed by the executive power, the Parliament who are the guardians and protectors of the people's liberties, always petition for redress of grievances, and enforce their petitions, by with-holding supplies until they are granted.

Our assembly, I am told, has applied for relief from these acts of parliament. But having nothing left to give, they could not enforce their application, by with-holding any thing.

It is, however, in our power, in a peaceable and constitutional way, to add weight to the remonstrance and petition of our representatives, by stopping the importation of goods from Britain, until we obtain relief and redress by a repeal of these unconstitutional acts.

But this, it may be said, is subjecting ourselves to present loss and inconvenience.

I would beg leave to ask, whether any people in any age or country ever defended and preserved their liberty from the encroachments of power, without suffering present inconveniencies. The Roman people suffered themselves to be defeated by their enemies, rather than submit to the tyranny of the nobles. And even in the midst of war, the Parliament of England has denied to grant supplies, until their grievances were redressed; well knowing that no present loss, suffering, or inconvenience, could equal that of tyranny or the loss of public liberty. To cite an example, which our own country furnishes; you all remember that in the height of the late terrible Indian war, our assembly and that of Maryland chose rather to let the country suffer great inconvenience, than immediately grant supplies on terms injurious to the public privilege and to justice.

As then we cannot enjoy liberty without property, both in our lives and estates; as we can have no property in that which another may of right take and dispose of as he pleases, without our consent; and as the late acts of parliament assert this right to be in them, we cannot enjoy freedom until this claim is given up, and until acts made in consequence of it be repealed. For so long as these acts continue, and the claim is kept up, our property is at their disposal, and our lives at their mercy.

To conclude, as liberty is the great and only security of property; as the security of property is the chief spur to industry, (it being vain to acquire what we have not a prospect to enjoy) and as the stopping the importation of goods is the only probable means of preserving to us and our posterity this liberty and security, I hope, my brethren, there is not a man among us, who will not cheerfully join in the measure proposed, and, with our brethren of Boston and New-York, freely forego a present advantage, nay, even submit to a present inconvenience for the sake of liberty, on which our happiness, lives, and properties depend. Let us never forget that our strength depends on our union, and our liberty on our strength. "United we conquer, divided we die."

The following paper was published in London, about the beginning of the Year 1768. By Dr. BENJAMIN FRANKLIN.

The waves never rise but when the winds blow. Prov.

As the cause of the present ill humour in America, and of the resolutions taken there to purchase less of our manufactures, does not seem to be generally understood, it may afford some satisfaction to our readers

If you give them the following short historical state of facts.

From the time that the colonies were first considered as capable of granting aids to the crown, down to the end of the last war, it is said, that the constant mode of obtaining those aids was, by *requisition* made from the crown, through its governors to the several assemblies, in circular letters from the Secretary of State in his Majesty's name, setting forth the occasion, requiring them to take the matter into consideration, and expressing a reliance to their prudence, duty and affection to his Majesty's government, that they would grant such sums, or raise such numbers of men, as were suitable to their respective circumstances.

The colonies being accustomed to this method, have from time to time granted money to the crown, or raised troops for its service, in proportion to their abilities; and during all the last war beyond their abilities, so that considerable sums were return'd them yearly by Parliament, as they had exceeded their proportion.

Had this happy method of requisition been continued, (a method that left the King's subjects in those remote countries the pleasure of shewing their zeal and loyalty, and of imagining that they recommend themselves to their sovereign by the liberality of their voluntary grants) there is no doubt, but all the money that could reasonably be expected to be rais'd from them in any manner, might have been obtained, without the least heart-burning, offence, or breach of the harmony, of affections and interests, that so long subsisted between the two countries.

It has been thought wisdom in a government exercising sovereignty over different kinds of people, to have some regard to prevailing and established opinions among the people to be governed, wherever such opinions might in their effects obstruct or promote public measures. If they tend to obstruct public service, they are to be changed, if possible, before we attempt to act against them; and they can only be changed by reason and persuasion. But if public business can be carried on without thwarting those opinions, if they can be, on the contrary, made subservient to it, they are not unnecessarily to be thwarted, how absurd soever such popular opinions may be in their natures.—This had been the wisdom of our government with respect to raising money in the colonies. It was well known, that the colonists universally were of opinion, that no money could be levied from English subjects, but by their own consent given by themselves or their chosen representatives: that therefore whatever money was to be raised from the people in the colonies, must first be granted by their Assemblies, as the money raised in Britain is first to be granted by the House of Commons: that this right of granting their own money, was essential to English liberty: and that if any man, or body of men, in which they had no representative of their chusing, could tax them at pleasure, they could not be said to have any property, any thing they could call their own. But as these opinions did not hinder their granting money voluntarily and amply whenever the crown by its servants came into their Assemblies (as it does into its Parliaments of Britain or Ireland) and demanded aids; therefore that method was chosen rather than the hateful one of arbitrary taxes.

I do not undertake here to support these opinions of the Americans; they have been refuted by a late act of Parliament, declaring its own power;—which very Parliament, however, shew'd wisely so much tender regard

regard to thofe inveterate prejudices, as to repeal a tax that had militated againſt them. And thofe prejudices are ſtill ſo fixed and rooted in the A-mericans, that, it has been ſuppoſed, not a ſingle man among them has been convinced of his error, even by that act of Parliament.

The perfon then who firſt projected to lay afide the accuſtomed method of requiſition, and to raiſe money on America by ſtamps, ſeems not to have acted wiſely, in deviating from that method (which the coloniſts look-ed upon as conſtitutional) and thwart-ing unneceſſarily the fixed prejudices of ſo great a number of the King's ſubjects.—It was not, however, for want of knowledge that what he was about to do would give them great offence; he appears to have been ve-ry ſenſible of this, and apprehenſive that it might occaſion ſome diſorders, to prevent or ſuppreſs which, he pro-jected another Bill, that was brought in the ſame ſeſſion with the ſtamp act, whereby it was to be made lawful for military officers in the colonies to quarter their ſoldiers in private houſes. This ſeem'd intended to awe the peo-ple into a compliance with the other act. Great oppoſition however being raiſed here againſt the bill by the a-gents from the colonies, and the mer-chants trading thither, the coloniſts declaring, that under ſuch a power in the army, no one could look on his houſe as his own, or think he had a home, when ſoldiers might be thruſt into it and mix'd with his family at the pleaſure of an officer, that part of the bill was dropt;—but there ſtill remained a clauſe, when it paſſed in-to a law, to oblige the ſeveral aſſem-blies to provide quarters for the ſol-diers, furniſhing them with firing, bedding, candles, ſmall beer or rum, and ſundry other articles, at the ex-pence of the ſeveral provinces. And this act continued in force when the

Stamp Act was repealed, though if obligatory on the aſſemblies, it equally militated againſt the American prin-ciple abovementioned, *that money is not to be raiſed on Engliſh ſubjects with-out their conſent.*

The colonies nevertheleſs being put into high good humour by the repeal of the Stamp Act, choſe to avoid a freſh diſpute upon the other, it being temporary and ſoon to expire, never, as they hoped, to revive again; and in the mean time they, by various ways in different colonies, provided for the quartering of the troops, either by acts of their own aſſemblies, without taking notice of the act of parliament, or by ſome variety or ſmall diminution, as of ſalt and vine-gar, in the ſupplies required by the act, that what they did might appear a voluntary act of their own, and not done in obedience to an act of parliament, which, according to their ideas of their rights, they thought hard to obey.

It might have been well if the matter had thus paſſed without no-tice; but a Governor having written home an angry and aggravating let-ter upon this conduct in the aſſembly of his province, the outed Premier of the Stamp Act and his adherents, then in the oppoſition, raiſed ſuch a clamour againſt America, as being in rebellion, and againſt thoſe who had been for the repeal of the Stamp Act, as having thereby been encou-ragers of this ſuppoſed rebellion, that it was thought neceſſary to inforce the quartering act by another act of par-liament, taking away from the pro-vince of New-York, which had been the moſt explicit in its refuſal, all the powers of legiſlation, till it ſhould have complied with that act. The news of which greatly alarmed the people every where in America, as (it has been ſaid) the language of ſuch an act ſeemed to them to be, *Obey im-plicitly*

plicitly laws made by the Parliament of Great Britain to raise money on you without your consent, or you shall enjoy no rights or privileges at all.

At the same time a person lately in high office, projected the levying more money, from America, by new duties on various articles of our own manufacture, as glass, paper, painters colours, &c. appointing a new Board of Customs, and sending over a set of Commissioners, with large salaries, to be established at Boston, who were to have the care of collecting those duties; which were by the act expressly mentioned to be intended for the payment of the salaries of Governors, Judges, and other Officers of the crown in America? it being a pretty general opinion here, that those officers ought not to depend on the people there for any part of their support.

It is not my intention to combat this opinion. But perhaps it may be some satisfaction to your readers, to know what ideas the Americans have on the subject. They say then, as to Governors, that they are not like Princes whose posterity have an inheritance in the government of a nation, and therefore an interest in its prosperity; they are generally strangers to the provinces they are sent to govern, have no estate, natural connection, or relation there, to give them an affection for the country;— that they come only to make money as fast as they can; are sometimes men of vicious characters and broken fortunes, sent by a minister merely to get them out of the way: that as they intend staying in the country no longer than their government continues, and purpose to leave no family behind them, they are apt to be regardless of the good will of the people, and care not what is said or thought of them after they are gone. Their situation at the same time gives

them many opportunities of being vexatious, and they are often so notwithstanding their dependance on the assemblies for all that part of their support that does not arise from fees established by law; but would probably be much more so, if they were to be supported by money drawn from the people without their consent or good will, which is the professed design of this new act. That, if by means of these forced duties, government is to be supported in America, without the intervention of the assemblies, their assemblies will soon be looked upon as useless, and a governor will not call them, as having nothing to hope from their meeting, and perhaps something to fear from their enquiries into and remonstrances against his mal-administration. That thus the people will be deprived of their most essential rights. That it being, as at present, a governor's interest to cultivate the good will, by promoting the welfare of the people he governs, can be attended with no prejudice to the mother-country, since all the laws he may be prevailed on to give his assent to are subject to revision here, and if reported against by the Board of Trade, are immediately repealed by the crown; nor dare he pass any law contrary to his instructions, as he holds his office during the pleasure of the crown, and his securities are liable for the penalties of their bonds if he contravenes those instructions. This is what they say as to *Governors.* As to *Judges* they alledge, that being appointed from hence, and holding their commissions *not* during *good behaviour*, as in Britain, but during *pleasure*, all the weight of interest or influence would be thrown into one of the scales, (which ought to be held even) if the salaries are also to be paid out of duties raised upon the people without their consent, and independent of

their

their Assemblies approbation or disapprobation of the judges behaviour. That it is true, judges should be free from all influence; and therefore, whenever government here will grant commissions to able and honest judges during good behaviour, the Assemblies will settle permanent and ample salaries on them during their commissions: but, at present, they have no other means of getting rid of an ignorant or an unjust judge (and some of scandalous characters have, they say, been sometimes sent them) but by starving him out.

I do not suppose these reasonings of theirs will appear here to have much weight. I do not produce them with an expectation of convincing your readers. I relate them merely in pursuance of the task I have imposed on myself, to be an impartial historian of American facts and opinions.

The colonists being thus greatly alarmed, as I said before, by the news of the act for abolishing the legislature of New-York, and the imposition of these new duties professedly for such disagreeable purposes; (accompanied by a new set of revenue officers with large appointments, which gave strong suspicions that more business of the same kind was soon to be provided for them, that they might earn these salaries;) began seriously to consider their situation, and to revolve afresh in their minds grievances which from their respect and love for this country, they had long borne and seemed almost willing to forget. They reflected how lightly the interest of all America had been estimated here, when the interest of a few inhabitants of Great Britain happened to have the smallest competition with it. That thus the whole American people were forbidden the advantage of a direct importation of wine, oil, and fruit, from Portugal, but must take them loaded with all the expen-

ces of a voyage 1000 leagues round about, being to be landed first in England to be re-shipped for America; expences amounting, in war time, at least 30 per cent. more than otherwise they would have been charged with, and all this merely, that a few Portugal merchants in London may gain a commission on those goods passing through their hands. Portugal merchants, by the by, that can complain loudly of the smallest hardships laid on their trade by *foreigners*, and yet even the last year could oppose with all their influence the giving ease to their *fellow subjects* labouring under so heavy an oppression!—That on a slight complaint of a few Virginia merchants, nine colonies had been restrained from making paper money become absolutely necessary to their internal commerce, from the constant remittance of their gold and silver to Britain.—But not only the interest of a particular body of merchants, the interest of any small body of British tradesmen or artificers, has been found, they say, to outweigh that of all the King's subjects in the colonies. There cannot be a stronger natural right, than that of a man's making the best profit he can of the natural produce of his lands, provided he does not thereby hurt the state in general. Iron is to be found every where in America, and beaver furs are the natural produce of that country; hats and nails, and steel, are wanted there as well as here. It is of no importance to the common welfare of the empire, whether a subject of the King's gets his living by making hats on this or that side of the water. Yet the hatters of England have prevailed to obtain an act in their own favour, restraining that manufacture in America, in order to oblige the Americans to send their beaver to England to be manufactured, and purchase back the hats, load-

ed

ed with the charges of a double tranf-portation. In the fame manner have a few nail-makers, and ftill a fmall-er body of fteel-makers (perhaps there are not half a dozen of them in Eng-land) prevailed totally to forbid by an act of parliament the erecting of flitting mills or fteel furnaces in Ame-rica, that the Americans may be obliged to take all the nails for their buildings, and fteel for their tools, from thefe artificers, under the fame difadvantages.

Added to thefe, the Americans re-membered the act authorizing the moft cruel infult that perhaps was ever offered by one people to another, that of emptying our gaols into their fet-tlements; Scotland too having within thefe two years obtained the privilege it had not before, of fending its rogues and villains alfo to the plantations. I fay, reflecting on thefe things, they faid to one another (their news papers are full of fuch difcourfes) thefe peo-ple are not content with making a monopoly of us, forbidding us to trade with another country of Europe, and compelling us to buy every thing of them, though in many articles we could furnifh ourfelves 10, 20, and even to 50 per cent. cheaper elfe-where; but now they have as good as declared they have a right to tax us *ad libitum* internally and externally, and that our conftitutions and liber-ties fhall all be taken away, if we do not fubmit to that claim. They are not content with the high prices at which they they fell us their goods, but have now begun to enhance thofe prices by new duties; and by the ex-penfive apparatus of a new fet of of-ficers, appear to intend an augmen-tation and multiplication of thofe bur-thens that fhall be ftill more grievous to us. Our people have been foolifh-ly fond of their fuperfluous modes and manufactures, to the impoverifh-ing our country, carrying off all our

cafh, and loading us with debt; they will not fuffer us to reftrain the luxu-ry of our inhabitants as they do that of their own, by laws: they can make laws to difcourage or prohibit the importation of French fuperflui-ties: but though thofe of England are as ruinous to us as the French ones are to them, if we make a law of that kind, they immediately repeal it. Thus they get all our money from us by trade, and every profit we can any where make by our fifheries, our pro-duce or our commerce, centers final-ly with them; but this does not figni-fy. It is time then to take care of ourfelves by the beft means in our power. Let us unite in folemn refo-lutions and engagements with and to each other, that we will give thefe new officers as little trouble as poffi-ble, by not confuming the Britifh manufactures on which they are to levy the duties. Let us agree to con-fume no more of their expenfive gew-gaws. Let us live frugally, and let us induftrioufly manufacture what we can for ourfelves: thus we fhall be able honourably to difcharge the debts we already owe them, and after that, we may be able to keep fome money in our country, not only for the ufes of our internal commerce, but for the fervice of our gracious Sovereign, whenever he fhall have occafion for it, and think proper to require it of us in the old conftitutional manner. For notwithftanding the reproaches thrown out againft us in their public papers and pamphlets, notwithftanding we have been reviled in their fenate as rebels and traitors, we are truly a loyal people. Scotland has had its rebellions, and England its plots a-gainft the prefent Royal Family; but America is untainted with thofe crimes; there is in it fcarce a man, there is not a fingle native of our country, who is not firmly attached to his King by principle and by affection. But a

new

new kind of loyalty seems to be required of us, a loyalty to Parliament; a loyalty, that is to extend, it is said, to a furrender of all our properties, whenever a House of Commons, in which there is not a single member of our chusing, shall think fit to grant them away without our consent; and to a patient suffering the loss of our privileges as Englishmen, if we cannot submit to make such surrender. We were separated too far from Britain by the ocean, but we were united to it by respect and love, so that we could at any time freely have spent our lives and little fortunes in its cause: but this unhappy new system of politics tends to dissolve those bands of union, and to sever us for ever.

These are the wild ravings of the at present half distracted Americans. To be sure, no reasonable man in England can approve of such sentiments, and, as I said before, I do not pretend to support or justify them: but I sincerely wish, for the sake of the manufactures and commerce of Great Britain, and for the sake of the strength which a firm union with our growing colonies would give us, that these people had never been thus needlessly driven out of their senses.   F. S.

The Report of the Lords Committees, appointed by the House of Lords to enquire into the several proceedings in the Colony of Massachusetts-Bay, in opposition to the Sovereignty of his Majesty, in his Parliament of Great Britain, over that Province; and also what hath passed in this House relative thereto, from the first day of January, 1764.

Die Mercurii, 20 *Aprilis,* 1764.

The Earl of Buckinghamshire reported from the Lords Committees appointed to enquire into the several proceedings in the Colony of Massa-

chusetts-Bay, in opposition to the sovereignty of his Majesty, in his Parliament of Great Britain, over that Province, and also what hath passed in this House relative thereto, from the first day of January, 1764, as follows:

That, in obedience to your Lordships commands, the committee have met, and taken into consideration the matters to them referred; and having attentively read, and considered, the several papers which have been laid before the House, relative to the proceedings in the colony of Massachusetts-Bay, in opposition to the Sovereignty of his Majesty, in his Parliament of Great Britain, over that province; and having also carefully inspected the Journals of the House, from the first day of January, 1764, to the present time; they find, that, on the second day of April, 1764, a bill was brought up from the Commons to your Lordships, intitled, ' An act for granting certain duties ' in the British colonies and planta- ' tions in America, for continuing, ' and amending, and making perpe- ' tual, an act passed in the sixth year ' of the reign of his late Majesty ' King George the Second, (intituled, ' an act for the better securing and ' encouraging the trade of his Majes- ' ty's sugar colonies in America; for ' applying the produce of such du- ' ties, and of the duties to arise by ' virtue of the said act, towards de- ' fraying the expences of defending, ' protecting, and securing, the said ' colonies and plantations; for ex- ' plaining an act made in the twen- ' ty-fifth year of the reign of King ' Charles the Second, intituled, an ' act for the encouragement of the ' Greenland and Eastland trades, and ' for the better securing the Planta- ' tion trade;) and for altering and ' disallowing several draw-backs on ' exports from this kingdom, and
                                ' more

'more effectually preventing the clan-
'destine conveyance of goods to and
'from the said colonies and planta-
'tions, and improving and securing
'the trade between the same and
'Great Britain.'

That this Bill passed the House
on the fourth of April, and received
the royal assent on the following
day.

The committee having perused the
report of the Board of Trade, of the
eleventh day of December, 1764,
and the papers laid before his Majesty
therewith; find, in the said papers,
the strongest assertions, by the assembly of the Massachusetts-Bay, of
their sole right to pass laws, particularly of taxation, and of their resolution to invite the other colonies to
combine with them in measures to
prevent the King, in his Parliament,
from passing any such laws; for instance, in a letter to Mr. Mauduit,
then agent of the province, which
was drawn up by a committee of the
House of Representatives, and afterwards approved by the House, they
use the following expressions: 'The
'silence of the province should have
'been imputed to any cause, even to
'despair, rather than be construed
'into a tacit cession of their rights,
'or an acknowledgement of a right
'in the Parliament of Great Britain,
'to impose duties and taxes upon a
'people who are not represented in
'the House of Commons.' And, in
the same letter, they avowed and au-
thenticated the doctrines advanced in
a certain pamphlet, intituled, The
Rights of the British Colonies asserted
and proved, written by James Otis,
Esq; which pamphlet, amongst other
things, says, 'That the imposition
of taxes, whether on trade, or on
land, on houses or ships, on real or
personal, fixed or floating, property,
in the colonies, is absolutely irrecon-
cileable with the rights of the colo-

nists, as British subjects, and as
men.'

The committee find, that on the
twenty-eighth day of February 1765, a
Bill was brought from the Commons,
intituled, 'An act for granting and
'applying stamp duties, and other
'duties, in the British colonies and
'plantations in America, towards
'further defraying the expences of
'defending, protecting, and securing
'the same; and for amending such
'parts of the several acts of Parlia-
'ment relating to the trade and re-
'venues of the said colonies and plan-
'tations, as direct the manner of de-
'termining and recovering the pe-
'nalties and forfeitures therein men-
'tioned.'

That the said Bill received the
royal assent on the 22d of the same
month.

That, on the 17th day of December, his Majesty declared, in his most
gracious speech from the throne,
that the matters of importance which
had lately occured in some of his colonies in America were the principal
cause of his Majesty's assembling his
Parliament sooner than was usual in
times of peace.

It appears to the committee, from
the votes of the House of Representatives of the colony of Massachusetts-
Bay, of the 6th of June 1765, that
they came to a resolution, that it was
highly expedient there should be a
meeting as soon as might be of committees from the Houses of Representatives, or Burgesses, in the several colonies on the American continent, to consult on their then present circumstances, and the difficulties to which they were reduced by
the operation of the late acts of Parliament, for levying duties on the colonies; and to consider of a general
address to his Majesty and the Parliament, to implore relief: and that
letters should be forthwith prepared

H h   and

and tranfmitted to the refpective Speakers of the feveral affemblies, to invite them to accede to this propofition; and further, that, on the 8th of June, they did actually elect three perfons to be their committees, and alfo voted 450*l.* to bear their expences.

Your committee find, in a letter from the Governor to the Lords Commiffioners for Trade and Plantations, dated Auguft 15th, 1765, an account of a violent riot at Bofton, in refiftance to a law paffed by the legiflature of Great Britain, in which an attack was made upon Mr. Oliver, diftributor of ftamps, and carried to the length of pulling down and deftroying his houfes, manifefting a refolution, if they could have found him, of putting him to death. Upon which occafion the backwardnefs and indifpofition of the council, to fupport the peace and good order of government, were very apparent. Alfo, in another letter from the Governor, dated Auguft 31ft, 1765, to the faid Board of Trade, they find that the mob attacked the houfe of Mr. Storey, Regifter of the Admiralty, which they demolifhed; they alfo took all his books and papers, amongft which were the records of the Court of Admiralty, and burnt them, and fearched about for him, with an intent to murder him; they alfo pillaged the houfe of Mr. Hollowell, comptroller of the cuftoms, but their moft violent proceeding was againft the Lieutenant Governor, whofe houfe, plate, books, and manufcripts, to a very great value, they totally deftroyed. And, in this great extremity, the council being, as the governor obferves, dependent upon the people, refufed even to concur with him in his propofition of giving notice to General Gage of the then fituation of the town of Bofton.

It is remarkable that this commo-

tion entirely arofe out of the town of Bofton; for though it was given out, that many people out of the country were concerned in this affair, upon enquiry, it was found that fuch perfons living out of Bofton, as were feen in the crowd, were there merely as fpectators.

In Governor Bernard's letter to the Board of Trade, October the twelfth, 1765, he fays ' That the real autho-' rity of the government is at an end; ' fome of the principal ringleaders, in ' the late riots, walk the ftreets with ' impunity; no officers dare attack ' them, no Attorney General profe-' cute them, no witnefs appear a-' gainft them, and no judges fit upon ' them.'

And during this general diforder, the Governor thought it neceffary for fome companies of the militia to be muftered, with the unanimous advice of the council, but that the militia refufed to obey his orders.

And we find, that fo little attention, was paid to an act of the Britifh legiflature, by the Council and Houfe of Reprefentatives, that they refolved in a joint committee, on the twentyfifth of October 1765, that it fhould and might be lawful to do bufinefs without ftamps, notwithftanding the act of Parliament to the contrary.

On the fourteenth day of January, 1766, upon the meeting of the Parliament, after the recefs of Chriftmas, his Majefty was pleafed to declare himfelf in a moft gracious fpeech from the throne, in the following terms:

My Lords and Gentlemen,

' When I met you laft, I acquainted ' you, that matters of importance had ' happened in America, which would ' demand the moft ferious attention ' of Parliament,

' That no information which could ' ferve to direct your deliberations in ' fo interefting a concern might be
' wanting,

' wanting, I have ordered all the pa-
' pers that give any light into the ori-
' gin, the progrefs, or the tendency,
' of the difturbances, which have of
' late prevailed in fome of the nor-
' thern colonies, to be immediately
' laid before you.

' No time has been loft, on the firft
' advice of thefe difturbances, to iffue
' orders to the governors of my pro-
' vinces, and to the commanders of
' my forces, in America, for the ex-
' ertion of all the powers of govern-
' ment, in the fuppreffion of riots and
' tumults, and in the effectual fup-
' port of lawful authority.

' Whatever remains to be done on
' this occafion, I commit to your wif-
' dom ; not doubting but your zeal for
' the honour of my crown, your atten-
' tion to the juft rights and authority
' of the Britifh legiflature, and your
' affection and concern for the welfare
' and profperity of all my people,
' will guide you to fuch found and
' prudent refolutions, as may tend at
' once to preferve thofe conftitutional
' rights over the colonies, and to reftore
' to them that harmony and tranqui-
' lity which have lately been inter-
' rupted by riots and diforders of the
' the moft dangerous nature.'

In the dutiful addrefs which was
voted the fame day, the Houfe affure
his Majefty of their hearty concurrence with his Majefty's moft falutary
intentions; that they would exert
their utmoft endeavours to affert and
fupport his Majefty's dignity and honour, and the legiflative authority of
this kingdom, over its colonies ; and
that they would take into their confideration the moft proper methods to
provide for the reftoration of the tranquillity of thofe colonies, which had
been difturbed by fuch violent and
dangerous commotions,

Upon the fame day, all the papers
relating to the informations and advices received from America, of the
riots and tumults there, were laid before the Houfe.

More papers relating to America
were laid before the Houfe, which,
together with the other papers, were
referred to a committee of the whole
Houfe, for Tuefday the 28th.

More papers were laid before the
Houfe the 27th of January, and referred to the faid committee.

The committee met, and, after feveral adjournments, on the 10th of
February following, the Chairman
reported feveral refolutions, which
were agreed to by the Houfe, as
follows :

I. Refolved, That the King's Majefty, by and with the advice and
confent of the Lords Spiritual and
Temporal, and Commons of Great-
Britain, in Parliament affembled, had,
hath, and of right ought to have,
full power and authority to make
laws and ftatutes, of fufficient force
and validity to bind the colonies and
people of America, fubjects of the
crown of Great-Britain, in all cafes
whatfoever.

II. Refolved, That it appears to
this committee, that tumults and infurrections, of the moft dangerous
nature, have been raifed and carried
on in feveral of the North American
colonies, in open defiance of the power
and dignity of his Majefty's government, and in manifeft violation of the
laws and legiflative authority of this
kingdom.

III. Refolved, That it appears to
this committee, that the faid tumults
and infurrections have been encouraged and enflamed, by fundry votes
and refolutions, paffed in feveral of
the affemblies of the faid provinces,
derogatory to the honour of his Majefty's government, and deftructive of
the legal and conftitutional dependency of the faid colonies on the imperial crown and parliament of Great
Britain.

H h 2   IV

IV. Refolved, That it is the opinion of this committee, that an humble addrefs be prefented to his Majefty, to defire that his Majefty would be gracioufly pleafed to give inftructions to the governors of the feveral provinces, where the above-mentioned tumults and infurrections have happened, That they fhould, in his Majefty's name require of the affemblies of the faid provinces, to make proper recompence to thofe who have fuffered in their perfons or properties, in confequence of the aforefaid tumults and infurrections; and to affure his Majefty, That this Houfe will, upon this, and all occafions, fupport the lawful authority of his crown, and the rights of Parliament.

V. Refolved, That it is the opinion of this committee, That all his Majefty's fubjects refiding in the faid colonies, who have manifefted their defire to comply with, or to affift in, carrying into execution the act for laying a duty on Stamps, or any other act of parliament in the Britifh colonies, in North America, have acted as dutiful and loyal fubjects, and are therefore intitled to, and will affuredly have, the favour and protection of this Houfe.

Ordered, That an humble addrefs be prefented to his Majefty, purfuant to the fourth refolution.

On the 5th of March, a bill was brought from the Commons, intituled, ' An act for the better fecuring ' the dependency of his Majefty's do- ' minions in America upon the crown ' and parliament of Great-Britain.' Which bill received the royal affent on the 18th of the fame month.

And alfo a bill, intituled, ' An act ' to repeal an act, made in the laft ' feffion of parliament, intituled, An ' act for granting and applying cer- ' tain ftamp duties and other duties ' in the Britifh colonies and planta- ' tions in America, towards further

' defraying the expences, of defend- ' ing, protecting, and fecuring the ' fame; and for amending fuch parts ' of the feveral acts of parliament, re- ' lating to the trade and revenues of ' the faid colonies and plantations, as ' direct the manner of determining ' and recovering the penalties and for- ' feitures therein mentioned.' Which bill received the royal affent on the 18th of March.

Whilft the bill for repealing the Stamp Act was under deliberation, petitions from the merchants of the city of Briftol, from the merchants of Glafgow, from Edward Montague, agent for the colony of Virginia, and from the merchants of the city of London, in favour of the faid repeal, were received and read.

On the 2d of June, a bill was brought from the Commons, intituled, ' An act for indemnifying perfons ' who have incurred certain penalties ' inflicted by an act of the laft feffion ' of parliament, for granting certain ' ftamp duties in the Britifh colonies ' and plantations in America; and ' for making valid all inftruments ex- ' ecuted or inrolled there on unftamp- ' ed paper, vellum, or parchment.' Which bill received the royal affent the 6th of the fame month.

It appears by a letter from Governor Bernard to the Earl of Shelburne, dated December the 24th, 1766, that the Governor, by advice of the council, ordered the mutiny act and three other acts, to be printed by the printer of the laws. In the interval of the adjournment of affembly, two companies of artillery being driven on fhore by diftrefs of weather, and the faid act of parliament having been confulted, the council advifed the governor to order the commiffary to fupply them with what they demand- ed under the act; which was done. Upon the meeting of the affembly. a meffage was fent to the council, and
carried

carried by five members, to enquire, 'By what authority acts of parliament were registered amongst the laws of that province; and whether they knew of any act (meaning of assembly) requiring the registering of ordinances, (their term for acts of parliament,) which their legislature never consented to.'

The committee find, That, on the 12th of March, 1767, the Lord Wycombe, by his Majesty's command, laid before the House copies of letters, &c. from his Majesty's governors in America, which were ordered to lie on the table.

That, on the third of April, more copies of letters from his Majesty's governors in America were laid before the House, and ordered to lie on the table.

That, on the 14th of May, it was ordered, that an humble address should be presented to his Majesty, That he would be graciously pleased to give directions that there might be laid before this House copies of all reports made to or by the commissioners of trade and plantations, together with all orders and proceedings made, or had, by the secretaries of state, or his Majesty's privy council, relating to the bill passed by the governor, council, and assembly of the Massachusetts-Bay, for granting compensation to the sufferers, and of free and general pardon, indemnity, and oblivion, to the offenders, in the late times, from the time of the receipt of the said bill.

That, on the 18th day of May, pursuant to the said address, the Lord Wycombe laid before the House a copy of the report of the committee of council, &c. which papers were ordered to lie on the table.

That, on the same day, it was ordered, that an humble address should be presented to his Majesty, That he would be graciously pleased to give directions that there might be laid before this House copies of such precedents as had been, or might be found, of orders in council, declaring acts of assembly in America to be null, illegal or void; together with reports of the several attornies and solicitors general, or either of them, in similar cases, read at the council board the 9th instant,

That, on the 22d of May, the Lord Wycombe, by his Majesty's command, laid before the House, copies of such precedents as had been found of orders in council, declaring acts of assemblies in America to be null, illegal, and void; together with reports of the several attornies and solicitors general, or either of them, in similar cases.

Which papers were ordered to lie on the table; and, from a perusal of them, we find, that several acts of different colonies have been, from time to time, declared, by his Majesty in council, to be null, illegal, and void.

That, on the 15th of June, a bill was brought up from the Commons, intituled, ' An act to enable his Majesty to put the customs and other duties, in the British dominions in America, and the execution of the laws relating to trade there, under the management of commissioners to be appointed for that purpose, and to be resident in the said dominions.'

Which bill received the royal assent on the 29th of the same month,

That, on the 18th of June, a bill was brought up from the commons, intituled, " An act for granting certain duties in the British colonies and plantations in America; for allowing a drawback of the duties of customs upon the exportation, from this kingdom, of coffee and cocoa nuts, of the produce of the said colonies, or plantations; for discontinuing the drawbacks payable on china earthen ware exported

exported to America; and for more effectually preventing the clandestine running of goods in the said colonies and plantations."

Which bill received the royal assent on the 29th of June.

The committee find, That, on the meeting of the assembly of the province of Massachusetts-Bay, on the 28th of January 1767, a message was sent to the governor, from the House of Representatives, desiring to be informed, whether any provision had been made, at the expence of that government, for the King's troops, lately arrived in the harbour of Boston; and that, after having had the minutes of council (by which it expressly appeared that the provision for the artillery companies at the castle was made in pursuance of the then late act of parliament) laid before them, they replied, that " In giving orders, with the advice of the council, for making provision for the artillery companies at the castle, the governor had acted in an essential point against the plain intention of the charter, by which alone, and that only, according to such acts as are or may be in force, within this province, the governor and council were authorised to issue money out of the treasury :" adding, " that it was still more grievous to them to find the governor stating, as the foundation of the proceeding, a late act of parliament, which to them appeared as great a grievance as the stamp act, which took away the unalienable right of freedom from all taxation, but such as they should voluntarily consent to, and grant."

Governor Bernard was obliged, in his rejoinder, 14th and 18th February 1767, carefully to avoid giving the act of parliament as the foundation of the provision made; he would otherwise not have had the concurrence of the council; for tho' the greater part, he believed, had a due

respect for acts of parliament, not one of them would have dared to avow it, in that instance, and at that time.

The committee find, That, on the second of March, 1768, a bill was brought up from the commons, intituled, " An act for the more easy and effectual recovery of the penalties and forfeitures inflicted by the acts of parliament relating to trade, or revenues, of the British colonies and plantations in America."

Which bill received the royal assent on the 8th of the same month.

It appears to the committee, that by a circular letter from the House of Representatives of the colony of Massachusetts-Bay, addressed to all the assemblies upon the continent of North America, " They desired the assent of those assemblies to their sentiments and proceedings, acquainting them that they had represented to his Majesty, that the acts of parliament of Great Britain, imposing duties upon that province, with the sole and express purpose of raising a revenue, are infringements of their natural constitutional rights, and desired them to point out any thing further that might be necessary to carry their system into execution."

In this year, the assembly, at the election of the council, left out all the crown officers, which measure had been before adopted in the years 1766, and 1767.

In the beginning of May, 1768, subscriptions were made, and associations entered into, for the non-importation of goods from Great Britain; but this last measure was, at that time, defeated by the merchants in the other colonies refusing to concur in it.

On the 9th day of May, 1768, regular seizure was made by the collector and comptroller of the customs of the sloop Liberty, belonging to

Mr.

Mr. Hancock of the town of Boston, which occasioned a most violent tumult; the collector and comptroller, with the son of the collector, were attached by a numerous and outrageous mob, who beat and abused them in a most cruel manner; and in the night attacked their houses, broke the windows, seized on a boat belonging to the collector, which they carried away in triumph, and afterwards burnt: the commissioners of the customs expecting the same treatment, the riot still continuing, thought it prudent to retreat for safety till midnight, with their families, to the houses of some persons in the neighbourhood, and afterwards, upon conviction that their lives were in danger, took refuge on board his Majesty's ship the Romney, then in the harbour of Boston; and, for their further security, from thence into Castle William. During the time of this their perilous situation, they applied several times by letter to the governor and council, for protection, but could procure no assistance whatsoever, and were finally told, in a letter from Governor Bernard, dated the 13th of June, That, after several hours deliberation of the necessity of taking some measures to preserve the peace of the town, and what those measures should be, the council had come to a resolution, That, as there appeared to be no immediate danger of further violences, they were of opinion, that it would be best to refer this matter to the consideration of a committee of both Houses, and that therefore the governor at present could not let them know what kind of aid and protection they might expect to receive. The consequence of which was, that they received no protection whatsoever. The disorder and confusion remained in this state unnoticed till the 22d of July, when the governor moved the council to take

into consideration some measures for restoring vigour and firmness to government, but, on the 29th of July, the council made a reply to what had been proposed to them by the governor, in which they state, "That the disorders, which happened, were occasioned by the violent and unprecedented manner, in which the sloop Liberty had been seized by the officers of the customs."

In consequence of this disorderly state at Boston, two regiments having been sent thither from Halifax, in order to support the execution of the civil power, and preserve the peace of the town, strict orders were given and repeated to the troops not to quarrel with the townsmen, by whom, they complained, they had been frequently ill-treated, and insulted.

On Monday the 5th of March 1768, at nine at night, the alarm bells were rung as in cases of fire, the fire said to be in King-street, and the people thereby led thither; where finding the alarm false, they joined a multitude, who had been braving two companies at the gates of their barrack, and threatened with death the centinel, who was posted at the Custom-house, where the King's treasure was lodged; the centinel, being surrounded, was forced to retreat, and call for aid, which brought Captain Preston, captain of the day, with a party, from the main guard, to extricate him: that officer used his utmost endeavours to prevent mischief, notwithstanding which, the rioters by blows, and every act of aggravation, drew upon themselves the fire of several of the soldiers, by which some persons were unfortunately killed; and, upon the governor's offering to obtain the commanding officer's consent to remove one of the regiments to the castle, and to station the other, so as no opportunity of disputes with the townsmen should remain; the council insisted, that both regiments

regiments fhould go, giving for a reafon, that the people would moft certainly drive out the troops, and that
the inhabitants of other towns would
join with Bofton in it; and feveral
of them declared, that they did not
judge from the general temper of the
people only, but they knew it to be
the determination, not of a mob, but
of the generality of the principal inhabitants; in confequence of which,
both regiments were accordingly removed.

In the petition prefented to the governor by feveral people of confideration, in purfuance of the refolution of
a town meeting held at that time,
they difavow the legiflative authority
of this country, and affert that it
would be better for them to ftruggle
againft it, than tamely to relinquifh
their rights.

And the affembly abfolutely refufed, by a great majority, to refcind
their former order of fending circular
letters to the other colonies, though
they had received a pofitive requifition from the crown to that purpofe.

An affociation was entered into
the beginning of Auguft, when moft
of the merchants of Bofton entered
into, and fubfcribed an agreement,
that they would not fend for, or import, any kind of goods or merchandife, from Great Britain, fome few
articles of neceffity excepted, from
the firft of January 1769, to the
firft of January 1770; and that they
would not import any tea, paper,
glafs, or painters colours, until the
act impofing duties on thofe articles
fhould be repealed.

It was alfo voted, in a town meeting of the freeholders and other inhabitants of Bofton, September 12,
that the levying money within that
province, for the ufe and fervice of
the crown, in other manner than the
fame is granted by the great and ge-

neral court of affembly of the province, was in violation of the faid
royal charter, and the fame was alfo
in violation of the undoubted natural
rights of fubjects, declared in the
aforefaid act of Parliament, (meaning the act of fucceffion) freely to
give and grant their own money for
the fervice of the crown, with their
own confent, in perfon, or by reprefentatives of their own free election.

They alfo voted, that as the Governor did not think proper to call a
general court, for the redrefs of their
(fuppofed) grievances, the town fhould
then make choice of a fuitable number of perfons to act for them, as a
committee in convention, with fuch
as might be fent to join them from
the feveral towns in that province,
in order that fuch meafures might be
confulted and advifed, as his Majefty's fervice, and the peace and
fafety of his fubjects in the province,
might require.

They alfo voted, that there was,
at that time, a prevailing apprehenfion in the minds of many of an approaching war with France, in order
that the inhabitants of that town
might be prepared in cafe of fudden
danger, that thofe of the faid inhabitants who might, at that time, be
unprovided, fhould be, and thereby
were, requefted duly to obferve at
that time the law of the province,
whereby it is required, that every
lifted foldier, and other houfeholder,
(except troopers, who by law are
otherwife to be provided) fhall be always provided with a well-fixed fire-
lock, mufket, accoutrement, and ammunition, as in the faid law is particularly mentioned, to the fatisfaction of the commiffion officers of the
company.

They alfo voted, that a letter
fhould be written to the feveral towns
in the province, as follows.

Gentlemen,

' *Gentlemen,*

' You are already too well acquaint-
' ed with the melancholy, and very
' alarming circumſtances, to which
' this province, as well as America
' in general, is now reduced; taxes,
' equally detrimental to the commer-
' cial intereſt of the parent country
' and her colonies, are impoſed on
' the people without their conſent;
' taxes, deſigned for the ſupport of
' the civil government in the colonies,
' in a manner clearly unconſtitutional,
' and contrary to that, in which, 'till
' of late, government has been ſup-
' ported by the free gift of the people
' in the American Aſſemblies or Par-
' liaments, as alſo for the mainte-
' nance of a large ſtanding army, not
' for the defence of the newly acquir-
' ed territories, but for the old colo-
' nies, and in time of peace. The
' decent, humble, and truly loyal ap-
' plications and petitions from the
' repreſentatives of this province, for
' the redreſs of theſe heavy and very
' threatening grievances, have hi-
' therto been ineffectual; being aſſur-
' ed, from authentic intelligence, that
' they have not yet reached the royal
' ear; the only effect of tranſmitting
' applications, hitherto perceivable,
' has been a mandate, from one of
' his Majeſty's Secretaries of State to
' the governor of this province, to
' diſſolve the general aſſembly, mere-
' ly becauſe the late Houſe of Repre-
' ſentatives refuſed to reſcind a reſolu-
' tion of a former Houſe, which im-
' plied nothing more than a right in
' the American ſubjects to unite in
' humble and dutiful petitions to their
' gracious Sovereign, when they found
' themſelves aggrieved : this is a
' right naturally inherent in every
' man, and expreſsly recognized at
' the glorious revolution as the birth-
' right of an Engliſhman.

' This diſſolution, you are ſenſible,
' has taken place; the governor has

' publicly and repeatedly declared
' that he cannot call another aſſem-
' bly; and the Secretary of State for
' the American department, in one
' of his letters communicated to the
' Houſe, has been pleaſed to ſay,
" that proper care will be taken for
" the ſupport of the dignity of go-
" vernment;" the meaning of which
' is too plain to be miſunderſtood.

' The concern and perplexity into
' which theſe things have thrown the
' people have been greatly aggravated
' by a late declaration of his Excel-
' lency Governor Bernard, that one
' or more regiments may be expected
' in this province.

' The deſign of theſe troops is, in
' every one's apprehenſion, nothing
' ſhort of enforcing, by military
' power, the execution of acts of Par-
' liament, in the forming of which
' the colonies have not, and can not
' have, any conſtitutional influence.
' This is one of the greateſt diſtreſſes
' to which a free people can be re-
' duced.

' The town, which we have the
' honour to ſerve, have taken theſe
' things, at their late meeting, into
' their moſt ſerious conſideration;
' and, as there is in the minds of ma-
' ny a prevailing apprehenſion of an
' approaching war with France, they
' have paſſed the ſeveral votes which
' we tranſmit to you, deſiring that
' they may be immediately laid before
' the town, whoſe prudentials are in
' your care, at a legal meeting, for
' their candid and particular atten-
' tion.

' Deprived of the councils of a ge-
' neral aſſembly in this dark and dif-
' ficult ſeaſon, the loyal people of this
' province will, we are perſuaded,
' immediately perceive the propriety
' and utility of the propoſed com-
' mittee of convention, and the ſound
' and wholeſome advice that may be
' expected from a number of gentle-
' men,

I i

' men, chosen by themselves, and in
' whom they may repose the greatest
' confidence, must tend to the real
' service of our most gracious Sove-
' reign, and the welfare of his sub-
' jects in this province, and may hap-
' pily prevent any sudden and uncon-
' nected measures, which, in their
' present anxiety, and even agony of
' mind, they may be in danger of fal-
' ling into.

' And it is of importance that the
' convention should meet as soon as
' may be; so early a day as the
' twenty-second of this instant Sep-
' tember, has been proposed for that
' purpose;—and it is hoped the re-
' motest towns will, by that time, or
' as soon after as conveniently may
' be, return their respective com-
' mittees.

' Not doubting but you are equally
' concerned with us and our fellow
' citizens, for the preservation of our
' invaluable rights, and for the gene-
' ral happiness of our country, and
' that you are disposed, with equal
' ardour, to exert yourselves, in every
' constitutional way, for so glorious a
' purpose.'

The committee observe, that it
does not appear to them that any
steps were taken to suppress these
measures, or that they were noticed
of, by the council, or any of the
civil magistrates.

The committee think it necessary
here to insert the following extracts.

The first extract is from his Majesty's most gracious Speech from the
throne, on the eighth day of November, 1768.

" At the close of the last Parliament,
I expressed my satisfaction at the ap-
pearances which then induced me
to believe, that such of my subjects
as had been misled in some parts of
my dominions, were returning to a
just sense of their duty; but it is with
equal concern, that I have since seen

that spirit of faction, which I had
hoped was well-nigh extinguished,
breaking out afresh in some of my colonies in North America, and in one
of them proceeding even to acts of
violence, and of resistance to the execution of the law; the capital town
of which colony appears, by late advices, to be in a state of disobedience
to all law and government, and has
proceeded to measures subversive of
the constitution, and attended with
circumstances that manifest a disposition to throw off their dependence on
Great Britain. On my part, I have
pursued every measure that appeared
to be necessary for supporting the
constitution, and inducing a due obedience to the authority of the legislature; you may rely upon my steady
perseverance in these purposes, and I
doubt not but that, with your concurrence and support, I shall be able
to defeat the mischievous designs of
those turbulent and seditious persons,
who, under false pretences, have but
too successfully deluded numbers of
my subjects in America, and whose
practices, if suffered to prevail, cannot fail to produce the most fatal consequences to my colonies immediately,
and, in the end, to all the dominions
of my crown."

The second extract is from your
Lordship's dutiful address to his Majesty, on his said most gracious Speech.

" We feel the most sincere concern, that any of our fellow subjects
in North America should be misled
by factious and designing men, into
acts of violence, and of resistance to
the execution of the law; attended
with circumstances that manifest a
disposition to throw off their dependence upon Great Britain. At the
same time, that we shall be always
ready to contribute to the relief of
any real grievance of your Majesty's
American subjects, we most unfeign-
edly gave your Majesty the strongest
assurances,

affurances, that we fhall ever zealoufly concur in fupport of fuch juft and neceffary meafures, as may beft enable your Majefty to reprefs that daring fpirit of difobedience, and to enforce a due fubmiffion to the laws; always confidering, that it is one of our moft effential duties to maintain inviolate the fupreme authority of the legiflature of Great Britain over every part of the dominions of your Majefty's crown."

The third extract is from his Majefty's moft gracious anfwer to your Lordfhip's addrefs.

"Your zealous concurrence in every meafure, that can bring relief to my people, is well known to me; nor do I doubt of the attention that you will always give to any real grievances of my American fubjects. The ftrong affurances I receive from you, at the fame time of your determination to vindicate the juft legiflative authority of Parliament, over all the dominions of my crown, deferve my warmeft approbation."

The committee find, that, on the fifteenth of November, the Lord Harwich acquainted the Houfe, that he had received his Majefty's commands to lay before the Houfe papers relating to the late difturbances in America; and that the fame would be laid before the Houfe in a few days.

That accordingly, on the twenty-eighth of November, the Lord Harwich laid before the Houfe, copies of all letters, &c. relating to the late proceedings of the colony of the Maffachufetts-Bay, together with a lift thereof, which was read by the clerk.

That on the fifteenth of December, the Houfe came to the following refolutions:

I. Refolved, by the Lords Spiritual and Temporal, in Parliament affembled, that the votes, refolutions, and proceedings, of the Houfe of Repre-

fentatives of Maffachufetts-Bay, in the month of January and February laft, refpecting feveral late acts of Parliament, fo far as the faid votes, refolutions, and proceedings, do import a denial of, or to draw into queftion, the power and authority of his Majefty, by and with the advice and confent of the Lords Spiritual and Temporal, and Commons, in Parliament affembled, to make laws and ftatutes of fufficient force and validity, to bind the colonies and people of America, fubjects to the Crown of Great Britain, in all cafes whatfoever, are illegal, unconftitutional, and derogatory of the rights of the Crown and Parliament of Great Britain.

II. Refolved, by the Lords Spiritual and Temporal, in Parliament affembled, that the refolution of the faid Houfe of Reprefentatives of the province of Maffachufetts-Bay, in January laft, to write letters to the feveral Houfes of Reprefentatives of the Britifh colonies in the continent, defiring them to join with the faid Houfe of Reprefentatives of the province of Maffachufetts-Bay, in petitions, which do deny or draw into queftion the right of Parliament to impofe duties and taxes upon his Majefty's fubjects in America; and, in purfuance of the faid refolution, the writing fuch letters, in which certain late acts of Parliament, impofing duties and taxes, are ftated to be infringements of the rights of his Majefty's fubjects of the faid province, are proceedings of a moft unwarrantable and dangerous nature, calculated to inflame the minds of his Majefty's fubjects in the other colonies, tending to create unlawful combinations repugnant to the laws of Great Britain, and fubverfive of the conftitution.

III. Refolved, by the Lords Spiritual and Temporal, in Parliament affembled

fembled, that it appears, that the town of Bofton, in the province of Maffachufetts-Bay, has, for fome time paft, been in a ftate of great diforder and confufion; and that the peace of the faid town has, at feveral times, been difturbed by riots and tumults of a dangerous nature, in which the officers of his Majefty's revenue there have been obftructed by acts of violence, in the execution of the laws, and their lives endangered.

IV. Refolved, by the Lords Spiritual and Temporal, in Parliament affembled, that it appears, that neither the council of the faid province of Maffachufetts-Bay, nor the ordinary civil Magiftrates, did exert their authority for fuppreffing the faid riots and tumults.

V. Refolved, by the Lords Spiritual and Temporal, in Parliament affembled, that, in thefe circumftances of the province of the Maffachufetts-Bay, and of the town of Bofton, the prefervation of the public peace, and the due execution of the laws, became impracticable, without the aid of a military force to fupport and protect the civil Magiftrates, and the officers of his Majefty's revenue.

VI. Refolved, by the Lords Spiritual and Temporal, in Parliament affembled, that the declarations, refolutions, and proceedings, in the town meeting at Bofton, on the fourteenth of June, and twelfth of September, were illegal and unconftitutional, and calculated to excite fedition and infurrections in his Majefty's province of Maffachufetts-Bay.

VII. Refolved, by the Lords Spiritual and Temporal, in Parliament affembled, that the appointment at the town meeting, on the twelfth of September, of a convention to be held in the town of Bofton, on the twenty-fecond of that month, to confift of deputies from the feveral towns and diftricts in the province of the Maffachufetts Bay, and the iffuing a pre-

cept, by the felectmen of the town of Bofton, to each of the faid towns and diftricts, for the election of fuch deputies, were proceedings fubverfive of his Majefty's government, and evidently manifefting a defign, in the inhabitants of the faid town of Bofton, to fet up a new and unconftitutional authority, independent of the crown of Great Britain.

VIII. Refolved, by the Lords Spiritual and Temporal, in Parliament affembled, that the elections, by feveral towns and diftricts in the province of Maffachufetts-Bay, of deputies to fit in the fame convention, and the meeting of fuch convention in confequence thereof, were daring infults offered to his Majefty's authority, and audacious ufurpations of the powers of government.

It was then ordered, that an humble addrefs be prefented to his Majefty, to return his Majefty thanks for the communication which he has been gracioufly pleafed to make to his Parliament, of feveral papers relative to public tranfactions in his Majefty's province of Maffachufetts-Bay.

To exprefs our fincere fatisfaction in the meafures which his Majefty has purfued for fupporting the conftitution, and inducing a due obedience to the authority of the legiflature.

To give his Majefty the ftrongeft affurances, that we will effectually ftand by and fupport his Majefty in fuch further meafures, as may be found neceffary to maintain the civil Magiftrates, in a due execution of the laws, within his Majefty's province of Maffachufetts-Bay.

And as we conceive, that nothing can be more immediately neceffary, either for the maintenance of his Majefty's authority in the faid province, or for the guarding his Majefty's fubjects therein from being further deluded by the arts of wicked and

and defigning men, than to proceed, in the moft fpeedy and effectual manner, for bringing to condign punifhment the chief authors and inftigators of the late diforders, to befeech his Majefty, that he will be gracioufly pleafed to direct his Majefty's governor of Maffachufetts-Bay, to take the moft effectual methods for procuring the fulleft information that can be obtained touching all treafons, or mifprifion of treafon, committed within his government fince the thirtieth of December laft, and to tranfmit the fame, together with the names of the perfons who were moft active in the commiffion of fuch offences, to one of his Majefty's principal Secretaries of State, in order that his Majefty may iffue a fpecial commiffion for enquiring of, hearing and determining the faid offences, within this realm, purfuant to the provifions of the ftatute of the thirty-fifth year of the reign of King Henry the Eighth, if his Majefty fhall, upon receiving the faid information, fee fufficient ground for fuch a proceeding.

And a meffage was fent to the Houfe of Commons, to carry down the faid refolutions and addrefs, and defire their concurrence thereto.

On the twentieth of January, 1769, the Lord Harwich, (by his Majefty's command) laid before the Houfe more copies of letters relating to America, which were ordered to lie on the table.

On the 9th of February, the refolutions and addrefs, fent to the Commons on the 15th of December laft, for their concurrence, were returned, agreed to, with fome amendments, which were read and agreed to, and notice thereof fent to the Commons; and the faid addrefs was ordered to be prefented to his Majefty by both Houfes.

On the 14th of February, the Lord Chancellor reported his Majefty's anfwer to the faid addrefs, as follows:

My Lords, and Gentlemen,

" The fincere fatisfaction you exprefs in the meafures which I have already taken, and the ftrong affurances you give of fupporting me in thofe which may be neceffary to maintain the juft legiflative authority, and the due execution of the laws in my province of Maffachufetts-Bay, give me great pleafure.

" I fhall not fail to give thofe orders which you recommend, as the moft effectual method of bringing the authors of the late unhappy diforders in that province to condign punifhment."

Which addrefs and anfwer were ordered to be printed.

It doth not appear to the committee, that the cenfure of the proceedings in the province of Maffachufetts-Bay, and of the conduct of the council and other civil magiftrates, expreffed by both Houfes of Parliament in their refolutions, and their approbation of the meafure of fending troops thither, to fupport and protect the magiftrates, and the officers of the revenue, produced the good effect that might reafonably have been hoped for; a difpofition to deny the authority, and refift the laws, of the fupreme legiflature, continued ftill to prevail, not only in flagitious publications in the daily news-papers, but alfo in a variety of violent and unwarrantable refolutions and proceedings of thofe merchants and others, who had fubfcribed to the agreements for non-importation of goods from Great-Britain.

Meetings of the affociators were reprefented to have been held in as regular a manner as any other meeting authorifed by the conftitution. Committees were appointed to examine the cargoes of all veffels arriving from
Great-

Great-Britain, and regular votes and resolutions of censure were passed in those meetings, upon all such as refused to concur in those unlawful associations; their names were published in the public news papers, as enemies to their country; and the mandates and decrees of those committees met with a respect and obedience denied to the constitutional authority of government.

In some cases goods imported from Great-Britain, were locked up in warehouses, under the care of these committees, in order to prevent their being sold; and, in one or two instances, they were re-shipped to Great Britain.

On the 31st of May, 1769, the general court met at the court-house at Boston, pursuant to his Majesty's writs, and the first step the assembly took, before they proceeded on any other business, was to send a message to the governor, asserting, that the having ships in the harbour, and troops in the town of Boston, was inconsistent with their dignity and freedom; and therefore, that they had a right to expect, that he would give orders for the removal of the forces by sea and land from that port, and from the gates of the city, during the session of the assembly; and, at the same time, the House came to several resolutions to the same effect, as the declarations contained in their message to the governor.

The governor having, in reply to their message, acquainted them, that he had no authority over his Majesty's ships in that port, or his troops in that town, nor could give any orders for the removal of them, they then proceeded to the election of counsellors, in which election, not only the lieutenant-governor, and other officers of government were excluded, but also several other gentlemen, who

had been of the former council, and who (the governor represents) shewed a disposition to support the King's government, to acknowledge the authority of parliament, and to preserve the people from a democratical despotism, and were otherwise distinguished by their integrity and ability.

On the 13th of June, the assembly sent an answer to the governor's message of the 31st of May, in which he had told them he had no authority over the King's ships, or troops.

In this answer they assert, that, " By the principles of the constitution, the governor of that colony has the absolute military command; that the sending a military force there, to enforce the execution of the laws, is inconsistent with the nature of government, and the spirit of a free constitution; that the unwillingness of a people in general that a law should be executed, was strong presumption of its being an unjust law; that it could not be *their* law, as the people must consent to laws before they can be obliged, in conscience, to obey them."

It appears, by a vote of the assembly, on the 8th of July, that they have declared, that all trials for treason, misprision of treason, or for any felony, or crime whatever, committed or done in that colony, ought, of right, to be had and conducted within the courts of the colony; and that the seizing any person or persons, residing in that colony, suspected of any crime whatsoever committed therein, and sending such person or persons to places beyond the sea to be tried, is highly derogatory of the rights of British subjects, as thereby the inestimable privilege of being tried by a jury from vicinage, as well as the liberty of summoning and producing witnesses on such trial, will be taken away from the party accused.

On the 6th of April 1770, a bill was brought up from the House of Com-

Commons to your Lordſhips, intituled, "An act to repeal ſo much of an act, made in the ſeventh year of his preſent Majeſty's reign, intituled, "An act for granting certain duties in the Britiſh colonies and plantations in America, for allowing a drawback of the duties of cuſtoms, upon the exportation from this kingdom, of coffee and cocoa nuts, of the produce of the ſaid colonies or plantations; for diſcontinuing the drawbacks payable on china earthen ware, exported to America, and for more effectually preventing the clandeſtine running of goods in the ſaid colonies and plantations;" as relates to the duties upon glaſs, red lead, white lead, painters colours, paper, paſteboards, millboards, and ſcaleboards, of the produce or manufacture of Great Britain, imported into any of his Majeſty's colonies in America; and alſo to the diſcontinuing the drawbacks payable on china earthen ware exported to America, and for regulating the exportation thereof."

Which bill received the royal aſſent on the 12th of April.

On the 30th of April it was ordered, That an humble addreſs ſhould be preſented to his Majeſty, that he would be graciouſly pleaſed to give directions, that there be laid before this Houſe copies of all narratives of any diſputes or diſturbances which have happened between his Majeſty's troops, ſtationed in North America, and the inhabitants of any of his Majeſty's colonies there, ſince the 24th day of June laſt, received by the commiſſioners of his Majeſty's treaſury, any of his Majeſty's ſecretaries of ſtate, or any other public offices, together with copies of all orders and inſtructions ſent to the governors, lieutenant-governors, deputy governors, preſidents of the council of any of his Majeſty's colonies in North America, or to the commander in chief of his Majeſty's

forces, or any officer, civil or military, within the ſame, relative to ſuch diſputes or diſturbances.

And that on the 4th of May, the Lord Harwich, by his Majeſty's command, laid before the Houſe ſeveral papers relative to the late diſturbances in America, purſuant to an addreſs to his Majeſty for that purpoſe, on the 30th of April laſt, together with a liſt thereof, which were ordered to lie on the table.

The committee find, That on the 7th of May, the Lord Harwich laid before the Houſe, by his Majeſty's command, a narrative of the late tranſactions at Boſton, and the caſe of Captain Thomas Preſton, of the 29th regiment of foot, which had been tranſmitted to his Lordſhip from the War-office; and the ſame were ordered to lie on the table.

On the 14th of May, it was ordered, That an humble addreſs ſhould be preſented to his Majeſty, that he would be graciouſly pleaſed to give directions that there be laid before this Houſe copies of the Earl of Hillſborough's letter of the 13th of May 1769, to the governors of the ſeveral colonies of North America, together with the ſpeeches of the governors referring to the ſaid letter, and the anſwers of the aſſemblies to the ſame, ſo far as they have been received.

And, on the 15th, the Lord Harwich laid before the Houſe, by his Majeſty's command, copies of the Earl of Hillſborough's letter of the 13th of May 1769, to the governors of the ſeveral colonies of North America, together with the ſpeeches of the governors referring to the ſaid letter; and the anſwers of the aſſemblies to the ſame, ſo far as they have been received, together with a liſt thereof, which were ordered to lie on the table; and the ſame, with the other America papers preſented in this ſeſſion, were alſo ordered to be taken

into

into confideration on Friday next, and the Lords fummoned.

The committee find, by lieutenant governor Hutchinfon's letter, of the 27th of March 1770, that when the troops were in the town, the commiffioners of the cuftoms were fenfible they could have no dependence upon them; for if any riot had happened, no civil magiftrate, that he knew, would have employed them in fuppreffing it; thofe who from a principle would have been difpofed to it, refufing, and giving this reafon, that they muft immediately after have left the country; and that juft the fame principles prevailed with refpect to the troops which were faid to be unconftitutional, although eftablifhed by an act of parliament, it being alledged that it was an act which did not bind colonifts.

Lieutenant-Governor Hutchinfon, in his letter to the Earl of Hillfborough, April the twenty-feventh, 1770, complains, "That he has never been able to obtain the advice or confent of the council, to any propofal made for the difcountenancing the ufurpation of the powers of government by the town of Bofton; that he had ufed the negative powers given him by charter, in excluding Mr. Hancock from being Speaker *pro tempore*, and Mr. Cufhing from the office of commiffary general, to which offices they had been elected;" but adds, " That this was doing but little, as he could not remove any of thofe who were actually in office, fome of whom were more inflammatory than any out of office." He further fays, " That they were then attempting to compel all the importers of what they call the contraband goods, to fend them back, and that he was not fure they would not fucceed: that all goods which they have not enumerated, are called contraband. That tea from Holland may

lawfully be fold: that it is a high crime to fell any from England: that Mr. Hancock offered to fend one or more of his fhips back, and to lofe the freight: that feveral of the importers pleaded, that they fhould be utterly ruined; but that the Bofton zealots had no bowels; and gave for anfwer, that if a fhip was to bring in the plague, nobody would doubt what was neceffary to be done with her; but the prefent cafe is much worfe than that. In the fame letter, the Lieutenant-Governor obferves, that the Bofton principles obtain more and more in the remote parts of the province, and the reprefentatives of feven-eighths of the town appear, in the prefent feffion, to be favourers of the nonimportation meafures: that their internal diftreffes may, in a courfe of years, force them to defift; but that the diftrefs at prefent, and it may be for fome time to come, lies principally upon the friends to government, who run the rifk of importing goods, and then are compelled by the ruling powers to keep them unfold, or to fhip them back: that he made an attempt that day to prevail upon a merchant of the firft eftate and character, to induce him to promote an affociation, but to no purpofe; and that he gave him for anfwer, that until Parliament made provifion for the punifhment of the confederacies, all would be ineffectual, and the affociates would be expofed to popular rage." He obferved further, " That the laft year, when the King's Speech, and the addreffes of the Lords, and of the Houfe of Commons, firft came to them, the heads of the oppofition were ftruck with terror, and the feditious news-paper writers laid afide their pens for five or fix weeks; but as foon as the apprehenfion of vigorous meafures ceafed, their fears were over, and they

became

became more assuming and tyranni-
cal than before; and although the
terror was not so great the present
year, yet it was visible; but now
that they expect nothing will be
done, they are recovering their spirits, knowing there is no power
within the government to restrain
them.

The resistance to the custom-house
officers still continued to manifest itself upon every occasion; in consequence of which, on the eighteenth
of May 1770, a tidesman of the customs, who had seized a small coast-
ing vessel, belonging to Connecticut,
and a few casks of sugar, for breach
of the acts of trade, in the evening,
was seized, stripped, and carted a-
bout the town, for three or four
hours, besmeared with tar, and then
covered with feathers, and followed
by a great number of disorderly people.

The committee do not find, in
your Lordships journals of the years
1771 and 1772, any material proceedings relative to the matters to
them referred.

Though, in the year 1771, things
remained tolerably quiet in the province of Massachusetts-Bay, yet the
disposition to disavow the authority
of Parliament occasionally broke out
in the House of Assembly and town
meetings; accordingly, in an answer
from the House of Representatives,
to a message from the Governor, on
the fifth of July 1771, they say, that
" They know of no commissioners of
his Majesty's customs, nor of any revenue his Majesty has a right to establish in North America; that they
know and feel a tribute levied and
extorted from those who, if they have
property, have a right to the absolute
disposal of it."

At the same time the disposition
to import goods, in defiance of the
laws of revenue and trade, and to

support such iniquitous practices by
insults and open violences upon the
officers, whose duty it is to carry the
said laws into execution, broke out
upon many occasions; and, as usual,
the magistrates declined giving their
assistance and support, though applied
to for that purpose, which appears
in the case of Arthur Savage, comptroller of his Majesty's customs at Falmouth, who was forcibly taken out
of his house in the night, by several
persons disguised, and armed with
pistols, and other dangerous wea-
pons, who put him in the utmost
danger of his life, and not only obliged him to divulge the name of
the person who had lodged an information, but also to swear the truth
of his information; declaring at the
same time, that if he discovered who
they were, they would take his life;
and that, upon his application to the
justices, who were then sitting, they
declined the examination of the evidence he brought to prove the fact.

Things remained much in the same
state in the year 1772; the continued
ill temper of the people at Boston,
was manifested by their instructions
to their Representatives.

Upon the news of his Majesty's
granting salaries to the justices of the
superior court, the most inflammatory
pieces were published in the news-
papers, and the selectmen of Boston
ordered a meeting to consider of measures upon that occasion, which meeting voted an address to the Governor, in which they say, " That the
freeholders and other inhabitants of
the town of Boston, legally assembled in Faneuil Hall, beg leave to acquaint his Excellency, that a report
has prevailed, which they have reason to apprehend is well grounded;
that stipends are affixed to the offices
of the judges of the superior court of
judicature, &c. of this province,
whereby they are become indepen-
K k   dent

dent of the grants of the general assembly for their support; contrary to the ancient and invariable usage."

" That this report has spread an alarm among all considerate persons who have heard of it, in town and country, being viewed as tending rapidly to compleat the system of their slavery, which originated in the House of Commons of Great Britain, assuming a power and authority to give and grant the monies of the colonists without their consent, and against their repeated remonstrances. And as the judges hold their places during pleasure, this establishment appears big with fatal evils, so obvious that it is needless to trespass on your Excellency's time, in mentioning them."

The town meeting afterwards appointed a committee of correspondence, to write circular letters to all the towns in the province, to induce them to unite in measures upon that occasion, which committee met the second of November, 1772, and made a report, containing several resolutions, contradictory to the supremacy of the British legislature: and, after setting forth, that all men have a right to remain in a state of nature as long as they please, they proceed to draw a report upon the natural rights of the colonists as men, christians and subjects, and from a list of infringements and violations of their rights; one of the first of which contains an assertion, that the British Parliament have assumed the powers of legislation for the colonies, in all cases whatsoever, without obtaining the consent of the inhabitants, which is ever essentially necessary to the rightful establishment of such a legislature.

They also consider it as an infringement of their rights, that a number of new officers, unknown to the charter, have been appointed to superintend the revenues, whereas the great and general court, or assembly of that province, had the sole right of appointing all civil officers, the election and constitution of whom is, in the said charter, expressly excepted, among whom these officers are not included.

They likewise complain of it as a grievance, that his Majesty has been pleased to apply 1500l. sterling annually, out of the American revenue, for the support of the government of this province, independent of the assembly, and that the judges of the Superior court, as also the King's Attorney and Solicitor General, are to receive their support from what they call this grievous tribute, which they say will, if accomplished, compleat their slavery.

Six hundred copies of this report were circulated in the towns of the province, with a pathetic letter addressed to the inhabitants, who are called upon not to doze any longer, or sit supinely in indifference, whilst the iron hand of oppression is daily tearing the choicest fruits from the fair tree of liberty.

On the sixth of May, a message was brought from the House of Commons to your Lordships, with a Bill, intituled, " An act to allow a drawback of the duties of customs, on the exportation of tea, to any of his Majesty's colonies or plantations in America, to increase the deposit on bohea tea, to be sold at the East India Company's sales, and to impower the commissioners of the treasury, to grant licences to the East India Company to export tea, duty-free," which Bill received the Royal Assent on the tenth of May.

It appears to the committee, in the answer of the council to the Governor's Speech, at the opening of the session, that they declare they are of opi-

opinion, that the Parliament cannot conftitutionally levy taxes, in any form, on his Majefty's fubjects in that province.

And the Houfe of Reprefentatives, upon the fame occafion, declare, that if there had been, in any late inftances, a fubmiffion to acts of Parliament, it has been, in their opinion, rather from inconfideration, or a reluctance at the idea of contending with the parent ftate, than from a conviction or acknowledgement of the fupreme legiflative authority of Parliament.

The committee of correfpondence appear to have ufed their utmoft endeavours to work up the minds of the people, not only of their own, but alfo of the fouthern governments, to prevent the importation of teas from the Eaft India Company; and accordingly, on the third of November, 1773, a mob, of about five hundred perfons committed feveral outrageous acts of violence, againft the perfons to whom it was fufpected the tea in queftion would be configned, infifting that they fhould engage and promife not to receive or fell it; that if they did, they would be voted enemies to their country, and muft expect to be treated as fuch hereafter. They then forced open the doors of the ware-houfes of Mr. Clark, and tore them off the hinges, and entered with great violence, attempting to force their way up to the compting-houfe, but were driven back by the perfons who were in it.

A committee then of the freeholders, and other inhabitants, attended Meffieurs Thompfon and Elifha Hutchinfon, fuppofed to be two of the confignees, and requefted them to refign their appointment; and upon their refufing, voted their anfwer unfatisfactory. Governor Hutchinfon did every thing in his power, without the council, for the prefervation of the peace and good order of the town, and thought, that if he had had the aid the council might have given, his endeavours would have been more effectual.

On the 17th of November, 1773, a large number of people befet the houfe of Mr. Hutchinfon, but not finding him at home, proceeded to Mr. Clarke's, another of the confignees, where they committed great diforders, broke the glaffes and frames of the windows, and did confiderable damage. After this riot, the Governor immediately fummoned a council, and laid before them the neceffity of fome meafures being taken, but the council declined advifing or directing any meafures for landing the tea, fuggefting that they then would, of courfe, advife to a meafure for procuring the payment of the duty, and therefore be advifing to a meafure inconfiftent with the declared fentiment of both Houfes, in the laft winter feffion of the general court, which they apprehend to be altogether inexpedient and improper.

After the arrival of a fhip loaded with tea, a meeting of the people of Bofton, and the neighbouring towns, was held on the 29th of November, and continued, by adjournment, till next day, when a motion was made and agreed to, nem. con. that the tea fhould not only be fent back, but that no duty fhould be paid thereon.

It was alfo voted, nem. con. that Mr. Rotch, owner of the veffel, and Captain Hall, the mafter of the fhip, at their peril, fhould not fuffer any of the tea to be landed. It was alfo voted, That Governor Hutchinfon's conduct, in requefting the Juftices of peace to meet to fupprefs all riots and unlawful affemblies, carried a defigned reflection upon the people there met, and was folely calculated to ferve the views of adminiftration. They afterwards voted, that the tea brought by Captain Hall fhould be returned by Mr. Rotch to England, in the fame bottom in which it came. It was alfo voted, *nem. con.* That fix perfons fhould be appointed to give due notice to the towns in the country; when they fhould be required fo to do upon any important occafion.

They alfo refolved, That if any perfon or perfons fhould, hereafter, import any tea from Great Britain, or if any mafter or mafters of any veffels in Great Britain fhould take the fame on board, to be imported to that place, until the faid unrighteous act fhould be repealed, he or they fhould be deemed, by that body, an enemy to his country; and that they would prevent the landing and fale of the fame, and the payment of any duty thereon; and that they would effect the return thereof to the place from whence it came.

They alfo refolved, That thefe their votes be printed and fent to England, and all the fea ports in the province. Before they feparated, they voted, that their brethren in the country fhould be defired to give their affiftance, upon the firft notice that fhould be given.

After the diffolution of this affembly of the people, what is called the committee of correfpondence called in committees of other towns, or other perfons to join with them; kept up a military watch and guard every night, to prevent the landing any teas; and appeared to be the executioners of the refolves, and orders, paffed at the aforefaid affembly.

The Configuees having retired to the caftle, the owner of the firft fhip that arrived was the principal perfon applied to; and he was fent for repeatedly by thefe committees, and was frequently required to fend back the fhip with the teas. He pleaded, that he could not obtain a clearance at the cuftom houfe, nor a pafs for

the caftle; and that if he fhould be able to get the fhip out of the harbour, both fhip and cargo would be forfeited in every part of the King's dominions. This was not thought fatisfactory, and the next morning, another affembly of the people met, and chofe a moderator. At this meeting it was determined that Mr. Rotch, the owner of the fhip, fhould demand, at the cuftom-houfe, a clearance of the teas for England, which was done the 15th, when the collector and comptroller refufed to grant it.

He then was obliged to demand a permit from the naval office to pafs the caftle; afterwards he was fent to the governor to apply to him for the permit, who foon fatisfied him that no permit could be granted, until the veffel was regularly cleared: he returned to town that evening, and reported this anfwer to the meeting. Immediately whereupon, numbers of the people cried out, *a mob! a mob!* left the houfe, repaired to the wharfs, where three of the veffels lay a-ground, having on board 340 chefts of tea, and in two hours time it was totally deftroyed; a fufficient number of people for doing the work,were difguifed, and thefe were furrounded by numbers, as well of the inhabitants of Bofton as of other towns.

The committee obferves that many perfons of confideration in the town of Bofton took the lead in the proceedings of this meeting, for whofe names they beg leave to refer your Lordfhips to the papers themfelves.

On the 4th of March 1774, the Earl of Dartmouth acquainted the Houfe, that his Majefty had given directions, That the feveral papers received from America relating to the difturbances there, with regard to the importation of tea, fhould be laid before the Houfe, and that the fame would be delivered on Monday next.   The

The Earl of Dartmouth acquainted the Houfe, That he had a meffage from his Majefty, under his royal fign manual, which his Majefty had commanded him to deliver to this Houfe; and the fame was read by the Lord Chancellor, and is as follows, viz.

GEORGE R.

"His Majefty, upon information of the unwarrantable practices which had been lately concerted and carried on in North America, and particularly of the violent and outrageous proceedings at the town and port of Bofton, in the province of Maffachufetts-Bay, with a view to obftructing the commerce of this kingdom, and upon grounds and pretences immediately fubverfive of the conftitution thereof, hath thought fit to lay the whole matter before his two Houfes of Parliament, fully confiding as well in their zeal for the maintenance of his Majefty's authority, as in their attachment to the common intereft and welfare of all his dominions, that they will not only enable his Majefty effectually to take fuch meafures as may be moft likely to put an immediate ftop to the prefent diforders, but will alfo take into their moft ferious confideration what farther regulations and permanent provifions may be neceffary to be eftablifhed, for better fecuring the execution of the laws, and the juft dependence of the colonies upon the crown and parliament of Great Britain."

G. R.

The Earl of Dartmouth alfo (by his Majefty's command) laid before the Houfe copies of all letters, &c. received from North America, relating to the difturbances there, with regard to the importation of tea, together with a lift thereof.

It was ordered, That an humble addrefs be prefented to his Majefty, to return his Majefty the thanks of this Houfe, for his Majefty's gracious meffage, and for the communication his Majefty hath been gracioufly pleafed to make to this Houfe, of feveral papers relative to the prefent ftate of fome of his Majefty's colonies in North America.

To affure his Majefty that this Houfe, truly fenfible that the peace and good government of the colonies, and the preventing any obftructions there to the commerce of this kingdom, are objects of their moft ferious attention, will enter upon the confideration of thefe papers with an earneft defire to make fuch provifions as, upon mature deliberation, fhall appear neceffary and expedient for fecuring the juft dependence of the faid colonies upon the crown and parliament of Great Britain, and for enforcing a due obedience to the laws of this kingdom throughout all his Majefty's dominions: and the faid papers, and his Majefty's moft gracious fpeech, were likewife ordered to be taken into confideration on Thurfday fevennight; and the Lords fummoned.

On the 11th of March, the Earl of Dartmouth (by his Majefty's command) laid before the Houfe more papers from America, relating to the difturbances there, with regard to the importation of tea, together with a lift thereof; and the fame was read, and ordered to lie on the table, and to be taken into confideration on Thurfday next.

On the 26th of March, a meffage was brought from the Houfe of Commons, with a bill, entituled, "An act to difcontinue, in fuch manner, and for fuch time, as are therein mentioned, the landing and difcharging, lading, or fhipping, of goods, wares, and merchandife, at the town, and within the harbour of Bofton, in the province of Maffachufetts-Bay, in North America.

Oa

On the 28th of March, a petition of Mr. Sayer and others, natives of America, was prefented and read, praying, that the faid bill may not pafs into a law, which was ordered to lie on the table. Then the Houfe took into confideration the feveral papers, and his Majefty's moft gracious meffage; and the faid bill was read a fecond time, and committed.

On the 30th of March, a petition of William Bolland, Efq; agent for the council of the province of Maffachufetts-Bay, was prefented to the Houfe and read; he was called in, and heard at the Bar; and being withdrawn, the faid bill was read a third time, and paffed *nem. diff.* and received the Royal affent on the following day.

It appears to the committee, that, on the 25th of January, a great number of rioters in the town of Bofton, committed a moft inhuman act of violence upon the perfon of John Malcom, a preventive officer for the port of Falmouth in Cafcobay, who had lately feized a veffel in that port for want of a regifter: no complaint of irregularity was made againft him; but it was thought proper, by the above rioters, to punifh him by tarring and feathering him, (but without ftripping him) and carrying him about in derifion. This unfortunate man having afterwards been frequently hooted at in the ftreets was provoked, on the 25th, by a tradefman, who, he alledged, had feveral times before affronted him, to ftrike him with his cane, in confequence of which a warrant was iffued againft him; but the conftable not being able to find him, a mob gathered about his houfe in the evening, and having broke his windows, he pufhed thro' the broken windows with his fword, and gave a flight fcratch to one of the affailants; foon after which the mob entered his

houfe, lowered him by a rope from an upper chamber into a cart, tore his cloaths off, tarred his head and body, feathered him, and dragged him through the main ftreet into King ftreet, from thence to Liberty Tree, and from thence, to the Neck, as far as the gallows, where they whipped him, beat him with fticks, and threatened to hang him. Having kept him under the gallows above an hour, they carried him back in the fame manner to the extremity of the north end of the town, and returned him to his own houfe, and fo benumbed by the cold, having been naked near four hours, and fo bruifed, that his life was defpaired of. It appears that none but the loweft clafs of the people were fufpected of having been concerned in it, and that Mr. Malcom having for fome time before been threatened by the populace with revenge for his free and open declarations againft the late proceedings, had occafionally, indifcreetly, given them provocation.

The Houfe of Reprefentatives of Maffachufetts-Bay, on the firft of February, required the Chief Juftice Oliver, and the four judges of the Superior Court, to declare, whether they would receive the grants of affembly for their falaries, or accept their fuppport from the crown, and were anfwered by the four judges (they being fearful of making themfelves objects of popular refentment, one of their number having been previoufly brought over to that confent), that they would receive their falaries from the province; but by the Chief Juftice, that he would continue to accept his fupport from the crown: on the 11th of February, they remonftrated to the Governor, that the faid Chief Juftice Peter Oliver, having received his falary and reward out of the revenue unjuftly and unconftitutionally levied and extorted

torted from the American colonies, and being determined to continue to receive it contrary to the known sense of the body of people of the province, had thereby proved himself an enemy to its constitution, placed himself under an undue bias, and rendered himself disqualified to hold his office any longer. And not having procured his removal from the governor, in consequence of their remonstrance, they passed a vote to adjourn the superior court, which by law, is to be held on the 15th of February, to the 22d of that month, to which the governor refused his assent; and complains, that he now considers himself as acting altogether on the defensive, avoiding his consent where he cannot justify it, destitute of any aid from any part of the legislature, or executive powers of government, in maintaining order when the breach of it is caused, or pretended to be caused, by such acts of parliament, or such exercise of his Majesty's authority, as the people are taught by their leaders to call grievances.

A true state of the proceedings in the Parliament of Great-Britain, and in the province of the Massachusetts-Bay, relative to the giving and granting the money of the people of that province, and of all America, in the House of Commons, in which they are not represented. Drawn up by Dr. BENJAMIN FRANKLIN.

On the 12th of November 1761, Governor Bernard made the following speech to both Houses of Assembly, in the province of Massachusetts-Bay:

"At the opening of this general court I had the pleasure to observe upon the happy and propitious circumstances that had attended the commencement of the present reign, and particularly the extinction of parties, and the general coalition of all parties in support of his Majesty's govern-

ment; and I could not but express my earnest desire that the same patriotic spirit which influenced Great Britain, might prevail throughout his Majesty's American provinces, and especially in this most ancient and most loyal of them.

"I was well persuaded, that while I was speaking to you on this subject, your sentiments and mine were the same. I have been fully confirmed in this, as well by your own declarations, as by your conduct consequent thereto; and I have now all the assurance that I shall be assisted and supported by you.

F. BERNARD."

On the 24th of April 1762, his Excellency made the following speech to the two Houses:

"The unanimity and dispatch with which you have complied with the requisitions of his Majesty require my particular acknowledgment, and it gives me additional pleasure to observe, that you have therein acted under no other influence than a due sense of your duty, both as members of a general empire, and as the body of a particular province.

"It will always be my desire that freedom and independence should prevail in your councils, and that the whole credit of your proceedings therein should be placed to your own account. It will be a sufficient honour for me to preside over a people whose motives to loyalty and public spirit arise from their own breasts.

FRA. BERNARD."

His Excellency again spoke as follows to the two Houses of Assembly on the 27th of May 1762:

"Whatever shall be the event of the war, it must be no small satisfaction to us, that this province hath contributed its full share to the support of it. Every thing that has been required of it hath been most readily complied with; and the execution

cution of the powers committed to me, for raising the provincial troops, hath been as full and complete as the grant of them was. Never before were regiments so easily levied, so well composed, and so early in the field, as they have been this year; the common people seemed to be animated with the spirit of the general court, and to vie with them in their readiness to serve the King.

" The ample provision which has been already made, leaves me nothing to ask for the immediate service of the King.

FRA. BERNARD."

The following is a true copy of the message which his Majesty sent down to the House of Commons every year, from 1759, till the conclusion of the war:

GEORGE Rex.
26° Die April's 1759°.

" His Majesty being sensible of the zeal and vigour with which his faithful subjects in North America have exerted themselves in defence of his Majesty's just rights and possessions, recommends it to this House to take the same into consideration, and to enable his Majesty to give them a proper compensation for the expences incurred by the respective provinces, in the levying, clothing, and pay of the troops raised by the same, according as the active vigour and strenuous efforts of the respective provinces shall appear to merit.

G. R."

Upon which the House resolved, April 30, " That a sum not exceeding two hundred thousand pounds be granted to his Majesty upon account, to enable his Majesty to give a proper compensation to the respective provinces in North America, for the expences incurred by them in the levying, clothing, and pay of the troops raised by the same, according as the active vigour and strenuous efforts

of the respective provinces shall be thought by his Majesty to merit."

Similar resolutions followed yearly every message. And though this compensation did not exceed one fourth part of what they expended, they were satisfied with these most honourable of all testimonies, that they had not been backward in contributing their share towards the general defence of the empire.

His Majesty's Surveyor-General of the Northern district in America, transmitted to the Lords of the Treasury in 1764, a charge of corruption in his office and collusion with smugglers, supported by the oaths of credible witnesses, against Governor Bernard; for which the surveyor general received the thanks of the treasury-board, and Governor Bernard was suffered still to hold that office he had abused, and has been admitted as the principal accuser and witness against the people of the Massachusetts-Bay.

On the 10th of March 1764, the House of Commons resolved, "That it may be proper to charge certain stamp duties in the colonies and plantations:" but did not at that time form any bill for the purpose.

On the 5th of April 1764, an act passed for imposing duties in America by the British parliament, for the purpose of raising a revenue.

In consequence of these proceedings, the House of Representatives of the Massachusetts-Bay came to resolutions, " That the sole right of giving and granting the money of the people of that province, was vested in them as their legal representatives; and that the imposition of duties and taxes, by the Parliament of Great-Britain, upon a people who are not represented in the House of Commons, is absolutely irreconcilable with their rights. That no man can justly take the property of another without

his

his confent, upon which original principle the right of reprefentation in the fame body which exercifes the power of making laws for levying taxes, one of the main pillars of the Britifh Conftitution, is evidently founded: that the extenfion of the powers of the court of admiralty within this province, is a moft violent infraction of the right of trial by jury,—a right which this houfe, upon the principles of their Britifh Anceftors, hold moft dear and facred, it being the only fecurity of the lives, liberties, and property of his Majefty's fubjects. That this houfe owe the ftricteft allegiance to his moft Sacred Majefty King George the Third,— and that they have the greateft veneration for the Parliament.

In February 1765, a Bill for raifing a revenue in America by duties on ftamps, &c. received the royal affent. Petitions from the feveral affemblies of America againft the paffing of this act, were rejected by the Parliament, or not received, on the pretence of a rule, that petitions fhould not be received againft a money bill, and this was a money bill.

Upon the arrival of this act in America, every affembly on the continent came to refolutions againft the right of impofing taxes upon them unreprefented and without their confent. The Houfe of Reprefentatives of the Maffachufetts-Bay, obferving the little attention paid to feparate petitions, refolved, ' That it was highly expedient there fhould be a meeting as foon as might be, of committees from the Houfes of Reprefentatives in the feveral colonies on the American continent to confult on the prefent circumftances, and the difficulties to which they were reduced by the operation of the late acts of Parliament for levying duties on the colonies, and to confider of a general addrefs to his

Majefty and the Parliament, to implore relief.' Letters were tranfmitted accordingly to the Speakers of the other Affemblies, and three perfons elected to attend a congrefs on the part of this province.

In the mean time fome difturbances arofe in the town of Bofton. The reprefentation of thefe difturbances was inflamed with the ftrongeft colouring in various letters from Governor Bernard to the Lords of Trade, though he knew the inhabitants had publicly condemned thefe proceedings, as appears from the following vote of the town:

' At a legal Meeting of the Freeholders and other Inhabitants of the Town of Bofton, at Fanueil Hall, Auguft 27th, 1765.

The town having an utter deteftation of the extraordinary and violent proceedings of a number of perfons unknown, againft fome of the inhabitants of the fame, the laft night,— vote unanimoufly, that the felect men and magiftrates of the town be defired to ufe their utmoft endeavours, agreeeble to law, to fupprefs the like diforders for the future, and that the freeholders and other inhabitants will do every thing in their power to affift them therein.

Voted, that the inhabitants of this town will be ready on all occafions to affift the felect men and magiftrates in the fuppreffion of all diforders of a like nature that may happen, when called upon for that purpofe.

Att. William Cooper, Town Clerk.'

In truth, the whole proved to be nothing more than fome injury offered to private property, for which the affembly afterwards voted a compenfation.

On the 25th of October 1765, there being no ftamp papers, the council and Houfe of Reprefentatives, to avoid the mifchievous confequences of a total ftop to all public

L l   bufinefs,

bufinefs, refolved, that it might be lawful to do bufinefs without ftamps.

The congrefs confifting of a Committee of Reprefentatives from feveral provinces, met at New York the firft of October 1765. The motives and views with which the congrefs was called, are thus ftated by the Houfe of Reprefentatives of Maffachufetts-Bay: 'Had the colonies been fully heard by the Parliament, it is poffible their decifions with refpect to the late acts for levying duties and taxes on the colonies, might have been different. However, the Houfe of Reprefentatives think it their duty not to ceafe petitioning, and have accordingly, this prefent feffions, wrote to the Speakers of the feveral Houfes of Reprefentatives of the feveral colonies on the continent, propofing a meeting at New York on the firft Tuefday of October next, of committees of the Houfes of Reprefentatives of the feveral colonies, to confult together on their prefent circumftances, and the difficulties to which they are and muft be reduced by the operation of the late acts of parliament, and to prepare a united, dutiful, humble, and loyal reprefentation of their condition to his Majefty and his Parliament, imploring relief. And it is humbly hoped, that decent and dutiful applications for the preventing or even altering fuch acts of Parliament as they apprehend can be made to appear to be grievous, will not be thought fufficient grounds to charge us with the want of the moft profound refpect for that auguft body. In confidence of having free accefs to that fountain of national juftice, the Houfe reft affured that all neceffary relief will be afforded, and that the liberties and privileges their conftituents at prefent enjoy, will remain fecure.

Signed, SAM. WHITE, Speaker.'
The congrefs fummoned upon thefe

principles, met and acted upon them. They refolved, ' That the only reprefentatives of the people of the colonies are perfons chofen therein by themfelves, and that no taxes ever have been, or can be, conftitutionally impofed upon them but by their refpective legiflatures. That all fupplies to the crown being free gifts of the people, it is unreafonable and inconfiftent with the principles and fpirit of the Britifh conftitution, for the people of Great Britain to grant to his Majefty the property of the colonifts. That it is the indifpenfable duty of thefe colonies to the beft of fovereigns, to the mother country, and themfelves, to endeavour, by a loyal and dutiful addrefs to his Majefty, and humble applications to both Houfes of Parliament, to procure the repeal of the act for granting and applying certain ftamp duties, of all claufes of any other act of Parliament whereby the jurifdiction of the Admiralty is extended, and of the other late acts for the reftriction of American commerce.'

They alfo drew up a petition to the King, in which they fay, ' Our fubordinate legiflatures are in effect rendered ufelefs by the late acts of Parliament impofing duties and taxes on thefe colonies, and extending the jurifdiction of the courts of admiralty beyond its antient limit: ftatutes by which your Majefty's commons in Great Britain undertake abfolutely to difpofe of the property of their fellow fubjects in America without their confent, and for the inforcing whereof they are fubjected to the determination of a fingle judge, in a court unreftrained by the wife rules of the common law, the birthright of Englifhmen, and the fafeguard of their perfons and properties.

' The invaluable rights of taxing ourfelves, and trial by our peers, of which we implore your Majefty's protection,

tection, are not, we moſt humbly conceive, unconſtitutional, but confirmed by the great charter of Engliſh Liberty. On the firſt of theſe rights, the Honourable the Houſe of Commons found their practice of originating money bills—a right enjoyed by the Kingdom of Ireland ; by the Clergy of England, till relinquiſhed by themſelves——a right, in fine, which all other your Majeſty's Engliſh ſubjects, both within and without the realm, have hitherto enjoyed.'

So far were they from any thought or deſire to draw into queſtion, or to deny the ſovereignty of his Majeſty in his Parliament, or to arrogate to themſelves the ſole right of making laws, that, in their petition to the Houſe of Commons, they declare the reverſe in theſe words :

' We moſt ſincerely renognize our allegiance to the crown, and acknowledge all due ſubordination to the Parliament of Great Britain, and ſhall always retain the moſt grateful ſenſe of their aſſiſtance and protection. We eſteem our dependence on, and connection with Great Britain, as one of our greateſt bleſſings, and apprehend the former will appear to be ſufficiently ſecure, when it is conſidered, that the inhabitants in the colonies have the moſt unbounded affection for his Majeſty's perſon, family, and government, as well as for the mother country, and that their ſubordination to the Parliament, is univerſally acknowledged.'

Theſe petitions however were not received, on pretence of their being from a body not legally aſſembled, and unknown to the conſtitution.

In January 1766, the Houſe of Repreſentatives were obliged to complain of Governor Bernard's having, together with his council, aſſumed a legiſlative power, in ordering an act of Parliament, or as he ſtiles it an ordinance, to be regiſtered among the laws of the province; which was never done before, but by act of Aſſembly *. This juſt complaint againſt the uſurpation of the Governor, has been individiouſly repreſented as an attack upon the authority of Parliament †, whereas in truth it had no relation to that authority.

In January 1766, petitions were preſented from the merchants of London, Briſtol, and Glaſgow, to both Houſes of Parliament, repreſenting the great injury that would accrue to their property, and to the commerce of this Kingdom, from the operation of the Stamp Act, and praying for its repeal.

The repeal of it took place accordingly on the 19th March following.

The Aſſembly of Maſſachuſetts-Bay, upon the repeal being known, formed and tranſmitted an humble addreſs of thanks to his Majeſty, and letters of the moſt grateful acknowledgement to their illuſtrious patrons and friends in either Houſe of Parliament. Soon after this paſſed a bill for granting compenſation to the ſufferers during the diſorders occaſioned by the Stamp Act; agreeably to his Majeſty's recommendation, in conſequence of the addreſs of both Houſes of Parliament, his Majeſty's pleaſure being ſignified to them by Mr. Secretary Conway.

The Aſſembly alſo conformed themſelves to the mutiny act, though it touched the privilege of granting freely their own money, for which they had ſo ſtrenuouſly contended. But they complyed, as well from an

* But the moſt intereſting objection, which is not avowed, and therefore cannot receive a formal anſwer, is, that an American repreſentation will take away all pretences for diſputing the ordinances of Parliament.' Governor Bernard's letter 1764, p. 59. And again, p. 72, and 54.

† See extract of Governor Bernard's letter in the Lords report, p. 7.

L l 2   abhor-

abhorrence of renewing the late dispute which had given them so much pain, as from a confidence in his Majesty's then servants, whom they regarded as friendly to their liberties and rights.

Their satisfaction in, and gratitude for the repeal of the stamp act, produced a conduct so studiously void of offence, that Governor Bernard could not avoid giving his testimony of it in his letters to the Earl of Shelburne, Secretary of State, as follows :

' The House from the time of opening the session to this day, has shewn a disposition to avoid all dispute with me; every thing having passed with as much good-humour as I could desire, except only their continuing to act in addressing the King, remonstrating to the Secretary of State, and employing a separate Agent. It is the importance of this innovation, without any willfulness of my own, which induces me to make this remonstrance, at a time when I have a fair prospect of having, in all other business, nothing but good to say of the proceedings of this House.

' They have acted in all things, even in their remonstrance, with temper and moderation; they have avoided some subjects of dispute, and have laid a foundation for removing some causes of former altercation.

' I shall make such a prudent and proper use of this letter, as I hope will perfectly restore the peace and tranquility of this province, for which purpose considerable steps have already been made by the House of Representatives.'

Such was the temper and moderation with which the people were disposed to seek relief from the grievances they felt. We shall presently see what steps were artfully taken to move them from that moderation, and compel the mob into riots and tumults, which were to be visited upon the town, and made the pretext for introducing a military force.

The new revenue act passed on the 29th of June 1767; a little more than a year after the repeal of the stamp act.

The House of Representatives, in their petition to the King, touching this act, expressly acknowledge the supreme power of Parliament. ' With great sincerity, permit us, (say they,) to assure your Majesty, that your subjects of this province ever have, and still continue to acknowledge your Majesty's High Court of Parliament the supreme legislative power of the whole empire.'

In their letters to the ministry, they say, ' The subjects in this province, and undoubtedly in all the colonies, however they may have been otherwise represented to his Majesty's ministers, are loyal; they are firmly attached to the mother state; they always consider her interest and their own as inseparably interwoven, and it is their fervent wish that it may ever so remain. All they desire is, to be restored to the standing upon which they were originally put, to have the honour and privilege of voluntarily contributing to the aid of their sovereign when required. They are free subjects; and it is hoped the nation will never consider them as in a tributary state.' And again, ' All they desire is to be placed on their original standing, that they may still be happy in the enjoyment of their invaluable privileges, and the nation may still reap the advantage of their growth and prosperity.

That their prayers might be more likely to obtain success from being united with the supplications of all the colonies, they transmitted a circular letter to the other assemblies, informing them—' That the House had humbly represented to the ministry niftry their own fentiments; that his Majefty's high Court of Parliament is the fupreme legiflative power over the whole empire; that in all free ftates the conftitution is fixed; and as the fupreme legiflative derives its power and authority from the conftitution, it cannot overleap the bounds of it, without deftroying. its own foundation. That the conftitution afcertains and limits both fovereignty and allegiance, and, therefore, his Majefty's American fubjects, who acknowledge themfelves bound by the ties of allegiance, have an equitable claim to the full enjoyment of the fundamental rules of the Englifh conftitution. That it is an affential, unalterable right in nature, ingrafted into the Britifh conftitution as a fundamental law, and ever held facred and irrevocable by the fubjects within the realm, that what a man has honeftly acquired is abfolutely his own, which he may freely give, but which cannot be taken from him without his confent. That the American fubjects may, therefore, exclufive of any confideration of charter rights, with a decent firmnefs adapted to the character of freemen and fubjects, affert this natural conftitutional right.' They add—' That as they have too much reafon to believe, that the enemies of the colonies have reprefented them to his Majefty's minifters and the parliament, as factious, difloyal, and fhewing a difpofition to make themfelves independent of the mother country, they have taken occafion, in the moft humble terms, to affure his Majefty and his minifters, that, with regard to the people of this province, and, as they doubt not, of all the colonies, that charge is unjuft.'

In confequence of this, Governor Bernard laid before the houfe, on the 21ft of June, 1768, the following requifition:

' It gives great concern to his Majefty to find, that the fame moderation which appeared by your letter to have been adopted at the beginning of the feffion, in a full affembly, had not continued; and that inftead of that fpirit of prudence and refpect to the conftitution, which feemed at that time to influence the conduct of a large majority of the members, a thin houfe at the end of the feffion fhould have prefumed to revert to, and refolve upon a meafure of fo inflammatory a nature as that of writing to the other colonies, on the fubject of their intended reprefentation againft fome late acts of Parliament. His Majefty confiders this ftep as evidently tending to create unwarrantable combinations, to excite an unjuftifiable oppofition to the conftitutional authority of Parliament, and to revive thofe unhappy divifions and diftractions, which have operated fo prejudicially to the true interefts of Great Britain and the colonies. It is the King's pleafure, that fo foon as the general court is again affembled, at the time prefcribed by the charter, you fhould require of the Houfe of Reprefentatives, in his Majefty's name, to refcind the refolution which gave birth to the circular letter from the Speaker, and to declare their difapprobation of, and diffent to that rafh and hafty proceeding. His Majefty has the fulleft reliance upon the affection of his good fubjects in the Maffachufetts-Bay, and has obferved with fatisfaction, that fpirit of decency, and love of order, which has difcovered itfelf in the conduct of the moft confiderable of its inhabitants.—If the new affembly fhould refufe to comply with his Majefty's reafonable expectation, it it the King's pleafure that you fhould immediately diffolve them.

Whitehall, April 22, 1768. HILLSBOROUGH.'

This letter produced univerfal apprehenprehenſion and diſcontent not only in the Maſſachuſetts-Bay, but in all America. A demand, attended with a penalty of diſſolution, ſeemed a command, not a requiſition, leaving no deliberative or diſcretionary power in the aſſembly; and the ground of it being a petition to the King, guarded with a moſt explicit declaration of the ſupreme legiſlative power of Parliament, it wore the ſevere and dreadful appearance of a penal prohibition againſt petitioning. It was in effect ſaying, you ſhall not even preſume to complain; and reducing them below the common ſtate of ſlavery, in which, if men complain, with decency, they are heard, unleſs their maſters happen to be monſters. It warmed moderation into zeal, and inflamed zeal into rage. Yet ſtill there appeared a diſpoſition to expreſs their grievances in humble petitions. All the aſſemblies on the continent, in anſwer to a requiſition of ſimilar import to that already mentioned, aſſerted the right of the ſubject to petition for redreſs of grievances. They joined in petitions, ſtating the impoſition of taxes upon them without their conſent, and the abolition of juries in revenue cauſes, as intolerable grievances, from which they prayed relief.

The Houſe of Repreſentatives of Maſſachuſetts-Bay drew up a letter to the Earl of Hillſborough, Secretary of State, in which they vindicate their conduct from the aſperſions thrown upon it in the Governor's letters; and add, ' It is an inexpreſſible grief to the people of this province, to find repeated cenſures falling upon them, not from Miniſters of State alone, but from Majeſty itſelf, grounded on letters and accuſations from the Governor, a ſight of which, though repeatedly requeſted of his Excellency, is refuſed. There is no evil of this life, which they ſo ſenſi-

bly feel, as the diſpleaſure of their ſovereign. It is a puniſhment which they are ſure his Majeſty will never inflict, but upon a repreſentation of the juſtice of it, from his ſervants, in whom he confides. Your Lordſhip will allow the houſe to appeal to your own candour, upon the hardſhip of their being made to ſuffer ſo ſevere a misfortune, without their ever being called to anſwer for themſelves, or even made acquainted with the matters of charge alledged againſt them; a right, to which, by the common rules of ſociety, founded in the eternal laws of reaſon and equity, they are juſtly entitled. The Houſe of Repreſentatives of this province have more than once, during the adminiſtration of Governor Bernard, been under the neceſſity of entreating his Majeſty's miniſters to ſuſpend their further judgment upon ſuch repreſentations of the temper of the people, and the conduct of the aſſembly, as they were able to make appear to be injurious. The ſame indulgence this houſe now beg of your Lordſhip; and beſeech your Lordſhip to patronize them ſo far as to make a favourable repreſentation of their conduct to the King our Sovereign: it being the higheſt ambition of this houſe, and of the people whom they repreſent, to ſtand before his Majeſty in their juſt character, of affectionate and loyal ſubjects.'

On the 10th of June a ſeizure was made of a ſloop faſtened to the wharf, with an armed force, and the ſeizure carried by violence to the Man of War. That this ſeizure was made with every circumſtance of violence and inſult which could irritate a mob, is proved by the oaths of 13 eye-witneſſes, whoſe credibility has never been impeached. Unhappily the irritation ſucceeded but too well. The collector and comptroller who made the ſeizure in that manner, were

were treated with great indignity and perfonal injury by the mob *.

About the fame time the Captain of the men of war lying in the harbour at Bofton, preffed fome feamen belonging to the town, in violation of an act of Parliament for the encouragement of trade to America, which fays, 6 Anne, chap. 27. § 9. " No mariner, or other perfon, fon, who fhall ferve on board, or be retained to ferve on board, any privateer, or trading fhip or veffel, that fhall be employed in any part of America, nor any mariner, or perfon, being on fhore in any part thereof, fhall be liable to be impreffed or taken away, by any officer or officers of or belonging to her Majefty's fhips of war."

The inhabitants of Bofton, to prevent the tumults which might be apprehended from fo dangerous an infraction of law, were affembled, and drew up a petition to the Governor, praying his interpofition to prevent fuch alarming outrages. The Governor, however, refufed upon various pretexts, to interfere.

The following words of their petition will fhew to what ftate of alarm, anxiety, and defpair, thefe proceedings had reduced them. ' Dutiful petitions, fay they, have been prefered to our moft gracious Sovereign, to which (tho' to the great confternation of the people, we now learn they have been cruelly and infiduoufly prevented from reaching the royal prefence) we have waited to receive a gracious anfwer, with the greateft attention to the public peace, until we find ourfelves invaded with an armed force, feizing, impreffing, and imprifoning the perfons of our fellow fubjects, contrary to exprefs acts of Parliament. Menaces have been thrown out fit only for barbarians, which already affect us in the moft fenfible manner, and threaten us with famine and defolation, as all navigation is obftructed, upon which alone our whole fupport depends, and the town is at this crifis in a fituation nearly fuch as if war were formally declared againft it.

' To contend againft our Parent State is, in our idea, the moft fhocking and dreadful extremity ; but tamely to relinquifh the only fecurity we and our pofterity retain of the enjoyment of our lives and properties, without one ftruggle, is fo humiliating and bafe, that we cannot fupport the reflection. We apprehend, Sir, that it is in your option, in your power, and we would hope in your inclination, to prevent this diftreffed and juftly incenfed people from effecting too much, or from the fhame and reproach of attempting too little.'

The riot upon the feizure of the floop was exaggerated into treafon and rebellion. The commiffioners fled from the town in pretended fear of their lives ; affidavits were taken in fecret and *ex parte*, and the comptroller Mr. Hallowell was difpatched home, to give adminiftration the moft horrible idea of the people. Governor Bernard's letters to the Secretary of State contained a direct charge of treafon againft forty perfons, not one of whom was profecuted, becaufe the whole was a forgery, calculated to meet the change of fyftem which Governor Bernard has fince informed us, they then knew had taken place at London, and

---

* That the feizure was unjuft is plain from this, that they were obliged to reftore the veffel, after detaining her a long time, not being able to find any evidence to fupport a profecution. The fuits too for enormous fums againft a number of perfons, brought in the court of admiralty, being found infupportable, were, after long continuance, to the great expence and trouble of their perfons, dropt, by a declaration of the King's advocate that his Majefty would profecute no farther ; ——but the profecuted could obtain no cofts or damages, for fo is the law.

and encourage the rigorous measures which the new system was to pursue.

Unhappily it succeeded too well. Troops were sent to Boston, where they landed the 1st of October 1768. But a difficulty now arose, about quartering the troops in the town contrary to an act of Parliament. The Governor, however, soon determined to cut the knot he could not untie. ' He therefore issued a commission, to dispense with the law and establish quarters for the troops in the town. I speak from his own letter.

Thus the people saw two acts of Parliament, made for their protection, wantonly and with impunity violated; while those which were to their feelings highly unjust and oppressive, were to be rigorously executed with a military force. Nothing could be devised more irritating, except the manner in which the quartering the soldiers was executed. They filled the general assembly room, the court house, and Fanueil hall, where the town meetings were assembled. When the general assembly met, the main guard was planted with a number of field pieces at, and pointed into the very door of the assembly house. Every species of insult and outrage was, as if purposely, practised to drive the people into some violent act, which should justify the letting loose the military upon them.

In consequence of the various violations of those laws which should have protected them, the minds of the people were in the most dangerous state of alarm and agitation. To prevent the destructive commotions which might be apprehended from such a disposition, the moderate and well disposed inhabitants of Boston petitioned the Governor to call an assembly, that the popular turbulence might be quieted by their confidence in and respect for their own legislature. The Governor, however, thought proper to refuse them this relief; they therefore summoned a convention of deputies from the different townships, as the only means of composing the agitation of men's minds, (from which they otherwise expected the worst consequences,) by their confidence in persons deputed by themselves, to enter into a wise and cool consideration of their grievances, and the constitutional means of obtaining redress. The select men of Boston have expressed these motives in the following passage of their circular letter:—' Deprived of the counsels of a general assembly in this dark and difficult season, the loyal people of this province will, we are persuaded, immediately perceive the propriety and utility of the proposed committee of convention, and the sound and wholesome advice that may be expected from a number of gentlemen chosen by themselves, and in whom they may repose the greatest confidence, must tend to the real service of our most gracious Sovereign, and the welfare of his subjects in this province, and may happily prevent any sudden and unconnected measures, which, in their present anxiety, and even agony of mind, they may be in danger of falling into.'

The convention met on the 22d of September 1768, and drew up an humble petition to his Majesty, imploring relief. ' With great sincerity, say they, permit us to assure your Majesty, that your subjects of this province, of which we are a part, ever have acknowledged and still continue to acknowledge your Majesty's high Court of Parliament the supreme legislative power of the whole empire. The superintending authority of which is clearly admitted in all cases that can consist with the fundamental rights of nature, and

and the conſtitution to which your Majeſty's happy ſubjects in all parts of your empire conceive they have a juſt and equitable claim.

' It is therefore with the deepeſt concern that your humble ſuppliants would repreſent to your Majeſty, that your Parliament, the rectitude of whoſe intentions is never to be queſtioned, has thought proper to paſs divers acts, impoſing taxes on your Majeſty's ſubjects in America, with the ſole and expreſs purpoſe of raiſing a revenue. If your Majeſty's ſubjects here ſhall be deprived of the honour and privilege of voluntarily contributing their aid to your Majeſty in ſupporting your government and authority in the province, and defending and ſecuring your rights and territories in America, which they have always hitherto done with the utmoſt chearfulneſs: if theſe acts of Parliament ſhall remain in force ; and your Majeſty's Commons in Great Britain ſhall continue to exerciſe the power of granting the property of their fellow ſubjects in this province, your people muſt then regret their unhappy fate, in having only the name left of free ſubjects.'

The troops which had landed at Boſton without the leaſt oppoſition, determined, as it was natural to expect, to make the diſturbance they were diſappointed in not finding. They offered a variety of inſults to the peaceable inhabitants, and one of their officers was detected in attempting to excite the Negroes to rebel; till at laſt a party of ſoldiers under the command of Captain Preſton, fired upon the people on the 5th of March 1769, killing ſix, and wounding many more. So intolerable an outrage aſſembled the people, who were ſo much incenſed, that it was thought prudent for the troops to evacuate the town.

The removal of the troops reſtored the tranquillity of the town and the good-humour of the people, the principal of whom exerted themſelves to palliate the conduct of Captain Preſton, and obtain for him a favourable trial. To this end, he was tried ſeparately from the ſoldiers, and he was acquitted, becauſe no evidence could depoſe that they heard him give orders to fire.—Indeed, the noiſe of the tumult was ſo great, that if he had given ſuch orders, which he denied, none could have heard him but the ſoldiers among whom he ſtood.—When the ſoldiers came to be tried, they pleaded the orders of their Captain, which they durſt not diſobey. And on the belief of this as a truth, the humane jury acquitted them alſo. An inſtance of great temper and equity in a people ſo exaſperated.

It was not however intended that the quiet of the town and province ſhould continue long. New modes of irritation were applied, to drive the people into violence and deſpair.

Mr. Robinſon, one of the commiſſioners who had attempted to aſſaſſinate Mr. Otis, was diſpatched to England immediately after the affair of the 5th of March, with a caſe ſaid to be that of Captain Preſton, though directly repugnant to what he had publiſhed under his own hand. This caſe had been ſecretly drawn up, and was as ſecretly tranſmitted. The purpoſe of it was to throw the charge of being the aggreſſors upon the people, and that the ſoldiers fired upon them in their own defence, and to ſave the cuſtom-houſe from being plundered. This ſtatement was accompanied by minutes of council framed by the Secretary himſelf, and ſecretly ſworn to, in which one of his Majeſty's council was repreſented, as declaring that there had been a premeditated deſign and plan of a general inſurrection formed by the people, of which this

M m attack

attack upon the guard was the firſt ſtep. Abſurd as it was to ſuppoſe that the people had planned and began to execute an inſurrection, and yet not a man appear in arms, for no ſuch thing was pretended, ſtill the example of the ſucceſs and impunity with which Governor Bernard had accuſed them ſpecifically of treaſon, without being able to prove a tittle of it, was enough to encourage Governor Hutchinſon, and his Brother-in-law the Secretary, to repeat a ſimilar charge on this occaſion, which they knew would operate for the time, and being made ſecretly, they truſted it would not be known, ſo as to meet a refutation. Mr. Commiſſioner Robinſon arrived in London, and his State, &c. was circulated through the miniſtry and members of parliament, and, ſupported by his perſonal applications, inflamed them againſt the province. In the mean time, the town proceeded to draw up their narrative of the affair founded upon affidavits taken openly, with notice given to all perſons concerned to attend and croſs-examine the witneſſes. Upon this open and fair enquiry, it appeared by the teſtimony of near an hundred perſons, that the ſoldiers were the aggreſſors, having fired upon the people without ſufficient provocation, and without the intervention of, or even application to the civil magiſtrate.

It was not until October 1770, that the repreſentation and affidavit of their ſecretary, Mr. Oliver, reached his Majeſty's council at Boſton, in a pamphlet which had been publiſhed in London, to juſtify the proceedings of the military on the 5th of March 1769, and accuſe the people. The member to whom he had imputed the words, which were calculated to convey the idea of an inſurrection having been planned by the people, publicly made oath, that the

Secretary had miſrepreſented his words, and that he never knew, or heard, or even thought of any ſuch Plan. The other members of council who were preſent alſo made oath, that Mr. Oliver's account was a miſrepreſentation; and the council came unanimouſly to the following reſolutions: " That Andrew Oliver, Eſq. ſecretary of this province, by ſecretly taking minutes at council, of what was ſaid by the members of the council, in their debates, alſo by ſigning a paper containing thoſe minutes, and further by giving his depoſition to the truth of it, has, in each and all thoſe inſtances, acted inconſiſtent with the duty of his office, and thereby is guilty of a breach of truſt.

Mr. Oliver, thus ſtigmatized, was ſoon after appointed lieutenant-governor of the province. Unhappily this wore the appearance of rewarding for his treachery to the council and his enmity to the people, which tended neceſſarily to diminiſh the confidence and reſpect due to government; and to ſpread diſcontent through the province.

On the 13th of May 1770, Governor Hutchinſon held the aſſembly at Cambridge, obliging them to quit Boſton, where all the public records and conveniences for carrying on buſineſs, were lodged. The two Houſes remonſtrated againſt this, not only as highly inconvenient and diſtreſſing to them, and an embarraſſment to public buſineſs, but an infringement of their chartered rights. Notwithſtanding this, the aſſembly was continued there for two ſeſſions without any reaſon being given but mere will and pleaſure (ſignified in inſtructions from the miniſter) and then it was adjourned to Boſton, not as an act of graciouſneſs, but of caprice. It was impoſſible but that ſuch proceedings muſt have irritated men's minds;

minds, and raifed among all ranks of people a fpirit of difcontent and diftruft.*

The proceedings in England were not more conciliating.

Governor Bernard had, by various falfe and inflammatory reprefentations concentered upon the province the whole force of royal and parliamentary indignation. He had exprefsly accufed certain perfons of a treafonable defign, their names, as he pretended, being enrolled for the purpofe, to feize the caftle and turn it againft the King's troops.

This intelligence produced the following addrefs from the Houfe of Lords to the King, on the 15th of December 1768, concurred in by the Commons on the 9th of February, 1769.

"As we conceive, that nothing can be more immediately neceffary, either for the maintenance of his Majefty's authority in the faid province, or from guarding his Majefty's fubjects therein from being further deluded by the arts of wicked and defigning men, than to proceed in the moft fpeedy and effectual manner for bringing to condign punifhment the chief authors and inftigators of the late diforders, to befeech his Majefty, that he will be gracioufly pleafed to direct his Majefty's Governor of Maffachufetts-Bay to take the moft effectual methods for procuring the fulleft information that can be ob-

* The Affembly of South Carolina was about the fame time removed from Charleftown to Port Royal, a remote place unfit to accommodate them. This method of harraffing affemblies into the meafures of a miniftry, feems borrowed from the favourite minifter of Henry III. who, " to work his ends (as Gafcoign tells us) caufed the Parliament to fit *in villibus et remotis partibus regni,* where few people, *propter defectum hofpitii et victualium,* could attend, and by fhifting that affembly from place to place to enforce (in the author's words) *illos paucos qui remanebunt de communitate regni, concedere regi quamvis peffima.*"

tained touching all treafons, or mifprifions of treafon, committed within his government fince the 30th day of December laft, and to tranfmit the fame, together with the names of the perfons who were the moft active in the commiffion of fuch offences, to one of his Majefty's principal fecretaries of ftate, in order that his Majefty may iffue a fpecial commiffion for enquiring of, hearing and determining the faid offences within this realm, purfuant to the provifions of the ftatute of the 35th year of the reign of King Henry the Eighth, if his Majefty fhall, upon receiving the faid information, fee fufficient ground for fuch a proceeding."

His Majefty's anfwer was:

" I fhall not fail to give thofe orders which you recommend, as the moft effectual method of bringing the authors of the late unhappy diforders in that province to condign punifhment."

But Governor Bernard thus armed with all the powers of government, was unable to fubftantiate his accufation againft a fingle perfon. The purpofes for which the accufation was devifed were fully anfwered. An odium had been fixed upon the people, a military force had been fent, which promifed to create the very rebellion he had falfely declared to exift, for the purpofe of procuring that force.

The manner in which he proceeded in his endeavours to ftir up refiftance and create diforders, is thus defcribed in the narrative of the town, and which he has never been able to contradict.

' Governor Bernard, without confulting the council, having given up the ftate houfe to the troops at their landing, they took poffeffion of the chambers where the reprefentatives of the province and the court of law held their meetings; and (except the

council

council chamber) of all other parts of that houfe; in which they continued a confiderable time, to the great annoyance of thofe courts while they fat, and of the merchants and gentlemen of the town, who had always made the lower floor of it their exchange. They had a right fo to do, as the property of it was in the town; but they were deprived of that right by mere power.—The faid Governor foon after, by every ftratagem and method, but a forcible entry, endeavoured to get poffeffion of the manufactory houfe, to make a barrack of it for the troops; and for that purpofe caufed it to be befieged by the troops, and the people in it to be ufed very cruelly; which extraordinary proceedings created univerfal uneafinefs, arifing from the apprehenfion that the troops, under the influence of fuch a man, would be employed to effect the moft dangerous purpofes; but failing of that, other houfes were procured, in which, contrary to act of Parliament, he caufed the troops to be quartered. After their quarters were thus fettled, the main guard was pofted at one of the faid houfes, directly oppofite to, and not twelve yards from the ftate-houfe, (where the general court and all the law courts for the county were held) with two field pieces pointed to the ftate-houfe. This fituation of the main guard and field pieces feemed to indicate an attack upon the conftitution, and a defiance of law; and to be intended to affront the legiflative and executive authority of the province.'

The general court, at the firft feffion after the arrival of the troops, viewed it in this light, and applied to Governor Bernard to remove fuch an offence, but to no purpofe. Difgufted at fuch an indignity, and at the appearance of being under dureffe, they refufed to do bufinefs in fuch a fituation, and were removed to another place, to the great inconvenience of the members.

Befides this, the challenging the inhabitants by centinels pofted in all parts of the town, occafioned many quarrels and great uneafinefs. It was fully proved againft Captain Wilfon of the 59th Regiment, that he was exciting the Negroes of the town to take away their mafter's lives and property, and repair to the army for protection. To thefe were added various outrages, fuch as the foldiers attacking and infulting the magiftrates of the town, refcuing their fellows from the peace officers, firing loaded mufkets in the ftreets to the great alarm and danger of the peaceable inhabitants, and wounding perfons frequently and wantonly with their bayonets and cutlaffes.

Thefe infults and outrages did not, however, produce the infurrection that was wifhed; but an humble petition from the reprefentatives of the people to his Majefty againft the author of all thofe evils Governor Bernard.

This petition was voted the 27th of June 1769. The Governor prorogued the affembly to January 10th, 1770, and came over to England. On the 25th of October, he prefented a petition to bring the charges againft him to a hearing. In the mean time orders were fent to the lieutenant-governor, Mr. Hutchinfon, to prorogue the affembly to the 14th of March, which was done accordingly. Notwithftanding the agent reprefented the impoffibility of the affembly even knowing that their petition was to be heard, much lefs tranfmitting evidence in fupport of the allegations it contained, that this impoffibility was created by the very perfon accufed, and who, in the face of that, called upon them to fupport their charge, to which the agent added

ded an humble prayer, that the hearing might be deferred till convenient time was given for the meeting of the assembly and transmission of evidence: yet the petition was ordered peremptorily to a hearing on the 28th of February, when, in default of evidence, the several charges in it were declared groundless, vexatious and scandalous, and that the petitioning could only be with a view of keeping up a spirit of clamour and discontent in the said province.

Thus the people had the grief and mortification to find, that whether they were the accusers or the accused, they were sure of being censured and condemned. This man had been instrumental in bringing upon them the odium of disaffection and rebellion; he had shut the ear of the King and parliament against their applications for redress of grievances; he had contributed to the having a military force sent to dragoon them; he had, in violation of an express act of parliament, quartered those troops in their town, with every circumstance of insolence and outrage; he had subjected them to the intolerable oppression of being dragged three thousand miles, upon mere suspicion, to struggle for their lives and property, without friends and without witnesses, against all the force of ministerial prosecution. Yet it was conceived that to petition against such a man could only flow from factious motives, and because his own agency in proroguing the assembly rendered it impossible they should even know it was required of them to support their charges against him, those charges were pronounced groundless and malicious. With the feelings of men they could not but be sensibly affected by these proceedings, which, to speak in the language of the poet, preaching to stones would make them capable.

To heighten the colouring of these

transactions, orders were sent in 1771 to the Governor, to refuse his assent to any tax bill which should include the commissioners of customs. These gentlemen, whose officious and incendiary zeal against that country had raised them to office, were to be distinguished more than the first men in this country, by an exemption from sharing in the common burdens of the community.

In 1772, the Judges salaries were ordered to be paid out of the extorted revenue, and not by grants from the representatives of the people, as had been the constant usage. Nothing could alarm the people more than this establishment, as it struck at once at the very root of the impartial administration of justice. The inhabitants of Boston say in their address to the Governor, that " as the judges hold their places *during pleasure,* this establishment was big with the most fatal evils."

Both Governor Bernard and Governor Hutchinson had repeatedly represented the discontent and opposition, as arising from a factious few in Boston; and that the province in general were averse to their measures, and satisfied with their situation. To ascertain the general sentiments of the people, a committee was appointed at Boston, to represent their sense of grievances to the rest of the townships, and take their opinion upon them. This was accordingly done, the 2d of November 1772. The rest of the towns concurred most unanimously in the same sense of grievances, and desire of having them redressed.

On the 6th of January 1773, Governor Hutchinson, in his speech to the two Houses of Assembly, challenges them to a controversy upon the supreme legislative authority of parliament. The assembly, in their answer, take up the question as a point
of

of argument and speculation, refuting his arguments, and controverting his conclusions. It was a question, which, of themselves, they had never ventured to agitate, and they entered into it now, when publicly provoked to it, with avowed reluctance.—"We have the highest respect," say they, "for that august body the Parliament, and do not presume to prescribe the exact limits of its authority. Yet, with the deference that is due to it, we are humbly of opinion, that as all human authority, in the nature of it, is and ought to be limited, it cannot constitutionally extend, for the reasons we have above suggested, to the levying of taxes in any form on his Majesty's subjects of this province. These are great and profound questions. It is the grief of this House, that by the ill policy of a late injudicious administration, America has been driven into the contemplation of them. And we cannot but express our concern, that your Excellency by your speech has reduced us to the unhappy alternative, either of appearing by our silence to acquiesce in your Excellency's sentiments, or of thus freely discussing this point."

The most charitable construction of this conduct in the Governor is, that it was prompted by indiscreet zeal; the most probable conjecture is, that it was a snare laid for the two Houses to draw them into such a denial of the supreme legislative authority of this country, as might expose them to its utmost indignation. Whether it arose from malice or indiscretion, most certainly it was courting the discussion of a question which common sense and common honesty would have wished to cover with a sacred and impenetrable veil. But the two Houses, though compelled into the discussion of the right as a speculative point, had no idea of drawing it into

question practically. For in March following, the House of Representatives transmitted a letter to the secretary of state, (the Earl of Dartmouth) in which they thus state the exercise of that power, which was questionable as to the right and grievous in its operation.

"Your Lordship is well acquainted with the several acts, by which the British Parliament have thought proper, within a few years past, to raise a revenue in America, without our consent. The many and weighty reasons against, and objections to those acts, are so well known and understood by your Lordship, that we shall not take off your attention to the great affairs of the nation, by particularly mentioning them at this time: we only beg leave to say that we apprehend they tend to injure our commerce and subvert our liberties, and therefore are unjust, impolitic, and destructive of the real interest of the whole empire."

The same temper and moderation appears in the letter addressed by both Houses to the Earl of Dartmouth.

Province of the Massachusetts-Bay,
June 29th, 1773.

My Lord,[*]

"The re-establishment of the union and harmony that formerly subsisted between Great-Britain and her colonies is earnestly to be wished by the friends of both. As your Lordship is one of them, the two Houses of the Assembly of this province beg leave to address you. The original causes of the interruption of that union and harmony may probably be found in the letters sent from hence to administration, and to other gentlemen of influence in parliament, since the appointment of Sir Francis Bernard to the government of this province; and there is great reason to apprehend, that he and his coadjutors originally re-

[*] The Right Hon. the Earl of Dartmouth.

commended and laid the plans for the establishing the American revenue, out of which they expected large stipends and appointments for themselves, and which, through their instrumentality, has been the occasion of all the evils that have since taken place.

" When we had humbly addressed his Majesty, and petitioned both Houses of Parliament, representing our grievances, and praying for the repeal of the revenue acts, the like instruments, and probably the same, exerted themselves to prevent those petitions being laid before his Majesty and the Parliament, or to frustrate the prayer of them. Of this we have just had some new and unexpected evidence from original letters of Governor Hutchinson and Lieutenant-Governor Oliver; in which the former particularly and expresly, by his letter of the 10th of December 1768, endeavoured, in co-operation with Governor Bernard, to frustrate a petition of a number of the council for the repealing those acts, and to procure his Majesty's censure on the petitioners; and the letters of the latter, by the disadvantageous idea conveyed by them of the two Houses of Assembly, manifestly tended to create a prejudice against any petitions coming from a body of such a character; and his letter of the 11th of May 1768 in particular, mentions the petition of the House of Representatives to his Majesty, and their letters to divers noble Lords, with such circumstances as had a tendency to defeat the petition, and render the letters of no effect.

" It is now manifest, my Lord, what practices and arts have been used to mislead administration, both in the first proposal of American revenue acts, and in the continuance of them: but when they had lost

their force, and there appeared, under the influence of your Lordship, a disposition in Parliament to repeal those acts, his Excellency Governor Hutchinson, in his speech at the opening of the last session of the general court, was pleased to throw out new matter for contention and debate, and to call on the two Houses, in such a pressing manner as amounted to little short of a challenge to answer him. Into such a dilemma were they brought by the speech, that they were under a necessity of giving such answers to it as they did, or having their conduct construed into an acquiescence with the doctrines contained in it, which would have been an implicit acknowledgment that the province was in a state of subjection differing very little from slavery. The answers were the effect of necessity, and this necessity occasioned great grief to the two Houses. The people of this province, my Lord, are true and faithful subjects of his Majesty, and think themselves happy in their connection with Great Britain.

" They would rejoice at the restoration of the harmony and good will that once subsisted between the parent state and them: but it is in vain to expect this happiness during the continuance of their grievances, and while the charter rights, one after another, are wrested from them. Among these rights is the supporting of the officers of the crown by grants from the assembly; and in an especial manner, the supporting of the judges in the same way, on whose judgment the province is dependent in the most important cases, of life, liberties, and property. If warrants have not yet been, or if they already have been issued, we earnestly beg the favour of your Lordship's interposition to suppress or recal them.

If

If your Lordſhip ſhould condeſcend to aſk what are the means of reſtoring the harmony ſo much deſired, we ſhould anſwer in a word, that we are humbly of opinion, if things were brought to the general ſtate in which they ſtood at the concluſion of the late war, it would reſtore the happy harmony which at that time ſubſiſted.

" Your Lordſhip's appointment to be principal Secretary of State for the American department has given the colonies the higheſt ſatisfaction. They think it a happy omen, and that it will be productive of American tranquility, conſiſtent with their rights as Britiſh Subjects. The two Houſes humbly hope for your Lordſhip's influence to bring about ſo happy an event, and in the mean time they can with full confidence rely on your Lordſhip, that the machinations of Sir Francis Bernard, and other known enemies of the peace of Great-Britain and her colonies, will not be ſuffered to prevent or delay it.

" This letter which has been agreed on by both Houſes, is in their name, and by their order, ſigned and tranſmitted to your Lordſhip, by, my Lord, your Lordſhip's moſt obedient, and very humble ſervant,

THO. FLUCKER, Secretary."

(COPY.)

In the mean time the repreſentatives of the people have omitted no opportunity of laying their griefs at the foot of the throne, with the moſt humble ſupplications for relief.

Their petition to the King in 1772 ſpeaks thus :—" The inhabitants of this province had long ſhared in the bleſſings of good government under the mild adminiſtration of your Majeſty and your royal predeceſſors, until your Britiſh Parliament ſaw fit to paſs divers acts for the expreſs purpoſe of raiſing a revenue in America, without the conſent of your ſubjects

inhabiting therein. It was this that filled the minds of your ſubjects of this province with diſcontent ; being grieved that your Majeſty's council ſhould adviſe to a meaſure, which in a great degree deprives them of the rights and liberties of free and natural ſubjects granted to them by the charter. The Houſe of Repreſentatives did, in the year 1768, demonſtrate to your Majeſty this grievous infraction of their deareſt rights of Engliſhmen. Our hearts are too deeply impreſſed with loyalty and affection to your Majeſty's perſon and family to imagine, that a failure of the redreſs then prayed for, can be imputed to any want of paternal regard in your royal mind for all your ſubjects. It becomes us rather to ſuppoſe, that the petition and complaint, unfortunately for us, did not reach the throne."

They repeat the ſame ſubject of complaint in their petition of 1773, in theſe words : " The Parliament of Great-Britain, in which your ſubjects here are not and cannot be repreſented, hath exerciſed a power of raiſing a revenue within the province, to the great grief and diſtreſs of your Majeſty's people, and, we conceieve, in repugnance to the royal charter. Your petitioners did, at the laſt ſeſſion of this aſſembly, make their humble ſupplication to your Majeſty, praying the interpoſition of your royal clemency for the redreſs of their grievances ; but we know not whether our petition was ever laid before your Majeſty."

Beſides the cauſes of uneaſineſs and irritation already mentioned, ſundry inſtructions have been ſent to the governor of this province, ſince the year 1770, which tended to keep the people in continual alarm and diſcontent. The nature of theſe inſtructions

tions is full explained in the following extract from a letter of the House of Representatives, to the Earl of Dartmouth.

" We cannot refrain from expressing our strongest apprehensions, that the instructions which have of late been given to the governor by the ministry, if persisted in, will entirely destroy our liberties, and subvert our happy constitution. In pursuance of instructions, the garrison of our principal fortress, Castle-William, has been withdrawn, and a garrison of his Majesty's regular troops, over whom the governor has declared he has no controul, placed in their stead. By this means the governor has no longer that command of this fortress, which he is vested with by the royal charter. Upon this occasion we would refer it to your Lordship's consideration, whether the establishment of the office, and power of a military commander in chief, not subordinate to, but independent of, uncontrouled by, and in some instances superseding the power and authorities already granted to the governors and captains-general of the provinces, with a jurisdiction extending over the whole continent of America, is not repugnant to law, and to the principles of prudence and sound policy; and must not be very alarming to all those who have any regard for the liberties of the constitution either of Great-Britain, or of the colonies.

" By virtue of instructions, the honourable his Majesty's council are forbid to meet and transact matters of a public concern, as a council of advice to the governor, unless called by the governor; and if they should so meet at any time, the governor is ordered to negative them at the next election.

" Notwithstanding the charter fully authorises and empowers the general court to impose and levy proportionable and reasonable rates and taxes upon the estates and persons of all and every the proprietors and inhabitants of the province, yet the Governor has been instructed not to give his consent to any law or laws, by which the commissioners, or any person employed in the King's service, whose offices have no peculiar relation to this province, shall be taxed. This we conceive is repugnant to the privilege granted by charter, which makes the general court the only proper judges, who are to be exempted from taxes.—By instruction also, the Governor is forbid to give his consent, upon any pretence whatever, to any vote or order for the payment of any salary or allowance to any person or persons appointed to negotiate the affairs of the province in Great Britain, other than such as shall be thereunto appointed by an act of the whole legislature, or by a vote of the House of Representatives, to which the Governor and council respectively have given their concurrence. Of what service can such an agent be to the province, especially while matters which so nearly affect the very fundamentals of the constitution are in dispute. For if he must receive his instructions from all the branches of the legislature, as may, and undoubtedly will be insisted on, can it be expected they will agree in a set of instructions in our present critical situation? If it should be said that either branch would have a right to instruct the agent separately, yet it may happen, especially if the agent be equally obliged to pursue his instructions from each branch, that in the most important matters the instructions will be various and contradictory, which must totally deprive us of any benefit from his agency, in all such cases. In short, it is de-

N n

defeating

feating us of every valuble purpofe, as we conceive, that might accrue to the province by an agent at the court of Great Britain. Moreover, with fuch an agent, under the direction of the three branches, will it not be utterly impracticable for the affembly ever to lay before their Sovereign their complaints againft the corrupt and arbitrary adminiftration of a Governor? Self-defence, my Lord, whether it regard individuals or bodies of men, is the firft law of nature. The right of defence includes all means requifite and proper for that defence, and confequently a right to appoint and fupport their own defender. It muft therefore appear, that the houfe has, more efpecially when their deareft rights are at ftake, a clear and juft right to appoint an agent for themfelves, without the concurrence of the Governor.

"It muft be apparent to your Lordfhip, that while our judges hold their commiffions during pleafure only, if they are to receive their fupport from the crown, independent of the free grants of the people, they will be dependent on the crown both for their places and fupport; and we fhould fubmit to your Lordfhip's confideration, whether this be not a fituation in which no man could wifh to be, who is properly impreffed with a fenfe of human depravity, or who has a due regard for juftice. In fuch a cafe, what decifions muft the people expect, when the difpute lies between prerogative and privilege?

"We beg your Lordfhip's candid attention to the unhappy circumftances of the province; and hope the reprefentation we have made of our grievances will meet with a favourable reception. The colonies are far from being infenfible of their happinefs, in being connected with the mother country, and of the mutual

benefits derived from it; and fhall at all times efteem it our glory to cultivate, as far as our influence may extend, the warmeft fentiments of loyalty and affection to his Majefty, and to promote a happy union and harmony between the fubjects of Great Britain and thofe of the colonies. We are greatly aggrieved. We think it our indifpenfable duty to point out to your Lordfhip our grievances; we have frequently done it heretofore to adminiftration. We have failed of fuccefs. Inftead of being relieved, our grievances have been increafed. Our conftituents are juftly and univerfally alarmed, and filled with anxious concern at the prefent poftue of affairs."

It is proper to fay a fingle word about agency, Mr. De Berdt was appointed by the Houfe only, 7th November 1765; he was admitted, without the leaft queftion, as agent, at the Board of Trade, under different adminiftrations, and Governor Bernard gave his affent to a Bill for paying his falary fo late as the year 1768. It happened to be the duty of the agent foon after to convey the complaints of his conftituents to the throne, both againft the minifter and the governor. In this bufinefs a faithful honeft agent was found exceedingly troublefome. Such reprefentations were therefore made by the governor, and fuch inftructions fent by the minifter, as incapacitated the Houfe from paying their agent, unlefs they would have one approved of by the very perfons againft whom it might be his duty to act. This meafure needs no comment. It is not in human depravity to devife an act of more grofs injuftice, than that of debarring men of the means of defending themfelves when accufed, or of complaining when injured.

With

With all these repeated disappointments and accumulated grievances rankling in the minds of the people, the House of Representatives received, through the hands of their agent, some original letters written by their Governor and Lieutenant Governor to persons of influence in England. These letters contained a most unfavourable representation of the principles and proceedings of the people, and of their representatives. They called for punishment upon individuals, and restraints upon the whole by an abridgement of their liberties. The means of altering the charter, and of new modelling the constitution of the colony, so as to render the crown absolute, were pointed out with a malignant ability. Strong injunctions were added of the necessity of finding out some way, " to TAKE OFF the original incendiaries," lest they should " continue to instil their poison into the minds of the people."

These letters were read with grief, astonishment, and indignation. The people viewed the writers of them in the most criminal light. They considered them as the intentional authors of all their past calamities, and the enemies of their future peace and happiness. What aggravated the crime was, that these men were their countrymen, had always professed the warmest wishes for the welfare of the province and of the people ; and in consequence of those professions, had obtained their highest confidence and respect. This character was peculiarly competent to one of the letter writers. He was the *Strafford* of his time. The secret manner in which the letters had been conveyed, made the treachery tenfold more terrible and offensive.

The House of Representatives

voted an humble petition to the King for the removal of these governors, " who had rendered themselves justly obnoxious to the people, and entirely lost their confidence."— His Majesty's council in the province resolved, at the same time, that it would be for his Majesty's service, and the peace of the province to remove them,

This petition was heard before a Committee of the Lords of the Privy Council, where an illiberal lawyer was hired and permitted to abuse the petitioners and their agent, in the grossest terms scurrility could invent ; and the Lords reported, " That the petition was groundless, vexatious and scandalous, and calculated only for the seditious purposes of keeping up a spirit of clamour and discontent in the province. That nothing had been laid before them which did or could, in their opinion, in any manner, or in any degree impeach the honour, integrity or conduct of the governor or lieutenant governor."

It is curious to observe that Mr. Hutchinson, in his history, has described his own situation in that of Governor Dudley, in the year 1705. " The people (says he) in general, looked upon him as an enemy, even to the privileges of the new charter. Sir *Henry Ashurst* procured an original letter, wrote by the governor's son *Paul*, who was then Attorney general, to Mr. *Floyd*, and sent it to *New England*, in which were these expressions, *the government and colledge are disposed of here in chimney corners, and private meetings, as confidently as can be—This country will never be worth living in, for gentlemen and lawyers, till the charter is taken away.* Copies were dispersed about the province, and the letter was soon after printed."

Sir

Sir Henry Afhurft was agent for the province, and a man of high character, credit, and honour. Mr. Hutchinfon paffes no cenfure on this action, neither does it appear to have been cenfured at the time. Not that Wedderburns were wanting, but that the times did not countenance their fcurrility.

In December 1773, a large quantity of tea, fhipped by the Eaft India company, with the duty impofed by Parliament to be paid in America, arrived at Bofton. All the colonies to which the tea under the fame circumftances was deftined, had publicly refolved that it fhould not be admitted. The directors of the Eaft India company had been forewarned of its fate, and an offer made before it was fhipped to pay the duty here. But the tea was deftined to produce the commotions it occafioned, and the offer was rejected. The people met in Bofton, and infifted on the tea being fent back. The governor refufed to permit the fhip to return, upon which fome perfons in difguife deftroyed it in the night. It is manifeft that the governor intended to urge them to this extremity, or elfe he would have acted, as General Haldimand writes he expected Governor Tryon would do, " to prevent dangerous extremities, rather chufe to permit the teas fhould be fent back to England." The fame was permitted at Philadelphia, and the tea actually fent back on the 27th of December. General Haldimand declares this was the determination of every colony. " The feveral governors (fays he) of other provinces, will undoubtedly make your Lordfhip acquainted with the oppofition intended, and made in their refpective governments againft the landing the tea; the whole proceeding

from an almoft unanimous refolution not to pay any new duties or taxes laid by the Parliament of Great Britain."

Governor Hutchinfon's fon and his near relation were the confignees of the tea, and the perfons moft interefted in the fale of it. As the confignees had refufed to refign the tea, their windows were broke by the mob. Upon this they applied to his Majefty's council for protection, who came to the following report upon the application.

" In council Nov. 27, 1773, the petition of Richard Clark, Efq; and others (to whom the Eaft India company have configned a quantity of their tea) being referred to this day, the fame was taken up; and after long debates, Mr. Danforth, Mr. Bowdoin, Mr. Dexter, and Mr. Winthrop, were appointed a committee thereon, who reported, and the report after debate was referred for further confideration to Monday next, at ten o'clock, A. M.

" Monday, Nov. 29, 1773. The faid report was again confidered, and after fome amendment unanimoufly agreed to. It is as follows:

" Previous to the confideration of the petition before the Board, they would make a few obfervations occafioned by the fubject of it. The fituation of things between Great Britain and the colonies has been for fome years paft very unhappy. Parliament on the one hand has been taxing the colonies, and they on the other have been petitioning and remonftrating againft it; apprehending they have conftitutionally an exclufive right of taxing themfelves, and that without fuch a right their condition would be but little better than flavery. Poffeffed of thefe fentiments, every new meafure of Parliament, tending to
eftablifh

establish and confirm a tax on them, renews and increases their distress; and it is particularly increased by the act lately made, empowering the East India company to ship their tea to America.

" This act in a commercial view they think introductive of monopolies, and tending to bring on them the extensive evils thence arising: but their great objection to it is from its being manifestly intended (though that intention is not expressed therein) more effectually to secure the payment of the duty on tea, laid by an act passed in the 7th year of his present Majesty, intitled, ' An act for granting certain duties in the British Colonies and Plantations in America;' which act in its operation deprives the colonists of the right above-mentioned (the exclusive right of taxing themselves) which they hold to be so essential an one, that it cannot be taken away, or given up, without their being degraded, or degrading themselves below the character of men. It not only deprives them of that right, but enacts that the monies arising from the duties granted by it may be applied " as his Majesty or his successors shall think proper or necessary, for defraying the charges of the administration of justice, and the support of the civil government, within all or any of the said colonies and plantations."

" This clause of the act has already operated in some of the colonies, and in this colony in particular, with regard to the support of civil government, and thereby has operated in diminution of its charter rights, to the great grief of the good people of it, who have been, and still are, greatly alarmed by repeated reports, that it is to have a further operation with respect to the defraying the charge of the administration of justice, which would not only be a further diminution of those rights, but tend in all constitutional questions, and in many other cases of importance, to bias the judges against the subject. They humbly rely on the justice and goodness of his Majesty for the restitution and preservation of those rights.

" This short state of facts the Board thought necessary to be given, to shew the cause of the present great uneasiness, which is not confined to this neighbourhood, but is general and extensive. The people think their exclusive right of taxing themselves by their representatives infringed and violated by the act above-mentioned; that the new act, empowering the East India company to import their tea into America, confirms that violation, and is a new effort, not only more effectually to secure the payment of the tea duty, but lay a foundation for the enhancing it; and in a like way, if this should succeed, to lay other taxes on America; that it is in its attendants and consequences ruinous to the liberties and properties of themselves, and their posterity; that as their numerous petitions for relief have been rejected, the said new act demonstrates an unwillingness in ministry that parliament should grant them relief; that this is the source of their distress that borders on despair; and that they know not where to apply for relief.

" These being the sentiments of the people, it is become the indispensable duty of the Board to mention them, that the occasion of the late demands on Mr. Clark and others (the agents for the East India company) and of the consequent disturbances,

turbances, might appear: and we mention them, not to juftify thofe difturbances, the authors of which we have advifed fhould be profecuted, but to give a juft idea of the rife of them.

"On this occafion, juftice impels us to declare, that the people of this town and province, though they have a high fenfe of liberty, derived from the manners, the example and conftitution of the mother country, have, till the late parliamentary taxations of the colonies, been as free from difturbances as any people whatever.

"This reprefentation the board thought neceffary to be made prior to their taking notice of the petition of the agents above-mentioned; to the confideration of which they now proceed.

"The petitioners ' beg 'leave to refign themfelves, and the property committed to their care, to his Excellency and the board, as guardians and protectors of the people, praying that meafures may be directed to for the landing and fecuring the tea, &c.' With regard to the perfonal protection of the petitioners, the board have not been informed, that they have applied for it to any of the juftices of the peace; within whofe department it is to take cognizance of the cafe of the petitioners, and of all other breaches of the peace; they being vefted by law with all the authority neceffary for the protection of his Majefty's fubjects. In the principal inftance of abufe,* of which they complain, the board have already advifed, that the authors fhould be profecuted according to law; and they do advife the fame in the other inftances mentioned in their petition.

"With regard to the tea committed to the care of the petitioners, the

* Some of their windows were broken.

board have no authority to take either that or any other merchandize out of their care; and fhould they do it, or give any order or advice concerning it, and a lofs enfue, they apprehend they fhould make themfelves refponfible for it. With refpect to the prayer of the petition, "that meafures may be directed to for landing and fecuring the tea," the board would obferve on it, that the duty on the tea becomes payable, and muft be paid, or fecured to be paid, on its being landed. And fhould they direct or advife to any meafure for landing it, they would of courfe advife to a meafure for procuring the payment of the duty, and therefore be advifing to a meafure inconfiftent with the declared fentiment of both Houfes in the laft winter feffion of the general court, which they apprehend to be altogether inexpedient and improper.

"The board, however, on this occafion affure your Excellency, that as they have feen, with regret, fome late difturbances, and have advifed to the profecuting the authors of them, fo they will, in all legal methods, endeavour, to the utmoft of their power, to prevent them in future.

"Whereupon advifed, That his Excellency renew his orders to his Majefty's juftices of the peace, fheriffs, and other peace officers, to exert themfelves to the utmoft for the fecurity of his Majefty's fubjects, the prefervation of peace and good order, and for preventing all offences againft the law."

On the 18th of February 1774, the whole Houfe of Reprefentatives waited on the governor with a fecond petition, for the removal of the chief juftice, who had rendered himfelf incapable, by accepting a falary from the crown, at whofe will he alfo held his place. They fay, "Your Excellency will pleafe to confider that
this

this House is well acquainted with the general sense of their constituents in this matter; and we can now assure, you, that the continuance of the chief justice in his place, will increase the uneasiness of the people without doors, and endanger the public tranquility. We therefore earnestly intreat your Excellency, that while we are in this instance employing the powers with which we are entrusted in promoting the tranquillity and good order of government, ' we may,' agreeably to your declaration in your speech to both Houses, ' find that you are ready to give your consent to a request of the House intended for that and other great and important purposes:' and that your Excellency will immediately take every step for the removal of the chief justice from the superior court."

The governor returned them a positive denial, accompanied with a curious piece of equivocation. The House had prayed that he would take the advice of his Majesty's council upon their petition, conformable to the charter.—To which he answers, That though he was by charter to act with the advice and assistance of his council, yet the summoning of the council was *in his discretion*. Thus was the protective provision of the charter effectually evaded.

This is a full and fair state of the proceedings in and respecting the province of the Massachusetts-Bay, from the year 1762 to 1774.

The candid reader will judge what causes of discontent have been given them, and whether they have operated beyond their natural bounds. If they have been particularly unquiet, they have also been particularly irritated and injured. Imagining ourselves in their situation, will, I believe, prevent us from severely censuring their conduct.

It is manifest that they have constantly expressed their complaints in petitions conceived in the most measured language of subordination and respect. That they have repeatedly acknowledged the supreme legislative authority of parliament. That the only instance in which they seem to have questioned it, was in a mere speculative dispute, purposely provoked by the governor. That the constant subject of their complaints has been the having their money taken from them without their consent; the substituting a dependent judge, bribed by being paid out of the forfeitures, to determine in all causes of revenue, by the rules of the civil law, and without a jury; and the violation of their security in the due administration of government and of justice, by rendering the governor and judges *totally* dependent on the crown. That their wish has been to return to the state in which they were before the passing these laws and sending these instructions, and not to become independent of Great-Britain. This appears not only from their repeated and authentic declarations, but from Governor Hutchinson's letters. ' The enemies of government (so is he pleased to stile the Council, the House of Representatives, and the people) gave out, that their friends in parliament were increasing, and all things would be soon on the old footing; in other words, that all acts imposing duties would be repealed, the commissioners board dissolved, the customs put on their old footing, and illicit trade be carried on with little or no hazard.' The malignity of this reflection upon the people, will plainly appear from the following declaration of Governor Bernard, whose testimony in their favour will hardly be questioned. ' I do not pretend, says he, that this province is *entirely* free from the breach of those laws (of trade,)

trade,) but only that such breach, if discovered, is *surely punished*.' What more can be said of the best country upon earth? Yet Governor Hutchinson does not scruple to charge them with having been all smugglers, and to throw an odium upon their struggling for their rights by the imputation of their sole object being to renew that illicit trade with impunity.

It must also appear from their proceedings, that their great crime has been their constancy in petitioning for redress of grievances; which has been attempted to be repressed, even by the most unjustifiable means of refusing them an agent to vindicate them when misrepresented, and support their complaints. While this common right of justice is denied them, persons are notoriously hired here to load them in the public papers with every species of opprobrium, falshood, and abuse. There are two things which deserve the most particular attention: 1st, That whenever affidavits were taken on the part of the people, they were taken in public, with summonses to all persons concerned to attend, and cross examine the witnesses: on the contrary, those which were obtained by the governor and commissioners, accusing the people, were made in secret, and the persons accused unapprized and totally ignorant of the proceeding, they were transmitted in secret, and the injured persons by mere accidents, and after they had operated to their hurt, had an opportunity of seeing and refuting them. The instances on both sides will be found in the affidavits taken on the seizure of the sloop Liberty, and the riot, and in Mr. Oliver's affidavit, and the narrative of the town, respecting the massacre on the 5th of March. 2d. That the chief and almost only continual witnesses against the people,

are, the Governors Bernard and Hutchinson: the former of whom has long laboured under an accusation upon oath of gross corruption in his office; the latter has been detected in the basest plot against their liberties; and both are at open enmity with the people, having been petitioned against by their representatives, as universally odious. How far the representatives of men so circumstanced can be presumed fair and impartial, or deserve credit, must be left to the candid to determine.

We have seen their petitions either intercepted, or treated with a contemptuous silence, or answered with the severest censures. Seven years supplication has brought no relief. And now, to fill up the measure of their misfortunes, their port is stopt up, their charter is to be subverted, and a lawless army let loose upon them. They have been tried, condemned and punished, unheard and unapprized of the whole proceeding. They are left to weep over their apprehensions, realized in the utter subversion of their liberties. This accumulation of calamities is heaped upon them, because high and strong resentments, as they naturally must, have followed severe and reiterated injuries: because discontent has arisen from disappointed and despised complaints; and violence from insulted discontent.

Whoever will take the trouble of reading, in the history of this most meritorious and unhappy people, the unparalelled hardships with which they purchased those liberties we have now torn from them; and view the deplorable, the desperate situation, to which they are now reduced—however obdurate, however prejudiced he may be, he must think, at least, *one human tear may drop, and be forgiven.*

INDEX.

I N D E X

TO THE

PRIOR DOCUMENTS.

New

INDEX,

F I N I S.